HOMELANDS

HOMELANDS

Shifting Borders and Territorial Disputes

Nadav G. Shelef

CORNELL UNIVERSITY PRESS   ITHACA AND LONDON

First published 2020 by Cornell University Press

Library of Congress Cataloging-in-Publication Data

Names: Shelef, Nadav G. (Nadav Gershon), 1974– author.
Title: Homelands : shifting borders and territorial disputes / Nadav G. Shelef.
Description: Ithaca [New York] : Cornell University Press, 2020. | Includes
    bibliographical references and index.
Identifiers: LCCN 2019044592 (print) | LCCN 2019044593 (ebook) |
    ISBN 9780801453489 (hardcover) | ISBN 9780801479922 (paperback) |
    ISBN 9781501712364 (pdf) | ISBN 9781501709722 (epub)
Subjects: LCSH: Boundaries. | Territory, National. | Boundary disputes. |
    Geopolitics. | Irredentism. | Nationalism.
Classification: LCC JC323 .S548 2020 (print) | LCC JC323 (ebook) |
    DDC 320.1/2—dc23
LC record available at https://lccn.loc.gov/2019044592
LC ebook record available at https://lccn.loc.gov/2019044593

To M., A., and R., with love

Contents

Illustrations and Tables

Illustrations

Tables

Acknowledgments

This book started where my previous one ended. That book, grounded in the Israeli context, consistently sparked questions about the potentially exceptional character of Israeli nationalism and its evolution: perhaps the kinds of transformations that shaped the ways Israelis thought about the fundamental aspects of their polity did not occur in other cases? While there was little theoretical reason to believe that was the case, I had no empirical basis from which to answer the question. This book is my answer. Focusing on a single dimension of nationalist ideology—the location of the homeland—it shows that nationalism evolves in other contexts as well.

I have benefited from the support and feedback of many friends and colleagues over the years that it took to complete this project. The data collection and empirical analysis could not have been completed without the painstaking and indefatigable help of a generation of students at the University of Wisconsin–Madison. Sam Alhadeff, Shaan Amin, Carlo Annelli, Adam Auerbach, Sanja Badanjak, Nick Barnes, Evgeny Finkel, Simon Haeder, Anne Jamison, Ian McQuistion, Clarence Moore, Susanne Mueller-Redwood, Erin Pelletier, and Katie Robiadek all made significant contributions to this project.

My colleagues, especially Mark Copelovitch, Yoi Herrera, Helen Kinsella, Andy Kydd, Jon Pevehouse, Nils Ringe, and Jessica Weeks, not only read parts of the manuscript but their feedback also shaped it in more ways than I can enumerate. I could not ask for better colleagues and friends. I also benefited from comments by Emanuel Adler, Boaz Atzili, Michael Barnett, Fabio Capano, Lars-Erik Cederman, Nisha Fazal, Stacie Goddard, Hein Goemans, Oded Haklai, Ron Hassner, Marc Lynch, Harris Mylonas, Wendy Pearlman, Bill Quandt, and Ken Schultz, among many others at conferences and workshops at which portions of the project were presented. They all made the work better. It goes without saying that any errors are my own and persist despite their best efforts. I am also grateful for the support, forbearance, and occasional prod from Roger Haydon. My thanks also go to the reviewers whose comments and suggestions made this a much better book.

Portions of chapters 1, 5, and 6 were published in "Unequal Ground: Homelands and Conflict," *International Organization* 70, no. 1 (2016): 33–63, Cambridge University Press, reprinted with permission. Portions of chapter 4 were previously published in "Which Land Is Our Land?: Domestic Politics and

Change in the Territorial Claims of Stateless Nationalist Movements," *Security Studies* 23, no. 4 (2014): 754–86 (with Harris Mylonas), https://www.tandf-online.com/. A version of some of the material in chapter 5 was published in "How Homelands Change," *Journal of Conflict Resolution* 64, no. 2–3 (2020): 490–517, https://doi.org/10.1177/0022002719863470. I thank these journals for permission to reprint versions of these articles.

Finally, I could not have completed this book without the love and support of my family. M., A., and R., thank you.

Abbreviations

AMG	Allied Military Government
CDU	Christian Democratic Party (Germany)
CSU	Christian Social Union (Germany)
DC	Christian Democracy Party (Italy)
EPLF	Eritrean People's Liberation Front
FBIS	Foreign Broadcast Information Service
FDP	Free Democratic Party (Germany)
FRG	Federal Republic of Germany
FTT	Free Territory of Trieste
GDR	German Democratic Republic
ICJ	International Court of Justice
ICOW	Issue Correlates of War
JCP	Jordanian Communist Party
MSI	Italian Social Movement
PCI	Italian Communist Party
PDFLP	Democratic Front for the Liberation of Palestine
PFLP	Popular Front for the Liberation of Palestine
PLO	Palestine Liberation Organization
PNA	Palestinian National Authority
PNC	Palestinian National Council
SED	East German Communist Party
SPD	Social Democratic Party (Germany)
TPLF	Tigray People's Liberation Front
UNRWA	United Nations Relief and Works Agency for Palestine Refugees in the Near East

HOMELANDS

INTRODUCTION

Few things are as instinctively durable as a nation's desire for its homeland. The Jewish pining for the land of Israel, the Palestinian struggle for the same territory, the Hungarian dream of the pre-Trianon borders, and the Serbian drive to regain Greater Serbia are all piercing reminders of the persistence of lost homeland territory in the national imagination—and of the conflict that often follows. Our instincts, however, are only partially right. Such poignant cases notwithstanding, there are many, often unnoticed, instances of once-voluble claims to lost homeland territory melting away. Indian nationalists no longer claim Lahore as part of Mother India. Germans rarely seek the return of the German homeland east of the Oder and the Neisse Rivers. Even Italian nationalists, whose aspirations for their *terra irredenta* (unredeemed land) along the Adriatic coast gave us the term "irredentism," no longer widely include Istria or Dalmatia within the geographical scope of the Italian homeland.

This book shows how such transformations in the area included in the homeland come about and explores their consequences for international conflict. It argues that contractions in the area included in what counts as the homeland occur as a result of a process rooted in domestic political competition. New, more modest, understandings of the homeland, where they are associated with domestic political success, displace more expansive ones. Over time, land left out of these understandings loses its status as part of the homeland. Such contractions in the area considered part of the homeland, in turn, are critical for parsing the variation in territorial partitions' ability to resolve conflict. Partitions work—that

1

is, they resolve existing conflict without leading to further irredentist conflict—when the parts of the homeland that remain on the other side of the new border cease to be seen as appropriately part of the homeland.

In addition to bringing homelands back into consideration, explaining how they contract, and detailing their role in international conflict, this book also aims to bridge the persistent gap between constructivist theories of nationalism and quantitative empirical analyses of international relations. Scholarship in each of these traditions too often fails to engage with the lessons and concerns addressed by the other. The emphasis by constructivist scholarship on the importance of ideas and meaning frequently comes at the expense of addressing questions about generalizability and even occasional hostility to positivist modes of analysis. Quantitative cross-national scholarship usefully identifies general trends and average effects, but rarely integrates key constructivist insights about the importance of ideas, meaning, and change into either explanations of these trends or into the data used to identify them. The result has been a persistent gulf between the widely accepted theoretical understanding of nationalism and of why territory matters, and the data used to evaluate its impact cross-nationally. I bridge this gap by developing an explanation of how homelands contract as well as providing systematic, comparable data about the homeland status of lost territory over time. Both the theory and these data are consistent with constructivist understandings of homelands and can be incorporated into positivist quantitative analysis.

This book advances three main theoretical arguments. First, not all territory is equal ground. The relevance of material differences between territories for conflict over them has long been recognized. Higher ground is easier to defend, dense jungles are harder to penetrate, and resource wealth, trade routes, or the presence of coethnics in a territory can spur neighbors to embark on irredentist projects.[1] This book makes the case that variation in the nonmaterial, ideational value ascribed to land designated as the homeland is also relevant for understanding the role territory plays in international conflict. The nonmaterial value of homelands matters because the "homeland" is not a tangible object. It is an idea whose territorial extent is intersubjectively defined by members of the national community. The homeland, as chapter 1 elaborates, is a nationalist form of territoriality. Part and parcel of the nationalist political project, the homeland delimits the area from which a nation has risen and in which it should fulfill its destiny. The categorization of particular territory as part of the national homeland endows it with value independently of its material characteristics because homeland territory plays a role in constituting the nation itself. As increasingly well-established insights from social psychology suggest, this nonmaterial value is likely to affect the strategic calculations actors make and the kind of political contestation that surrounds the redrawing of borders.

Second, the value of homelands notwithstanding, the idea of what constitutes the appropriate geographic extent of the national homeland can change. Like all other shared ideas and social facts, homelands are not static; they are malleable, though not infinitely so. While significant constructivist scholarship acknowledges the possibility of change in the abstract, in practice, homelands are nonetheless often treated as if they were static. This book offers a theory that accommodates both the value of homelands and their transformations and traces such modifications empirically. Taking seriously the possibility that a homeland's boundaries can change directs our attention to questions about how and under what conditions such transformations take place. Asking these questions allows us to move beyond the debate about whether or not territory's role in conflict is due to its perceived indivisibility to an explicit investigation of the mechanisms that drive changes in what counts as part of the homeland and the conditions that make such change more likely.

Third, drawing inspiration from dynamics of change characterized as emergent or evolutionary, the book contends that a key process of contraction in the homeland's boundaries relies on the presence of variation, differential success in the domestic political arena, and time for relatively more successful variants to displace less successful ones. This process is an evolutionary one because the presence of these elements—variation, differential success, and time—produce evolutionary change in any context.[2] Such evolutionary dynamics are common in the social and political worlds.[3] They also apply to homelands.[4] Domestic political actors frequently disagree about what constitutes the homeland and why certain parcels are part of it (variation); some political movements promoting alternative variants of what the homeland looks like succeed more than others; and in the right institutional context, there is sufficient time for the positive political returns from this success to enable the variants associated with political success to spread more widely in a society (even if they are not the reason for the success per se). Both the case studies and the cross-national analysis that follow show how this process, one rooted in the consequences of domestic political contestation, explains when and how lost parts of the homeland come to be excluded from definitions of the homeland's extent.

Outline of the Book

Chapter 1 begins with an elaboration of the theoretical arguments that homelands matter, that their contours can change, and that evolutionary processes arising from domestic political contestation could account for such transformations. I start by arguing that nationalism calls homelands into being. It is the nationalist project that transforms mere land into homeland and sanctifies it. I then show that, despite its importance to nationalists, two aspects of the homeland are often domestically contested: (1) exactly which tracts of land are part of it; and (2) what logic or combination of logics is used to designate land as part of the homeland. It is the outcome of the political competition between movements that vary in the answers they provide to one or both of these questions that selects which shape of the homeland becomes taken for granted in the wider society and whether lost lands come to be excluded from it. I then develop the empirically observable implications of this theory as well as alternative explanations for contractions in the homeland's scope. These implications serve as the foundation for the empirical exploration in both the cases studies and the cross-national statistical analysis that follow.

The three case studies in chapters 2–4 undertake a fine-grained investigation of the pattern of stability and change in the conceptions of the area that counted as part of the homeland in the post–World War II German, Italian, and Palestinian contexts. The West German setting explored in chapter 2 is especially useful because it features the simultaneous loss of territories that differ in their ethnic composition; in economic value; whether they came to be excluded from the homeland, and, if they did, when this redefinition of the homeland occurred. As chapter 2 shows, political movements in the Federal Republic of Germany (FRG) also differed in when, and even whether, they withdrew homeland territoriality from the various parts of the homeland Germany lost. This chapter traces the withdrawal of homeland territoriality from Germany's lost lands and, leveraging the internal variation that characterizes the German experience, explains the timing of the changes that took place, and accounts for the absence of change where we might have expected it to occur. This historical process tracing shows that different logics of legitimation and domestic political mechanisms played a crucial role in explaining the pattern of stability and change in conceptions of the German homeland.

The division of Venezia Giulia investigated in chapter 3 is a paradigmatic case in which the partition of homeland territory in the aftermath of war came to be accepted as appropriate by those on both sides of the border. At the end of World War II, American intelligence services identified the border between Italy and Yugoslavia as particularly problematic and as a likely location for violent confrontations between East and West.[5] They had good reason to think so. Trieste and the Istrian Peninsula were at the heart of the Italian nationalist claim to the "unredeemed lands" that motivated much of the conflict in the Balkans in the early part of the twentieth century. Yugoslav (and Slovenian and Croat) nationalists also saw these same territories as unambiguously part of their respective homelands. Alongside the raging international conflict of the Second World War, this border zone was the site of an ethnic civil war between Slavs and Italians that was as bloody and bitter as any other. Yet, by the 1970s, this region became a model for regional cooperation. While individual claims for compensation for lost property remain, mainstream Italian nationalists no longer claim the areas they once fought for so passionately as appropriately part of their homeland. In chapter 3, I argue that this acceptance was not automatic or inevitable. Rather, I show how the efforts of the governing Christian Democracy Party (DC) to stem additional territorial losses after the war and to overcome the short-term political challenges it faced in the new republic shaped the timing and process of the withdrawal of homeland territoriality from once-sacred land.

The drawing of a new border clearly failed to resolve the conflict over Palestine. Chapter 4 shows, however, that the same domestic political mechanisms that governed changes to the definition of the homeland in the German and Italian contexts operated in the setting of a stateless nationalist movement as well. Focusing on the extent (and limits) of the changes in the territorial claims of the main Palestinian nationalist movements, this chapter expands our view beyond the conventional focus on states in studies of territorial conflict. Doing so is useful because, by definition, the main actors in most secessionist conflicts are stateless. A more complete understanding of the role homelands play in conflict thus requires including those secessionist movements that are conventionally excluded from analyses pitched at the level of the state.

The case studies in this book were selected for a number of reasons. At one level, they are intended to expand our conceptualization of what partitions can look like. Most discussions of the division of homelands focus on a few canonical cases like India or Cyprus. Yet, as the cross-national section of the book shows, systematically identifying partitions in terms of the loss of land to which homeland territoriality had been applied yields many more cases than are usually considered. Many of these, like the partition of Cape Verde from Guinea Bissau, are significantly smaller and less consequential in world-historical terms, if not necessarily to the people that live through them, than the cardinal cases of India and Palestine. Nonetheless, the omission of a very large number of cases from the scholarly imagination raises the possibility that our intuitions about the impact of homelands on both domestic and international politics are tinged by the focus on a few large and significant cases at the expense of the modal one. I return to these themes in greater detail in the conclusion.

These cases also provide additional out-of-sample testing of the theory about how the ideologies of nationalist movements change, which was developed largely in the Israeli context.[6] The selection of cases in which domestic political dynamics played a critical role in explaining the empirical pattern (including the timing, actors, and process) of the withdrawal of homeland territoriality from lost lands also follows Evan Lieberman's recommendation to select "on the line" cases that can provide a check against spurious correlations and address questions about causal order and quality of measurement which may be raised by the quantitative analysis in the second half of the book.[7]

Finally, the detailed process-tracing deployed in the case studies also enables a more nuanced consideration of the impact of the Cold War than is possible in the quantitative analysis. As will be described in chapter 5, the data used in the quantitative analysis spans the period from 1945 to 1996. The influence of the Cold War on nearly every international dynamic for most of this period raises the possibility that the findings of the large-N analysis are limited to that historical era. Although work that explicitly engaged in asynchronous comparison suggests that this is not so, the case studies are nonetheless able to tackle this possibility explicitly.[8] They show that, even where superpower influence should theoretically have mattered, its impact was filtered through the dynamics of domestic political competition (where such competition existed).

Chapters 5 and 6 broaden the view and undertake a systematic cross-national exploration of the correlates and consequences of the withdrawal of homeland territoriality from lost lands. This investigation reinforces the findings of the case studies by showing that their main findings are broadly generalizable. These chapters demonstrate that the ideational designation of land as part of the homeland makes conflict more likely, that the withdrawal of homeland territoriality from lost lands is a regular feature of our world, and that the exclusion of lost territory from the homeland's scope is more likely where the conditions that produce evolutionary dynamics are also likely to be present.

To do so, in chapter 5 I present a replicable, systematic, cross-national measure of the homeland status of lost territory which is consistent with the ideational character of homelands and captures the possibility that their scope can change. This indicator is based on the systematic tracing over time of the way in which domestic media on both sides of every new international border drawn between 1945 and 1996 spoke about the land newly located on the wrong side of the border. This measure enables the inclusion of the homeland status of lost territory in quantitative analysis of conflict in ways that bridge the gap between political science theory and existing proxies for the homeland status of territory.

I then use a survival analysis to explore the general purchase of explanations of the withdrawal of homeland territoriality from parts of the homeland left on the wrong side of new international borders. This analysis shows that those conditions which produce evolutionary dynamics—namely, the sustained presence of meaningful institutionalized domestic political competition over time—are consistently associated with withdrawing homeland territoriality from lost parts of the homeland, even when controlling for the other factors that shape whether territory is included in the homeland.

In chapter 6, I use the measure of the homeland status of lost lands to test the critical implication of the argument that homelands matter. The chapter demonstrates that the rhetorical delineation of the homeland is not inconsequential talk. Losing territory that is discursively defined as part of the homeland is associated with more subsequent conflict than losing territory that is not categorized as part of the homeland, even when the material (economic, strategic, and demographic) aspects of the territory and the characteristics of the states facing each other across the new border are accounted for. The converse is also true. The withdrawal of homeland territoriality from lost lands is also associated with a reduction in many forms of international conflict.

The book concludes by using the lessons from the empirical exploration of homelands and their contraction to reevaluate how we identify partitions and to reassess the question of whether partitions can be used to resolve conflict.

UNDERSTANDING HOMELANDS

Humans, it is sometimes asserted, are territorial animals.[1] While this claim is undoubtedly accurate, the tremendous historical variation in the types of spaces we seek to control, the ways we delimit these areas, and the tactics with which we exercise this control cannot be accounted for by human nature. Human territoriality is better characterized as a strategy with which this control is exercised. It is "the attempt by an individual or group to affect, influence, or control people, phenomena, and relationships, by delimiting and asserting control over a geographic area."[2] As a strategy, the particular ways territoriality is deployed vary over time and are sensitive to historical, ideational, and technological developments.[3]

For example, the shifting conceptions of space engendered by modern mapping technologies changed how states pictured, demarcated, and sought to control their realms.[4] Likewise, for most of modern history the unpopulated atolls in the South China Sea were relevant largely as obstacles to seafaring vessels. It was only after the invention of the internal combustion engine and the discovery of oil underneath these atolls that the application of various strategies of territorial control to these once-forsaken areas accelerated (along with the international conflict over them).[5]

Homelands are also the product of a historical development; in this case ideational rather than technological. The categorization of land as part of the homeland is a specific form of territoriality engendered by the idea that a particular group of people (the nation) ought to control a particular territory because that land is part of who the people are. Homelands, in other words, are a product of the nationalist project. In terms of its effect, the emergence of nationalism was like the discovery of oil; it was a change that revamped the way territory was valuated.[6]

At its core, nationalism defines the appropriate bounds within which the mundane politics of who gets what and how should take place. It delimits the people from whom sovereignty should derive and the territory over which this sovereignty ought to extend. Many colloquial uses of nationalism, and not a few scholarly ones, emphasize the impact of the lines nationalism draws between the in-group and out-groups over those it draws on the map. Patterns of exclusion are certainly consequential. However, understanding the ways homelands shape domestic politics and international conflict requires also paying attention to nationalism's territorial dimension.[7] It is this dimension that endows the homeland with value and shapes conflict over its loss.

The territorial aspect of nationalism is inherent in the concept itself. As Hans Kohn argued, nationalism "presupposes the existence, in fact or as an ideal, of a centralized form of government over a distinct and large territory."[8] Ernest Gellner's conceptualization of nationalism as the drive to make the cultural and political borders of the nation congruent assumes a territorial component to these borders.[9] Similarly, Benedict Anderson's cardinal definition of the nation as a political community that is "imagined as both inherently limited and sovereign" requires a geographical location in which this sovereignty is to be exercised.[10] The importance of territory to the national project led John Agnew to conclude that territorial "borders are kit and caboodle, then, to everyday nationalism."[11]

While abstract nations are not necessarily anchored in any particular geographical location, they do have to be tied to some place. This territorial imperative leads nationalists to identify a particular piece of land as their home land. To be sure, groups have long had locations that they were from, in which they resided, and to whose landscapes they were emotionally bound (what geographers term cultural regions).[12] People have also long sought to control particular locations for material reasons (as in the apparently age-old conflict between farmers and ranchers).

Nationalism, however, renders homelands more than these locations. Nationalism transforms cultural regions (whether actual or imagined) into "the physical and legal embodiment" of collective identity and into the very essence of a people.[13] It does so by providing a story that "tie[s] together the fate of the nation and the territory . . . [; and] explain[s] why a given territory belongs rightfully to the nation, how the nation arrived at the present territorial situation, and which territory would fulfill [the nation's] destiny."[14] The nationalist political project imbues territory designated as the homeland with so much meaning that its defense becomes the nation-state's cardinal duty and control of homeland territory becomes the sine qua non of national existence. This binding of nation and territory constrained the territorial horse-trading that had been the norm until that point, and transformed the loss of homeland territory into a grave injustice whose remedy justified tremendous sacrifice.[15] This attachment is so great that nationalists' willingness to sacrifice for the homeland is sometimes seen as irrational.[16]

This is the case, importantly, for all nations and all nationalisms. Even so-called civic or inclusive nationalisms—nationalisms that use the borders of the state rather than ethnic criteria to define their membership boundaries—are territorially grounded.[17] They too seek exclusive sovereignty over a homeland.

This understanding of homelands implies that the rhetorical designation of land as part of the homeland plays a critical role in calling the homeland into being. Actors apply homeland territoriality to land by saying (in words or images) that a particular parcel of land is part of the homeland. This is why nationalists devote so much costly energy to maps, geography textbooks, and seemingly quixotic battles over the names used to label particular places. The need to rhetorically delineate the location of the homeland also leads nationalists to speak differently of land that is part of the homeland than of land that is not part of it. As Walker Connor pointed out, nationalists routinely use familial metaphors to "mystically convert what the outsider sees as merely the territory populated by a nation into a motherland or fatherland, the ancestral land, land of our fathers, this sacred soil . . . the cradle of the nation, . . . and most commonly, the *home*—the *home*land of our particular people—a Mother Russia, an Armenia, a Deutschland, an England (Enga land: land of the Angles), or a Kurdistan (literally, land of the Kurds)."[18] The resulting depictions of the homeland generate an "instantly recognizable, everywhere visible" logo that penetrates the popular imagination and forms a powerful emblem for the nation.[19]

If the applications of homeland territoriality to land embodied by these map-images are (or become) socially resonant—that is, if they spread widely in a society—the territory to which they are applied becomes part of the homeland. Conversely, territory omitted from these logos ceases to be part of the homeland.

There are certainly concrete, material, ways of applying homeland territoriality to land. Physical conquest, the erection of border fences, checkpoints, passport controls, the sowing of minefields, the settlement of conationals, and the extension of state services, including legal, tax, and education regimes, into new spaces are all tangible ways of saying that "this land is ours." These methods of applying homeland territoriality are available, however, only when a state actually controls the territory in question. Maintaining the homeland status of land in the absence of sovereignty over it is an almost exclusively rhetorical act.

Assessing the conditions under which homeland territoriality is withdrawn from lost homeland territory thus requires paying attention to the pattern of articulation about that territory.

Understanding homelands as a nationalist form of territoriality also has two additional implications. First, homelands are valuable because of their ideational categorization as homelands rather than having their value derived from some other attribute of the territory (such as its material characteristics or the presence of coethnics). As a result, the potential impact of the ideational value of homelands on conflict (or on any outcome of interest) should be considered alongside the other dimensions of nationalism and the material features of territory. Second, since the claim that a particular territory constitutes the homeland is part of the nationalist political project to configure politics and societies in particular ways, the designation of land as part of the homeland is as likely to be subject to the same kinds of contestation and potential changes over time as other political projects. The remainder of this chapter takes up each of these implications in turn.

The Ideational Value of Homeland Territory

So that my generation would comprehend the Homeland's worth,
Men were always transformed to dust, it seems.
The Homeland is the remains of our forefathers
Who turned into dust for this precious soil.

Cholpan Ergash, Uzbek poet[20]

How can an amputated man sleep comfortably at night?

Somali liberation song[21]

Understanding homelands as a nationalist form of territoriality—as a rhetorical strategy of asserting the nation's control over a particular space—does not render them epiphenomenal or rob them of their power. In fact, it is difficult to overstate the value nationalists place on their homelands. Their loss "touch[es] the main nerve center of popular feeling" because the establishment of a link between the nation and a territory identified as the homeland fundamentally transforms an otherwise unexceptional piece of real estate into something worth dying for.[22] The German nationalist philosopher Johann Herder was thus exaggerating only slightly when he exclaimed that if you "deprive [nationalists] of their country, you deprive them of everything."[23] Indeed, nearly all nationalisms echo the

Uzbek poem quoted in the epigraph that calculates the worth of the homeland in the currency of the sacrifices of earlier generations.[24] As Connor notes, "The homeland is much more than territory. . . . [It is] intermeshed with notions of ancestry and family. This emotional attachment to the homeland derives from perceptions of it as the cultural hearth and, very often, the geographic cradle of the ethno-national group. In Bismarckian terminology, 'Blut und Boden!', blood and soil have become mixed."[25]

Important strides have been made in integrating homelands' ideational value into research on territorial conflict. Most notably, the Issue Correlates of War (ICOW) project includes the categorization of a territory as the homeland by representatives of the state among the factors that make up its index of "intangible value."[26] Other studies flag the ability of a territory's symbolic value to increase the salience of territories in conflict and to shape the politics of such cases by mobilizing domestic support, enabling state leaders to fight off domestic challengers, and constraining their ability to make territorial concessions.[27]

Yet, too often the role of ideational attachment to territory continues to be overlooked in contemporary studies of international conflict.[28] For example, Gary Goertz and Paul Diehl's discussion of a territory's "intrinsic value" is conceptualized primarily in economic terms, minimizing its independent ideological importance.[29] Other studies categorize international territorial conflict as taking place over largely tangible assets.[30] Paul Huth's valuable disaggregation of the issues at stake in territorial conflicts as strategic location, minorities in the territory with ethnic ties to the challenger, and the economic value of the territory, similarly excludes the ideational value of the land in its own right from the list of potential reasons for conflict.[31] This was also the case for an important account of the rise of the territorial integrity norm in international relations.[32] Scholarship on enduring territorial conflict sometimes dismisses the ideational value of homelands as cheap talk by leaders seeking to mobilize support. From this perspective, because leaders "can easily embed symbolic value onto claimed territory," whether the territory has symbolic value is irrelevant for testing alternative explanations of conflict.[33] Ideational attachment to the land is also sometimes dismissed as a constant that cannot explain variation in the existence, onset, or severity of conflict.[34] Even work on "what makes territory important" excluded nationalist attachment to homelands as a potential answer to this question.[35]

Studies of irredentism also tend to minimize the impact of the ideational value of the territory itself. The dominant understanding of irredentism assumes that a state demands the incorporation of territory outside its borders primarily because the territory is populated by its coethnics.[36] The possibility that the territory could be desired because its value is derived directly from being part of the homeland separately from its demographic characteristics is rarely considered.[37]

The omission of ideationally based nationalist attachment to the homeland as a relevant variable also characterizes the logic of many supporters of partition and accounts that assume nationalist conflict is driven by the security concerns created by ethnic intermingling.[38] While these arguments acknowledge the importance of a territory's demographic and strategic characteristics, they tend to downplay the importance of nationalists' ideological attachment to homelands. They see territory as fungible; any territory will do for the location of the national state as long as it has relatively defensible borders and is reasonably ethnically homogeneous.

The elision of the ideational value of homelands is problematic because this value likely affects the ways in which nationalists calculate the costs and benefits of territorial conflict and compromise. Indeed, experiments in the field have shown that the sanctity of homelands structures the preferences of nationalists in very much the same way that religious values structure the preferences of believers.[39] The homeland, in other words, constitutes a nationalist sacred value.[40] As a robust psychological literature has demonstrated, sacred values shape decision making because, while intangible, they still possess great worth—worth that is measured along a nonmaterialist metric.[41]

The sanctity of the homeland for nationalists implies, therefore, that materialist considerations about the value of territory (such as its economic utility, strategic importance, or even lives lost in its pursuit) could take a back seat to value considerations. Once consecrated as sacred ground, compromising on homelands in exchange for material gain becomes more difficult, even taboo, since to do so would rob it of its sanctity. This is why the German nationalist poet Ernst Moritz Arndt could subvert Jesus's call for supreme loyalty (Matthew 10:37) and aver that "the highest form of religion is to love the fatherland more passionately than laws and princes, fathers and mothers, wives and children."[42]

As a sacred value, the importance of homelands is thus analytically independent of their size, or economic, strategic, or demographic weight. Just as the importance of the Black Hills of South Dakota to the Lakota Sioux is not reducible to their real-estate value and the value of the Kaaba in Mecca is not pegged to the riyals spent by pilgrims, territory categorized as the homeland is valuable primarily in terms of the nationalism that calls the homeland into existence. This is why even a committed Marxist, like the leader of the Palestinian Democratic Front for the Liberation of Palestine, Nayef Hawatmeh, could argue that the value of the homeland is not determined by its economic potential. "We are fighting," he declared, "for what is our land, even if it were a barren desert in which only thorns grew."[43] Homeland claims should thus be understood not simply as a measure of the intensity of attachment to territory (though they certainly are that), but as reflecting a distinct reason for the existence of such attachment in the first place. While material reasons could still shape the scope of homelands and conflict over them, there are good theoretical reasons to believe that the value of homelands is not reducible to these material calculations.

While homelands function like religious sacred values, it is worth emphasizing that they are nationalist sacred values, not religious ones. This distinction shapes who it is that cares about a particular territory (conationals rather than cobelievers), which territory they care about (the national homeland rather than sites of miracles or prayer), and why it has symbolic value (because it constitutes the nation rather than because it is the place where the human world and the divine intersect). While both homelands and holy sites are sacred to their believers, not all sacred religious sites are part of the nationalist homeland and the homeland may not be religiously sanctified. This distinction enables systematic study by ensuring that we are studying similar phenomena and not muddying the waters by comparing, for example, the German desire for *Ostdeutchland* with Sikh concerns about desecrating the Golden Temple.

Understanding homelands as a sacred value does not mean that the application of homeland territoriality to lost lands cannot be deployed instrumentally. For example, Idi Amin's sudden affirmation in 1974 that the Ugandan homeland extended all the way to the Kagera River was clearly intended to legitimate the invasion of Tanzania. However, such applications of homeland territoriality in the context of a conflict with a neighbor imply that, at least domestically, they are more than merely cheap talk. In order to serve as an informative signal to international audiences, these audiences would have to believe that the claim was credible. Since leaders are rational, we would thus be unlikely to observe the use of homeland claims where leaders know they would fail.[44] That is, the effective instrumental use of homeland claims in the international arena depends on the assumption that such claims would resonate domestically. Consistent with this possibility, chapters 5 and 6 show that the application of homeland territoriality across new international borders does not occur as frequently as we would expect if it was only cheap talk.

Finally, even if deployed insincerely, the application of homeland territoriality to lost lands is always implicated in domestic political contestation over the appropriate extent of the homeland. At a minimum, the use of homeland discourse, like political speech in general, shapes "people's minds about what goals are valuable and about the roles they play (or should play) in social life."[45] Public applications of homeland territoriality to lost lands foster the sense that others see those territories as part of the homeland. The more individuals believe that everyone else believes these territories are part of the homeland, the less likely they are to challenge those notions even if they privately disagree.[46] Since the application of homeland territoriality to lost lands is a rhetorical act, the public designation of the lost lands as part of the homeland effectively reinforces the continued homeland status of these lands.

One implication of the ideational value of homelands is that their loss ought to lead to more international conflict than the loss of nonhomeland territory. Chapter 6 takes up this hypothesis. Consistent with the view of homelands as discursively defined sacred ground, it demonstrates that losing homeland territory is systematically associated with more international conflict, including violent conflict, than losing nonhomeland territory.

Domestic Contestation over the Homeland

Just because nationalists attribute tremendous value to the homeland does not mean that they necessarily agree on its extent or on the reason particular parcels of land are part of it. All nationalisms deny the existence of these disagreements. However, as Crawford Young noted, nationalisms actively suppress such disagreements precisely because the definition of the nation, including its homeland, is so contested.[47] While the degree of actual internal variation is likely to fluctuate between cases and over time within them, given the commonplace expectation of contestation over other aspects of nationalism and social identity, there is good reason to expect that domestic actors can disagree about the homeland as well.[48]

There are at least two different kinds of domestic variations regarding the homeland that are especially relevant. The first, and most direct, is over exactly which parcels of land ought to be included in the homeland. The empirical existence of domestic variation on this question has been identified in a variety of cases around the globe, including in the Croatian, Ethiopian, Indian, Irish, Israeli, Macedonian, Palestinian, Pakistani, Polish, Romanian, and Russian contexts.[49] As Joya Chatterji noted with some exaggeration, there "were almost as many images of Pakistan as Jinnah had followers."[50] Figures 1.1 and 1.2 illustrate a typical example, from the Ethiopian case, in which different political movements display different map-images of the homeland. Figure 1.1 depicts the cover of the pamphlet declaring the establishment of the provisional military government (the Derg) that overthrew Emperor Haile Selassie in 1974. Over their slogan of "Ethiopia Tikdem," or Ethiopia First, is a map-image of the Ethiopian homeland as they delimited it. Figure 1.2, by contrast, depicts the cover of a booklet published by the Tigray People's Liberation Front (TPLF)—the leading faction in a civil war waged against the Derg—a decade later. The map-image of the homeland for which it is fighting is denoted by the area in which its soldiers are depicted. Crucially, unlike the Derg's conception of the bounds of Ethiopia, the TPLF excludes the area of present-day Eritrea. In other words, unlike the Derg, the TPLF did not consider Eritrea to be part of the Ethiopian homeland (even if they would have liked to have control of the territory for other reasons).[51] The existence of different map-images of the homeland within a society matters for at least two reasons. First, they reflect variation in the ideational value of particular parcels of land within a society and thus the possibility of different calculations about how much should be sacrificed to regain them. Second, as I will elaborate below, the existence of domestic variation opens the door to the possibility that change in the homeland's scope can take place through an evolutionary process.

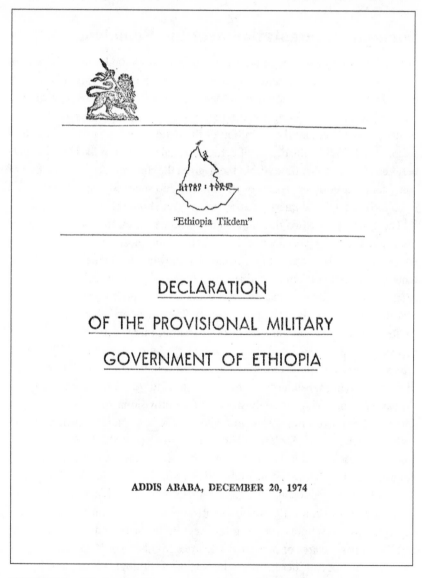

"Ethiopia Tikdem"

DECLARATION

OF THE PROVISIONAL MILITARY

GOVERNMENT OF ETHIOPIA

ADDIS ABABA, DECEMBER 20, 1974

FIGURE 1.1 Map-image of the homeland by the Ethiopian Derg, 1974. Pamphlet cover, Michigan State University Libraries, DT387.9.A32.

9th ANNIVERSARY

OF THE

TIGRAY PEOPLE'S LIBERATION FRONT

T.P.L.F.   FEB. 18, 1975 -1984

FIGURE 1.2 Map-image of the homeland by the Tigray People's Liberation Front, 1984. UCLA Library.

A second kind of variation is over *why* particular parcels of land are part of the homeland. Despite the common view of nationalists as inherently territorially expansionist, their territorial aspirations are not unlimited. Nationalists do not seek to conquer the world; their nationalist territorial ambitions, while perhaps revanchist, are limited to territory that they understand to be part of their homeland. As noted above, delimiting the homeland's scope is a central part of the nationalist project. As a result, nationalists devote a lot of energy to justifying why particular land is part of the homeland. They deploy a range of logics with which to do so, including historical, legal, religious, demographic, security, and economic rationales, often in combination.[52]

These different logics of legitimation are not equally available to all parts of the nationalist political spectrum. Some of this variety stems from nationalism's multidimensional character.[53] While homelands are valuable, nationalists care about more than a "place under the sun"; they may also seek ethnic homogeneity or the creation of a particular political regime, among other cardinal goals. These additional commitments shape the rationales particular movements prefer to use to justify the application of homeland territoriality to particular parcels. Secular nationalists, for example, are less likely to use religious justifications. Ethnic nationalists are less likely to use demographic rationales if the land in question is populated by non-coethnics. Other ideological commitments also matter. For example, as will be shown below, for decades after World War II, the West German Christian Democratic Party (CDU), which was committed to integrating West Germany into the West as a way of regaining German sovereignty, justified its continued claims to the Saar, to East Germany, and to the lands east of the Oder-Neisse boundary in terms of international law and the rights of people to self-determination. The Social Democratic Party (SPD), which was more skeptical of Western integration, appealed to the historical German presence in those lands and to preventing the resuscitation of the territorial revanchist desires that helped trigger World War II.

Different logics of legitimation matter because they can have divergent territorial implications and domestic political consequences. For example, ethnically based justifications are relatively more difficult to sustain with regard to areas that do not contain significant numbers of coethnics (or that no longer do), while religious and historical justifications can be applied with less regard for demographic realities. Logics of legitimation also limit what those deploying them can credibly do. For example, while the CDU's emphasis on international law and self-determination helped legitimate the reunion of West Germany with the Saar and East Germany, it undermined their ability to claim the lands east of the Oder-Neisse Line after Poland's transition to democracy. Finally, as Stacie Goddard showed, different logics of legitimation also mobilize different constituencies, who may have differing levels of attachment to particular territories.

These mobilizational consequences of alternative logics of legitimation can therefore shape who is part of a ruling coalition and limit leaders' flexibility on territorial issues.[54]

Domestic variation in the definition of the homeland's extent or the logic used to justify claiming it can arise in a number of ways. If the contours of the homeland are selected as solutions to coordination dilemmas,[55] the observed variation could arise either because multiple potential focal points are available (i.e., there are multiple past boundaries or natural features around which coordination is possible) or because such coordination takes time and our observation happens to occur during this interregnum.

Variation can also emerge when a nation loses access to parts of its homeland, as there is likely to be a distribution of responses to the new political landscape. Some may be willing to accommodate the new reality, while true believers are motivated to change it. It is also possible that political leaders could introduce new variants when responding to external pressures or seeking to stay in power in the new circumstances.[56] Variants of either kind can also emerge as novel solutions to local political problems. As I have shown in my earlier work, new variants can begin as tactical steps taken to gain power or as short-term stratagems to enable cooperation between political movements with different territorial ambitions.[57]

The importance of domestic variation in the definition of the homeland implies that the conventional focus on the ethnic group or the state as the unit of analysis in studies of territorial conflict would be usefully complemented by analyses that capture the impact of this variation. For this reason, the process tracing in the case studies focuses on domestic political movements.[58] Political movements are the actors who choose one strategy of legitimation over another and reap the benefits (or pay the costs) of their decisions.[59] These movements, and their leaders, are also the actors who are socially empowered to articulate homeland claims and to modify them.[60] As a result, it is in and by these movements that the vision of the homeland's extent is actually constructed. Focusing on political movements is especially useful because it enables the examination of processes, like outbidding and evolutionary dynamics, that require variation in order to operate.[61] This is especially so for evolutionary dynamics because the mechanism of selection (political success or failure) usually takes place at the level of the political movement rather than at the individual, ethnic group, or state level.

Evolution and the Contraction of the Homeland

The importance of national territory underlies the substantial agreement among scholars that, at least as an empirical matter, contenders in territorial conflict tend to view territory as if it were indivisible.[62] Many scholars rightly make the case that it is the *perception* of indivisibility that is critical and that leaders act *as if* territory is indivisible. This is certainly how nationalists understand their homeland. Ahmed Shukeiri, the first leader of the Palestine Liberation Organization, could have been speaking on behalf of all nationalists when he demanded all of the "Holy Land ... because it cannot be a Holy Land if it is partitioned; holiness is indivisible."[63] It is not just the present contours of the homeland that are seen as immutable, but, as Thongchai Winichakul wryly showed, nationalists can extend the stable existence of their homeland back into history, even into periods where it did not actually exist.[64]

As Winichakul intimates, there is no need to accept such nationalist claims at face value. Indeed, among contemporary scholars of nationalism and geography, the view that homelands are immutable is a minority position. This is the case because the identification of a particular territory as the national homeland is a fundamentally social and political act.[65] The link between a nation and its homeland may be based on some perceived historical tie to the land (i.e., some cultural region), but this link can be more or less historically tenuous. For example, the Boers believed South Africa was their divinely promised homeland despite being settlers from another continent.[66] French nationalists assume that *l'Hexagone* is the French homeland despite having had to engage in a century-long project to forge a French nation from the multiple groups in the area to inhabit it.[67] Similarly, the fact that the forefathers of Uzbek nationalists are unlikely to have thought of themselves as Uzbek before their consolidation as an ethnonational group in the early 1920s, does not prevent contemporary Uzbek nationalists from calculating the worth of the homeland in terms of "the remains of our forefathers / Who turned into dust for this precious soil."[68] Even German nationalism, often taken as representing the archetype of a well-established nationalism, engaged in an explicit project of constructing the homeland's extent.[69] The initial identification of a particular territory as the homeland may even be essentially random, as in the argument that the boundaries of homelands may have originated as solutions to coordination dilemmas arising from the need to provide collective defense.[70]

The same theoretical underpinnings that recognize the importance of homelands also provide the scaffolding for expecting it to be mutable. Since mere land is transformed into homeland through the application of nationalist territoriality, homelands can be transformed back into mere land through its withdrawal. After all, territoriality is, as Robert Sack reminds us, a strategy used to control space, not a feature of the natural or physical world, "and as a strategy, territoriality can be turned on and off."[71] Concretely, this means that the geographic scope of the homeland expands when homeland territoriality is applied to new parcels of land and contracts when it is withdrawn from areas to which it had been previously applied. Though, as will be shown below, such change is rarely as instantaneous or Manichaean as Sack's metaphor implies. Rather, the exclusion of the lost lands from the rhetorical depictions of the homeland occurs when once-canonical familial metaphors applied to a territory fade from use, when domestic actors no longer care enough about the territory to explicitly lament its loss, or when they exclude it from the commonly articulated map-images of the homeland. That is, change in the extent of the homeland takes place when the familiar rhetorical emblem of the homeland morphs into a new one. As with the internalization of norms more generally, the eventual absence of debate over the exclusion of lost lands in a society is a marker of its acceptance.[72]

While claims that nations are infinitely fluid have little empirical traction, the reality of some change in the geographic scope of the homeland has been documented in a wide variety of contexts. As noted above, despite the early twentieth-century Italian nationalist definition of the "geographical, historical and ethnographical boundaries of Italy" as including "Trentino, Eastern Friuli, Trieste with Istria, Fiume and Dalmatia," few Italian nationalists currently argue that Italy ought to extend its sovereignty over the parts of Croatia and Slovenia that were once seen as such vital parts of the Italian homeland.[73] In the Israeli case, the heirs of the right-wing Herut movement no longer claim Jordan as appropriately part of their homeland. Similarly, Israeli religious nationalists originally identified the homeland as corresponding to the divinely promised land "from the River of Egypt . . . to the great river, the River Euphrates" (Genesis 15:18), a claim that included present-day Israel, the West Bank, the Gaza Strip, Jordan, Lebanon, and parts of Egypt, Syria, Iraq, and Turkey. The view of the appropriate extent of the homeland they articulate today includes present-day Israel, the West Bank, the Gaza Strip, and the Golan Heights, but tends to exclude areas in Jordan, Lebanon, Egypt, Syria, Iraq, and Turkey that were once included.[74] Slovenian nationalists once claimed not just contemporary Slovenia, but parts of present-day Italy, Austria, Hungary, and Croatia. Today, however, most Slovenian political movements accept the legitimacy and appropriateness of the borders between Slovenia and its neighbors.[75] Macedonian nationalist movements have also shifted the areas they include within the scope of the state they desired.[76] Likewise, while Indian nationalists ardently rejected the partition of the British Raj in 1947 and still include Kashmir within the bounds of the Indian homeland, the equivalent claims once made with regard to Lahore and Dhaka are no longer commonly raised.[77] This list could go on. Herder, in other words, was only partially right; homelands matter a great deal, but the loss of homeland territory can sometimes be accommodated.

This book shows that the withdrawal of homeland territoriality from lost lands is often driven by an evolutionary dynamic in which the short-term political success of rhetorical variants of the homeland's extent, or of logics of legitima-tion that implicitly exclude lost lands, enables these variants to displace more expansive ones as long as these returns are sustained. As in other contexts, evo-lutionary dynamics drive change wherever there is variation along some dimen-sion of interest, differential success between these variants in their reproduction (often termed "selection"), and time for a relatively more successful variant to displace less successful ones.[78]

Homelands are frequently characterized by all three elements required for change to take place through evolutionary dynamics. As I have already high-lighted, domestic variation in the precise extent of the homeland and in the logic of legitimation used to apply homeland territoriality is commonly observed and may be especially likely when nations lose access to parts of their homeland. Such domestic variation is also more likely the more open a society is. While authori-tarian regimes are rarely internally monolithic, they can more easily repress or otherwise limit the articulation of different map-images of the homeland or of inconvenient logics used to justify homeland claims. Democratic settings, by contrast, are comparatively more likely to provide political space for the articula-tion of domestic disagreement over the appropriate extent of the homeland and the particular logic used to justify those claims.

Variation, however, is not enough to bring about change through evolutionary dynamics. It is the intersection of variation with the consequences of domestic political competition that drives the transformation of notions of the homeland. Change takes place when one particular variant is systematically associated with more success in the domestic political game than other variants for long enough. This political success means that the variant would be articulated more and more commonly (differential success) than the alternatives. The association with success occurs when positive political returns accrue to a movement articulat-ing a variant which, implicitly or explicitly, withdraws homeland territoriality from lost lands. These positive political returns mean that these variants will be repeated more often than others, reframed as right and just, and, if successful for long enough, eventually displace (though usually not eliminate) other visions of the homeland's extent. As Neta Crawford showed in a different context, in this way, relatively small initial changes—such as shifting the logic of legitimation with which homeland territoriality is applied or deploying a more ambiguous rhetorical map-image of the homeland—"may avalanche into large, unantici-pated, openings for reform, further argument, and institutionalization."[79]

The positive domestic political returns that drive this process can accrue in a number of ways. For example, where rhetorical variants are introduced in order to help a political movement achieve what may even be a short-term goal, to the extent that this goal is achieved, both the political benefits of maintaining the modulation as the ideological standard and the cost of returning to the original position increase. Likewise, when a more ambiguous territorial formulation enables the formation of a particular coalition, the more ambiguous formula will become harder to abandon because doing so risks breaking up the coalition that led to success in the first place.[80]

Political failure also matters. Perfectly sensible legitimating logics or variants of the extent of the homeland are less likely to spread if the movements articulating them lose the domestic political battle (even if this occurs for reasons unrelated to territorial issues).[81] For example, in the context of the case studies to follow, the communist parties in West Germany, Italy, and Palestine all accepted the loss of homeland territory relatively quickly. However, their domestic political failure meant that positive political returns did not accrue to their views and their map-image of the homeland did not spread widely.[82]

In another pathway, positive returns to new variants can accrue as a movement becomes reliant on the support of a constituency mobilized by a particular variant. As political movements become dependent on these constituencies for their political fortunes, it becomes harder to shift away from the legitimating logic that mobilized them.[83] While Goddard uses such a lock-in effect to explain how previously divisible territory becomes conceptualized as indivisible, this book demonstrates that similar processes can also trap political movements into making less, rather than more, expansive claims.

Changing contexts can also mean that a logic used to claim homeland territory in the past may come to hinder the application of homeland territoriality to particular territories at a later date. For example, as chapter 2 shows, the CDU's appeal to the legal provisionality of the FRG's borders and primacy of the right of self-determination of the individuals living in Germany's lost homeland territories proved to be tremendously successful in securing the return of the Saar to Germany in 1957 and undergirding the unification with East Germany in 1990. However, it ultimately undermined the CDU's ability to apply homeland territoriality to the lands under Polish and Russian rule when these states democratized. Similarly, chapter 3 shows that Italy's leaders' decision to emphasize ethnicity as the legitimating principle underlying their application of homeland territoriality to Istria and Dalmatia after World War II made it much harder to continue claiming those territories as part of the homeland after the Italian exodus from Yugoslavia.

The view of change as a process that results from the interplay of variation, differential success, and time implies that the withdrawal of homeland territoriality can occur even in so-called "settled times" and in the absence of exogenous shocks. This is the case because variation and differential success characterize politics in both settled and unsettled times. As Ann Swidler argued, all "real cultures contain diverse, often conflicting symbols, rituals, stories, and guides to action."[84] Settled times, as Jack Snyder rightly elaborated, are thus never actually "entirely settled. Every discourse of legitimation is plagued with internal contradictions stemming from its multivocality. . . . In a pluralistic marketplace of ideas, these contradictions become the basis for incessant jockeying and debate, animated both by broader social trends and by the logic of the discourse itself."[85]

The actual conduct of this jockeying can also facilitate the withdrawal of homeland territoriality from lost lands (subject to the presence of positive returns to the new variant), and its presence can be used to distinguish this mechanism of the withdrawal of homeland territoriality from more mechanical alternatives that are not as rooted in domestic politics. Because of the homeland's cardinal importance to nationalists, it is very difficult to hide modulations to its map-image.[86] Nationalists, well aware that the application of homeland territoriality is a fundamentally rhetorical act, are quite sensitive to the implications of new rhetorical formulations that could be understood as withdrawing homeland territoriality from lost lands. As the conflict between Greece and the Republic of Macedonia (now called the Republic of North Macedonia) over the very name of the latter suggests, nationalists invest so much energy in fights over place names, maps, and other rhetorical applications of homeland territoriality precisely because they fear that a new rhetorical formula would undermine a location's status as part of the homeland.[87]

As a result, when new variants, of either kind, emerge, ideological truth tellers will invariably exclaim that the proponents of these variants are sinning against the nation itself.[88] In the German context, for example, Konrad Adenauer was accused of betraying the German nation for prioritizing "unity in freedom" over the immediate reunification of Germany. Willy Brandt suffered analogous accusations when promoting his New Ostpolitik. Yitzhak Rabin was assassinated by an Israeli nationalist for working toward the partition of the land of Israel. A Palestinian advocate of agreeing to a partition of Palestine even had a rocket fired at his house.

Advocates of new variants want to survive, politically as well as physically. As a result, they tend to deploy three common tactics along with the new rhetorical variant: arguments that the variant, rather than reflecting any underlying change, is actually the best way to achieve the original goal; increasing ambiguity about where homeland territoriality is applied; and rhetorical coercion. Where these rhetorical gambits succeed, they reinforce the viability of the variant in whose name they are deployed. Where such rhetorical gambits are missing, it is unlikely that change is the product of a politically based evolutionary dynamic.

The first tactic—framing the new variant as the best way to achieve a traditional goal—is often used to justify practical policies that are ideologically distasteful. For example, as the next chapter shows, the German SPD vigorously championed its New Ostpolitik in the late 1960s and early 1970s as the best way of keeping alive the possibility of reunification even if it appeared to foreclose the possibility by de facto recognizing the East German state. Such justifications may be insincere stratagems used to gain support for unpopular policies. However, even when deployed sincerely, that is, even when there is no prior intention to withdraw homeland territoriality from lost lands, the political success of these policies renders them and the variant of the homeland associated with them harder to abandon. In such contexts, over time, the ideological definition of the homeland will come into closer alignment with what works in the domestic political context.

The second tactic, the blurring of the map-image of the homeland, often takes the form of replacing an explicit application of homeland territoriality to land with a more generic and ambiguous formula. Such blurring may be especially attractive if it helps movements simultaneously appeal to multiple, even opposed, constituencies. For example, the secular Israeli Right, in the process of withdrawing homeland territoriality from the East Bank of the Jordan River, replaced the comparatively specific claim to "both banks of the Jordan" with the comparatively more ambiguous claim to "the whole land of Israel."[89] The resulting ambiguity about exactly where homeland territoriality is applied allows proponents of the new formula to plausibly deny that any change has taken place even as the failure to explicitly flag the homeland status of the lost lands (in the absence of other ways of applying homeland territoriality) amounts to its withdrawal. The smuggling of the withdrawal of homeland territoriality from lost lands into familiar justifications of well-established ideas allows homeland territoriality to be withdrawn from lost lands even while appearing to maintain fidelity to old norms.[90]

Finally, the withdrawal of homeland territoriality from lost lands is often defended and promoted through the use of rhetorical coercion. Rhetorical coercion is the use of an opponent's own normative commitments to trap them into acceding to positions that they would otherwise reject.[91] Rhetorical coercion is available for use by proponents of more modest rhetorical variants of the homeland because nationalism is multifaceted. As noted above, although the homeland is a sacred value for nationalists, it is not the only one. Nationalists also desire control over their political destiny or, in some cases, an ethnically homogeneous state. They may also be committed to establishing a particular political regime. Advocates of new variants can deploy rhetorical coercion by framing the truth tellers who adhere to maximalist views of the homeland as undermining the achievement of these other, equally important, nationalist goals. The trade of the explicit claim to the lost parts of the homeland for the achievement of these other nationalist goals can be used to render the accommodation to territorial losses more palatable. In effect, successful rhetorical coercion enables the application of a (nonmaterial) cost-benefit analysis to the continued application of homeland territoriality to lost lands—an analysis that may be critical in eventually excluding the lost parts of the homeland from its scope.[92]

It is worth emphasizing that the possibility of a trade of claims to lost homeland territory for some other ideologically valuable goal is built into the nationalist understanding of homelands as a sacred value. As I have already noted, sacred values, including those of the homeland, are not those with infinite utility, but rather values whose relative utility is measured along a nonmaterialist metric.[93] As Philip Tetlock's pioneering work found, the restriction against comparisons associated with sacred values only prevents tradeoffs "with bounded or secular values" not trading among things that all have sacred value.[94] This means that, while attempting to trade a sacred value for a nonsacred one will almost certainly elicit a backlash, it is possible to trade sacred ground for other, equally sacred, nationalist principles. The use of rhetorical coercion effectively specifies the currency of the side payments that can render homelands effectively divisible. While the economic or strategic value of territory, or even the costs of conflict, may not transform indivisible homelands into divisible territory, side payments in values that are equally important to nationalists, such as sovereignty, national homogeneity, or the preservation of other parts of the homeland, may do so.

The acceptability of trading sacred values against each other has been validated experimentally in a variety of settings, including in nationalist contexts. In pioneering work, investigators found that even just acknowledging Palestinian refugees' right of return, a pillar of Palestinian nationalism, made Palestinians more amenable to agreeing to a division of their homeland.[95] Scholars have also found that the desire for an ethnically homogeneous state can check irredentist desires despite the value of the homeland on the other side of the border.[96] Some homeland territory can also be sacrificed to maintain control of other parts of the homeland. For example, in the 1920s and early 1930s, Labor Zionists were willing to shift their attention away from actualizing their claim to the East Bank of the Jordan River in order to cement their presence in the area to the west of the river.[97] As will be shown in chapter 2, Willy Brandt and Helmut Kohl defended the abandonment of the claim to the German homeland east of the Oder and the Neisse Rivers as the price to be paid for the unification of the German homeland to its west. Chapter 4 will also show how Fatah, the main Palestinian nationalist movement, was willing to trade its overt claim to part of the homeland in order to maintain the principle of Palestinian control over their national movement.

The possibility that homeland territoriality can be withdrawn from lost lands is one element that distinguishes this book's argument from the other work on symbolic values in international relations.[98] Like that body of work, the theory of homelands and their impact presented in this book recognizes that understanding the power of homelands requires viewing them from the inside out—that is, from the perspective of the people involved. The symbolic values literature, however, often roots these views in basic personality traits—traits that are, for better or worse, very difficult to change. As a result, a symbolic politics theory of homelands might recognize that different groups of people could have different views of the homeland's extent but would not expect those views to change unless basic personality traits changed as well.

Instead of looking for change in personality traits, this book contends that mundane political competition plays a critical role in the withdrawal of homeland territoriality from lost lands. New variants of either the rhetorical map-image of the homeland or of the logic of legitimation used to apply homeland territoriality to lost lands may arise in response to external events, geopolitical considerations, or the exigencies of everyday politics. Domestic political competition forces political actors to defend and justify these variants against accusations of ideological betrayal and heresy. In the course of this defense, proponents of the new variant will often claim that the variant, rather than reflecting any change, is actually the best way to achieve the original goal, increase ambiguity about where homeland territoriality is applied, or deploy rhetorical coercion—all of which, if successful, serve to mute the original claim and enable the new variant to be articulated more commonly. Where the new variant is associated with domestic political success, it becomes harder for a political movement to abandon it, regardless of the original intention behind its introduction. Over time, the newly successful variant will displace the articulation of more expansive rhetorical formulas. The corresponding withdrawal of homeland territoriality from the lands omitted from the new rhetorical delimitation of the homeland effectively reshapes the homeland's scope.

Alternative Explanations for the Withdrawal of Homeland Territoriality

Scholarship in comparative politics and international relations offers a number of potential explanations for how and why homeland territoriality could be withdrawn from lost lands that do not rely on the combined impact of variation, differential success in the domestic political arena, and time. Broadly speaking, these alternatives tend to emphasize the dominant role of either the passage of time, rational adaptation to new information, or leaders' instrumental considerations on their own. These alternatives and their empirically observable implications are summarized in table 1.1.

TABLE 1.1 Observable expectations of alternative processes of contraction in the scope of the homeland

EXPLANATION OF CHANGE	ACTOR	TIMING	CONSISTENT
Evolutionary dynamic	Any movement	Linked to political success of the new variant	No (Gradual displacement of old variant)
Passage of time	Ruling party, cohorts born after loss of homeland territory, or all movements	Linked to generational change, regime institutionalization, or historical era	Yes
Adaptation to new information about the world	All movements exposed to the new information	Immediately	Yes
Instrumental considerations	Ruling party	Immediately	Yes

The first alternative explanation points to the various effects of the passage of time on its own and comes in a number of guises. For example, some arguments focus on the replacement of individuals as older generations die off and are replaced by younger cohorts.[99] From this perspective, even if there are legacy effects or if the current population does not or cannot change its views for some other reason, cohorts who grow up after the loss of homeland territory are more likely to abandon claims to lost lands because actual control of these parts of the homeland was never part of their lived experience. As they replace older generations in the body politic, their vision of the homeland is expected to displace the one held by their parents.

Other arguments that highlight the passage of time point to world-historical effects such as the declining international legitimacy of challenging international borders in the second half of the twentieth century. The rise and internalization of the norm of border fixity, to use Boaz Atzili's term, implies that the loss of homeland territory would be accommodated as time passes.[100] Contractions in the homeland's scope in this account would come about either through generational replacement as younger cohorts grow up in a world characterized by this new norm, because leaders have internalized the new norms, or because leaders recognize that the international community's reduced tolerance of transgressions against this norm means that they are less likely to be successful if they do challenge it.[101] In all these varieties, the withdrawal of homeland territoriality from lost lands is a function of the time since the rise of the territorial integrity norm.

Another argument based on world-historical effects points to the secular devaluation of territory that accompanied globalization. The de-linking of power and territorial control as a result of economic integration implies that as global integration increases, territoriality of all kinds, including nationalist territoriality, should decrease. As a result, from this perspective, states that are highly integrated into the global economy would be expected to be relatively less concerned with territory and therefore less likely to continue applying homeland territoriality to lost lands.[102]

A fourth version points to the institutionalization of regimes over time. As Edward Mansfield and Jack Snyder persuasively argued, political leaders where ruling coalitions are fragile (mostly in new democracies and during periods of transition) face increased incentives to use nationalist appeals, including territorial claims, to gain mass allies.[103] From this perspective, the institutionalization of the regime leads to the waning of applications of homeland territoriality to lost lands as the need to use nationalist rhetoric to shore up the ruling coalition also declines.

Time surely matters. However, rather than linking its impact to structural features of the world, evolutionary dynamics allow it to matter through the time it takes for new variants to displace older ones. This different view of what time is doing has a number of empirically observable implications. Explanations that focus on the inexorable and one-way passage of time necessarily expect the withdrawal of homeland territoriality to be monotonic. Depending on the particular version of the time-based arguments, such arguments would also anticipate the withdrawal of homeland territoriality to be more or less mechanistic. Evolutionary dynamics do not necessarily expect either. Linking the role of time to the cadence of the domestic political success of new variants implies that change can take place more quickly than through generational replacement or before a regime is institutionalized. Nor does change have to be monotonic. While time flows in only one direction, politics does not. Losing variants can regain political strength, and homeland territoriality can be reapplied to lost lands even after it is withdrawn. Indeed, as chapter 5 will show, on average, the application of homeland territoriality to lost lands both wanes over time and experiences a significant resurgence.

A second set of alternative accounts of the withdrawal of homeland territoriality is based on a kind of preference updating to new information about the world. From this perspective, new realities created by the imposition of a new border, population movements, changes in military capacities, or information about a territory's resource endowment can shift the otherwise path-dependent definition of the homeland's scope off its track by offering an incentive to change and punishing intransigence. Sometimes, for instance, drawing a border is assumed to be enough. For example, some have argued that the creation of the Irish (para) state led Unionists to constrict their focus to Northern Ireland and withdraw homeland territoriality from the rest of the island.[104] People, in this perspective, simply adjust to the new reality.

Other than the drawing of the border itself, shifts in the geographical distribution of coethnics are perhaps the most influential trigger that this set of explanations points to. This view builds on the assumption that the location of coethnics shapes the borders of the homeland in the first place;[105] an assumption consistent with both the association between separating warring populations and reduced conflict, and the presence of economic "border effects" along ethnic lines.[106] From this perspective, demographic changes (such as the expulsion of coethnics from lost homeland territory) could reasonably be expected to lead to the internalization of new borders that encompass current concentrations of coethnics. Conversely, according to the same logic, the continued presence of coethnics in a particular territory or mass migration into it, would make it less likely that homeland territoriality would be withdrawn from lost lands.[107]

A similar account could point, not to changes in who lives in a territory, but to the material value of the land itself. Some pieces of land host important industrial centers, others oil wells or diamond mines, yet others have strategic relevance.[108] According to this line of reasoning, when the tangible value of a piece of land that is contiguous to the national movement's territorial base changes—as a result of the discovery of new resources or a change in the geostrategic environment—the imagining of the desired national state will also change to accommodate the new information.[109]

While new information about the real state of the world clearly shapes behavior, the analysis below shows that adaptation to reality is not automatic. This is the case because the lessons imparted by changing realities are the product of interpretation by political actors.[110] The interpretation of new realities is shaped by the beliefs of those experiencing them and the legitimating logics they use to apply homeland territoriality. These can lead to very different reactions to the same reality. In the Irish case, for example, while Unionists may have adapted to the new reality, Irish nationalists in Northern Ireland clearly did not. More broadly, those applying religious or historical forms of legitimation to justify the application of homeland territoriality are less likely to be persuaded by ethnic cleansing that a particular place is no longer part of their homeland than those who rely on ethnic demography to justify their claims. Variants of the map-image of the homeland or alternative logics of legitimation that are relatively more congruent with the dictates of observable reality are more likely to generate positive political returns than claims that are not buttressed by reality, but simple congruence with objective observable reality is not enough to explain change.

The impact of new realities also depends on the distribution of preferences among the public whose support generates the political returns.[111] Where the

relevant public remains committed to a more expansive vision of the homeland, deviating from it, even if doing so would be more congruent with observable reality, could be political suicide. This helps explain why the Communists
in West Germany, Italy, and Palestine, despite offering a more realistic version
of the homeland, did not succeed. In such cases, or where expansive territorial
claims are a relatively easy way to successfully establish one's nationalist creden-
tials, outbidding dynamics could lead to the continued application of homeland territoriality to lost lands even at great cost.[112] However, if public opinion is
more moderate than the leaders of a particular political movement, or if domestic political success is associated with a less expansive vision of the homeland,
the increasing returns to such variants can lead to the spread of more moderate
claims.[113] Finally, these arguments face significant concerns about endogeneity.
For example, it is possible that the presence of coethnics in a territory leads to
including that territory as part of the homeland. However, as the settlement projects carried out by China, Indonesia, Israel, Iraq, Morocco, and the United States,
to name a few, demonstrate, it is also possible that the presence of coethnics in a
territory is a product of the prior belief that it is part of the homeland.[114]

A third set of alternative explanations for how homelands contract emphasizes the instrumental considerations of leaders. For instance, power considerations could matter. Since, ceteris paribus, more territory is better than less, we
might expect leaders to expand the definition of the homeland to accommodate
what they can get if they are strong enough to take it.[115] By the same token, since
leaders are strategic actors, the manifest inability to reassert control over lost territory ought to aid the elision of that territory from the homeland's scope.

In an environment of strategic interactions, information about resolve conveyed through the application or withdrawal of homeland territoriality by one
side could also shape the likelihood that homeland territoriality would be withdrawn by the other side. In this scenario, for example, a desire to signal resolve
during a conflict may encourage the application of homeland territoriality to lost
lands. The context in which the border was drawn might also play a role. Because
it might be easier to mobilize populations around land ripped away due to war as
opposed to land ceded through bilateral negotiations or legal proceedings, these
conditions could also affect the likelihood that homeland territoriality would be
withdrawn from lost lands.

Ethnic geography and regional dynamics can play an important role in shaping these considerations. The agitation for independence, autonomy, or collective
minority rights by coethnics in the lost homeland territory (such as, for example,
the mobilization of the Russian Bloc party in Crimea) could pressure leaders of
the society that lost the territory to apply homeland territoriality to it in an effort
to support the struggle of their coethnics.[116] Likewise, the presence of shared

coethnics in other neighboring states may trigger a competition for regional power or for the right to speak for the ethnic group as a whole. This competition, in turn, could induce leaders to apply homeland territoriality to lost lands.

The map-image of the homeland and the logic of legitimation deployed by leaders could also be shaped by pressure exerted by external patrons. This is certainly the case for stateless nationalist movements, who are relatively weak by definition. It is also a plausible influence on state-based political actors, as was especially the case during the Cold War. The refraction of nearly every international dispute through the lens of superpower competition meant that the superpowers sometimes had an outsized influence on the domestic politics (and even the political positions) of their clients. The desires of the superpowers (or external patrons more broadly) to ensure stability, reduce overall conflict, and prevent future entanglements may mean that patrons might have different geographical interests than those of the client. In such cases, withdrawing homeland territoriality from lost lands may be the price of securing or maintaining the support of these patrons.[117]

While surely important on their own, instrumental mechanisms of change in the definition of the homeland are missing both a process by which the elite-led modulations spread and become internalized beyond the narrow group of decision makers and an account of why changes in the homeland's scope are not as common as fluctuations in leaders' instrumental considerations. Evolutionary dynamics provide these missing steps. First, it is not enough for leaders to have an incentive to initiate a change. The new variants must be domestically politically successful as well. This success allows variants to be articulated more commonly, shaping the perceptions of the public at large about what their leaders and society in general believe. The political success of new variants, at least in democracies, is an indication of their social and political resonance. Second, unlike the expectation of nearly immediate impact of elite responses to new exigencies, evolutionary dynamics highlight the fact that it takes time for new variants to displace older ones. An evolutionary dynamic thus does not require that populations switch their view of the homeland status of territory at once; instead, it expects the relative frequency of more successful variants to increase, perhaps eventually displacing older alternatives entirely.

The empirical analysis which follows takes advantage of the fact that each alternative explanation has a distinctive combination of empirically observable expectations about the domestic actors who drive the change, the timing of the withdrawal of homeland territoriality, and its consistency. The use of multiple elements of change to evaluate the plausibility of each explanation also helps disentangle alternative explanations where they have similar expectations when it comes to one particular element, but differ on another.[118] These differing expectations are summarized in table 1.1. An explanation that accounts for more components is preferable to one that explains fewer because it passes a higher threshold for hypothesis testing.

I focus on three empirical characteristics of change: who carries it out, its timing, and consistency. Evolutionary dynamics do not have strong prior expectations about who it is that withdraws homeland territoriality from lost lands because new variants can be articulated for many reasons. They do not, however, expect all movements to necessarily change in the same way at the same time. By contrast, transformation driven by a kind of Bayesian updating to new information about the territory or circumstances would expect everyone exposed to the new information to withdraw homeland territoriality from the lost lands more or less simultaneously. This explanation can accommodate domestic variation in the withdrawal of homeland territoriality from lost lands where there is variation in the access to the new information. If the information is only available to some, we can expect only those with privileged access to that information to lead the change and to defend it. Usually, this would be the party in power. For example, parties in government may be expected to change before those in the opposition if governing parties have better insight into, for example, the lack of international support for regaining lost territories by force. Explanations based on the passage of time predict that the withdrawal of homeland territoriality would be concentrated in the ruling party, the age-period cohort that comes of age after the loss of the territory, or widely distributed, depending on the particular pathway through which time is expected to exert its force. Finally, instrumentally based accounts would anticipate that change would be concentrated in ruling parties, who are more likely to be exposed to superpower diktat and strategic considerations.

The timing of change refers to when the withdrawal of homeland territoriality is institutionalized within a movement.[119] Explanations based on either instrumental considerations or adapting to new information about reality expect the withdrawal of homeland territoriality from lost lands to begin relatively close to the time of exposure to the triggering event and to become institutionalized relatively quickly. For example, if the drawing of a new international border is hypothesized to trigger the withdrawal of homeland territoriality from lost lands, the timing of this transformation should closely follow the drawing of the border and be carried relatively quickly throughout the movement. Likewise, if the trigger of change is a shift in information about relative capacity brought about for any reason—new allies, new technologies, and the like—the timing of changes in claims of the appropriate scope of the national state ought to correspond to fluctuations in the relative capacity. Evolutionary explanations based on domestic political competition, however, link the timing of change to the domestic political success associated with the articulation of the new variant. Instrumentally based processes of transformation might point to the same triggering event, but pay much less explicit attention to the success or failure of the resulting actions. Consequently, they expect a close correspondence between the timing of the change and the timing of the trigger. Explanations that highlight the passage of time would point to age-period cohort replacement, the pace of regime institutionalization, or the rate of norm internalization as the factor determining when the change would actually take place.

The alternative explanations also predict that the withdrawal of homeland territoriality would proceed in different ways. When it occurs as a result of updating to new information, the replacement of one map-image of the homeland by another ought to proceed smoothly and consistently among those with access to that information. If, given new information or incentives, it is irrational to continue articulating the old territorial claims, once initiated, the ideological change ought to be consistent. Evolutionary dynamics, by contrast, do not expect consistency even by those promoting the new variants. Since the initiation of the process of withdrawing homeland territoriality may be orthogonal to territorial issues, or even unintentional, there are good reasons to expect the pattern of articulation in such cases to be inconsistent. Moreover, since any change is linked to the accrual of positive domestic political returns to excluding lost lands from the scope of the homeland, and since such positive returns take time to manifest, this intervening period may be characterized by inconsistent applications of homeland territoriality to lost lands.

The case studies that follow examine the ability of each explanation to account for these empirically observable elements of the withdrawal of homeland territoriality from lost lands by tracing the process (or its absence despite expectations to the contrary) in the German, Italian, and Palestinian contexts. The statistical analysis in the second half of the book complements this approach by identifying cross-national proxies for these alternative explanations of change and investigating the generalizability of the lessons from the case studies.

THE SHIFTING CONTOURS OF THE GERMAN HOMELAND

Germany, opined Gustav Heinemann, West Germany's former president, is a "troublesome fatherland."[1] The trouble was caused by the persistent mismatch between the area to which German nationalism applied homeland territoriality and the actual territory controlled by the German nation-state. The German homeland was commonly described, as the German nationalist poet Ernst Moritz Arndt put it, as extending "Where'er resounds the German tongue, Where'er its hymns to God are sung."[2] More specific map-images of the German fatherland depicted it as spanning the area between the Meuse River in the west, the Vistula River in the east, the Alps, and the North Sea.[3] A similarly expansive vision of the German homeland was embedded in the German national anthem, which, until 1945, identified the homeland as extending over the (smaller) area roughly corresponding to the 1871 borders of the German Empire (see figure 2.1). Regardless of how it was defined, for most of the twentieth century, significant portions of the German homeland were left outside the borders of the German nation-state.

The mismatch between the vision of the homeland's extent and the reality of the territory that was part of the German state increased after World War II. As a result of its defeat, Germany lost East Prussia to the Soviet Union, Pomerania and Silesia to Poland, and the Saar to France. These losses were emotionally and economically devastating.[4] The "Eastern Territories" that were ceded to Russia and Poland constituted nearly a quarter of Germany's land. Observers believed that this loss of Germany's breadbasket would inevitably undermine Germany's economic capabilities.[5] No less important, East Prussia had been the heart of

German nationalism and the core around which the German state had been organized.[6] Indeed, as the label of *Ostdeutschland* (Eastern Germany, often referred to as the Eastern Territories) suggests, at the time, "East Germany" referred to the land east of the Oder and the Neisse Rivers rather than to what would later become the German Democratic Republic (GDR) (see figure 2.1).

Anthony Eden, then the British foreign secretary, openly worried that these partitions of Germany would lead to another war. He contended that Germany's "very extensive territorial losses, which she will regard as unjust and intolerable and to which she will never become resigned, would gravely diminish any hope there may be that Germany might eventually become reconciled to the settlement of Europe."[7] As late as 1961, *Time* magazine argued against Western recognition of either the Oder-Neisse Line or the division between East and West Germany because in the "threeway dismemberment of Germany lie the seeds of future war."[8] Underlying these concerns was the widespread understanding that the phantom-limb pain caused by German territorial losses after World War I precipitated both the Nazi's rise and the Second World War.[9]

The historical importance attributed to the German homeland reflected in these assessments makes the German experience an especially unlikely one

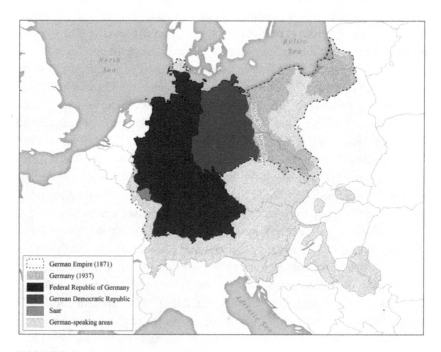

FIGURE 2.1   Germany's shifting borders

in which to illustrate the idea that what counts as the homeland's geographic extent can change over time. The German context is also a useful setting in which to investigate how and why the withdrawal of homeland territoriality occurs, because it is characterized by the simultaneous loss of multiple parcels of homeland territory that displayed significant variation in whether such a withdrawal took place, the actors who carried it out, and its timing.

This chapter argues that an evolutionary dynamic based in domestic political competition best accommodates the variation in the withdrawal of homeland territoriality across territories, the timing of those changes, and the variation in who it was within West Germany that withdrew homeland territoriality from lost lands. Variants—of legitimating strategies used to apply homeland territoriality and of rhetorical map-images of the homeland—that were associated with short-term positive political returns became harder to abandon by the political movement that articulated them. These positive returns effectively locked the political movement articulating the new variants into a new, more modest, understanding of the extent of their homeland.

The chapter begins by tracing the continued application of homeland territoriality to the lands Germany lost after the Second World War by the two main West German political parties and illustrating the particular logics of legitimation they deployed to do so. It then highlights how the political success and failure associated with particular map-images and logics of legitimation shaped their continued use and the timing of change. I conclude the chapter by evaluating the ability of the main alternative explanations to account for the variation in the German case and its empirical features.

Among these alternatives, explanations based on rational adaptation to new information may be especially plausible given the shocks caused by Germany's total defeat in World War II, the construction of the Berlin Wall, and the expulsion of Germans from the lands Germany had lost to the east. Time may have also mattered, as succeeding generations grew less attached to land that was never part of Germany in their lived experience. Finally, the central role Germany played in the Cold War raises the possibility that superpower influence shaped the application of homeland territoriality to lost lands. While these had an effect, on its own each fails to account for important aspects of the withdrawal of homeland territoriality accounted for by evolutionary dynamics.

The Lost Lands in the West German Imagination

At the end of the Second World War, Germany was a humiliated, dismembered, and occupied society. Large and valuable parts of its territory were sliced off and awarded to its neighbors. Even the German state itself ceased to exist. What remained was ruled by four occupying powers; states that cared more about preventing the resurgence of a militant Germany and balancing each other's power than about the future of Germany per se. "It seemed to be," as Peter Alter wrote, "finis Germaniae."[10]

As a result, in addition to the tremendous challenges of postwar reconstruction and reckoning with German responsibility for the Holocaust, Germany's leaders also faced the task of achieving two paramount nationalist goals: reestablishing German independence and regaining control of the lost parts of the homeland. Nationalism in post–World War II Germany was a touchy subject. There was certainly a discomfort with open displays of national pride, as the link between the Nazis and German nationalism discredited militant and openly expansionist forms of nationalism.[11] This discomfort notwithstanding, there was not a rejection of nationalism per se. Had this been the case, Germans would not have been interested in unification or, for that matter, independence. That they still sought these fundamentally nationalist goals demonstrates that German nationalism persisted.

Postwar Germany was characterized by a national consensus that the lands it had lost ought to be redeemed. This consensus was reflected in the nearly unanimous support for reunification. For example, in September 1949, 93 percent of those surveyed in the American zone favored reunification. A decade after the end of the war, reunification still dominated West German political discourse and was seen as the most important issue facing the country.[12] Into the 1960s, all political parties in West Germany except for the Communists called for the reunification of Germany in all its parts, and the Communists' failure to do so was a key reason for their marginalization.[13] Reflecting both the political and popular consensus, Konrad Adenauer, West Germany's dominant postwar leader, wrote to President Eisenhower in 1953 that, although Germany sought to settle the issue peacefully, no German government would ever be in a position to recognize the Oder-Neisse Line nor, it went without saying, the GDR.[14] Consistent with the prevailing view, the preamble of the 1949 West German Basic Law (which functioned as West Germany's constitution) mandated that the West German republic work toward the reunification of Germany.

The continued widespread application of homeland territoriality to the lost lands was also evident in official maps and geography textbooks. Both stressed the unity of Germany in its 1937 borders and labeled the entire area as *Deutschland* (Germany, literally land of the Germans) for decades after the war. The inclusion of the lost lands in the definition of the homeland was also reflected in the refusal to acknowledge the GDR in these cartographical representations of the homeland. If it was named at all, it was labeled the "Soviet Occupied Zone."

The "Eastern Territories" were likewise routinely identified as under temporary Polish or Soviet "administration" rather than as part of those states.[15] As late as 1970, the maps on the evening television weather forecasts still included Silesia, Pomerania, and East Prussia within Germany. That year, a survey found that 70 percent of respondents agreed that "what happened after the war in the East is not final. A peace treaty will decide what things will be like."[16]

While there was wide agreement within German society about the virtues of sovereignty, independence, and reunification, the two main West German political trends, led by the Social Democratic Party (SPD) on the left and the Christian Democratic Party (CDU) on the right, offered almost diametrically opposed strategies for how to achieve these goals and justified the continued application of homeland territoriality to the lost lands in meaningfully different ways.

The SPD, led by Kurt Schumacher, argued that Germany had an undiminished natural right to the lost parts of its homeland. The SPD held that, because nations require their homeland in order to fully exist, full sovereignty for Germany was impossible to achieve without reunification with the lost parts of its homeland.[17] As Erich Ollenhauer, Schumacher's successor at the helm of the SPD, put it, "Without the assurance of the national existence of our people [i.e., unification], just as that of every other people, neither the construction of a viable Europe nor the realization of democracy in socialism is possible."[18] Anything that interfered with German reunification, including European integration or an alliance with the West, was interpreted as undermining German national existence.

Schumacher and the SPD also saw the reunification of Germany as a requirement for peace. Like Eden, Schumacher interpreted Germany's loss of homeland territory in light of twentieth-century German history. German unification, because it would forestall the resurgence of the irredentist impulses that drove Germany to war in the first place, was seen as the best way of preventing Germany from threatening Europe in the future. From this vantage point, a commitment to a peaceful Germany required the reunification of Germany within its 1937 borders.

For these reasons, the SPD placed the goal of reunifying Germany within its 1937 borders above nearly everything else. In the very first Bundestag debate, Schumacher urged that all decisions be judged by their effect on this singular goal. The SPD's attitudes toward a whole range of critical issues, including sovereignty for the Federal Republic of Germany (FRG), nuclear weapons, European unification, and membership in international organizations (including NATO), among others, were subordinated to calculations about their impact on this single issue.[19] For example, in the debate over the potential rearmament of Germany, the SPD declared its willingness to support rearmament, only as long as "the efforts for the reunification of Germany be continued without respite . . . [and as long as] treaties through which the Federal Republic obligates itself to military efforts [i.e., NATO and the European Defense Community] are revocable by the Federal Republic if they should become an obstacle to the reunification of Germany."[20]

In sum, the SPD during this period adhered to a map-image of the homeland that corresponded to the 1937 borders of the German state (see figures 2.2–2.4). It justified this claim using a nationalist logic of legitimation as well as the idea that German sovereignty over its homeland was the only way to ensure a lasting peace and the maintenance of freedom.

The CDU under Konrad Adenauer took an almost diametrically opposed approach to the same goals. While also seeking reunification, the CDU believed that the reestablishment of German sovereignty and firm integration into the Western alliance had to come first because both sovereignty and reunification depended on the occupying powers. Gaining the support of the occupying powers, however, required convincing them that Germany was no longer a threat to world peace. In this context, the CDU believed that the SPD's strident calls for unification at (nearly) any cost undermined their objective by reminding the occupying powers of the territorially revanchist positions of the Third Reich. Instead, Adenauer's CDU promulgated a two-step approach to reunification.

In the first step, West Germany would regain full state sovereignty by convincing the Allies that such a state would not threaten the world order. This phase had three interlocking components: support for European unification, the establishment of a democracy in West Germany, and firm integration into the Western (rather than Soviet) orbit. Binding Germany to Europe was a way of trying to credibly commit the future German state to peace even in the absence of full unification. Democracy and Western integration went hand in hand. Both were, they believed, crucial for convincing the (Western) occupying powers that the FRG no longer posed a threat to the world. Consistent with these goals, the CDU legitimated its claims to the lost lands in terms of the freedom of the population to achieve self-determination. "Reunification of Germany in freedom" became one of its slogans, where "in freedom" signaled (among other things) a Germany firmly and unquestionably anchored in the West.

As a result of this strategy, the CDU consistently rejected plans for resolving Germany's division that would drive a wedge between Germany and the West. These rejections were understood not as a rejection of unification or of the homeland status of the lost lands, but as affirmations of what the CDU believed to be the only way to get them back.[21] Anything that weakened the link between the FRG and the West was seen as undermining the likelihood of reunification.[22] Such plans, Adenauer contended, "would not liberate the seventeen million Germans in the Zone [i.e., East Germany], but rather would send the fifty-two

FIGURE 2.2 SPD map-image of the homeland, 1948: "The whole of Germany should be it." Archiv der sozialen Demokratie, ©SPD/AdsD.

FIGURE 2.3   SPD map-image of the homeland, 1949: "SPD—Forward for a free Germany." Archiv der sozialen Demokratie, ©SPD/AdsD.

million who now live in freedom into the same slavery."[23] Integration into the West was also seen as helping bring about unification because it would enable them to make use of the Marshall program to reconstruct Germany's economy and build a democratic political sphere.

FIGURE 2.4 SPD map-image of the homeland, 1955: "SPD 4 reunification of Germany." Archiv der sozialen Demokratie, ©SPD/AdsD.

The second step of this approach assumed that the political and economic benefits which would accrue from democracy and integration into the West would make West Germany so attractive relative to the impoverished Soviet system that the Soviet Union would eventually capitulate and allow reunification to take place from a position of weakness.[24] This strategy was captured in the slogan of "unity through strength." Strength mattered, Adenauer explained to the CDU party congress in 1952, because "a totalitarian state—we know this from history—does not even consider it worthwhile to talk to a weak country, but it will speak responsibly with a strong country, and for this reason, the West must be strong."[25]

In practice, however, the commitment to Western integration in the context of the Cold War implied delaying reunification because it made Soviet support for reunification less likely.[26] Nonetheless, the CDU consistently contended that their policy of a firm alliance with the West and integration into NATO were actually, in the words of their 1961 platform, "the best for our objective of Germany's reunification in freedom. In fact, we believe that this policy is necessary in order to achieve this objective."[27] Conceding that achieving "unity through strength" would take "ten to fifteen years," Adenauer counseled patience.[28] Still, in 1969, the CDU chancellor Kurt Kiesinger continued to maintain that more time was needed. He exhorted Germans "to offer resistance to long drawn-out processes of attrition and not to become indifferent or lose our nerves when there seems to be no end to our efforts or when they appear to be in vain."[29]

In the meantime, the CDU pursued an essentially defensive policy of preventing actions that would foreclose the possibility of future reunification. The vigorous rhetorical support for reunification that this included had three main components: (1) continuing to publicly apply homeland territoriality to the lost lands, including the refusal to recognize the GDR; (2) emphasizing a legal doctrine holding that the final disposition of the lands lost by Germany after World War II could not take place until a final peace agreement; and (3) appealing to democratic legitimacy and to the rights of the population living in the lost lands to decide to which state they and the lands in which they lived ought to belong.[30] These largely symbolic gestures, they believed, would prevent the creation of irreversible facts on the ground while giving the process of "unity through strength" time to operate.

Consistent with this approach, the CDU continued to ritually flag the homeland status of the lost lands and of reunification as the end goal through the 1980s (see figures 2.5–2.7). Even if their private beliefs differed, in public Adenauer and the CDU consistently applied homeland territoriality to the lost lands, reinforcing their continued status as part of the homeland.[31] Whenever a public figure hinted that the lost lands were of secondary importance, they were quickly

FIGURE 2.5 CDU map-image of the homeland, 1947: "Never agree to the Oder-Neisse Line: Vote CDU." Konrad Adenauer Foundation, Archive for Christian-Democratic Policy (ACDP), poster collection, 10-012-5.

FIGURE 2.6 CDU map-image of the homeland, 1953: "The whole of Germany should be the undivided fatherland." Konrad Adenauer Foundation, Archive for Christian-Democratic Policy (ACDP), poster collection, 10-001-14.

FIGURE 2.7   CDU map-image of the homeland, 1980: "What is Germany?" Konrad Adenauer Foundation, Archive for Christian-Democratic Policy (ACDP), poster collection, 10-031-20001.

forced to walk the utterance back and declare their fealty to the continued homeland status of those lands.[32] In any case, as argued above, the private beliefs of CDU leaders were secondary in this context. Since the application of homeland territoriality is a rhetorical act, the public designations of the lost lands, including both the area of the GDR and the Eastern Territories, as part of the homeland effectively maintained their status as homeland territory.

Adenauer candidly deployed these rhetorical positions "to clear away any notion that Germany could grow accustomed to the existence of two German states."[33] This was also the motivation behind the Hallstein Doctrine, according to which the FRG would not maintain diplomatic relations with any state that recognized the GDR. Adenauer openly acknowledged that their actions were driven by the fear that any formal recognition of the GDR would start them on a slippery slope to the institutionalization of the division between the two Germanies and the loss of the ability to reunite the homeland. In a memorandum to the USSR in May 1957, his government stated that they were "unable to recognize that regime [i.e., the GDR] and negotiate with it, even if it were only because that, by so doing, it would be taking the decisive step in partitioning Germany."[34]

Again in 1961, the CDU-led government responded to a Soviet proposal for a treaty with the FRG by arguing that,

> even apart from the legal impossibility of concluding a peace treaty with a divided Germany, a procedure of this nature would not be understood by the German people, who ardently desire to be reunited. The German people would regard the conclusion of a peace treaty as proposed by the Soviet Government as a deepening of the division of Germany. In declaring that such a peace treaty would not demand any kind of sacrifice of the Federal Republic, the Government of the Union of Soviet Socialist Republics overlooks the fact that it is demanding of the Federal Republic the sacrifices [sic] of the main concern of the German people, i.e., their reunification.[35]

This attitude was reflected in the CDU's election platforms as well. Its Hamburg Programme (1953) declared that "our main task continues to be the peaceful reunification of all Germans in their own fatherland."[36] The CDU's 1957 manifesto began with the declaration that "the Christian Democratic Union aims at the unity of the fatherland, freedom for the nations and peace in the World" and repeated the idea that the latter goals required the "reunification of the divided fatherland in peace and freedom."[37] A version of this theme, and the application of homeland territoriality to their lost lands, especially to the land of East Germany, that it reflected characterized every CDU platform through the 1980s.

The continued application of homeland territoriality to the land on the other side of the de facto borders was also evident in the CDU's explicit consideration of the "Soviet Occupied Zone" (i.e., the GDR) and the "German Eastern Territories now under Polish administration" as worthy of representation in the party's institutions. Both of these territories were allocated Lander representation as well as twenty delegates to represent "the territories beyond the rivers Oder and Neisse" and seventy-five delegates for the Soviet Occupied Zone.[38]

The second way in which homeland territoriality was applied to lost lands was encoded in the emphasis on the temporary legal status of the FRG's borders.[39] This is what the German missive above labeled the "legal impossibility" of a peace agreement with a divided Germany. As the CDU-led German government declared in 1950,

> the decision on the eastern German territories at present under Polish and Soviet administration cannot and will not be taken until a peace treaty is concluded with a united Germany. The German Federal Government, as the spokesman for the entire German nation, will never

accept the annexation [to Poland and the USSR] contrary to every principle of law and humanity, of these purely German territories. The Federal Government will seek a just solution of this question in future peace negotiations between a genuinely democratic Poland and a democratic, united Germany.[40]

In 1960 the CDU undersecretary of the Ministry for All-German Affairs, Franz Thedieck, summarized "the Federal Government's legal standpoint and political conception in regard to the German Eastern Territories" as follows:

1. The Government of the Federal Republic of Germany is the only German government which has been freely and legally established; therefore it alone is entitled to represent the people in international affairs. The most basic and the principal goal of the Federal Government is and remains the restoration by peaceful means of Germany's unity as a state.
2. In regard to the territorial state of Germany, the borders of the state as they existed on December 31, 1937, are determinant.
3. The German people does not recognize the Oder-Neisse Line as the present or future border of Germany.
4. The final determination of the borders of Germany is postponed pending a settlement reached in a freely agreed treaty of peace.
5. Only an all-German government, a representation of the people that has been elected by the whole people, is authorized to confirm a decision on the future German borders in the East.
6. The right of homeland and the right of self-determination are inevitable presuppositions for the solution of the German East problem.[41]

Even West Germany's "Peace note" of March 1966—which proposed reaching renunciation-of-force agreements with the Warsaw Pact countries—began with an affirmation of German territorial claims and the legal justification for these claims. While articulating a desire for closer relations with Poland, West Germany nevertheless decried Poland's support for

> the continued division of Germany and . . . [Poland's] calls upon the Federal Government to recognize the Oder-Neisse Line, though it is generally known that, under the allied agreements of 1945, the settlement of frontier questions has been postponed until the conclusion of a peace treaty with the whole of Germany and that, according to International Law, Germany continues to exist within its frontiers of 31 December 1937 until such time as a freely elected all-German government recognizes other frontiers. . . . For in this question neither emotions nor alone the power of the victor, but rather reason, must prevail.[42]

Poland did not interpret this legal position as mere talk. It clearly understood the FRG's reluctance to formally accept the Oder-Neisse boundary as evidence of its continued territorial claim to the land east of the Oder-Neisse boundary.[43] As will be shown below, despite the friction this caused, the CDU continued to deploy the legal logic of legitimation until 1990.

The third rhetorical aspect of the CDU's application of homeland territoriality to the lost lands was the appeal to the rights of the inhabitants of those territories to choose the state in which they lived—rights that could only be exercised if they lived in real democratic regimes. For example, in 1961 the CDU-led government demanded that Germans be "allowed to exercise the right of self-determination.... A separate peace treaty with only one part of Germany, would violate the right of self-determination of peoples that has been recognized as one of the leading principles of the United Nations. . . . The right of self-determination as an inalienable fundamental right of all nations can also be claimed by the German people who uphold their traditional national unity and would unanimously confirm their will to that effect in a free election."[44]

The insistence on the right of self-determination was understood as both the precursor of and the mechanism for reunification. As the precursor, this rhetoric signaled West Germany's firm commitment to Western values and its opposition to Soviet tutelage. The appeal to the right of self-determination may have also been intended to signal that the nationalism displayed by the CDU differed from the prior incarnation of German nationalism, despite its continued territorial revanchism.[45] As a mechanism, the "attractiveness" model at the heart of Adenauer's long-term strategy left him with little doubt that, given the choice, the population in the lost lands would opt for reuniting with the FRG. Finally, in an act of rhetorical coercion directed against the West, the CDU's emphasis on "reunification in peace and freedom" also sought to use the West's own values (especially the notion that people are entitled to have a say in their political fate) to prevent the Western powers from making any final decisions about the location of Germany's borders without consulting Germany.

The different approaches of the SPD and CDU first played out in the debate over the Saar in the early 1950s. As with the other territories Germany had lost after the war, West Germans continued to apply homeland territoriality to the Saar and to believe that it should be returned to German control. A 1952 survey, for example, showed that about 70 percent of West Germans favored reunification with the Saar even at the cost of harming relations with France.[46] Consistent with its more general approach, the SPD vocally and unambiguously called for its immediate return. Opposing a separate Saar membership in the Council of Europe, Schumacher argued that the Saar must be returned to Germany in order to avoid weakening the German people's enthusiasm for international cooperation—a euphemism for the threat of another war. The SPD was also concerned that allowing European integration to proceed without a unified Germany, especially if the Saar was recognized as a distinct actor in Europe, would provide implicit German sanction for the ripping of the Saar from Germany and prejudice Germany's ability to regain the Eastern Territories.[47]

The CDU under Adenauer, while also wanting reunification with the Saar, prioritized the relationship with the Allies and achieving sovereignty, as long as no permanent facts on the ground were created. The CDU government's 1950 white paper on the Saar forcefully applied homeland territoriality to it, claiming the Saar as "German by history, by language and by custom." Also applying the legally based logic of legitimation, the white paper maintained that the Saar was "part of Germany" by "both constitutional and international law. . . . Pursuant to the declaration of 6 June 1945 by the four occupying powers regarding the assumption of supreme authority in Germany, that country's frontiers are as they existed on 31 December 1937." Finally, repeating the theme of "reunification in freedom," the white paper contended that the repressive measures of the French occupation authorities rendered any decisions reached by the "Saar state parliament" neither free nor democratic.[48]

Adenaeur's government was, however, willing to countenance the Europeanization of the Saar in the short term if it would serve their other goals of regaining sovereignty and integration into the West. Adenauer worried that insisting on immediate reunification at all costs would jeopardize German integration into the West, which, in turn, would undermine their ability to regain all the lost lands. The Europeanization of the Saar was seen as an acceptable interim solution because it would forestall both the integration of the Saar into France and the creation of a fully independent Saarland—developments that, he believed, would make eventual reunification impossible. Europeanization, by contrast, was thought not to have any bearing on the final settlement of who was sovereign over the territory.[49]

The CDU's emphasis on individual freedom and the right to self-determination of the people living in the lost lands bore fruit when, in an October 1955 referendum, the Saar's population decisively opted to rejoin Germany (91 percent voted to do so, while fewer than 1 percent supported joining France). As a result, following the conclusion of the Saar Treaty in 1956, the Saarland rejoined Germany the following year. Adenauer's approach of "unity in strength and freedom" was thus shown to be effective and consistent with the achievement of both of the key nationalist goals of sovereignty and reunification.

The domestic appeal of Adenauer's approach was reinforced by the economic success that came along with Western integration and participation in the Marshall Plan. The "German economic miracle" transformed West Germany from a war-ravaged state to a thriving economy and to a position of global economic leadership in only a few years. Achieving sovereignty, successful economic reconstruction, democracy, and actual reunification with some of its lost lands led to the crowning of Adenauer as Germany's preeminent postwar leader. This success also generated tremendous positive political returns for the CDU and cemented its status as the driving force of postwar German politics. As a result, the CDU governed West Germany from 1949 until 1969.

These positive returns made changing either the map-image of the homeland as Germany within its 1937 borders or the logics of legitimation used to apply homeland territoriality to the lost lands very difficult, even as domestic and international conditions were changing. As Ronald Granieri notes, by 1956 the CDU "had spent seven years promising their constituents that membership in the American-led West would bring 'freedom, peace, and reunification.'" The political risks of deviating from this strategy were too great.[50] Their 1957 election slogan of "No Experiments" reflected, among other things, their reluctance to abandon a strategy that had been so successful up to that point.

The CDU did soften its tone somewhat when it was forced into a coalition with the SPD in 1966, but it did not fundamentally change its song. Needing to navigate between the SPD, who were now advocating for greater dialogue with the GDR, and their internal truth tellers, who maintained a full-throated application of homeland territoriality to the lost lands, Kurt Kiesinger, the CDU chancellor, argued briefly that détente was a prerequisite for reunification rather than the other way around.[51] In this vein, his government relaxed the Hallstein Doctrine and established trading relationships with Eastern Europe, including with Poland. However, the Soviet invasion of Czechoslovakia in 1968 led CDU leaders to conclude that there was no chance for détente and to curtail further modifications that might have heralded a more significant shift in their position. At the end of the day, therefore, as Clay Clemens concluded, the CDU's approach on issues of the homeland changed relatively little between 1949 and 1969.[52]

The SPD's "Reunification through Peace" and Its Consequences

The flip side of the CDUs dominance was the SPD's persistent failure. By the mid-1950s, the SPD feared becoming a permanent minority. This fear was compounded by the 1957 elections, in which, for the first time in German history, the CDU won an absolute majority in the Bundestag. Seeking to break through their 30 percent ceiling in national elections, the SPD modified its position on a number of issues. These changes included shifting to the center on social and economic policy, signaling their full acceptance of West German integration into the Western alliance, and reevaluating their approach to reunification.[53] Starting with the party's 1959 Bad Godesburg programme, the SPD sought to show that it would no longer cling to a foreign policy in which reunification was the overriding focus. While the party still contended that "the division of Germany is a threat to peace," that ending the "division is a vital interest of the German People," and that Germany could not be fully sovereign until it was unified, reunification was now presented as one of a number of foreign policy goals.[54] The SPD also increasingly adopted the rhetoric of "unification in freedom," which had been used to such good effect by the CDU, to signal its commitment to Western democracy and support for integration into the Western alliance in order to counter accusations that it was too sympathetic to the Soviets.[55]

The erection of the Berlin Wall in August 1961 accelerated the reevaluation of the SPD's foreign policy positions and its attitude toward how to achieve unification. This was especially the case for Willy Brandt who, as the SPD mayor of West Berlin, experienced the city's physical partition in a particularly visceral way. Rather than continue to "run their heads against this wall" by demanding unification as a precondition for any other policy, as Brandt put it, he sought a new approach.[56] Rejecting both the CDU's "unification through strength" and the SPD's prior insistence that unification would lead to peace, Brandt began to argue that peace would lead to German unification.

Such "reunification through peace" had two interlocking components. The first was reaching a modus vivendi with East Germany that would prevent the complete separation of the German people and the potential creation of two distinct nations. Like the CDU's policies, this was primarily a defensive stance meant to forestall the institutionalization of partition in the minds of the German people. Unlike the CDU, however, the SPD was willing to go much farther in terms of recognizing the GDR to do so. The second component of "reunification through peace" required convincing the Soviet Union that West Germany sincerely wanted better relations with the East. Soviet opinion mattered because no modus vivendi between the Germanies could occur without its approval. Eliciting Soviet approval for the maintenance of the German nation in the face of partition, argued Brandt, required openly withdrawing homeland territoriality from the Eastern Territories and giving up the goal of reestablishing German control over them.[57] In effect, "reunification through peace" was based on a trade of the Eastern Territories for the possibility of future reunification between East and West Germany.

Following this logic, under Brandt's leadership, the SPD began to withdraw the application of homeland territoriality from the Eastern Territories. The SPD openly acknowledged the territorial cost for holding open the possibility of reunification with East Germany and for maintaining the "unity of the German people." "Reunification," the party conceded in 1966, "will call for sacrifices *relating to the drawing up of the frontiers of the reunited country.*"[58] Egon Bahr's 1969 working paper laying out the framework of the New Ostpolitik explicitly noted that their reunification strategy required recognition of the Oder-Neisse boundary. As Timothy Ash summarized, "the firmer the acceptance of the German-Polish frontier, the greater the chances of opening the German-German frontier."[59]

As part of the withdrawal of homeland territoriality from the Eastern Territories, the SPD increasingly emphasized the needs of the German nation, defined in terms of the people, over territorial unification. German unification remained a goal, but it was increasingly measured using an ethnic rather than territorial metric. If, in the 1940s and 1950s, the unification of German land was the way to preserve the German nation and ensure peace, by the 1960s, the unity of the nation was framed as more important than the unity of the land.[60] This theme would come to play an increasingly significant role in the SPD's understanding of the "German problem" as time went on. Given the expulsion of most of the Germans from the areas east of the Oder-Neisse boundary, the shift to focusing on the unity of the German people implied less concern for those territories in which there were significantly fewer coethnics.

Reflecting the withdrawal of homeland territoriality, the Eastern Territories were also increasingly excluded from the SPD's discussions of German unity. For example, at the time (1966), Brandt refused to recognize the "other part of Germany [i.e., the GDR] as foreign territory" because it is part of Germany itself. That he saw no such obstacle to recognizing Poland implied that he did not consider the Eastern Territories to be part of Germany. Indeed, Brandt repeatedly invoked the division of the "two parts of Germany," referring to the FRG and GDR, and excluding the Eastern Territories from the implied map-image of Germany in the process.[61]

While the overt withdrawal of homeland territoriality from the Eastern Territories incensed the SPD's opponents, the SPD was nonetheless able to carry it out because it was successfully framed as required for the achievement of (future) reunification with the rest of the lost lands and for enabling the unity of the German people. It was portrayed as a trade of a part of the homeland for other, equally sacred, nationalist goals; a trade of something, as Brandt repeatedly emphasized, they did not, in any case, actually possess.

This strategy would eventually be encapsulated in what came to be known as Brandt's New Ostpolitik. Yielding a complex of three treaties in the early 1970s (the Moscow Treaty with the Soviet Union, the Warsaw Treaty with Poland, and the Basic Treaty with the GDR), Brandt's New Ostpolitik normalized relations between West Germany and these states. In territorial terms, in these treaties West Germany formally accepted the "inviolability" of borders and the territorial integrity of its neighbors.

Brandt's political opponents (and many observers) interpreted the New Ostpolitik as fundamentally burying German territorial revisionist claims and enshrining the partition of Germany.[62] These interpretations were, however, only half right. With the New Ostpolitik, the SPD did cease applying homeland territoriality to the Eastern Territories, but it had no intention of doing so vis-à-vis East Germany.[63] Brandt's acknowledgment that his government "accept[ed] the results of history," powerfully delivered during his historic visit to Warsaw, applied only to the land east of the Oder-Neisse boundary. His government explicitly did not cease striving for the unification of the Germanies to the west of that line.[64]

Instead, Brandt and his allies maintained that the New Ostpolitik was a temporary (if open-ended) measure that would bring about the reunification of the FRG and the GDR, even if it appeared to push it into an indefinite future. At heart, the goal of the New Ostpolitik was to reduce tensions with the East in order to bring about German reunification. Elaborated already in 1963 by Egon Bahr, Brandt's key aide and one of the architects of the New Ostpolitik, this approach was intended "to regulate the relations between the two German states *until their unification*," even at the cost of acting *as if* they accepted the division of Germany in practical terms.[65] As Brandt argued at the 1966 SPD conference, reunification "will not be realized in a single act, but in the course of a process." In the meantime, they should "consider the possibility of a qualified, regulated, and *temporally limited* co-existence of the two areas [i.e., East and West Germany]. ... It would be a modus vivendi accompanied by the firm intention of arriving at further positive solutions [i.e., unification]."[66]

Underlying this "process" was Bahr's concept of *Wandel durch Annäherung* (change through rapprochement). The main assumption was that reducing tensions between West Germany and the Soviet Union would make the latter more likely to allow its client to loosen restrictions on contacts between the people in East and West Germany. Deepening these human relationships would keep the German nation linked together despite its political division into two states. When relations between the peoples were sufficiently thawed and the states involved no longer perceived each other as threats, the attractiveness of the lives of West Germans would lead the Germans in the East to organically seek reunification. In a way, this strategy operationalized the paradox, first formulated by the Kennedy administration, and taken by Brandt and Bahr as one of the main lessons of the Berlin Wall, that recognition of the status quo was the first step to overcoming it.[67]

Reminiscent of the CDU's defensive orientation, the New Ostpolitik was seen as the lesser of two evils—as a way of *stopping* the institutionalization of the distinction between the two Germanies and of maintaining the status of East Germany as part of the German homeland. The architects of the SPD's New

Ostpolitik feared that a continual progress of estrangement between the FRG and the GDR and the continuing growing apart of the people in them would lead to the disappearance of the German nation and prevent reunification once and for all because Germans would no longer feel that they belonged together.[68] In this vein, Bahr argued in the 1969 working paper laying out the basic logic of the New Ostpolitik that the division between East and West Germany was getting deeper and increasingly permanent. "We must reckon with it [i.e., the division] for the foreseeable future. The necessity increases to adapt to this position without abandoning the goal of reunification."[69]

The continued application of homeland territoriality to East Germany was evident in the tireless efforts by German negotiators to weaken the commitment to maintaining existing state borders in the Moscow Treaty. As Egon Bahr put it, there was "a real conflict of interests" with the Soviets on this issue. "The Soviet goal is to legalize the [territorial] status quo. Our goal is to overcome it."[70] The problem was solved by fudging the description of the borders in the Treaty and appending a "letter on German unity" affirming that "this treaty does not conflict with the political objective of the Federal Republic of Germany to work for a state of peace in Europe in which the German nation will recover its unity in free self-determination."[71] Some creative translation helped as well. The Soviet text referred to the "recognition" of borders, while the German version used the term "acknowledgment" instead.[72] This would allow Brandt to argue that the inviolability of borders "is not identical with their finality."[73] Bahr noted that convincing the USSR to accept the West German "letter on German unity" meant that "the East was able to tell itself that once the status quo had been confirmed and consolidated, one need not worry about a few Germans striving for unity. At that time, I wrote to a friend that the opposite was in fact true, and that I would not have initiated this policy had I not been convinced that it was a real starting point for the long-term development of the German question."[74]

Brandt understood the long-term impact of the New Ostpolitik in similar terms. His notes for the talks with Brezhnev on the occasion of the signing of the Moscow Treaty listed what he thought each would get from the treaty. The West German part of the list began: "-Bln [Berlin], -DDR [East Germany]."[75]

The long-term goal of Brandt's Ostpolitik was thus to lead to change in the Warsaw Pact countries, even in the Soviet Union, from the inside, and, eventually, to bring about the peaceful alteration of Europe's borders. Brezhnev was not fooled. He also understood that the strategy behind the Moscow Treaty was to use Soviet domination to force East Germany into closer ties with West Germany. He told Erich Honecker, the SED's general secretary, that Brandt "hopes in this way to realise his goals in relation to the GDR" and urged him to do everything to resist this influence and to "concentrate everything on the all-sided strength-ening of the GDR."[76] The GDR also correctly interpreted the New Ostpolitik as a change in tactics by the FRG, not a sincere renunciation of its claim to East Germany. It was, they remarked, "aggression in felt slippers." In response, the GDR further fortified the intra-German border, built up the Stasi apparatus and intensified their campaign for a separate GDR-based identity.[77]

Perhaps unaware of how transparent its intentions were, the SPD believed that its grand strategy would fail if openly discussed. As Martin Hillenbrand, the US assistant undersecretary of state summarized at the time, "Brandt cannot articulate his grand design clearly because this might negatively affect its realiza-tion."[78] As a result, the language with which Brandt and the leaders of the SPD approached the issue of reunification with East Germany became "inspiration-ally vague" and contradictory.[79] For example, Brandt simultaneously declared that "the Federal Republic of Germany has no territorial demands," and that "the renunciation of every attempt to overcome by peaceful means the unnatural condition of the division of Germany" is "a renunciation of common sense."[80] Reflecting the new vagueness, mentions of unification all but disappeared from the SPD's election platforms by the 1970s and 1980s. As Bahr would later reveal, such vagueness and contradictory statements were intentional.[81] The shift in the SPD's rhetoric about unification reflected the belief that, in "the long-run . . . German unity could only be achieved if one ceased to demand it!"[82]

These changes were most strongly reflected in the growing willingness of the SPD to de facto recognize the GDR as a distinct state. Whereas the CDU feared that doing so would institutionalize the loss of homeland territory, the SPD now pointed out that this institutionalization was taking place whether or not West Germany recognized the East German state. Recognition of the GDR would, moreover, allow for the creation of functional mechanisms for limiting the impact of the division by facilitating cross-border interactions. Together with enabling East Germany to feel secure enough to allow contact between the popu-lations, these cross-border interactions would keep the door open for reunifica-tion in the future.

Helmut Schmidt, who succeeded Brandt as the SPD chancellor, maintained this view of the New Ostpolitik's goals. "Our policy on Germany," he asserted in 1976, "is free from illusions. We shall, by dint of tough, patient work, preserve the cohesion of the people in Germany. This is the purpose of the policy we pursue with regard to the other German State under the Treaty on the Basis of Rela-tions. Everyone knows that the aim of our policy is to work for a state of peace in Europe in which the German nation will regain its unity through free self-determination."[83] The recognition of the GDR as a state, at least in de facto terms, was thus not understood by the SPD leadership as the withdrawal of homeland territoriality from the land over which the GDR existed; but it was a tactical retreat.

The process of de facto recognition began with the initially contested labeling of the GDR as a "state," while still rejecting the possibility of formal recognition.[84] If, in 1961, the SPD stridently rejected the idea that two states existed in the German fatherland, by 1969 Brandt would concede the application of the "state" label to the GDR, even though he still publicly opposed formal recognition of the GDR by the Federal Republic.[85] A few months later, in his address on the state of the German nation, Brandt repeated this formulation, but now added that they ought to seek "a regulated coexistence between the two *states* in Germany in this phase of history." In a relatively transparent attempt at rhetorical coercion, he argued that "patriotism calls for realizing the facts and trying over and over again to seek new possibilities"—facts and possibilities that, he continued, required negotiating with the East Berlin government and therefore recognizing its existence.[86] By the time the Basic Treaty was signed three years later, Brandt openly spoke of the two German states as equals.[87] By 1976 Schmidt could report with significantly less uproar that they would continue to implement existing treaties and agreements between the "two German states."[88] Accordingly, the SPD's platform that year (and those that followed) emphasized the normalcy of relations between the two states.[89]

The changes initiated in the late 1950s and early 1960s by the SPD worked— at least in terms of their domestic appeal. By 1966 the SPD had convinced the German public, and the CDU, that it was sufficiently committed to Western integration that it was possible to include them in the governing coalition. The popularity of the New Ostpolitik, and of Willy Brandt, led the party in 1969 to its high-water mark of the postwar era and to gaining the chancellery for the first time since the war. The SPD then governed West Germany (in coalition with the centrist Free Democratic Party [FDP]) for more than a decade.

This same success, however, trapped the SPD into a catch-22 when it came to maintaining the application of homeland territoriality to the lost lands. Its political success was based on the argument that preserving the idea of a single German people required the cooperation of Moscow and the GDR. This cooperation, in turn, required that West Germany mute overt claims to lost parts of the homeland as being appropriately theirs. However, since the application of homeland territoriality to lost lands is fundamentally a rhetorical act, such muting was tantamount to withdrawing homeland territoriality from the lost lands and therefore reduced the nationalist imperative to regain sovereignty over them. The association of this muting with the SPD's political success meant that it became increasingly difficult to abandon. Over time, maintaining good relations with the GDR was transformed from a step toward reunification into a desired outcome in its own right.[90] In effect, the variant of the map-image of the homeland promoted by the SPD increasingly omitted East Germany as well as the Eastern Territories despite the initial intent to treat those parts of the homeland differently.

Demonstrating the power of this political lock-in effect, when the SPD lost power in 1982, it doubled down on the approach that had brought it success in the 1960s and effectively abandoned reunification as a policy objective.[91] It intensified its contacts and cooperation with the SED (the East German Communist Party), and developed a position akin to a "Two-State-Patriotism" rather than a vision of ultimate unification. Its 1983 and 1987 platforms, for example, openly called for respecting the self-sufficiency and independence of the GDR.[92] During the 1987 election campaign, an aging Brandt even promised the SED that West Germany would recognize a separate GDR citizenship—thereby formally recognizing the distinctiveness of the people living in the two states—if the SPD emerged victorious.[93]

These developments were reinforced by two additional factors. First, by then a closer relationship with the GDR was one of the few things that the increasingly fractious SPD could agree on. Since raising the issue of reunification exacerbated the party's internal cleavages, party leaders sought to keep it off the agenda—an act which, in any case, was consistent with the general strategy of muting the application of homeland territoriality to the GDR. Second, the SPD found itself having to counteract the emergence of the Green Party which, in 1983, garnered 5.6 percent of the national vote. The Greens threatened to outflank the SPD on the left, further reinforcing the political gains of neglecting to apply homeland territoriality to the GDR.[94]

The extent of the withdrawal of homeland territoriality, even from East Germany, within the SPD was vividly displayed when the Berlin Wall fell and reunification emerged as a real possibility. Rather than celebrating the opportunity to reunite the homeland, the SPD sought to slow the process down and emphasized concerns about its social and economic costs. Oskar Lafontaine, the SPD's candidate for chancellor, even viewed the potential movement of East Germans into West Germany in terms of "immigration"; East Germans were seen as outsiders, not as conationals. In fact, it was the endorsement by the Social Democrats–East of "the unity of the German nation" rather than its own initiative that compelled the SPD-West to endorse reunification.[95] In summary, the success of the tactical step at the heart of the New Ostpolitik, the muting of the claim to East Germany in order to facilitate better relations with it, made it difficult for the SPD to maintain the status of the GDR as part of the homeland.

The CDU: Rhetorical Consistency and Practical Change

For the CDU, the period between the introduction of the New Ostpolitik in 1969 and the collapse of the Berlin Wall twenty years later was characterized by contradiction. On the one hand, the CDU maintained its traditional application of homeland territoriality to the lost lands. Its election platforms, for example, consistently raised the issue of unification. On the other hand, the CDU simultaneously pursued engagement with the Soviet Bloc and increasingly came to advocate policies that, in practice, hewed ever more closely to those at the heart of Brandt's New Ostpolitik. Downplaying earlier concerns about a slippery slope, these policies focused on ameliorating the "consequences of the division" for the Germans in the GDR even at the cost of de facto recognizing the East German state and a commitment to maintaining its stability.

Given the predictions of an evolutionary dynamic, we would expect the popularity and political success associated with these practical politics to put pressure on the CDU to bring its ideological commitments into alignment with its practical positions. Indeed, the withdrawal of homeland territoriality from the lost lands did spread within the party. Additional time and the continued accrual of positive political returns, might have led the CDU to follow the SPD in withdrawing homeland territoriality from the lost lands. However, this process was cut short by the unexpected collapse of the Berlin Wall and the reemergence of the realistic possibility of (partial) reunification. Once the wall came down, the CDU's maintained application of homeland territoriality to the land of the GDR meant that it was relatively well positioned to actively pursue unification. At the same time, its reliance on legal and democratic logics of legitimating the application of homeland territoriality to the lost lands simultaneously undermined its ability to do so for the Eastern Territories.

The contradictions displayed by the CDU during this period reflected its internal division between truth tellers and reformists about how to best achieve reunification.[96] Until the late 1970s and early 1980s, the party was dominated by its truth-teller wing. Determined to maintain both the original map-image of the homeland and Adenauer's approach of "reunification through strength," this wing of the party maintained its vocal rhetorical commitment to reunification and opposed even a de facto acknowledgment of the territorial status quo. The truth tellers in the party were largely composed of expellees (the German label for German residents of the Eastern Territories who were forced to leave after World War II), conservatives from relatively homogeneous, middle class, Catholic, and southern regions, or rural parts of the Rhineland, as well as many North German and Protestant conservatives, and the entire Christian Social Union (CSU).[97] Many truth tellers within the CDU were also sensitive to the risk of being outflanked by the National Democratic Party on the right. They believed that continuing to apply homeland territoriality to the lost lands would help them regain the roughly 4 percent of the vote received by the more radical National Democratic Party, and, therefore, the majority in the Bundestag.[98]

The so-called "reformist" wing of the CDU, though it agreed that reunification should remain the ultimate goal, argued for more tactical flexibility in how to deal with the East in the short-term. Like the SPD, it highlighted the concern for the well-being of Germans in the GDR and for the plight of the divided families. The reformists contended that tactical, symbolic concessions such as some limited status for the GDR and some formal acknowledgment of the Oder-Neisse Line, were a reasonable price to pay to address these concerns because they did not bear on the ultimate resolution of the German question.

The reformists also worried that the insistence on the absolute rejection of the GDR carried political costs. They shared "the growing sense that ordinary Germans were ready for a greater degree of normalcy in FRG foreign policy. They believed the public was wearying of an emphasis on reunification that came at the expense of tangible measures to ameliorate the division's effects."[99] Not coincidentally, they tended to hail from regions that were closely contested between the CDU and the SPD, and thus had to compete with the latter to attract voters who were sympathetic to the flexibility displayed by Brandt. Finally, the reformists were also concerned that, in an era when the United States was seeking détente, a completely intransigent West German position would weaken the US's support of West Germany, thus undermining one of the central components of the CDUs overarching strategy for achieving reunification.[100]

The divide between the two wings of the CDU restricted the ability of party leaders to formulate a cohesive position.[101] The result was an inconsistent, even incoherent, internal compromise, in which the CDU maintained the rhetorical application of homeland territoriality to the lost lands and simultaneously supported policies that implicitly recognized the distinctiveness of the GDR and the Eastern Territories.

This pattern was already visible in its reaction to the Basic Treaty in 1972. The conclusion of this treaty placed CDU leaders in a difficult position. On the one hand, they were ideologically committed to "unity through strength"—a strategy which required that they not do anything—including recognizing the GDR—that might forestall unification in the future. On the other hand, they did not have enough support to prevent the ratification of the Ostpolitik treaties. The November 1972 elections confirmed the popularity of Brandt's new approach and further weakened the CDU's political position. These elections, seen as a referendum on Brandt's New Ostpolitik, resulted in a gain of sixteen seats for the SPD and its partner, the FDP, at the expense of the CDU/CSU. The CDU was also under tremendous pressure from Washington not to derail the process of European conciliation.[102]

Caught in this bind, the CDU acceded to a compromise that sought to maintain party unity while simultaneously acknowledging public support for the New Ostpolitik and navigating between its dual commitment to the Western alliance and to the homeland. In this deal, the CDU agreed to abstain on the vote to ratify the Ostpolitik treaties rather than oppose them outright. In exchange, the CDU secured the SPD's agreement to a joint Bundestag resolution stressing the treaties' temporary character and the interpretation that they were not a legally binding peace settlement for Germany. Interpreting the treaties as merely guaranteeing that Germany would not use force to change the border, this resolution thus applied the conventional CDU legal strategy of legitimation to enable the continued application of homeland territoriality to the lost lands.[103] "The Federal Republic of Germany," the resolution declared,

> has assumed in its own behalf [i.e., not on behalf of a future united German state] the obligations it undertook in the treaties. The treaties proceed from the frontiers as actually existing today, the unilateral alteration of which they exclude. The treaties do not anticipate a peace settlement for Germany by treaty and do not create any legal foundation for the frontiers existing today.... The inalienable right to self-determination is not affected by the treaties. The policy of the Federal Republic of Germany aiming at the peaceful restoration of national unity within the European framework is not in contradiction to the treaties which do not prejudice the solution of the German question.[104]

This compromise enabled the CDU to avoid voting against treaties that were domestically popular (even among CDU voters), to avoid bearing the political cost of obstructing policies that would improve the conditions for Germans in the East, and to minimize any damage caused by openly disregarding American interests.[105] Internally, this compromise provided the reformists with the practical flexibility they desired in dealing with East Germany and the hardliners with the upholding of the rhetorical application of homeland territoriality to the lost lands. The emphasis of their legal logic of legitimization also addressed the truth tellers' concern that the Warsaw Treaty could be interpreted as giving up their claim to the Eastern Territories.[106]

This combination of tactical flexibility on actual policies while maintaining the rhetorical application of homeland territoriality to the lost lands was popular with the German public. The position of keeping "the German question . . . open legally and politically," as their 1976 election platform framed it, while displaying policy flexibility in dealing with the GDR and Eastern Europe, enabled the CDU to regain its position as the largest party in 1976, though not the chancellor's seat.[107] Boding well for the success of this mixed approach, the following year, almost half the population (49 percent) favored a tougher stance toward the GDR than that pursued by the SPD.[108]

The CDU continued this approach in the 1982 elections, this time succeeding in regaining the chancellery. Consistent with the terms of the compromise between the wings of his party, Helmut Kohl's government combined a pragmatic approach to dealing with the East with a "blunt neo-Adenauerian reaffirmation of the absolute priority of Western integration . . . and of the long-term commitment to reunification."[109] Kohl's "uncompromising and confrontational rhetoric" emphasized the legal basis of German claims to reunification and the right of Germans to self-determination.[110] As the 1983 coalition agreement stated, the CDU-led government was committed "not only to keep the German question theoretically open, but also to be actively engaged for the German right to unity in freedom."[111]

Kohl's address on the state of the German nation in 1983 chastised the prior SPD governments for muting references to the division of Germany. By contrast, the CDU-led government, he promised, would take a very different approach. "We do not accept our German compatriots being denied the right to self-determination and their human rights being violated. We Germans do not accept the division of our Fatherland. We shall continue to strive with determination and perseverance to comply with the precept of our constitution to achieve through free self-determination the unity and freedom of Germany. We shall not resign because we know that history is on our side."[112]

However, consistent with the compromise that characterized the CDU's approach during this period, Kohl combined the rhetorical affirmation of the homeland status of the lost lands with the simultaneous de facto recognition of the existence of two German states, an SPD-like emphasis on maintaining the unity of the nation (rather than of the land per se) in the present, and a focus on making the "division more bearable and less hazardous through practical measures in a spirit of humanity and responsibility towards the Germans in the GDR."[113] In other words, when it came to practical policy, Kohl's government was virtually indistinguishable from its SPD-led predecessor. It too pursued a policy of small steps, and sought to improve the lives of the GDR's population, even at the cost of de facto recognizing the GDR and providing it with financial and diplomatic support.[114] This aspect of the compromise was reinforced by the fact that the FDP remained the main coalition partner and controlled the Foreign Ministry in both SPD- and CDU-led governments. The FDP, by the 1980s, had, like the SPD, largely given up on the articulation of overt demands for unification.[115]

Kohl's (and the CDU's) contradictory positions were even displayed within a single speech. For example, in his 1985 address on the German nation, Kohl hinted that they accepted the boundary with Poland, declaring that "we, the

Federal Republic of Germany and the People's Republic of Poland, have no territorial claims whatsoever on one another and will not make any in the future. The territories beyond Poland's Western boundary have become home to two generations of Polish families. We shall respect and never question this fact."[116] The apparent relinquishing of the claim to the Eastern Territories, however, was undermined by both the claim that the Oder-Neisse territories lay "beyond Poland's Western boundary," and the continued use of legal logics of legitimation that lay claim to them. In the same address, Kohl thus maintained that their "policy on Germany remains determined by the Basic Law for the Federal Republic of Germany, the Convention on the Relations between the Three Powers and the Federal Republic of Germany, the Moscow and Warsaw Treaties of 1970, the Quadripartite Agreement of 1971, the Letters on German Unity as well as the Joint Resolution of the German Bundestag adopted on May 17, 1972, the Basic Treaty with the GDR and the judgments handed down by the Federal Constitutional Court in July 1973 and July 1975," all of which affirmed the right of a united German state to the lands east of the Oder-Neisse territories. Kohl could split these hairs because of the claim that he was speaking only for the FRG. Since, in the CDU's legal conception, the FRG could not speak for a unified German state which did not yet exist, the CDU could simultaneously claim the Eastern Territories as part of a united Germany and argue that the FRG had no territorial claim on them.

The duality of the CDU's treatment of the land under East German control was prominently displayed during Honecker's visit to West Germany in September 1987. On the one hand, the visit looked just like the visit of any foreign head of state. "Two different German flags hung before the Federal Chancellery, the West German army band played two different anthems, two German leaders stood to attention side by side."[117] Yet, in his speech, Kohl affirmed his commitment to the unity of Germany, presuming the dissolution of the state led by the dignitary to his side.

Attempting to square the circle, CDU leaders argued that negotiating the promotion of human contact across the existing border, and the legal case for self-determination and the provisionality of that border, were both part of the same policy. In this vein, Alois Mertes, the chairman of the CDU's foreign policy working group, praised the "necessary efforts to hold together the German people [so long as] such steps did not work against the long-term goal of unification."[118]

The political success of this compromise meant that, for all of its inconsistency, party leaders had little incentive to come down on the side of either the reformists or the truth tellers within the party. Since either emphasizing or downplaying reunification demanded too high a cost in terms of party unity and existing foreign policy commitments, the CDU had little incentive to actively tilt in either direction. Instead, a "comfortable ambiguity" and policy of "deliberate vagueness" prevailed.[119] While the CDU never gave up on reunification, it also almost never spelled out how to achieve it.

This duality, and the ambiguity it embodied, might have eventually led to an institutionalization of the withdrawal of homeland territoriality that paralleled the developments in the SPD. Indeed, the reformist wing was ascendant within the party.[120] Their position was reinforced by the social integration of expellees and the concomitant decline of the expellee associations. This population, which had upheld the hard line on territorial issues, began to lose its distinctive political positions and its political attitudes increasingly resembled those of West Germans more generally.[121] By the late 1980s, the lack of attention the reformist wing of the party paid to reunification was nearly indistinguishable from the SPD's position. For example, a 1986 essay about the CDU by its national party manager and the campaign manager for the 1987 elections made no mention of unification as a goal for the party (or otherwise).[122] The reformists increasingly subordinated the concern with the right of self-determination to a concern with human rights more broadly. By 1989 (before the fall of the Berlin Wall), Horst Teltschik, Kohl's advisor, had come to understand German unification "principally [as] . . . the means to realise human rights and the right of self-determination for all Germans."[123] If, for Adenauer, self-determination was the means to achieve unification, by the late 1980s the reformist wing of the CDU saw unification as the means to realize human rights; a goal that might be achieved in other ways as well. Teltschik even argued that, "for us, the German question is not primarily a matter of seeking a territorial solution. . . . Now the question is one of harmonizing German goals and desires with developments throughout Europe."[124] Consistent with these developments, the initial draft of the CDU's 1988 party program, drafted by the reformists within the party, omitted the term "reunification" entirely![125]

The reformists, however, were ultimately unable to change the overall tenor of the CDUs approach. Kohl and other party leaders saw the continuing division within the party as a real danger to their ability to maintain power and subordinated any private desire to withdraw homeland territoriality from the Eastern Territories and the GDR to the imperative of maintaining party unity. Responding to pressure from the truth tellers in the party, the initial draft of the 1988 party program was scrapped in favor of maintaining the party's, by now traditional, contradictory approach. The revised version opened by appealing to Adenauer's statement that "the reunification of Germany in freedom was and is the most urgent goal of our policy." The goal of reunification reappeared throughout the document, as did a catalog of the legal basis for German unity and the provisionality of the border.[126]

This internal standoff and any process of accommodation to the partition of Germany on the part of the reformists was upended by the collapse of the Berlin

Wall in September 1989. The reappearance of reunification as a realistic possibility caught everyone by surprise. As Wolfgang Schäuble, minister of the interior and one of Kohl's closest advisors on all-German policy, recalled, "We sat there like children in front of the Christmas tree and rubbed our eyes."[127] It took the CDU a few weeks to recover.

The delay was at least partly the product of the absence of a real operational strategy for unification.[128] While the basic compromise within the party maintained the rhetorical application of homeland territoriality to the lost lands, in practical terms, the CDU's policy positions reflected an accommodation of the division. The continued application of homeland territoriality mattered, as it kept the nationalist desire for unification alive. It maintained the notion of the extent of the homeland latent, such that when the GDR began to implode, "the sense of national identity, that it was 'natural' for there to be a single German state, could now come to the surface."[129] Rhetoric, however, can only go so far, and the failure to think through the practical aspects of unification shaped the CDU's initial response to the possibilities created by the fall of the Berlin Wall. It was hard to shift away from a decade of supporting practical policies geared toward ameliorating the consequences of the division rather than the division itself. As James McAdams noted, "If East Berlin's openness to ever greater contacts between the German populations was contingent upon its leaders' confidence in the internal stability of the GDR, then the CDU/CSU cannot have helped but acquire a stake in what transpired within East Germany in the process."[130] CDU leaders, in other words, initially worried that undermining the GDR by pressing for reunification would make the lives of its residents even worse.

However, by December 1989, Helmut Kohl released his ten-point plan for German unification. While still supremely cautious, if only because Kohl sought to allay concerns in both Western and Eastern Europe that a united Germany would threaten the European order, this plan nonetheless set out a practical path to reunification—a path that reflected the logics used by the CDU to apply homeland territoriality to the lost lands.[131] It emphasized "unity in freedom" and self-determination. It was, in Kohl's words, a way of "working toward a state of peace in Europe in which the German people can regain its unity in free self-determination. Reunification—that means retaining the national unity of Germany—remains the political aim of the Government of the Federal Republic."[132] Indeed, in accordance with the process outlined by Kohl, the GDR held free elections in March 1990—elections decisively won by the East German branch of the CDU on a platform of unification. In July 1990, a unification treaty between East and West Germany was negotiated. It was ratified in September 1990, and the following month the GDR was resorbed into West Germany.

The unrest in Eastern Europe and the possibility of reunification with "the other part of Germany" also raised questions about the status of the Eastern Territories. The truth tellers within the CDU had persistently applied homeland territoriality to these lands as well. The legal arguments used by the CDU to legitimate its claims to Germany's lost lands also consistently included the Eastern Territories. However, the reliance on a legally based legitimation strategy and on the right to self-determination ultimately undermined the ability of even the truth tellers within the CDU to sustain the claims to the Eastern Territories.

To begin with, the sanction given to the reunification of Germany by the superpowers, Britain, and France, formally put the legal issues to rest. The legal argument had been based on the contention that the final borders of Germany could only be settled by the four powers in a peace treaty ending the Second World War. In the Two Plus Four Treaty, the four powers did just that and formally set the borders of the united Germany along the Oder-Neisse boundary. As a result, advocates of the legal justification for the claim to the Eastern Territories were left with no leg to stand on.

Moreover, part of the rationale for applying the legal logic of legitimation to the Eastern Territories even after the conclusion of the Warsaw Treaty was that not doing so would undermine West Germany's claim to East Germany. This was the argument deployed by CDU leaders as they unsuccessfully tried, in a series of meetings in the 1970s, to convince their Polish interlocutors that they accepted the Oder-Neisse Line despite their simultaneous insistence that the German question remain open.[133] Once the unification of the GDR and FRG took place, this motivation also lost its power.

The argument for "unity in freedom" showed its power when East Germans overwhelmingly voted for pro-unification parties in the March 1990 elections. However, this same logic of legitimation could no longer be convincingly used to apply homeland territoriality to the Eastern Territories after Solidarity's victory in the 1989 Polish elections and Poland's subsequent transition to democracy. The Poles were now free to choose, and they displayed little interest in modifying the border.

Finally, the collapse of the Berlin Wall provided the reformists within the CDU with the political leverage to overcome the truth tellers' lingering resistance to accepting the Oder-Neisse boundary. Kohl and the reformists now deployed rhetorical coercion to frame the issue in terms of a choice between reunification with the GDR or claiming the Eastern Territories. "The historic opportunity to complete the unity of Germany in freedom would have been lost," Kohl argued on the day before unification, "if we had not given a clear answer to the question of Poland's western border."[134] Kohl, in effect, carried out the trade that was at the heart of Brandt's New Ostpolitik and the CDU's vision of the scope of the German homeland changed accordingly (see, for example, figure 2.8).[135] With the exception of the fringe right of the German political spectrum, the Eastern Territories were henceforth effectively elided from the German definition of the extent of their national homeland.

Christliche Demokratische Union Deutschlands ∗ Otto-Nuschke-Str. 59. 1080 Berlin

FIGURE 2.8   CDU map-image of the homeland, 1990: "Turning to the future." Konrad Adenauer Foundation, Archive for Christian-Democratic Policy (ACDP), poster collection, 10-024-5055. Note the exclusion of the "Eastern Territories" from this image.

In summary, the variation in the withdrawal of homeland territoriality from Germany's different lost territories, the timing of these withdrawals, and the actors who carried them out is most consistent with the expectations of an evolutionary dynamic based in domestic political competition. The political success that accrued to the CDU as it articulated a map-image of Germany in the 1937 borders explains why it persisted in applying homeland territoriality to the lost lands for so long. Political failure provided the SPD with more reason to experiment. For them, starting in the early 1960s, the withdrawal of homeland territoriality from the Eastern Territories was part of a conscious trade for the ability to pursue reunification with East Germany—a gambit that itself was part of an attempt to reverse its political misfortunes. This was initially a contested move, defended using both the blurring of the map-image of the homeland and rhetorical coercion. The political success of the SPD's new approach reinforced the exclusion of these territories from the map-image of the homeland for the SPD. The CDU, by contrast, did not withdraw homeland territoriality from the Eastern Territories until 1990 when the logics with which it had claimed these territories were no longer sustainable. This variation in the timing of when homeland territoriality was withdrawn from lost lands between the two main political parties cannot be accounted for by any single structural change.

The pattern of continued application of homeland territoriality to, and its withdrawal from, the land across the Elbe River was similarly varied. As was shown above, West Germans remained overwhelmingly committed to reunification for nearly two decades after the partition. However, starting in the late 1960s and early 1970s, the SPD muted its application of homeland territoriality to East Germany, even though its leaders still sought—in the long run—to undo the partition of Germany. By the 1980s, this muting was becoming institutionalized as the SPD doubled down on the approach that had brought it success in the past— so much so, that the once-tactical goal became an end in its own right. While the CDU was subject to the same external pressures as the SPD, the internal divisions within it led the party to adopt a compromise that maintained the rhetorical application of homeland territoriality to lost lands but allowed for the pursuit of practical policies that implicitly recognized their distinctiveness. The continued rhetorical inclusion of East Germany in its map-image of the homeland meant that the CDU was ultimately better positioned to articulate a plan—based on the logics of legitimation that it had deployed—for actual reunification.

Alternative Explanations

This section considers the ability of alternative explanations to account for the variation in the timing, actors, and process of the withdrawal of homeland territoriality from lost lands in the post–World War II German setting. I focus on the three main categories of alternative explanations for the withdrawal of homeland territoriality from lost lands identified in chapter 1—those that highlight rational adaptation to new information, the passage of time, and leaders' instrumental considerations.

Explanations based on rational adaptation to new information may be especially plausible in the German context. The consequence of Germany's total defeat in World War II and the construction of the Berlin Wall were both tremendous shocks that could have shaped notions of the homeland's extent.[136] Likewise, the demographic changes that took place after the war—particularly the expulsion of Germans from the Eastern Territories—could also have caused the withdrawal of homeland territoriality from them.[137] The replacement of about four million Germans with Russian and Polish speakers transformed the Eastern Territories from a territory with a significant German-speaking population into territories with a much smaller German presence.[138] It is not far-fetched to assume that the archetypically ethnic German nationalism, which placed such a strong emphasis on shared language, culture, and descent as criteria for membership, could be shaped by such demographic changes. A final version of this category of alternative explanations could point to the economic value of the territories to account for the variation in their treatment.

There is no doubt that the German defeat in World War II and the German reckoning with the crimes of the Holocaust had deep and wide repercussions for German politics and culture. At the same time, partially because such explanations attribute change to a singular event rather than to dynamic processes, they cannot fully accommodate the variation in the timing of withdrawal of homeland territoriality from lost lands across lost territories, between parties within West Germany, and between East and West Germany.

While the preceding discussion focused on West Germany, the East German treatment of the various territories lost after World War II exhibited variation of its own. For example, although the rapid, almost instantaneous, acceptance of the loss of the Eastern Territories by the SED is consistent with an explanation based on acceptance of the reality of the border as a result of Germany's total defeat, the failure to simultaneously accept the partition along the Elbe is not.[139] Despite the information conveyed by the border between East and West Germany, the SED, especially its leader, Walter Ulbricht, continued to apply homeland territoriality to the area of West Germany long after the war.[140] As scholars have noted, "Everything from the GDR's national anthem to the songs of the People's Police was meant to show that the Communists were the true, all-German nationalists."[141] Still, in 1953, the East German Politburo argued that its policies were enacted "with an eye toward the great goal of restoring the unity of Germany."[142] Ulbricht, East Germany's dominant postwar leader, continued to promote reunification (and therefore the application of homeland territoriality to West Germany) well into the 1960s. In 1967, even as the concept of "GDR consciousness" was introduced in an attempt to foster a specifically East German national identity, Ulbricht continued to argue that "unification of the German states" remained their chief goal. "We . . . have never written off the unitary, peaceful and progressive German state . . . and we will never do so."[143] Attributing the withdrawal of homeland territoriality from the Eastern Territories to the German defeat or to the erection of new de facto borders cannot explain the absence of such a withdrawal across the other new borders that were drawn at the same time.

The same challenge is posed by the persistent desire for reunification in West Germany. It may be, as Hans Kohn argued, that with "the total collapse" of Germany as a result of World War II, "the myth of the Reich lost its hold over the German mind."[144] However, this did not, at least not automatically, extend to their conception of the extent of the homeland. As shown above, West German public opinion consistently supported the return of the lost parts of the homeland. Well into the 1980s, more than two-thirds (and occasionally as much as 80 percent) of West Germans continued to support unification with East Germany, even if they thought it was not a particularly realistic objective.[145] The continued application of homeland territoriality to lost lands reflected in this desire is inconsistent with a change in the definition of the homeland triggered by Germany's total defeat and dismemberment in 1945.

The onset of the SPD's New Ostpolitik in the early and mid-1960s could be consistent, however, with the possibility that the entrenchment of the Cold War, symbolized by the erection of the Berlin Wall, finally convinced West Germans that the postwar territorial order was here to stay. While clearly a smaller cognitive shock than Germany's total defeat, it nonetheless plausibly conveyed new information about the willingness of the West to support German unification. As Brandt would later write in his memoirs, when the wall went up "a curtain was drawn aside to reveal an empty stage. To put it more bluntly, we lost certain illusions that had outlived the hopes underlying them. . . . Ulbricht had been allowed to take a swipe at the Western super-power, and the United States merely winced with annoyance. My political deliberations in the years that followed were substantially influenced by this day's experience, and it was against this background that my so-called Ostpolitik—the beginning of détente—took shape."[146] He now realized that "even the powerful United States couldn't help us. Instead, we had to take cognizance of the fact that the border through the city was equivalent to a border between the superpowers of this world. Whoever, subsequent to this . . . had believed that he could achieve something by running with his head against this hideous wall has unfortunately had to recognize that his head comes away worse than the wall does."[147] In other words, the Berlin Wall plausibly conveyed information, not about the border per se, but about the willingness of West Germany's allies to support its territorial ambitions.[148]

The growing public resignation to the separateness of the GDR in the 1960s is also consistent with this possibility. If, in 1963, 42 percent of West Germans still considered reunification to be the most important problem facing Germans, in 1971 only 3 percent did so.[149] According to some observers at the time, West Germany was turning inward and West Germans increasingly ceased to consider the two Germanies as provisional units.[150] Starting in the early 1970s, official maps even began to portray the boundary with the GDR as an international rather than an intranational boundary.[151]

This change was even more pronounced when it came to the Eastern Territories. By 1969 68 percent of West Germans (including 62 percent of expellees) agreed that Poles have a "right to a homeland" in the formerly German territories beyond the Oder-Neisse Line. That same year, for the first time, a majority of 53 percent (including 44 percent of expellees) agreed that the FRG should accept the German-Polish border.[152] By 1979 only a tenth of West Germans identified Germany as extending beyond the Oder-Neisse.[153] Indeed, by the late 1980s, some observers of Germany concluded that the claim to the Eastern Territories was no longer a relevant issue in German politics and society.[154] These developments are consistent with the gradual acceptance of the international norm of border fixity by the German population and German policy makers following the construction of the Berlin Wall.[155]

This explanation, however, cannot account for the domestic variation in who updated their publicly articulated beliefs to the new information. First, as McAdams noted, for nearly a decade after the wall was erected, the leadership in both Bonn and East Berlin continued to adhere to their respective "policies of strength."[156] That is, even if the SPD withdrew homeland territoriality from lost lands in response to the erection of the Berlin Wall, the party in power did not do so. The different geography textbooks each party authorized provide one striking example of the variation in their reactions. As Guntram Herb noted, "Lander [German subnational administrative units akin to provinces] that had an SPD majority refused to approve atlases that featured the 1937 boundary while those with a CDU/CSU majority mandated that all maps of Germany show it."[157] An appeal to the impact of a singular event, like the erection of the Berlin Wall, cannot explain the variation across party lines.

Such variation is doubly problematic because this explanation would predict that change would be most likely among those exposed to the new information; and the party in power would have been more directly exposed to the practical consequences of the new environment. The opposition, by contrast, always has more leeway to ignore inconvenient truths in the name of ideological purity. Yet, it was the party out of power that was willing to experiment with a new approach.

The ruling CDU, for whom "unity in strength" was associated with political success, had little incentive to change.[158]

Even the evidence consistent with an adaptation to a new, post–Berlin Wall
reality presented above is not as clear cut as it initially appears. For instance, the
negative reaction to the decision by West German atlas publishers to change the
depiction of the Eastern Territories was so strong that, a few years later, the 1937
boundary reappeared in all atlases and the land east of the Oder-Neisse Line was
again labeled as "Deutschland."[159] While some public opinion surveys showed a
declining interest in the lost lands, others did not. As shown above, support for
unification remained consistently high. German public opinion on homeland
matters was also notoriously contradictory. For example, in a July 1970 survey,
63 percent agreed fully or partly that "the German division and the loss of the
Eastern territories are results of the last war that we cannot undo. There is no
point in pretending they are not final." This response would be consistent with
the increasing acceptance of the Oder-Neisse Line. However, in this same survey, 70 percent of respondents also agreed fully or partly that "what happened
after the war in the East is not final. A peace treaty will decide what things will
be like." Unlike the preceding response, this one suggests that the status of the
Oder-Neisse territories is open for negotiation.[160] As one scholar concluded,
"Little doubt existed that the German question" was still on the table despite the
recognition of the de facto border.[161]

Compounding the difficulty with attributing the timing of change to new
information conveyed by the Berlin Wall is the fact that information about the
weakness of Allied support for West German claims had already been available
to the German leadership for years. Already in 1958, Secretary of State Dulles's
commitment to "hold West Berlin" was correctly interpreted in Bonn as implying
a lack of commitment to include the rest of the city as part of West Germany.[162] If
the Allies could backtrack on their treaty commitments to all of Berlin, there was
no reason to believe they would continue to support other West German interests. Indeed, in 1959, the three Western Allies agreed to no longer consider "the
[West German] impractical demand for reunification."[163] German policy makers
noticed. Heinrich Krone, one of Adenauer's advisors, concluded that "the West
wants to have quiet. With Berlin, the Kremlin has gotten the German question
rolling. We will not come out of this struggle without some losses."[164] However,
rather than change his mind, or withdraw homeland territoriality from the lost
lands in response, Adenauer went shopping for a new Western patron instead.
The worry about the reliability of the US's support for German unification drove
Adenauer to conclude the Éylsée Treaty with France despite the tension it caused
with the United States.[165]

The appeal to the construction of the Berlin Wall as the trigger of change is problematic even in the case of the SPD. The SPD had already laid the foundations for its transformation by 1959, in response to its continued political drubbing, and before the erection of the Berlin Wall in 1961. Indeed, party leaders admitted in a closed meeting in 1959 that they saw no chance for West Germany to regain the lost eastern territories, though they stressed that they could not divulge this stance to the public at large.[166] The Berlin Wall did have an impact, but it did so by reinforcing the political prospects of a variant consistent with withdrawing homeland territoriality from lost lands not by initiating the withdrawal on its own.

Finally, and consistent with the insight that events do not speak for themselves, more than one lesson was taken from the construction of the Berlin Wall. While it conveyed information about the relative lack of support from the Western powers (even if this was not new information per se), it also revealed a new path for attacking the GDR and bringing about reunification. Brandt's declaration that the Berlin Wall shaped his approach is thus better interpreted as leading to a change in the tactics with which to achieve the desired goal rather than directly affecting the goal itself. In 1963 Bahr summarized the lesson that he and Brandt took from the erection of the Berlin Wall: "We have said that the Wall was a sign of weakness. One could also say, it was a sign of the communist regime's fear and urge for self-preservation. The question is whether there are not possibilities gradually to diminish the regime's quite justifiable fears, so that the loosening up of the frontiers and the Wall will also become practicable, because the risk will be bearable. This is a policy which one could sum up in the formula: *Wandel durch Annäherung* (change through rapprochement)."[167]

A third version of the rational adaptation to new information explanation could point instead to the demographic transformations in the lost lands as the explanation for the variation in the withdrawal of homeland territoriality from them. From this perspective, homeland territoriality continued to be applied to the Saar and East Germany because they continued to be populated by ethnic Germans. Homeland territoriality was withdrawn from the Eastern Territories because most of its German-speaking population was expelled after the war.

This account, however, also suffers from a number of empirical shortcomings. First, an explanation based on a change in ethnic geography alone cannot explain why East Germany and the West German SPD ultimately accepted the partition along the Elbe despite the continued presence of ethnic Germans on the other side (not to mention the border with Austria).

Second, ethnic Germans remained in the Eastern Territories. The German Red Cross estimated the German population of the Eastern Territories at about four hundred thousand, and other estimates yielded a figure of more than a million.[168]

(The roughly one million Germans who migrated from the east to Germany in 1988–90 suggests that these figures were not far-fetched.) Thus, while the proportion of Germans relative to non-Germans certainly declined, a significant German population remained across the border.

One could, perhaps, argue that it is the proportion of coethnics to non-coethnics that matters. Such an argument, however, runs into at least two difficulties. First, German nationalism always included territories that were largely populated by non-coethnics within the map of the German homeland.[169] As a result, it is not clear why a lower proportion of Germans would necessarily have an impact now when it did not before. Second, such explanations would need to articulate how many coethnics need to be in a territory (or to no longer be in a territory) in order for homeland territoriality to be applied (or withdrawn). As I argue in chapter 5, since there is little prospect of answering this question, ethnic geography on its own is a less useful explanation of the application of homeland territoriality.

The geographic distribution of coethnics did matter in the German case, but its impact was mediated by the degree to which domestic political movements used an ethnic strategy of legitimization to designate land as part of the homeland. Since the CDU emphasized legal and self-determination logics to legitimate its application of homeland territoriality to lost lands and did not exclusively rely on an ethnic one, it was able to continue laying claim to lost lands even when their ethnic composition changed. Ethnic geography had more of an impact on the SPD's position once it started to define the problem in primarily ethnic rather than territorial terms. That is, the German exodus from the Eastern Territories facilitated the withdrawal of homeland territoriality from these lands for the SPD once it began focusing on the welfare of the German *Volk* rather than German land. Framing the concern as over the German people reduced the imperative to control territory with fewer coethnics in it. This was, importantly, a product of the introduction of a new variant of the strategy of legitimation, not its cause.

A final version of an explanation focusing on adaptation to new information could point to the variation in the economic value of the different territories. In the German context, however, the variation in the treatment of the lost lands does not correspond to their value. Of all the territories Germany lost after World War II, the Eastern Territories ceded to Poland were perhaps especially economically valuable. They were a key part of Germany's food production, and contained significant mineral deposits as well as the economically vital port of Danzig.[170] Yet, if anything, these were the territories from which homeland territoriality was more easily withdrawn.

An appeal to the economic value of territory is also complicated by the presence of competing economic imperatives. Economic interest in the resources of the Eastern Territories was counterbalanced by the potential economic gains to be had from trade with the Eastern Bloc. Indeed, West Germany's export interests, for whom the old territorial claims were seen as hindering trade with Eastern Europe, reinforced the New Ostpolitik and their preferences may help explain the CDU's agreement to accept it in practice.[171] This suggests that economic interests other than the material value of territory might also shape the application of homeland territoriality to lost lands.

Economic considerations even played a relatively minor part in considerations of unification with either the Saar or East Germany. In both cases, West Germany was willing to pay dearly to regain sovereignty over these homeland territories. The agreement returning the Saar to Germany provided France with the opportunity to mine 66,000,000 tons of coal from the Warndt, guaranteed delivery of 1.2 million tons of coal annually starting in 1962, and a third of the total output of the Saar mines. Nonetheless, Germans were willing to pay.[172]

The same was true for reunification with East Germany. In 1990 the projected cost of reunification was estimated at around 3 percent of West German GDP or 40 percent of private domestic savings.[173] A later study put the cost of reunification at $1.9 trillion over twenty years.[174] One economic analysis calculated the net burden of transfers from West to East Germany at about 0.7 percent of German GDP annually.[175] Indeed, the expected costs of reunification were part of the argument put forth by those, including the SPD, who sought to slow it down.[176] Yet, despite its anticipated economic cost, in 1991, 79 percent of the West German public approved of reunification; in 2009, 77 percent still did so.[177]

The second main category of alternative explanations focuses on the passage of time. In this vein, generational change has been pointed to as the driver of the withdrawal of homeland territoriality from lost lands in the German context.[178] The delay in the timing of the reduced salience of the lost lands in West Germany makes this explanation especially attractive. Indeed, there is substantial evidence to support this perspective. For example, notwithstanding Willy Brandt's protestations of a decade earlier, by 1979 nearly half of young West Germans described the GDR as a *foreign* country.[179]

Here too, however, the available public opinion evidence is contradictory. While it may be the case that relatively more of the younger generation was willing to cease applying homeland territoriality to lost lands than older generations, a majority of them continued to do so. A 1981 survey, for example, found that 56 percent of those under twenty-one did not consider the GDR to be a foreign country. In 1982 only 12 percent of those under thirty supported deleting the paragraph in the constitution's preamble that emphasized the German nation's right to self-determination and reunification.[180] Nor can an explanation linking the passage of time and generational replacement to the elision of the Eastern

Territories and the area of the GDR from the imagination of what counted as Germany account for the widespread support for reunification in both East and West Germany. Even if there were generational differences, they were not large enough to swamp the overall continued desire for reunification.

The rise of the norm of border fixity certainly had an impact—one visible in the rejection by West German leaders of all stripes of the legitimacy of changing borders by force.[181] While acceptance of this norm may account for this change in the tactics with which to pursue national sovereignty over lost parts of the homeland, it cannot account for the variation in whether homeland territoriality was withdrawn. Specifically, even if an appeal to the rising importance of this norm can account for the withdrawal of homeland territoriality from the Eastern Territories, it still cannot explain the continued desire for the erasure of the border between the FRG and the GDR.

The third form of alternative explanation focuses instead on the instrumental considerations of German leaders. These explanations would expect elements like the consolidation of the German regime or superpower diktat to account for the withdrawal of homeland territoriality. However, the consolidation of West German democracy does not convincingly account for the withdrawal of homeland territoriality from lost lands for at least two reasons. First, it cannot account for the variation either between the two main parties in West Germany or between the various territories Germany lost. Second, German leaders continued to apply homeland territoriality to the lost lands for decades after West German democracy was fully institutionalized and, from this perspective, would no longer need to do so.

The constraints placed on German leaders by the superpowers provide a more plausible explanation. This explanation has a great deal of support in the case of the GDR. The Soviet vision of a postwar Eastern Europe composed of peaceful, cooperative, and subservient states had no room for contested territories. All over Eastern Europe, borders were redrawn, and the Soviet's client states forced to accommodate themselves to the new reality. The GDR also had little choice but to fall in line.[182] As Brezhnev would make clear to Honecker, "We have troops [stationed] with you in the GDR. Erich, I tell you frankly, and never forget this: The GDR cannot exist without us, without the S[oviet] U[nion], its power and strength. Without us there is no GDR."[183]

West German policy makers were also very sensitive to the US's positions. On both the left (after 1959) and the right, the desire to align their positions with the United States constrained the application of homeland territoriality to lost lands by the parties in power.[184]

At the same time, political actors in both states displayed an ability to resist the desires of their patrons. As McAdams concluded, both German governments "acted in ways that defied the international consensus that was taking shape around them."[185] The consistent West German concern with reunification contradicted the very premise of American plans for Europe. The American policy of "double containment," which sought to restrain both Soviet and German expansionism, meant that the United States was at no time prepared to let the German desire for reunification threaten the international order.[186] International pressure on Germany to accept the Oder-Neisse Line, including by Britain and the United States, began to be felt in earnest in the mid- and late 1950s, with only limited influence on the CDU's position on the issue.[187] West Germany, in other words, continually pressed for reunification against the wishes of its superpower patron.

Moreover, rather than simply acceding to the interests of the United States, Adenauer was consumed with the fear that the Allies would strike a deal with the Soviets without consulting the Germans at all. His "nightmare scenario" of another Potsdam Conference led him to prioritize Germany's ties with France over the Atlantic alliance when he felt that the United States was paying insufficient attention to German interests.[188] This patron-shopping complicates the story of West Germany simply following the orders of its superpower patron.

The historical record also shows that, when the SPD undertook the New Ostpolitik, the initiative belonged to the client state rather than to the superpower.[189] Indeed, as cited above, contrary to the image of a superpower imposing its will on the client state, Brandt attributed the change in his thinking not to a directive from the United States, but precisely to the opposite, to relative American weakness. He also had to work hard to convince a skeptical Nixon administration that his Ostpolitik did not contradict American interests or undermine its position in the Cold War.[190] Had the New Ostpolitik been a response to American pressure, he would not have needed to do so. The United States itself was also well aware of its limited ability to shape German views on territorial issues. Both Henry Kissinger and Willy Brandt agreed that Bonn did not "ask permission" before undertaking the New Ostpolitik. As Kissinger noted in 1969, Brandt "was asking not for our advice but for our cooperation" with a policy course that had already been decided upon.[191]

The position of the superpower mattered, but its impact was indirect. The SPD used the congruence between its (new) position and that of the Kennedy and Johnson administrations as part of their signal to the German public that the New Ostpolitik was not inconsistent with remaining firmly part of the West.[192] If anything, then, the impact of superpower influence was filtered through domestic politics by facilitating the political success of a new variant of the map-image of the homeland.

Even in the most likely case of Soviet influence over the GDR, the ability of the superpower to dictate the withdrawal of homeland territoriality was constrained by the domestic politics of the client state. In this particular case, the limit was imposed by Ulbricht's personal commitment to reunification across the Elbe. As the lone decision maker of consequence on this issue in the GDR hierarchy, his views shaped the application of homeland territoriality to lost lands even against the countervailing pressure of Soviet interests.[193]

Ultimately, however, the GDR and its leaders followed the Soviet lead. Despite Ulbricht's continued commitment to reunification, the GDR began a project of distinguishing itself from the FRG and establishing its own, separate identity. This project, known as demarcation (*Abgrenzung*), was an attempt to replace the claim to the territory across the border with a map-image of the homeland of the socialist nation in the GDR as limited to the areas east of the Elbe.[194] Some have suggested that concept of delimitation was originally intended as an assault on Ulbricht's policy of seeking eventual reunification.[195] Indeed, looking back in 1992, Honecker conceded that the *Abgrenzung* had been carried out at Moscow's behest.[196] In any case, ultimately, the Soviets replaced Ulbricht with someone more amenable to their interests. As this took place, the GDR increasingly ceased applying homeland territoriality to the land under West German control.[197] In the GDR, superpower diktat clearly mattered.

The German experience reinforces the book's main theoretical arguments. First, the value of homelands shaped its post–World War II domestic politics and international relations. While the loss of homeland territory did not lead to conflict as Eden feared, it still structured politics for decades. Second, notwithstanding the importance of the lost parts of the homeland, there was significant domestic contestation in West Germany between political movements advocating different ways of applying homeland territoriality to lost lands.

Third, homeland territoriality was eventually withdrawn from (some) lost lands and this withdrawal was intimately linked to the domestic contestation between these political movements. The variation in whether homeland territoriality was withdrawn from the lost part of the German homeland, the timing of any withdrawal, and the variation between the two main German political movements on these questions, allow for a particularly nuanced comparison of the expectations of alternative mechanisms with the historical record. This comparison shows that, at least in the West German setting, the expectations of evolutionary dynamics rooted in the consequences of variation and differential political success over time are consistent with more aspects of the historical record than the alternative explanations. The decision to use particular legitimating strategies, modulations made to gain power, and explicit trades among sacred values, shaped the pattern of the withdrawal of homeland territoriality and its continued application.

ITALY'S FORGOTTEN PARTITION

The history of the conflict over the Istrian Peninsula reads like that of many other territorial disputes. As Italian and Slav nationalisms emerged, both included this area in the scope of their respective national homeland.[1] These clashing applications of homeland territoriality were evident in the conflicting labels applied to the area; Slavs called it the "Julian March" (*Julijska Krajina*), for Italians the region was *Venezia Giulia*.[2]

While the Italian application of homeland territoriality to the region was already evident when Italian nationalism emerged as a political force in the 1830s and 1840s, it accelerated with the formation of the Italian state in 1860, and became especially prominent after its 1866 expansion into Lombardy and Venice.[3] In a typical delimitation of the scope of the Italian homeland, Giuseppe Mazzini, the father of Italian nationalism, declared that the Italian fatherland, without which Italians would have "neither names, nor distinctive marks, nor votes, nor rights and not even acceptance as brothers among peoples," and without which they would be the "the bastards of humanity . . . stretches from the Alps to the southernmost tip of Sicily."[4] The desire for the *Italia irredenta* (unredeemed Italy) that remained outside the nation's sovereignty became so emblematic of a nation's desire to control its homeland that the word "irredentism" has come to mean the drive to redeem lost parts of the homeland more generally.

During World War I, Italians and Slavs fought to gain sovereignty over this territory from the ruins of the Austro-Hungarian Empire. Building on Mazzini's vision of the homeland, Italian nationalists affirmed that the "holy soil of the fatherland" extended to the Alps, and that these formed Italy's natural borders (see, for example, the depiction of Italy's northeastern border in figure 3.1).[5] The slogan of "Trento e Trieste" (Trento and Trieste), in which the latter stood for all of Istria, mobilized a mass irredentist movement intent on asserting Italian control over these regions.[6] The Rapallo Treaty (1920) after World War I gave Italy control of most of the region and, under Mussolini, Italy engaged in an active process of nationalizing it. This process included converting Slavic surnames to Italian, banning the use of Slovene in schools and churches, and even chopping down Linden trees, which had become a symbol of Slovene nationalism.[7] The Yugoslavs, when they regained control of the region in the waning months of World War II, exacted their revenge by throwing Italian "fascist collaborators" into *foibe* (geological chasms) in the Karst.

Partition was seen as a way to resolve this conflict almost as soon as the guns fell silent. The first new border was drawn in June 1945 to separate the Yugoslav and Allied troops who had raced to liberate Trieste (with the latter arriving a day after the former). The so-called Morgan Line, drawn by Lieutenant General Sir William Duthie Morgan, began just south of the city of Trieste, and then curved north along the Isonzo River (see figure 3.2). The Morgan Line placed the Italian provinces of Trieste and Gorizia, a strip of land east of the Isonzo River, and the region surrounding Pola, at the tip of the Istrian Peninsula, under control

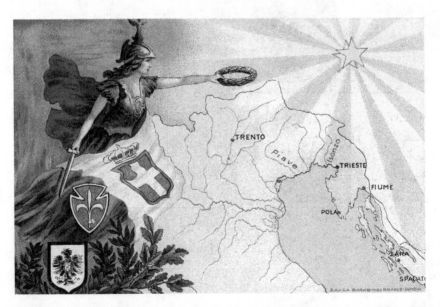

FIGURE 3.1 Map-image of the Italian homeland, 1916: "Light on unredeemed Italy"

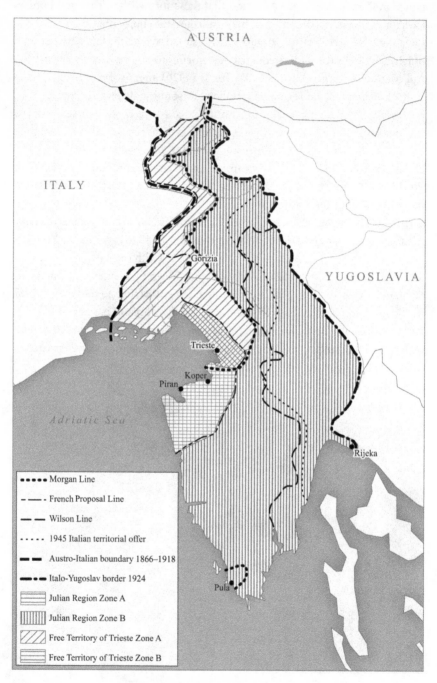

FIGURE 3.2 Borders in Venezia Giulia

of the Allied military. The remainder of the territory was placed under Yugoslav military administration.

The border between Italy and Yugoslavia moved again as part of the September 1947 peace treaty between Italy and the Allies. The peace treaty established the border along the so-called French line (see figure 3.2), which assigned Pola and a strip of territory east of the Isonzo River to Yugoslavia. The peace treaty also envisioned the creation of a new sovereign entity, the Free Territory of Trieste (FTT) on the eastern shore of the Gulf of Trieste. Until its actual incorporation, the FTT was to comprise two areas: Zone A, administered by the Allied Military Government (AMG), consisting of the city of Trieste and a narrow strip connecting it to Italy; and Zone B, administered by Yugoslavia, consisting of a portion of the northwestern part of the Istrian Peninsula. The FTT was never established because both the Soviet Union and the United States feared that the other would gain control of the strategically important area and, as a result, consistently vetoed the others' proposed governor. As a result, the line between the FTT's two zones (along with the rest of the 1947 border) eventually constituted the basis for the border between Italy and Yugoslavia. The terms of the de facto partition were set out in the 1954 Memorandum of Understanding (also known as the London Memorandum). This agreement, between the United States, Great Britain, Italy, and Yugoslavia, transferred administrative control of Zone A from the AMG to Italy and formally ratified Yugoslav civil administration of Zone B.

Despite the decades of ethnic and nationalist conflict over this territory, its division was, in the words of one observer, "that rare success story, the apparently definitive liquidation of one of the old world's historically most serious, dangerous, and long-lived territorial disputes."[8] In fact, this partition has been so successful at resolving the conflict between Slavs and Italians that it is usually omitted from contemporary studies of partitions and their ability to resolve conflict.[9]

This success reflects the fact that both Italy and Yugoslavia eventually withdrew homeland territoriality from the areas they had lost. This chapter explains the process by which Italy did so. The Italian withdrawal of homeland territoriality from the majority of Venezia Giulia occurred in two steps. The first, undertaken immediately after the war (1945–47), involved the constriction of the application of homeland territoriality by the dominant Christian Democracy Party (DC) to the area of the FTT rather than to the entire territory they had lost. This step was marked by a rhetorical shift from claiming Istria, Dalmatia, and Fiume, or "Venezia Giulia," to claiming "Trieste"; a conveniently ambiguous shorthand that during World War I stood for the entire region, shifted to refer to the area of the FTT after World War II, and was eventually reinterpreted as standing only for the city itself. The initial contraction of the scope of the homeland also involved a shift in the logic with which the homeland was delimited. Instead of the prior use of a combination of nationalist, ethnic, and historical logics, Italy's leaders adopted a logic of legitimation that emphasized the ethnic dimension almost exclusively. This narrowing of the logic of legitimation had significant downstream consequences. By lowering the domestic political cost of articulating visions of the homeland that excluded the lost lands once most Italians left the area under Yugoslav control, it set the table for the subsequent withdrawal of homeland territoriality from the Yugoslav-controlled parts of the FTT.

The second step did not begin until 1953. This timing, as well as the inconsistency about whether or not the lost lands were part of the homeland that characterized Italian discourse until 1975, cannot be fully explained independently of the DC's political concerns. The withdrawal of homeland territoriality by the DC began when agreement to the de facto partition of the Istrian Peninsula became politically useful. Following a liminal stage in which the DC's policies and pattern of articulation about the extent of the homeland were inconsistent, the de facto border became institutionalized as the new boundary of the Italian homeland because it was associated with continued DC rule. The institutionalization of the border as appropriate was marked by the 1975 Osimo Treaty, which recognized the de facto partition de jure, and officially ended the territorial dispute between Italy and Yugoslavia.

The process by which Italian homeland territoriality was withdrawn from most of Venezia Giulia is a hard case for an evolutionary dynamic rooted in domestic political contestation because the alternative explanations for what could shape the withdrawal of homeland territoriality from lost lands also strongly point in the same direction. Italy was under tremendous international pressure from the West to accept the postwar borders. The territorial partition was also accompanied by a significant shift in ethnic geography as Italian speakers left areas under Yugoslav control en masse. Moreover, postwar Italy was governed by a dominant political party that might reasonably have been expected to be immune to the need to experiment by articulating a new variant of the homeland's map-image or legitimating strategy that could become institutionalized as the new vision. Yet a careful examination of the Italian experience demonstrates that, although the consequences of domestic political processes may not account for all the variation in how societies accommodate themselves to the loss of homeland territory, they play a critical role in mediating the ability of external realities to drive such processes. As in the German context, the dramatic change in the ethnic composition of the territory and the international pressure on Italy to acquiesce to the new border shaped the way the main actors thought about this land. This impact, however, was felt only after endorsing the new border made short-term domestic political sense and depended on the prior shift to using an ethnic logic of legitimization almost exclusively to apply homeland territoriality to the Istrian Peninsula.

The remainder of the chapter proceeds as follows. The next section describes the first step in the Italian withdrawal of homeland territoriality from the lost parts of Venezia Giulia. This step was an adaptation to the reality that they would lose some territory after World War II. In an attempt to stem the extent of these losses, Italian leaders shifted the logic with which the Italian state legitimated its territorial aspirations. The following section illustrates the role that domestic political calculations had in accounting for the timing of the onset of the withdrawal of homeland territoriality from the lost lands and for the inconsistency that characterized this process. The final section considers the ability of alternative mechanisms to account for the empirical timing, actors, and consistency of the withdrawal of homeland territoriality from these parts of Italy's terra irredenta.

Adopting an Ethnic Line

In the immediate aftermath of the Second World War, Italian leaders worried that they would suffer additional territorial losses, especially in the Istrian Peninsula. This region, which had traded hands several times over the previous century was now largely in Yugoslav hands and Italy's leaders feared that the Allies would ratify this state of affairs. It was in this context that Italian leaders began withdrawing homeland territoriality from the eastern part of the Istrian Peninsula. This first step in the transformation of the scope of the Italian homeland corresponded to the withdrawal of homeland territoriality from the area to the east of the line marked as the Italian offer in figure 3.2. While initially modest in territorial terms, this step was notable primarily because the language with which it was pursued represented a transformation in the way Italian nationalism legitimated its territorial aspirations. Seeking to appeal to the world powers carving up Europe at the time, Italy's leaders opted to advance a territorial claim based on the ethnic composition of the territory rather than deploying the older argument that the area was innately Italian.

Although the Italian claims to Venezia Giulia always had an ethnic component, it was traditionally secondary to the innate Italian-ness of the land.[10] The Italian nationalist political project was built on the idea that the borders of the Italian homeland predated the ethnic Italianness of the population. It assumed the political unification of the area of "Italy" would lead the population within it to become "Italian." Mazzini's nationalism was guided by the idea that the cooperation of all the people in the "crucible of unification" would itself forge the national character. This was the logic behind the famous 1861 declaration by

Massimo D'Azeglio, the former prime minister of Piedmont: "We have made Italy; now we must make Italians."[11]

In other words, like many other nationalisms, the Italian nationalist project started by positing an Italy and then sought to meld the diverse people within it into a cohesive Italian nation.[12] If Venetians, Tuscans, and Romans could all be turned into Italians by Italian nationalism, there was little reason to believe that the inland population of Istria and Dalmatia would be any different.[13] Linguistic barriers were no obstacle to this project. By some estimates, only 3 percent of the population spoke Italian when the Italian state was founded; linguistic homogeneity would also follow political unification.[14] For this reason, although the population of Italian speakers was concentrated in the coastal areas of the Istrian Peninsula (especially in the cities of Fiume, Pola, and Trieste, and in the area west of the Isonzo River), the distinction between these areas and the rest of Istria and Dalmatia was initially politically irrelevant.[15] Consistent with the broader Italian nationalist project, Italian claims to the Istrian Peninsula assumed that the Slavs who lived in the region would ultimately assimilate and become Italian.[16] Indeed, the nationalizing efforts of the Italian state in the interwar period described above represented the application of the principle that the people on the land could be transformed into Italians.

After World War II, Italy's leadership turned this logic on its head. Instead of having Italian nationalism dictate the ethnic affiliation of the population within the homeland, the ethnic character of the population was now used to delimit the boundaries of Italian nationalism. As a result, Alcide De Gasperi, Italy's dominant postwar politician and the leader of the Christian Democracy Party, focused Italian territorial claims not on the entire territory that gave rise to Italian irredentism in the first place, but on those locations with significant Italian populations. Responding to the emphasis placed on ethnic balance by the Council of Foreign Ministers in their deliberations about the fate of Axis territories, he advocated for the inclusion in Italy of the major Italian urban centers and the intervening Slovenian land along the Adriatic coast. The border, he protested, should follow a "continuous ethnic line." He warned against "repeating the mistake of Versailles" by truncating Italian territory and decried the planned "assignation to Yugoslavia of the Italian zone of Western Istria as far as Pola particularly . . . [as] a terrible blow to Italy's national conscience."[17]

In a representative example of the ethnically based territorial claim that came to dominate their discourse, Ivanoe Bonomi, former premier and the Italian representative to the Political and Territorial Commission for Italy, contended that

> a partition of Venezia Giulia according to a clearly recognizable ethnic line would undoubtedly be accepted, sooner or later, by the two

neighbouring states and would thus ensure the re-establishment of mutually trusting relations between them. On the contrary the existence of a territory which, because of its very nature, will not cease to be coveted by one side and the other, will have the result of weighing heavily on the relations between the two states thus being a permanent threat to the peace between them and, in consequence, to world peace in general. The establishment of the new frontiers touches so deeply Italian feelings, that any judgment they may pass on the Peace Treaty will be heavily influenced by this decision. Nations can bear the heaviest blows: but those decisions which cut through their flesh, such as a transfer of their population to another state, remain engraved in the national conscience and determine the future course of history.[18]

Exactly which territory was included within this "continuous ethnic line" shifted over the course of the immediate postwar period. In 1945 and 1946, Italian leaders argued that such a border should be drawn largely based on the line Woodrow Wilson suggested in 1919 (see the Wilson Line and the Italian offer in figure 3.2).[19] The Italian endorsement of the Wilson Line is especially notable because Italy had vigorously rejected Wilson's proposal when it was initially made. At the time, they castigated this proposal for neglecting to include the rest of Istria on the grounds that the land was innately Italian and ethnicity should not be the dominant consideration.[20] As they increasingly relied on an ethnic logic of legitimation to claim their lost lands, between 1947 and 1953 the application of homeland territoriality was increasingly restricted to the area of the FTT, where the bulk of Italians resided. This area to which homeland territoriality was still consistently applied corresponds to the areas with checkered and diagonal hatching in figure 3.2.

Given its timing and consistency, it is likely that the decision to demand a border corresponding to the "ethnic composition of the territory" was initially an instrumental one. It took place too rapidly and uniformly to be consistent with the expectations of an evolutionary dynamic. Italian leaders believed the Allied Powers would be more sympathetic to ethnically based claims (as they were after the First World War) and that this could be the starting point for subsequent unification with any territory Italy might lose. There is also some evidence that it was a quickly made tactical decision intended to prevent Yugoslavia from gaining the entire territory.[21]

The possibility that this change was a rational response to Italy's weak bargaining position in the aftermath of its being on the losing side of the Second World War cannot be completely discounted. However, this explanation suffers from three difficulties. First, Italian leaders in the immediate postwar era argued that, since they resisted the Fascist government in Italy, they were actually on the side of the winners and, as such, should not be punished for Italy's role in the war. The "founding ideology of the Italian republic," noted the writer Sergio Romano, was built on the public lie that Italy had not lost the war.[22] Second, the actual line they initially proposed, while deviating modestly from the prior border, still included significant territory that was actually firmly under Yugoslav control. If they were acting as a defeated power, we might have expected them to acquiesce to the reality posed by the new postwar border—a shift that only occurred a few years later. Third, there was significant domestic variation in whether the new border was accepted among political movements in Italy. The neofascist Movimento Sociale Italiano (Italian Social Movement, or MSI), for example, continued to apply homeland territoriality to the entire Istrian Peninsula into the 1990s. On the other side, the Italian Communists were considerably more willing to accept the de facto postwar border, rather than any ethnic line. This variation is problematic for an explanation based on accommodation to the reality of the possible because all three groups were subject to the same information about Italy's weak international position.

Despite its instrumental origins, the decision to cast Italian territorial claims in ethnic terms had significant consequences. The choice of an ethnic logic of legitimation promulgated in the hopes that it would resonate with the global powers bled into other, domestic, arenas.[23] The DC's legitimation of territorial claims by referring to the ethnic composition of the territory meant that the mass exodus of Italians from the region in subsequent years weakened their ability to successfully apply homeland territoriality to this territory. The highlighting of the ethnic component in the Italian nationalist "repertoire of commonplaces" made their territorial ambitions more dependent on ethnic geography than in the past.[24] In this way, the instrumental choice to frame the desire for territory in primarily ethnic terms set the stage for the withdrawal of homeland territoriality from the entire region. This potentiality, however, was not actualized until domestic political considerations prompted the DC to agree to a provisional partition of the FTT.

Domestic Politics and the Institutionalization of a "Provisional" Solution

Italian politics in the immediate postwar period was dominated by the DC and, more specifically, by Alcide De Gasperi.[25] De Gasperi understood his basic mission as the (re)establishment of the Italian Republic and its protection from both fascism and communism. The DC saw itself as the only bulwark against these twin dangers. "We are the largest, most responsible party that the Italian nation has at present," declared De Gasperi in 1953, "and if the Christian Democrat [sic] Party's organizational, internal strength collapsed, democracy would be lost in Italy."[26] Despite its dominance, the political balancing act required to hold both fascism and communism at bay while maintaining its position in the center of the Italian political spectrum eventually drove the DC to acquiesce first to a provisional partition and, eventually, to cease applying homeland territoriality to the lost parts of the homeland.

Objectively speaking, it was evident already in 1947 that Italy would be unable to recover the territory that had come under Yugoslav control. This realization was common among Italy's diplomatic corps. Italy's ambassador to France, for example, criticized their "obsession" with Trieste, Pola, and other issues as irrelevant given their weakness.[27] This perspective gained even more credence after the Soviet-Yugoslav split in 1948 and the subsequent American attempts to integrate Yugoslavia into the Western defense orbit.[28]

Yet the DC's political leadership, and Italians more generally, initially showed few signs that they were willing to recalibrate their view of the homeland and accept the 1947 border. Expansive Italian claims could be maintained because, their significant disagreements notwithstanding, the noncommunist parts of the Italian Resistance agreed with the Fascists that the appropriate borders of the Italian homeland included Trieste and the Istrian Peninsula. The domestic legitimacy of this view was anchored in the postwar Italian regime's framing of the resistance to fascism in terms of a regenerative experience for the entire nation. From this perspective, the Fascist "interlude" was seen as a deviation from the path of Italian nationalism. Adopting the mantle of the heirs of the Risorgimiento, the nineteenth-century project of unifying Italy, the noncommunist parts of the resistance and the Italian Republic it founded appealed to an Italian nationalism that sought to defend the territorial integrity of the Italian homeland, including its terra irredenta.[29]

As a result, rather than automatically acquiescing to the reality of the new border, Italians across the political spectrum overwhelmingly identified the prospective loss of Venezia Giulia as the most painful one facing Italy. The future of Trieste became a focal point of Italian politics after the war.[30] Observers described the desire to regain the lost parts of the homeland as the "test of national dignity for the new democratic republic," "the lodestar of Italian foreign policy, the issue that conditioned almost every other choice," and as a "religious imperative."[31] De Gasperi argued that "Trieste is for Italians . . . more than a city and a harbor: it is a national feeling" and the "the polar star of [my] democratic policy." Italy's defense minister in the 1950s and the national party secretary of the DC, Paolo Taviani, wrote in his journal that the value of Trieste was sanctified to Italians by the fact that "over half a million Italian families had sacrificed a son to Trento and Trieste"—the project to redeem the Italian homeland that had been under Hapsburg (and now Yugoslav) control.[32]

In line with these sentiments, both Italian public opinion and a majority of the Italian parliament initially opposed the 1947 peace treaty, criticizing it for depriving Italy of her "dignity and legitimate pride."[33] Bonomi denounced the territorial provisions of the treaty as "cutting into the nation's living flesh" and as intended "to mortify and degrade Italy."[34] Popular resentment over Italy's loss of Trieste was spontaneous, sincere, and crossed party lines.[35] Still, in 1950, an observer noted that "you cannot talk long with an Italian about his country's future without the conversation turning to Trieste. . . . Trieste is to Italy a beloved child lost to an anguished mother."[36] The widespread resonance of the issue was demonstrated by the mass celebrations that erupted throughout Italy, even as far away as Palermo (all the way in the southern tip of Italy), in response to the 1948 Tripartite Declaration by the United States, Great Britain, and France that the entire FTT should be placed under Italian sovereignty.[37] In 1951 the New York Times correspondent wrote that "Italian public opinion is greatly exercised over the possibility that Italy may be called upon to accept further territorial sacrifices in [the Free Territory of] Trieste. Only this morning large demonstrations were held in Rome and other cities to urge the Government to defend Italian rights over the Trieste Free Territory at all costs."[38] Still, in 1953, it was an open question whether "the political climate in Italy would permit any Italian prime minister to renounce Zone B of the FTT, even if he could simultaneously celebrate the return of Trieste to Italy."[39]

Although Italy's parliament eventually narrowly approved the peace treaty, it did so because De Gasperi convinced them that, unjust as its territorial dimensions were, the peace treaty was a necessary first step toward regaining Italy's international position and, therefore, its ability to regain its lost territories.[40] The day after signing the peace treaty, the Italian government protested against it, declaring that Italy maintained the "right to rely on a radical revision of elements which could paralyze or poison the life of a nation of forty-five million human beings crowded into a land that cannot feed them."[41] On the occasion of Italy's admission to the Council of Europe in February 1949, De Gasperi repeated this argument, commenting that "finally . . . we emerge from the peculiar situation in which we have been since the war and like others, reenter the European family of nations in which . . . we will be able to say a word on those postwar questions [i.e., control of the FTT] which have not yet been solved."[42]

Indeed, Italy set about trying to change the territorial aspects of the peace treaty even before they were implemented.[43] The restoration of national sovereignty over Trieste and its hinterland remained a formal foreign policy goal of the new republic. Intuitively understanding the role of rhetorical applications of homeland territoriality to lost lands in the absence of sovereignty over them, the Italian government funded a network of Italian irredentist movements in Trieste under the umbrella of the "Second Irredentism." Their task, as articulated by the *Associazione Nazionale per la Venezia Giulia e Dalmazia* (National Association for Venezia Giulia and Dalmatia), the umbrella union of Italian irredentist organizations, was to preserve "the unquenching faith in the return of Venezia Giulia and of Dalmatia to the fold of the mother country."[44] They did so by routinely and consistently flagging the status of the lost lands as part of the Italian homeland.

As part of the continued drive to regain Italy's lost homeland territory, De Gasperi tried to leverage the American preoccupation with the spread of communism into support for Italian claims to Venezia Giulia. He repeatedly argued that, unless Italy regained its lost homeland territories, the DC would lose power and Italy would succumb to the Communists. For example, during a visit to Washington in September 1951, De Gasperi warned that if Italians thought that "their allies could not save Trieste for Italy, the result would be a dangerous trend toward neutralism" and "his coalition would lose votes to the left and right."[45]

All told, the DC's political leadership and Italian diplomats looked at the same geopolitical reality but reached different conclusions. Rather than focus on Italy's weakness or the geopolitical implications of the rift between Yugoslavia and the Soviet Union in June 1948, the DC's political leaders emphasized the 1948 Tripartite Declaration supporting the incorporation of the entire FTT into Italy.[46] Indeed, at least initially, the rupture between Yugoslavia and the USSR aroused confidence in Italy that it could regain its lost territory. For example, *Il Corriere della Sera*, a pro-government newspaper, saw Tito's weakness as an opportunity to advance their interests on the border question.[47] De Gasperi also minimized the importance of the Yugoslav-Soviet split as either a scam or a temporary disagreement. He continued to believe that the process of European unification would strengthen Italy's hand and enable it to obtain a better territorial outcome.[48]

This variation highlights one of the difficulties with ascribing the withdrawal of homeland territoriality from the lost lands in the Italian context to new information. New realities are usually complicated and new information ambiguous or contradictory. This makes it difficult to a priori predict which strands of reality will be used to update prior attitudes and which will be ignored. Confirmation bias, moreover, makes it more likely that new information would be ignored if it were inconvenient or contradicted earlier positions.[49]

The DC's political leadership was also predisposed to reach different conclusions because they were primarily concerned with the domestic political implications of abandoning the claim to the entire FTT. De Gasperi accused the diplomats advocating an agreement to partition (even one that would allow Italy to regain Zone A of the FTT) of underestimating the importance of domestic public opinion on the issue. He reprimanded them, saying that, regardless of the view from outside Italy, they "should always take account of the internal situation of the country." "Our position as democrats caught in the crossfire" between fascism and communism, he wrote, "is already bad enough without having to add the lack of understanding and impatience of friends."[50]

Indeed, both the Left and the Right highlighted Italy's failure to recover its terra irredenta and pressed the DC to demonstrate its continued fealty to an expansive (but still smaller than in the recent past) territorial claim. As one reporter noted at the time, "Trieste is rapidly developing into an important weapon in the hand of Premier de Gasperi's political enemies. There is no doubt about its being a question very close to the heart of all Italians and Belgrade's stubborn refusal even to discuss it is building up considerable resentment against the government."[51] The DC worried that pro-fascist sympathizers would use the issue of Trieste to gain support at its expense. A weaker DC, they feared, would allow the Italian Communist Party (PCI), the DC's most significant political opponent and the only other viable contender for national leadership, to take over.[52]

Two political developments in the early 1950s changed the DC's political calculus and drove it to agree, as a tactical measure, to a de facto partition: the rise of the FTT's Independence Front, and the political instability of the Italian regime. While the idea of an independent Trieste dated back to at least 1905, the political movement promoting it gained significant traction in the late 1940s. The leaders of the FTT's Independence Front contended that Trieste's economic survival depended on the city serving as central Europe's main shipping port. Since this required good relations with both East and West, they maintained that an independent Trieste would benefit by being able to remain neutral. In 1949 the Independence Front was the third largest party in Trieste, after the DC and the Communists. In the 1952 municipal elections, the Independence Front nearly doubled its vote share to 12 percent. This gain was seen as especially strong given the extremely unfavorable conditions in which it contested the elections, including, not least, the open hostility of the AMG.[53]

Despite the Independence Front's arguably modest political success, the DC was highly sensitive to the challenge it posed. As noted above, De Gasperi was guided by a very strong slippery-slope perspective, whereby any weakening of the DC would inevitably result in a Communist takeover of Italy. The Independence Front's apparent momentum changed the way the DC's leadership saw the impact of the passage of time on their territorial prospects. Initially, the DC believed that the unresolved status of the FTT provided time for Italy to regain its international status and therefore improved the likelihood that they would recover all the lost territories. As Italy's ambassador Pietro Quaroni had put it in

1947, their imperative was to "give up as little as possible until things change[d] in [Italy's] favor so that [Italy might] outlive [its] current state of weakness with the fewest losses and amputations." Likewise, Italy's ambassador to France argued that "we must postpone the Trieste question. The longer we postpone it the more we stand to gain."[54]

The Independence Front's momentum motivated the DC to start seeing time as working against them. Its leaders began to worry that if Italy did not cement its hold on the city of Trieste, its amorphous status and the city's practical economic needs would continue to strengthen local calls for an independent FTT. A stronger independence movement in Trieste, in turn, would increase the probability that Italy would lose the entire territory to an independent FTT.[55] If that were to happen, the DC feared not just the permanent loss of homeland territory, but the loss of support to the neofascist Right and, as a result, the Communist takeover of Italy.

The second main challenge the DC faced at the time was posed by its inability to translate its electoral dominance into political stability. The postwar republic adopted a nearly pure system of proportional representation. The resulting fractured character of Italian party politics meant that the DC was unable to maintain a stable government despite receiving nearly 49 percent of the vote and an outright parliamentary majority in the 1948 elections (even with thirty-five other parties on the ballot). De Gasperi, animated by his desire to forestall both the Communists and the neofascists, formed a broad centrist coalition rather than establishing a DC-only government. However, unable to sustain agreement on basic elements of domestic policy, De Gasperi's coalition was ultimately deserted by both its right and left flanks.[56] As a result, despite his parliamentary majority, De Gasperi was forced to form four separate governments between 1948 and 1953.

Seeking to ease the translation of popularity into political stability, the DC changed Italy's election law to provide a supermajority to any coalition that garnered more than 50 percent of the votes. While the DC argued that this reform would inject needed stability into the Italian political system, it was widely interpreted as an attempt to consolidate the DC's power at the expense of other parties. As a result, this gambit backfired and the DC was punished in the 1953 elections. Although it maintained its status as the largest party, its share of the vote declined to 40 percent. Coming on the heels of local elections in 1951 and 1952 in which the DC lost ground to both the Communists and to the Far Right, the 1953 success of these parties at the DC's expense seemed to confirm De Gasperi's worst fears.[57]

The idea of a provisional agreement that would allow Italy to gain direct control of Zone A of the FTT, including the city of Trieste, provided a way for De

Gasperi to respond to both of these challenges. In the city itself, such an agreement was expected to undercut the Triestine independence movement while, at least rhetorically, appeasing the Triestine desire to maintain the claim to the rest of the FTT. In Italian politics more broadly, a provisional solution would enable the DC to better compete with the resurgent Fascist Right by giving the DC a concrete victory, namely, the actual return of Zone A to Italy, while simultaneously insulating it from the charge that it was jeopardizing Italian claims to the rest of the lost territory.[58]

The timing of the change in De Gasperi's position on the question of a provisional partition of the FTT is striking. The idea of a provisional arrangement for the FTT had been promoted by Italian diplomats since at least August 1951. De Gasperi, however, steadfastly refused to consider such an arrangement both because it could be construed as the withdrawal of the claim to Zone B of the FTT and because he believed that it would hurt the DC electorally. Still, in April 1953, two months before the elections, he considered a provisional solution to be political suicide because no one would believe that it was really provisional. Maintaining the application of homeland territoriality to the entire area of the FTT, De Gasperi even rejected a proposal by the United States that offered Italy all of Zone A of the FTT, along with the cities of Koper, Izola, and Piran in Zone B—a proposal that would have given Italy more than it would ultimately accede to in 1954. In other words, until the 1953 elections, De Gasperi believed that the decision not to abandon Zone B of the FTT was more electorally valuable than the restitution of Zone A.[59]

However, ten days after the 1953 elections and the popular rebuke of the DC, De Gasperi quietly accepted the recommendation of Vittorio Zoppi (the secretary general of the Foreign Ministry and a longtime proponent of a provisional solution) that Italy seek a provisional solution despite his recent rejection of precisely such a formula. It appears that the DC's relatively poor showing convinced him that inaction would be as electorally damaging as a provisional solution. The formal Italian objective (though one kept private from the Italian population) was henceforth modified to seek Italian control of Zone A of the FTT, while keeping the future of Zone B of the FTT open for future negotiations.[60]

The DC continued to pursue this objective even after De Gasperi was forced to resign later that summer. His successor, Giuseppe Pella, approved De Gasperi's decision to seek a provisional settlement. The political logic that drove De Gasperi's willingness to seek a provisional solution was reinforced by Pella's even more precarious political position. His governing coalition depended on the support of monarchist and neofascist parties—parties that had pledged during the 1953 campaign "to create a climate of irredentism to recover Trieste, Istria, and the other Adriatic lands unjustly taken from [Italy]."[61] Maintaining their support thus depended on his promise "to defend national interests," that is, on the continued application of homeland territoriality to the lost parts of the homeland. At the same time, given the danger posed by the DC's weakening political fortunes and the momentum of the Independence Front in Trieste, Pella believed that the reacquisition of Zone A would be a political boon that would undercut the Independence Front and solidify support for a government widely viewed as merely transitional.[62]

Mario Scelba, who became prime minister in February 1954 after Pella was forced to resign because of factional disputes within the DC, picked up where his predecessors had left off. Scelba, according to British diplomats, was less "obsessed with Trieste" than Pella and De Gasperi, but he too continued to emphasize that any agreement would be merely provisional and not a renunciation of Italy's claims to Zone B.[63] He did so because the idea of a final partition of the FTT was deeply unpopular. In November 1953, for example, one study found that only 14 percent of Italians supported a partition of the Free Territory of Trieste.[64] The unpopularity of this idea makes it easy to understand why Italy's political leaders kept insisting that the agreement was merely provisional and not a fundamental change in their view of the lost lands.

Italy's agreement to a provisional partition was formalized in the 1954 London Memorandum, which transferred administrative control of Zone A from the AMG to Italy and formally ratified Yugoslav civil administration of Zone B. Formally, the agreement left the question of who was ultimately sovereign over these areas open for future negotiations. However, the public agreement was accompanied by a secret exchange of letters in which the United States affirmed that, from its perspective, the provisional partition was, in fact, final, and that they would accept the annexations by Italy and Yugoslavia of the relevant territories provided they took place peacefully.

The Italian debate over this agreement was quite contentious. Even with the arguments that it was the best Italy could do at the time, that the alternative was losing Zone A entirely, that it accomplished the formal return of the city of Trieste and Zone A to Italian control, and that the fate of Zone B was, in any case, only provisional, the opposition to it was so fierce that the London Memorandum was not formally ratified by the Italian parliament. (It was subsequently approved by the parliament while voting on the budget of the Foreign Ministry).[65] Both the Italian Right and Left accused the government of betraying Italy's national interest by agreeing to a de facto partition of the Italian homeland. The DC government only narrowly withstood a motion of no confidence on the agreement in the Chamber of Deputies after a marathon session punctuated by two fistfights.[66]

Broadly speaking, however, the political strategy that drove the acceptance of the provisional solution worked. The integration of the city of Trieste into Italy took the wind out of the sails of the Independence Front. Likewise, the Italian Far Right lost the issue of the city of Trieste and Zone A, and could not mobilize the same degree of fervent popular support for the claim to the yet-to-be-redeemed Zone B of the FTT. As a result, it grew correspondingly weaker. In the 1958 election, its support declined by nearly 20 percent. Indeed, observers noted that the "Trieste arrangements, coupled with the withdrawal of occupying troops from that city, have lessened the appeal of the more strident nationalists everywhere [in Italy] except in the Alto Adige [i.e., South Tyrol]."[67]

The DC's insistence on the provisional character of the London Memorandum is often portrayed as mere window dressing used to obscure a more fundamental acceptance of the border. From this perspective, the agreement was "deliberately based on ambiguity so that the border problem would be removed from the attention" of Italian public opinion.[68] To be sure, many in Italy's leadership understood the London Memorandum as signifying the final settlement of the border issue. Scelba, for example, noted in a 1955 Washington meeting with John Dulles, the US secretary of state, that the "Trieste question had finally been solved after being an irritant ever since the end of World War II."[69] Italy's ambassador to the United States also conceded that the accord "had merely a resemblance of being provisional while in reality it was final."[70]

Although Italy's decision makers may have privately understood the arrangement as permanent, perhaps because they were aware that the United States saw it as such, this view was not broadly shared at the time. The Italian press emphasized that the London Memorandum was the first step in regaining all of Istria. The pro-government *Il Messagero* pointed out that the pro-Western policies of the government had finally borne fruit and that "the brothers in Zone B [could] rekindle their hopes" because "Italy would never waiver from her firm request for a plebiscite in both zones." The headline in the right-wing *Il Secolo* put it more directly: "Italy is in Trieste with eyes on Istria."[71]

In public, DC leaders consistently emphasized the provisionality of the agreement. Even if this was merely window dressing, the fundamentally rhetorical character of the application of homeland territoriality to lost lands meant that portraying the agreement as provisional was still consequential. Since the homeland status of lost lands is maintained by claiming them in those terms, the reputed provisionality of the agreement sustained the status of the lost lands as part of the Italian homeland.

Many of the actual policies pursued by the DC and DC-led governments were also inconsistent with the perspective that the provisionality of the agreement was mere window dressing. To be sure, some Italian policy supported the implication that they had already withdrawn homeland territoriality from Zone B of the FTT. For example, in the early 1960s, Italy transformed its mission in

Capodistria into an Italian consulate, an institution by definition located out-side the national borders. In 1963 Italy created the autonomous region of Friuli-Venezia Giulia in new borders wholly within Italy, despite criticism that doing so recognized the division of the FTT as permanent.[72] In so doing, the Italian state effectively rebranded Venezia Giulia to refer to the new (truncated) territory rather than to the region as a whole.

Other policies, however, signaled the continued application of homeland ter-ritoriality to Zone B of the FTT. For example, the DC-led Italian government continued to financially support a range of irredentist groups well into the 1970s. Italy also continued to consider the Italian residents of Zone B to be Italian citi-zens and the southern extension of the former FTT as the international border between Italy and Yugoslavia.[73] Reflecting this position, DC-led governments regularly protested Yugoslav moves (like the conscription of its residents in 1956) intended to integrate Zone B into Yugoslavia. Indeed, it is hard to understand the formal protests Italy lodged when Yugoslavia mounted signs reading "SFR Yugo-slavia–SR Slovenia" at crossings between it and Zone B in 1974, if the 1954 agree-ment was taken as the final word on the fate of the lost lands. If Italy had already accepted the border twenty years earlier, this act ought to have passed beneath notice as mundane road maintenance inside Yugoslavia. Instead, suggesting that it had not yet ceased applying homeland territoriality to the lost lands, Italy pro-tested that "Yugoslav sovereignty has never been expanded to Italian territory labeled as 'Zone B' of the unrealized Free Territory of Trieste."[74] Indeed, the Ital-ian protest note explicitly defined Zone B of the FTT as Italian territory.[75]

These diplomatic protests reflected the reality that the DC was still willing to affirm the homeland status of the lost lands well into the 1970s, especially when it was politically expedient to do so. Historically, northeastern Italy, including the regions of Veneto, Friuli, and Trieste, was a bastion of support for the DC. For example, between 1946 and 1968, the DC received more than 50 percent of the vote in northeast Italy, well above its average in the country as a whole.[76] The party's fear of alienating this key domestic constituency played a key role in its 1963 decision to provide financial support to irredentist associations, and espe-cially to the Alleanza Tricolore Italiana (Italian Tricolor Alliance).[77]

The continued application of homeland territoriality to the lost lands, how-ever, cannot be attributed only to local political expediency because it also con-tinued in contexts far from the public gaze. For example, the delimitation of the continental shelf boundary in the Adriatic Sea, formalized in a highly technical and largely obscure 1968 treaty, began in the middle of the Gulf of Trieste rather than at the land border between Italy and Yugoslavia because Italy insisted that the border was not yet established.[78] Italy also continued to apply homeland ter-ritoriality to the lost lands throughout the first five years of the *secret* negotiations it carried out with Yugoslavia starting in 1969. It was only in the last round of negotiations that Italy abandoned its substantive territorial claims to sovereignty over Zone B.[79] One observer noted that, as late as the 1970s, "there was no shortage" of those, including in the DC's executive committee, who did not want to see the London Memorandum replaced with a treaty which would put the question to rest.[80] For these reasons, Bogdan Novak could worry as late as 1970 that "any serious crisis in Yugoslavia might be a temptation for Italy to regain at least the lost territory of the former Zone B [of the FTT] to which she had never renounced her claims, if not the entire western part of Istria. On such an occasion would a democratic Italian government have the strength to resist the nationalistic forces, which would demand that the opportune moment not be lost?"[81]

This persistent concern reflects the fact that the eventual withdrawal of homeland territoriality from Italy's lost lands is not easily attributed to an automatic, inevitable, or quick consequence of the London Memorandum or to the drawing of the border. Rather, the institutionalization of the view of the provisional border as permanent was driven by a combination of domestic political developments and external events that, over time, raised the costs of continuing to apply homeland territoriality to Zone B of the FTT and increased the benefits of withdrawing homeland territoriality from it. As discussed earlier in this chapter, some of the initial political benefits included undercutting the Triestine Independence Front and shoring up the DC's ability to counter the Communists by blunting the appeal of the neofascists.

By the end of the 1960s, shifting Italian political dynamics provided additional rewards to this position. Foremost among these was the pragmatic turn taken by the PCI. The moderation of its positions and the growing gap between its views and those of Moscow rendered the PCI an increasingly legitimate actor in Italian politics.[82] Part of the DC, led by Aldo Moro, sought to reinforce these changes and to benefit from them by using a grand alliance with a reformed PCI to preserve the DC's power. The price of such an alliance was the renunciation of the lingering claim to the lost territories. As Moro would later confirm, "the definitive renunciation to [sic] Italian formal rights over the ex–zone B was dictated by the necessity to safeguard the prospective inclusion of the Communist party in a governing coalition."[83]

There were also economic benefits to the new regional arrangement that reinforced the returns to the improved relations with Yugoslavia enabled by the withdrawal of homeland territoriality from the lost lands. In Gorizia, for example, trade volume increased by 900 percent in the first five years after the liberalization of cross-border traffic in 1955.[84] During the sharp economic downturn of the mid-1970s, Trieste became dependent on Yugoslavia for business, reducing support for irredentist claims even there.[85] The promotion of a relatively permeable border and a dense network of cross-border ties aided the acceptance of the loss of homeland territory by draining the loss of much of its practical implications for the Triestine population. In the words of the Triestine socialist Bruno Pincherle, "By metaphorically drawing this border with a pencil instead of a pen, the artificial frontier . . . dissolve[d] into a space of brotherhood, equality, and freedom."[86] In effect, facilitating cross-border relations on a regional level de-emphasized the national borders in favor of regional cooperation.[87] The resulting increasing openness of even segments of the Triestine population to the idea of renouncing Zone B if it would bring economic benefits reduced the appeal of continuing to apply homeland territoriality to the lost lands.[88]

External factors also raised the costs of returning to the old territorial claims. The tepid reaction to Soviet aggression, especially the invasion of Hungary in 1956 and the repression of the Prague Spring in 1968, led Italy's leaders to conclude that the West was too afraid of nuclear war to challenge the Eastern Bloc. This conclusion had two important consequences. First, even the territorially hawkish wing of the DC concluded that the era of open confrontation between East and West was over. As a result, "peaceful coexistence" could become a legitimate political objective for the DC rather than simply the Communist catchphrase that it had been until then.[89] Brandt's détente policies, which appeared to imply that European border revisionism was passé, further reinforced this view.

Second, the DC-led governments became increasingly invested in preserving and consolidating Tito's role as a buffer between Italy and the Warsaw Pact countries.[90] For example, after the Soviet invasion of Czechoslovakia in 1968, the Italian government guaranteed the inviolability of the border with Yugoslavia, despite the fact that the border was still formally provisional, in order to enhance Yugoslavia's domestic stability and forestall the possibility of Soviet troops on Italy's borders. Reflecting the same logic, a 1973 report by the Italian intelligence agency concluded that the rise of ethnonationalism and the possibility of Soviet intervention in Yugoslavia posed direct threats to Italy. The "report confirmed that the Italian government could simultaneously strengthen its security and Yugoslav stability by recognizing the territorial provisions of the London Memorandum as a definitive solution and establishing the Italian southeastern border along the demarcation line."[91] Indeed, when the Osimo Treaty was eventually concluded, Moro justified it by arguing that strengthening Yugoslavia was in Italy's strategic interest.[92]

All these factors reinforced the view within the party that the continued efforts to reincorporate the ex–Zone B of the FTT into Italy were harming their interests. Moro categorized these efforts as a "needless element of contentiousness amid the Adriatic friendship."[93] Even Amintore Fanfani, who led the DC faction most identified with the desire to maintain the claim to the lost parts of the homeland, suggested to Moro in 1967 that they "cautiously re-open negotiations with the Yugoslav government and, when dealing with the demand for Italian sovereignty over the ex-zone B, 'to conceal the fact that the Italian government would be ready for a future formal recognition of Yugoslav sovereignty [in Zone B of the FTT] without appropriate compensation.'"[94] By the early 1970s, both the DC and political parties of the Center Left were openly advocating the formal resolution of the dispute over the border. For some, especially on the left, the border issue had even become "quite irrelevant."[95] Even the irredentists recognized that popular support for their cause was waning. For example, Gianni Bartoli, the irredentist DC mayor of Trieste, warned the president of the National Italian Irredentist Association in 1970 that the public's growing apathy toward the Istrian Peninsula was endangering their territorial rights.[96]

The leadership of the DC, especially Moro, sought a way out of the conundrum posed by the mounting costs of continuing to apply homeland territoriality to the lost lands (including the opportunity cost of an alliance with the PCI) and their continued flagging of the lost lands as part of the homeland.[97] Rather than an open disavowal of the homeland status of the lost lands, the DC built on the ethnic legitimation of the claim to the lost lands that came to dominate after World War II, and reframed the issue as primarily one of the protection of individual Italians in those territories, rather than of the intrinsically Italian nature of the land. Instead of the loss of homeland territory per se, they increasingly affirmed the irredentists' concerns with the fate of Italians in those territories. To do so, the DC government started to provide significant financial support to Triestine cultural circles that promoted social reconciliation between Italians and Slovenes. These right-wing, but not strictly irredentist, associations focused on the well-being of Italians living in Yugoslavia rather than on issues of sovereignty and territorial control. The DC itself also subtly shifted its focus from claiming the territory on which Italians had lived to a concern with protecting the Italians who remained regardless of who controlled the territory itself. Now, it portrayed improved relations with Yugoslavia (at the cost of Zone B of the FTT), not as the abandonment of parts of the homeland, but as the best way of defending the interests of the Italian minority living in ex–Zone B.[98]

This pivot was so successful that the 1975 Osimo Treaty codifying the existing border between Italy and Yugoslavia was adopted with barely any opposition. While the agreement was challenged by some DC deputies from Venezia Giulia and by the neofascist Right, it was supported by the rest of the Italian political spectrum. The issue was so noncontroversial in Italian politics that fewer than twenty-five members of parliament bothered to participate in the debate over the treaty. Unlike the London Memorandum, Italy's parliament overwhelmingly approved the Osimo Treaty. The lower chamber approved the treaty 349–51, and in the senate, the vote was 211–11. Observers noted that the ratification of the treaty passed "almost unnoticed" by the great majority of Italians.[99]

While the breakup of Yugoslavia in the early 1990s was accompanied by a resurgence of the territorial debate, it was brief and marginal, even on the right.[100] Many of those who called for the revision or abrogation of the Osimo Treaty focused on compensation for displaced Italians rather than the reassertion of Italian sovereignty.[101] Reflecting the withdrawal of homeland territoriality from the lands Italy lost, in 1992 it recognized Slovenia and Croatia despite these states' encompassing parts of what had been the Italian homeland.

In summary, the Italian withdrawal of homeland territoriality from its "unre-deemed land" occurred in two steps. In the first, occurring immediately after World War II, the scope of the lands Italy sought to reclaim shrank from the entire Istrian Peninsula to the area of the Free Territory of Trieste. This was a move undertaken by Italy's political leadership in response to the immediate postwar environment. As important as the more constricted map-image of the homeland this represented was the attendant shift to using a predominantly ethnic rather than nationalist logic to legitimate this territorial claim. The second step, in which homeland territoriality was withdrawn from Zone B of the FTT, began in response to the political challenges faced by the DC in the early 1950s. This change was increasingly adopted by the party (and the Italian state it controlled) as the costs of maintaining the old position increased and the political benefits of the new vari-ant increased. This gradual process of the differential political returns accruing to the new variant helps account for the notable inconsistencies in the DC's policies and pattern of articulation about the homeland status of the lost lands.

Alternative Explanations

There are a number of other factors that could also account for the withdrawal of homeland territoriality from the lands that Italy lost to Yugoslavia after World War II, including the impact of new information, the passage of time, and super-power influence. In addition to these, there is a strain of scholarship that high-lights the idiosyncratic "weakness" of Italian nationalism. From this perspective, the loss of homeland territory could be easily accommodated because the Italian nation-building project never succeeded in creating a fully integrated, unitary, national identity in the first place.[102] From this perspective, it is not surprising that homeland territoriality was withdrawn from lost lands.

This argument, however, has both empirical and theoretical drawbacks. To begin with, an argument premised on a feeble Italian nationalism cannot account for the irredentist component of Italy's (very costly) entry into World War I. More fundamentally, the assumption that internal variation and contestation within a nation denote the failure of the nationalist project is misplaced. As chapter 1 argued, the presence of internal variation is a common feature of nationalism more broadly and not a marker of its failure. Finally, from an empirical perspective, an argument premised on the uniform weakness of Italian nationalism provides little purchase on the particular features of the withdrawal of homeland territoriality, including its timing or the variation among actors within Italy.

Stronger alternative explanations for the withdrawal of homeland territoriality from the lost lands emphasize the role of new information about ethnic geography or the reality of the border, the passage of time, or instrumental reactions to the constraints imposed by geopolitical considerations as the primary drivers and portray politics as merely incidental.

Of these, the appeal to a changing ethnic geography is especially strong. Dennison Rusinow, for example, argued that the Trieste question was resolved largely because "the Italians [in Istria] have gone away."[103] This perspective is supported by the congruence between the timing of the population changes and the declining salience of claims to Venezia Giulia. The first wave of the Italian exodus from Istria began after the signing of the peace treaty in 1947. A second wave began in October 1953, following the Allied decision to formally turn over Zone B to Yugoslavia. By the 1960s, when the DC was in the process of changing its views, the vast majority of Istria's Italian-speaking population had left Yugoslav-controlled territory.[104] By 1971 the Yugoslav census would only find 22,000 Italians in all of Yugoslavia.[105]

There are, however, a few reasons to be skeptical that the demographic change in the Istrian Peninsula would have been sufficient on its own to lead to the withdrawal of homeland territoriality. First, as in the German case, the reality of the demographic change was messier than acknowledged by Rusinow's sweeping assessment. As many Italians remained in areas controlled by Yugoslavia to which homeland territoriality continued to be applied (Zone B of the FTT) as in the area that became Yugoslavia in 1947 (Zone B of Venezia Giulia) and ceased to be claimed. In 1947 there were an estimated 30,000 Italians in Zone B of the FTT. However, there were an estimated 70,000 Italians (by language) in the area that was annexed to Yugoslavia in 1948.[106] If the withdrawal of homeland territoriality was a response to demographic changes, we would have expected the treatment of these areas to be broadly similar, if not actually reversed. As in the German case, without additional specification of how to weigh different groups of coethnics, an appeal to ethnic geography cannot account for the abandonment of the claim to Zone B of Venezia Giulia but the simultaneous maintenance of the claim to Zone B of the FTT, since both contained roughly similar numbers of Italians.

The variation between Italy's political parties also suggests that the impact of the demographic changes depended on the degree to which an ethnic logic of legitimation was used to justify the application of homeland territoriality to the lost lands. Where homeland territoriality was justified primarily in ethnic terms, as was the case for the DC by the 1960s, demographic changes facilitated the withdrawal of homeland territoriality. However, where ethnic logics of legitimation were secondary, changes in ethnic geography had less of an impact. This helps explain the difference between the DC and the neofascists. The latter consistently maintained the original blend of logics of legitimation to justify their claims of the lost lands. As a result, they were able to sustain the application of homeland territoriality despite demographic changes. For example, as Yugoslavia was imploding in the early 1990s, the neofascist MSI resuscitated the irredentist project. In November 1992, it campaigned for a "New Irredentism" and for the return of Istria, Fiume, and Dalmatia to Italy. Sailing into the narrow Bay of Buccari near Fiume (and eluding the Italian navy), they tossed bottles into the sea with the message: "Istria, Fiume and Dalmatia: Italy! . . . An unjust border separates . . . Istria, Fiume, Dalmatia, Roman, Venetian, [and] Italian lands. . . . Yugoslavia dies war-torn: the unjust and shameful peace treaties of 1947 and Osimo 1975 no longer apply today. . . . It is our oath: "Istria, Fiume, Dalmatia: come back to us!"[107]

The continued application of homeland territoriality by such groups in the face of the demographic transformation of the region demonstrates that, on their own, such changes do not automatically result in the withdrawal of homeland territoriality. Movements that justify the application of homeland territoriality using nonethnic logics are able to continue claiming the land regardless of who actually lives there. Indeed, movements that do not rely primarily on ethnic logics of legitimation to apply homeland territoriality can even use changes in ethnic demography to spur contemporary claims. In the Istrian context, for example, the Italian exodus from Pola encouraged the Italian National Liberation Committee (the umbrella organization of the Italian resistance movement led by the DC) to redouble their efforts to regain Istria and Zone B for Italy before their shift to a largely ethnic logic of legitimation.[108]

There is considerably less support for the argument that the drawing of the border in 1947 itself triggered an automatic updating and accommodation to the loss of homeland territory. First, as was shown above, Italian claims to the lost parts of the homeland continued long after 1947. The DC-led Italian state remained committed to changing the territorial clauses of the peace treaty and funded irredentist groups intent on restoring the lost lands to Italy for decades after the de facto border was drawn.[109] Nor can an explanation based on adaptation to information about the new border account for the variation in the responses to this information between the DC's political leadership and its diplomatic corps, all of whom were exposed to the same information. Even the perceived need to present the London Memorandum as provisional suggests that, still, in 1954 and for decades afterward, the leading Italian politicians felt constrained by public opinion even if they privately agreed that it was likely to be permanent.[110]

Moreover, although Moro eventually presented the territorial losses entrenched in the Osimo Treaty as the final price for Italy's defeat in World War II, this was not a commonly held view in the 1940s and 1950s. Rather, as noted above, the "Italian approach to the Trieste question since the end of World War II was shaped by two deeply held beliefs: 1) Italy had a right to the FTT which transcended the limits imposed by the realities of international politics and, 2) it was the Allies' duty to help recover it because of the commonality of interests deriving from the fact that Italy, unlike Yugoslavia, was a democracy and part of the Western camp."[111] The shock of being on the losing side of World War II did not trigger a process of adaptation because, as mentioned earlier, the postwar Italian republic was built on the conception that it was on the side of the victors. Since Italians believed that they were on the winning side, there was no reason to pay a price for being on the losing side beyond switching to an ethnic logic of legitimation.

There is a strong argument to be made that the passage of time mattered in the Italian case.[112] Many in Italy's leadership certainly believed that the passage of time would lead to the acceptance of the territorial losses. Taviani made this point explicitly to Claire Luce, the US ambassador to Italy. He told her that they needed to avoid "a definitive solution which no Italian government would be able to survive and made clear that "once Trieste was returned, the highly emotional state would subside since most of [sic] Italians had no idea where Capodistria or Pirano were located."[113] However, leaving aside the possibility that Taviani was interested in preventing the United States from publicly imposing a definitive solution on Italy, the belief that time on its own would reduce the salience of the issue ignores the fundamentally rhetorical character of the application of homeland territoriality to lost lands. If anything, emphasizing the provisionality of the agreement maintained the homeland status of the lost lands by continuing to portray their redemption as a realistic possibility. The resulting ambiguity, however, did have an impact. It provided space for the DC to pour new content into an old vessel by maintaining the claim to Trieste and de-emphasizing the homeland territoriality of the rest of Istria and Dalmatia.[114]

Generational change may also have mattered. After 1954 the proportion of Istrian refugees among the Triestine political leadership declined and those born in the rest of Italy increased.[115] It is likely that these generational shifts reinforced the acceptance of the border (if only by reducing the numbers of those supporting irredentism in Trieste itself). These effects became even more significant after the Osimo Treaty. Miklavcic thus found that younger Triestine cohorts took the border for granted in ways that those who remembered different territorial configurations did not.[116]

However, neither the passage of time nor generational change had an unmediated impact on the withdrawal of homeland territoriality from the lost lands. After all, the DC leaders who carried out the changed treatment of the lost lands all came of age while Italy still controlled those territories. Rather, the impact of time and generational replacement was filtered through the changing landscape of costs and benefits that accrued to the alternative strategies of legitimation and notions of the homeland. As the attachment of new cohorts to the lost lands waned as a result of generational replacement, so did the political costs of promoting a vision of the Italian homeland that excluded these lands.

The final alternative explanation points to a change in response to pressure from external patrons, especially in the context of the Cold War. Italy was certainly subject to significant pressure from the Allies to abandon its territorial claims after the war. It was also unambiguously dependent on the United States in the late 1940s and early 1950s.[117] Attributing the change in the Italian claims of the homeland to external pressure would also be consistent with the strain of scholarship that sees external influences as having been the dominant factor in shaping Italian nationhood.[118] US influence was especially evident in the views of Italy's diplomatic corps, who were most closely exposed to Allied thinking about the matter. However, Italian diplomats doubted that the United States would help Italy recover its lost lands already in 1947. They saw the very establishment of the FTT by the United States and the USSR over the objections of both Italy and Yugoslavia as evidence that the United States could not be trusted.[119] By 1951, when the United States began to openly prod the Italians to enter into direct negotiations with Yugoslavia, it was evident even to the Italian public at large that US policy on Trieste had shifted and no longer supported the return of the entire FTT to Italy.[120] Yet little change in the homeland status of the lost lands took place at that time.

External pressures notwithstanding, Italy's political leadership was unwilling to accept the provisional solution until it also served a domestic political purpose. Despite Italy's weakness and dependence on the United States, De Gasperi consistently sought to pressure the United States to support expansive Italian territorial claims.[121] As noted above, De Gasperi and the leaders of the DC even sought to transform their dependence on the United States into a lever with which to obtain political support to achieve its aims. It was only after the decision to seek a provisional solution had already been made that external pressures reinforced the utility of resolving the future of the FTT.[122]

Soviet pressure certainly shaped the positions of the PCI. Even here, however, while the PCI's stance toward Venezia Giulia always had to account for Moscow's preferences, it still pursued Italian nationalist objectives within the scope permitted by Moscow.[123] It did so because the border issue was so salient among its supporters that the PCI could not overtly abandon the lost lands without alienating its base.[124] Moscow understood this dynamic and permitted the Italian Communists to claim Trieste even against its own formal position so as not to undermine the PCI's political support.[125] In other words, even where superpower diktat was clearly influential, it did not automatically shape the homeland claims of the local political movement.

Finally, the attribution of the change to pressure from foreign patrons is also complicated by the fact that Italian policy at the time was subject to influence from two international patrons, each of which pushed Italy in a different direction regarding Trieste. Even if the United States was prodding Italy to reach an accommodation with Yugoslavia, the position of the Catholic Church wasn't nearly as clear. At least until the Second Vatican Council in 1962, the Catholic Church implicitly supported Italian claims to Zone B by, among other things, maintaining the unitary character of the Triestine dioceses as extending over both Trieste and ex–Zone B.[126] The Triestine irredentist claims were also supported by the local Catholic bishop Antonio Santini, who was, perhaps not accidentally, removed from this post in 1975.[127] Given the tremendous influence of the Catholic Church in nearly every aspect of Italian politics at the time, it is not a priori evident that US interests would necessarily dominate in this context.[128]

The Italian experience shows that even the most contested of lost homeland territories, in this case ones that served as the archetype of irredentist motivations and that saw bitter ethnic violence, can lose their status as part of the homeland. The Italian withdrawal of homeland territoriality took place in two stages. The first constricted the application of homeland territoriality by the dominant Christian Democracy Party to the area of the FTT rather than to the entire territory they had lost. The rapidity and uniformity of this first transformation is most consistent with a withdrawal of homeland territoriality as a result of leaders' instrumental considerations.

The process of the second step in the withdrawal of homeland territoriality from the land Italy had lost after World War II was much more consistent with the operation of an evolutionary dynamic. The withdrawal of homeland territoriality by the DC began when agreement to the de facto partition of the Istrian Peninsula became politically useful domestically. Following a liminal stage in which Italian policy and the pattern of articulation about the extent of the homeland by the governing DC were inconsistent, the de facto border became institutionalized as the new boundary of the Italian homeland because it was associated with positive political and economic returns.

The Italian case highlights how the particular logic with which homeland territoriality is applied, and that is used to rhetorically transform land into homeland, matters. The decision to emphasize an ethnic logic of legitimation after the Second World War, even if it was intended primarily as a response to the international political exigencies of the moment, constrained the DC's subsequent ability to maintain the application of homeland territory to land that was no longer characterized by a significant population of coethnics. The narrowing of the logic of legitimation to an ethnic one did so by lowering the domestic political cost of withdrawing homeland territoriality from the remaining areas under Yugoslav control once most Italians had left the area.

HOMELANDS AND CHANGE IN A STATELESS NATION

This chapter turns to the question of whether and how homelands contract in the context of a stateless nation.[1] This setting is especially important because these are the groups which engage in secessionist and self-determination conflicts and there is little reason to believe that these conflicts will wane.[2] The resolution of such disputes often depends on the willingness of both the group seeking self-determination and the state they are challenging to accept the continued presence of at least some homeland territory under the other's sovereignty. To succeed, strategies of conflict resolution that involve drawing new international borders thus require one or both sides to modify the area they claim as appropriately theirs. Since most prior research, including most of this book, focuses on nations with states, we know relatively little about how stateless nations respond to this situation. This chapter helps fill the gap.

Using the Palestinian context, I show that the same domestic political dynamics that shape the withdrawal of homeland territoriality from lost lands in nation-states also explain the withdrawal of homeland territoriality by nationalist movements belonging to stateless nations. This is the case because stateless nations also tend to contain multiple political movements (variation) that compete for both institutional survival and their nationalist goals and experience differential success over time. As a result, their vision of the homeland's scope is also subject to change brought about through evolutionary dynamics.

The Palestinian setting is especially useful for a number of reasons. First, it is substantively important. The Palestinian drive for national independence has been a key component of the conflict in the Middle East for the last century. Understanding Palestinian views of the homeland, how and why they have changed, and the limits of those transformations, is thus crucial for understanding the prospects for conflict resolution in this cardinal case. Second, from an analytical perspective, the Palestinian nationalist movements displayed meaningful variation in the extent to which they accepted a state in a divided homeland. This variation provides analytical leverage that can be used to evaluate the plausibility of alternative explanations of change.

Third, the Palestinian failure to gain independence provides a least likely context in which to expect evolutionary dynamics to drive change. The absence of the most significant prize in the politics of stateless nations, independence, means that the biggest source of positive domestic political returns to more moderate variants of the homeland or logics of legitimation is also missing. Palestinian political leaders cannot, in effect, credibly contend that a bird in the hand is better than two in the bush. Indeed, perhaps for this reason, unlike the cases in chapters 2 and 3, in which the withdrawal of homeland territoriality from lost lands is well entrenched, the changes that were underway in the main Palestinian nationalist movement until the first decade of the twenty-first century are precarious. The process tracing that follows shows both that evolutionary dynamics shaped the withdrawal of homeland territoriality even in this least likely setting and that they can account for its potential retrenchment.

The first part of this chapter demonstrates how Fatah, the main movement in the Palestinian political spectrum since the 1960s, envisioned the area of the state it sought and how the need to respond to political challenges led it to articulate a more modest variant of its geographical scope. The political success of that variant, one which initially accepted the partition of Palestine as a tactical measure, explains the degree of its institutionalization within Fatah. By the same token, the limits of that political success, especially the failure to gain actual sovereignty over the West Bank and Gaza Strip, also explain why this variant has been unable to decisively marginalize more expansive alternatives.

The second part of the chapter focuses on the territorial aspirations of Hamas, a religious nationalist political movement. While Hamas has not changed its view of the homeland, the chapter shows that political dynamics analogous to those that impelled Fatah to endorse a more modest variant of the homeland apply to Hamas as well. Here too, however, the limited political returns to this variant imply that it is less likely to fully displace more expansive variants.

Fatah's Acceptance of Partition

From very early on, Palestinian nationalism concentrated its application of homeland territoriality to the area of the post-1922 British Mandate of Palestine (corresponding to the area of Israel, the West Bank, and Gaza Strip in figure 4.1).[3] When the fighting over the territory subsided after the 1948 war, the British Mandate of Palestine was divided into three parts: the state of Israel, the Gaza Strip, which was administered by Egypt, and the area that came to be known as the West Bank, which was annexed by Jordan in 1951. These territorial divisions were codified in armistice agreements between Israel, Jordan, and Egypt, but not in formally recognized international borders. In 1967 Israel conquered the West Bank and Gaza Strip and, in 2005, withdrew from the interior of the latter.

FIGURE 4.1 Borders of Mandatory Palestine

Despite theoretical expectations that the new de facto borders would serve as powerful foci for coordinating their demands, Palestinian nationalists refused to accept the de facto international borders drawn through their homeland after the 1948 war. Ahmad Shukeiri, the first leader of the Palestine Liberation Organization (PLO), repeatedly declared into the 1960s—that is, before Israel had conquered the West Bank and Gaza Strip and referring to the area which became Israel in 1948—"Our objective is the liberation of the homeland from Israeli occupation" and "[We will] not negotiate our home, [and] neither will we compromise our homeland."[4] Mobilized Palestinian nationalists outside of Jordan (where the political activities of Palestinian nationalists were severely curtailed) rejected the Jordanian presence in the West Bank as well. The short-lived Government of All Palestine, established in the Gaza Strip in 1948, asserted that its goal was "the full independence of all Palestine bounded by Syria and Lebanon to the north, Syria and Transjordan to the east, the Mediterranean to the west and Egypt to the south."[5]

Fatah (which means "conquest" or "opening," and is the reverse acronym of the Palestinian National Liberation Movement) also applied homeland territoriality to the entire area of Mandatory Palestine. Founded in the late 1950s, Fatah was animated by two, equally important goals. Like all other Palestinian nationalist movements, they sought the creation of a Palestinian state in the borders of the 1922 British Mandate. To this goal they added, however, an abiding concern with the activation of a specifically Palestinian national identity and the transformation of Palestinians from objects of the historical struggle over Palestine to authors of their own destiny. In contrast with the Arab nationalist ideologies that animated other movements at the time, Fatah "proposed a *Palestinian* nationalist ideology in which Palestine would be liberated by *Palestinian* action, with Palestinian refugees taking matters into their own hands."[6] In practical terms, this meant demonstrating that there was a distinct Palestinian nation whose desire for national self-determination needed to be acknowledged. It also meant guarding against the subordination of the Palestinian struggle to the needs of other Arab states. Fatah quickly rose to power within the PLO, taking over its leadership in 1968 and dominating the Palestinian national movement until 2006 (and arguably since).

Fatah's continued application of homeland territoriality to the entire area of Mandatory Palestine was plainly evident in all its public articulations for decades after its emergence. Its first political manifesto (issued under the name of al-Asifah [the Storm]), clearly understood the existence of Israel as occupying its homeland and set the goal as liberating Palestine in its entirety.[7] Like Shukeiri, Fatah's leaders and pronouncements routinely reflected the stance that Israel's very existence entailed an occupation of land that should rightfully be under Palestinian sovereignty.

Their position did not change in the immediate aftermath of the 1967 war.[8] Fatah's continued application of homeland territoriality to all of Mandatory Palestine was evident, for example, in the main rationale its leaders used for rejecting UN Resolution 242. This resolution, passed by the United Nations Security Council at the end of the 1967 war, affirmed that a just and lasting peace in the Middle East required Israeli withdrawal from occupied territories, respect for the territorial integrity of every state in the area, and recognition of the right of those states to live in peace within secure and recognized borders. Until the mid-1970s, Fatah rejected this resolution primarily because of the latter clauses. Fatah equated the acceptance of Israel required by UN Resolution 242 with "agree[ing] to surrender and accept[ing] humiliation and shame."[9] Following Fatah's lead, the Fourth Palestinian National Assembly in 1968 formally rejected this resolution because guaranteeing "secure and mutually agreed frontiers involves the de facto recognition of Israel, and an encroachment on the unconditional right of the Palestinian Arab people to the whole of Palestine."[10]

The continued application of homeland territoriality to the entire area of Mandatory Palestine was more directly encoded in the rejection of partition as a strategy for conflict resolution whenever it was raised. For example, in the immediate aftermath of the civil war in Jordan (1970–71), Yasser Arafat, Fatah's leader and the face of Palestinian nationalism for decades, was approached by a delegation of West Bank notables who raised the possibility of calling for an independent Palestinian state in the West Bank and Gaza Strip. Arafat rejected the idea as "the most dangerous proposal that could be made. In the name of the Palestinian revolution I hereby declare that we shall oppose the establishment of this state to the last member of the Palestinian people, for if ever such a state is established it will spell the end of the whole Palestinian cause."[11]

At the time, Arafat even rejected the idea, most publicly articulated in 1965 by Tunisia's president Habib Bourguiba, that the Palestinians should accept partition as a tactical measure in the context of a phased struggle with Israel. Reminiscent of the arguments made by De Gasperi regarding the provisionality of the border in Trieste, according to this phased approach, accepting partition as a temporary measure would allow for the establishment of a Palestinian state that would, in turn, enable the Palestinians to fight for the liberation of the rest of Palestine from a stronger position.[12] In an interview with the Tunisian press in 1970, however, Arafat argued that "our situation cannot be compared to Tunisia's in its struggle against France. The Tunisian revolution was able to accept some compromises; but what we are asked in exchange for a state is to give up part of our land. And that we cannot do."[13] He also continually rejected any "whiff of peaceful solutions, or rather surrender solutions" which would have led to "the establishment of a Palestinian state and entity side by side with the Zionist state and entity."[14] Demonstrating the fidelity to the desire for all of Palestine, that same year Arafat coined the slogan of "Haifa before Jerusalem."[15]

Fatah's absolute refusal to consider partition began to change in early 1974, when it began articulating a willingness to accept a Palestinian state in part of Palestine.[16] This new rhetorical formula allowed for the establishment of a state on "the part of Palestinian territory that is liberated" or "on Palestinian national soil" rather than in all of it. This new variant distinguished between proximate goals and ultimate ones consistent with the phased approach advocated by Bourguiba.

This new variant, and the at least temporary acquiescence to partition that it implied, was explicitly understood as a short-term response to the political and military realities Fatah faced rather than a change in its ultimate goal. That is, the initial acceptance of partition did not reflect a withdrawal of homeland territoriality from the homeland territory that would remain under Israeli sovereignty. The advocates of the phased approach consistently argued to the truth tellers, both within Fatah and in other Palestinian guerrilla movements, who opposed any semblance of concession to Israel that it was a temporary tactical measure that made the end goal of "the liberation of all Palestinian soil" easier to achieve. They saw a truncated Palestinian entity as their Piedmont, as a springboard from which the liberation of the entire territory could proceed.[17] Nabeel Shaath, then the head of the PLO Planning Center, explained that their acquiescence to an interim state in the West Bank and Gaza Strip did not change their "maximum goal" and that they agreed to this "minimum goal" only "so long as that does not compromise our right to the rest [of Palestine]."[18] Salah Khalaf (also known as Abu Iyad), Fatah's second-in-command, similarly argued that the acceptance of a ministate implicit in the phased approach was simply an interim phase. "It was clear," he contended, "that we should make the distinction between compromise and surrender, that we should know how to take what was offered us without renouncing our strategic objective of a democratic state in all Palestine [sic]."[19] He sought to correct the misimpression that their acceptance of a ministate was anything but tactical. "We were misunderstood when we proposed an interim solution. . . . Some people have understood that the state was an end in itself. But we say No; when we proposed the state as an interim settlement we did not mean that we wanted a state at any price. Therefore we will have nothing to do with resolution 242 or its amendment."[20]

Farouk Kaddoumi, another of Fatah's leaders, also emphasized that their acceptance of a state in the West Bank and Gaza Strip was only an interim step—one motivated by their goal of preserving Palestinian identity: "Our goal of establishing a Palestinian state in part of our territory is part of an acknowledged strategy to ensure the survival of the Palestinian identity. If we cannot fully achieve our goals at this stage we must leave the Palestinian banner . . . in the hands of coming generations to lead them to the liberation of the rest of our territory."[21] Even when speaking to the UN Security Council, he emphasized that "this new phase in our struggle will see the establishment of Palestinian national authority on every part of the Palestinian national territories liberated from the Zionist occupation, and will constitute a step towards the establishment of the secular democratic state in Palestine."[22]

Regardless of its ultimate aims, the new variant provided political space for the withdrawal of homeland territoriality from areas that would be excluded from it to grow. It did so by legitimating intermediate steps—including, eventually, an independent state in part of Palestine—as acceptable goals. In other words, while previously taboo, over time, settling for less in the short term became compatible with maintaining their overall goal.[23]

The formula that implicitly accepted the partition of Palestine, even if only as an intermediate step, generated immediate and significant political returns for Fatah. These included the recognition of the PLO as the sole representative of the Palestinian people, increased international recognition, and the political support of the West Bank population. As the returns to the tactical acquiescence to partition grew, the idea of a Palestinian state whose territorial scope would be limited to the West Bank and Gaza Strip increasingly became seen as a goal in its own right. By 1986 the Fatah-led PLO openly reformulated what had been an explicitly tactical step as a national goal in and of itself. "The PLO believes that its first and foremost goal is to achieve the Palestinian people's inalienable national rights. The restoration of the land is not merely a tactical option subject to priority calculations but a national goal to be achieved by the PLO, side by side with its people and its Arab nation."[24] Consistent with this shift, by the mid-1980s the Fatah-dominated PLO began dropping the common affirmation of the PLO covenant—which demanded all of Palestine—as the starting point for all their decisions.[25]

No longer simply a step on the way to the total liberation of Palestine, in 1988 the Fatah-dominated PLO argued that a "*just* peace" would "be embodied by our people's return to their land and also by the establishment of a free and independent state on our Palestinian national soil with holy Jerusalem as its capital"; justice, in other words, no longer demanded the entire national soil.[26] That same year, the PLO also accepted UN Resolution 242, implicitly recognizing Israel and affirming Israel's right to exist. In the years prior to this announcement, Fatah and its leaders had shifted the terms with which they rejected the UN resolution. If the initial rejection had been based primarily on the recognition of Israel inherent in the resolution, by the 1980s the rejection of the UN resolution was increasingly justified instead by reference to its failure to recognize Palestinian national identity, and its treatment of Palestinians solely as individual refugees rather than as a nation deserving of self-determination.[27]

The 1988 Palestinian declaration of independence in the West Bank and Gaza Strip was celebrated as "the natural climax of a daring and tenacious popular struggle that started more than seventy years ago."[28] The so-called ministate once sought as a step toward the end goal was now portrayed as the end goal itself—as the climax of the Palestinian struggle for independence. Fatah's acceptance of the 1993 Oslo Accords, which explicitly recognized Israel, also presented what had been initially seen as the first step in a multistage process as the final goal. While its Revolutionary Council continued to argue that the creation of the Palestinian Authority established by the accords was a springboard with which to achieve other goals, unlike earlier declarations these goals were now framed as the establishment of a state in part of Palestine, rather than its complete liberation.[29]

Consistent with this change, in 2009 the Fatah General Congress redefined the territorial scope of their ambition as extending only to the West Bank (including East Jerusalem) and Gaza Strip. Its political platform declared that "the liberation of the homeland is the central axis of the Fatah movement struggle, including the right of the Palestinian people to self-determination as an inalienable right. . . . This includes the right to establish its own sovereign and independent state with Jerusalem as its capital on the liberated Palestinian land occupied by Israel since June 4, 1967, the right of the refugees to return and to compensation."[30]

The claim of the rest of Palestine as part of the homeland is absent from this platform. Moreover, rather than assert a desire to control the territory on which the Palestinians continued to reside in Israel, they limited their responsibility toward "Our People in '48"—that is, toward Palestinian citizens of Israel—to adopting "the demands of our Palestinian people in the territory of '48 to be recognized by Israel as full citizens with full rights."[31] In a 2012 interview with an Israeli news program, Fatah's leader, Mahmoud Abbas, affirmed that "Palestine now for me is [the 19]67 borders, with East Jerusalem as its capital. This is now and forever. . . . This is Palestine for me."[32]

How Fatah Accepted Partition

The withdrawal of homeland territoriality from the area that became Israel in 1948 implied by such statements was a by-product of the tactical steps Fatah took in its drive to reestablish Palestinian national identity and protect its position in Palestinian politics. Specifically, Fatah's eventual endorsement of a "ministate" in the West Bank and Gaza Strip as a short-term way station on the path to complete liberation was the unanticipated consequence of its response to three overlapping threats in the early 1970s that, individually and collectively, raised the specter of subordinating the Palestinian cause and weakening the PLO. These threats were posed by the independent political organization of the Palestinian population in the West Bank, Jordan's renewed claim to sovereignty over the West Bank, and the possibility that the Palestinians would be excluded from the negotiations to resolve the Middle East conflict which were expected in the aftermath of the 1973 war. The rhetorical formula of accepting partition as a phase in their struggle enabled Fatah to deepen its presence in the occupied territories both institutionally and politically and to signal a willingness to engage the international community, both of which ultimately contributed to the establishment of the PLO as the undisputed representative of the Palestinians. The benefits that accrued to Fatah (including political success, legitimacy, international recognition, and resources) reinforced the institutionalization of the idea of the ministate, eventually leading to an increased acceptance of partition as the final destination of their national project.

In the immediate aftermath of the 1967 war, the Palestinian public in the newly occupied territories hoped that the Arab states and Palestinian guerrilla organizations would bring about a quick end to the occupation. This expectation, however, faded after the Jordanian military defeated and expelled the armed Palestinian groups from Jordan. This so-called Black September conflict (1970–71) exposed the weakness of the Palestinian guerrillas and revealed the neighboring Arab states to be unreliable allies in a particularly spectacular fashion. Realizing that the Arab states would not bring about the end of the occupation in the near future, Palestinians in the territories undertook their own social and political organization aimed at improving their lives in the meantime.[33]

This grassroots organization in the West Bank posed a challenge to Fatah's leadership of the Palestinian nationalist movement for two reasons. First, unlike Fatah's leadership, which by the early 1970s was based in Lebanon, it was located in Palestine itself and thus could credibly claim to speak for the people there. As a result, it threatened to displace Fatah from the leadership of the Palestinian national cause. Second, the focus of the emerging civil society organizations and professional associations on improving daily life for Palestinians living under Israeli occupation stood in sharp contrast to the PLO's long-term goal of destroying Israel. As Israel succeeded in attracting Palestinians to its labor market and engaged in policies of de facto annexation, Fatah became increasingly concerned that the Palestinians in the territories would agree to compromises, such as autonomy, that would improve their daily lives but fall short of independence and thereby undermine the cardinal goal of the Palestinian national movement.[34]

Fatah was initially poorly positioned to compete with these grassroots political organizations. As Yezid Sayigh observed, until the mid-1970s the Fatah-led PLO was "guilty of a striking lack of interest in the occupied territories," focusing instead on building its institutional presence outside Palestine.[35] Fatah's initial engagement with the territories after the 1967 war was limited to attempts to create guerrilla cells intended to mobilize the population in a mass popular uprising—an approach that failed to establish Fatah as a significant political presence in the territories. Fatah's weakness was fully exposed in the (Israeli-organized) March 28, 1972, local council elections. Despite their rejection of the elections as a recognition of Israeli legitimacy, threats to treat anyone who stood for office as traitors, and calls to boycott the elections, more than 80 percent of those eligible turned out to vote.[36]

Fatah responded to the challenge by investing more time, energy, and resources in the West Bank than it ever had before. This new emphasis was evident in a wide range of activities and institution-building efforts, including creating its own newspaper and establishing (and taking over existing) trade unions and other civil society organizations in the West Bank.[37] These institutions enabled Fatah to extend its influence in the West Bank—an influence that was further reinforced by the significant influx of Arab funds after the Baghdad summit of 1978. Fatah's control of these funds (through its control of the PLO) enabled it to extend its rentier politics to an even wider constituency. The budgetary problems faced by the United Nations Relief and Works Agency for Palestine Refugees in the Near East (UNRWA) and its declining ability to provide services also prompted the PLO to deepen its rudimentary social welfare system in the West Bank. Fatah's institutional investment in the territories thus enabled it to create foci of political power that could resist compromises, such as autonomy, that fell short of its desired goals.[38]

The rhetorical acceptance of a state in the West Bank and Gaza Strip as a first step toward the complete liberation of Palestine complemented these institutional moves by signaling to Palestinians in the territories that Fatah shared their concern with improving their immediate situation and ending the occupation as soon as possible. Fatah had to send this signal because, by the early 1970s, the Palestinian population in the West Bank was much more willing to reach an agreement with Israel based on partition than were diaspora Palestinians.[39] For example, as described above, prominent leaders from the West Bank had already approached Arafat with the idea in the immediate aftermath of Black September. Again, in July 1973, over one hundred West Bank and Gaza notables publicly appealed to the secretary general of the United Nations calling for the self-determination of the population of the West Bank and Gaza Strip and for sovereignty over their territory.[40]

Seeking to rally this relatively more moderate population behind its banner, Fatah chose a strategy that would appeal to it. The phased approach allowed Fatah to accommodate the desires of the West Bank population for immediate relief without abandoning the commitment to the ultimate liberation of Palestine in its entirety. It also allowed them to compete more effectively with their main political rival in the territories at the time, the Jordanian Communist Party (JCP), because the Communists had already accepted the principle of partition.[41] The phased approach effectively insulated Fatah from the accusation that they put the, arguably unattainable, dream of liberating all of Palestine ahead of the concrete grievances of the West Bank population.

The need to appeal to a constituency whose primary goal was getting out from under the occupation and the fact that Fatah's main competition in the territories had already accepted partition help explain how the outbidding dynamics that were so evident in the strident rejections of even the possibility of anything other than the full liberation of Palestine were replaced by a process that reinforced moderation. As I noted in chapter 1, the presence of outbidding depends on, among other things, a public that is less moderate than the leadership of a political movement. Since this was not the case in the West Bank, outbidding dynamics were curtailed.

The increased attention paid to the occupied territories by Fatah and the self-conscious attempt to gain the support of its population were also intended to counter the possibility that Jordan would successfully assert its sovereignty over the West Bank and be recognized by the international community as responsible for the Palestinians. This possibility was made concrete in Jordan's 1972 proposal to establish a "United Arab Kingdom" on both banks of the Jordan River; a proposal that was intended to establish Jordan as the recognized speaker for the Palestinian cause.[42]

The belief that Jordan sought to subsume Palestinian identity permeated the Palestinian nationalist movements in the aftermath of Black September.[43] The Palestinian defeat at the hands of the Jordanians reinforced Fatah's perception of Jordan as a rival claimant to the West Bank. Abu Iyad (Salah Khalaf) even argued that King Hussein had attacked the Palestinians as part of a plan to restore to himself the right to negotiate the future of the occupied territories.[44] Arafat was similarly convinced that the expulsion of the guerrillas from Jordan was part of a secret deal between Israel and Jordan in which Israel would relinquish "parts of the West Bank that will revert to the Hashemite throne, so that [King] Husayn Bin Talal will become the only interlocutor on behalf of the Palestinian people in any coming settlement."[45] In a report to the PLO executive committee on March 16, 1972, Khalid el-Hassan, one of Fatah's founders and the head of its political department, concluded that the "essential aim" of the proposal for a

United Arab Kingdom "was: a) eliminating the fighting Palestinian personality; and b) putting an end to the existence of the Palestinian people" by incorporating them into Jordan.[46]

The phased approach offered a rebuttal to Jordan's claim to sovereignty over the West Bank. Indeed, its adoption was frequently justified as a way of preventing the Arab states, especially Jordan, from determining the fate of the Palestinians. Yasser Arafat began to argue that they faced a choice between losing the West Bank to Jordan or establishing a state in part of Palestine: "What is called the West Bank and Gaza Strip . . . now faces two possibilities: one, to go to king Husayn . . . as to the second possibility, it is to set up a Palestinian authority on it."[47] This concern also shaped his eventual endorsement of UN Resolution 242. He believed that if they did not do so, "the Jordanian option [meaning an Israeli-Jordanian agreement over the West Bank] will come back through the door we left wide open."[48] Similarly, Abu Iyad, Arafat's deputy and one of the main proponents of the phased approach inside Fatah, stressed that the main intent of the phased approach was to ensure that "the West Bank and [Gaza] Strip . . . not revert to king Husayn. . . . Concerning this phase, the basic object is to extract [the West Bank] from the regime of king Husayn."[49] Linking the danger that Jordan would become the representative of the Palestinians and the need to gain the support of the population in the territories, he argued that "the question we must ask ourselves is whether, by our refusal to accept anything less than the full liberation of all Palestine, we are prepared to abandon a portion of our patrimony to a third party. Is it possible to let King Hussein, the butcher of our people, negotiate in the name of the Palestinians? Do we have the right to turn our backs on the fate of the West Bank and Gaza populations, who are suffering from the oppression of occupation?"[50]

Finally, the attempts to reach a political settlement after the 1973 war reinforced Fatah's fear that Jordan would marginalize the Palestinians and return Palestinian nationalism to the days when the Arab states determined the Palestinians' fate.[51] Since most of these attempts envisioned Jordan reasserting control over the West Bank, Fatah's leadership sought to demonstrate that they, not Jordan, were the main voice of the Palestinians in the territories and that, as such, they could not be ignored.[52] Securing the support of other Arab states also required a rhetorical acceptance of partition. Since by that point Egypt, the most important player in the region, was interested in ending the conflict based on a partition, maintaining its support for the recognition of the PLO as the sole representative of the Palestinians required the PLO to take a stance that would not undermine the Egyptian desire to get its territory back from Israel. Likewise, the cost for being allowed into the realm of legitimate international politics was at least a rhetorical openness to the possibility of partition rather than the rejection of any solution short of Israel's destruction.

While deeply contested within Palestinian politics, the advocates of the phased approach found it appealing because it enabled Fatah to respond to these political challenges without changing their ultimate goals. As shown above, there is little evidence that, when this formula was introduced, its authors intended it as anything other than a temporary, tactical, response. This was plainly evident even in the 1974 Palestinian National Council (PNC) decisions that approved the establishment of a "national authority" on "the part of Palestinian territory that is liberated." These same decisions were preceded by the explicit declaration that "any step taken towards liberation is a step towards the realization of the PLO's strategy of establishing the democratic Palestinian state specified in the resolutions of previous National Councils."[53] As Sabri Jiryis highlighted, these previous resolutions uniformly declared that this state would be established after the "complete and total liberation of Palestinian soil from the occupation of Zionism and its base, Israel."[54] Similarly, Yezid Sayigh concluded that the willingness to accept a state in only part of Palestine "emerged incrementally, out of measures undertaken for reasons of short-term political expediency in response both to external challenges and the striving for internal control. Its beginnings were not the result of conscious design, therefore, and arose amidst deep internal divisions over the nature of the problem and its solution."[55] Muhammad Muslih reached the same conclusion, showing that, rather than an open and consistent transformation, the acceptance of a truncated Palestine took place haltingly, unevenly, and over the course of fifteen years.[56] The introduction of the rhetoric of a phased approach maintained the homeland status of the lands that would be lost as a result of accepting partition, but introduced a new rhetorical variant that, as it was associated with political success, became harder to abandon.

What began as an explicitly tactical short-term position intended to solidify Fatah's position in the territories and ensure that the Palestinians would be at the forefront of the struggle for Palestine, became more firmly entrenched within Fatah's discourse because it brought increasing political returns. Fatah's softened territorial claim opened the door to significant international recognition of the PLO in the 1970s and 1980s and to winning the battle for the political support of the West Bank's population.[57] The Arab recognition of the PLO as the sole legitimate representative of the Palestinian people was the most immediate result, coming just three months after the PNC's endorsement of a phased approach. Much of the international community also interpreted the adoption of a phased approach as a positive step since it theoretically enabled a political settlement in the Middle East. As a result, the PLO was increasingly recognized as a legitimate organization in capitals around the world. In October 1974, the PLO was recognized by the UN General Assembly as the representative of the Palestinian people. A month later, the PLO was granted nonstate observer status in the UN. By the time Jordan relinquished its claim to the West Bank in 1988 and the challenges for which the idea of the phased approach was adopted as the solution had dissipated, the returns (international legitimacy, resources) of maintaining the acceptance of partition were too great to abandon and the internal constituency supporting the creation of a Palestinian state and ending the occupation of the West Bank and Gaza Strip was sufficiently strong to promote the once-interim goal as the final one.

The domestic political rewards that accrued to the new territorial formula played a significant role in this development. In a process nicely captured by Stacie Goddard's description of lock-in effects, Fatah's success in gaining the support of the Palestinian population in the territories created a political constituency in a position of power within the movement that could eventually contest a return to the status quo ante.[58] For example, as part of the attempt to co-opt the West Bank leadership and to ensure that they would acknowledge the PLO as the only legitimate representative of the Palestinian people, Fatah began to include West Bank Palestinians in leadership positions.[59] In perhaps the most overt example, three of the signers of the appeal sent by West Bank notables to the UN secretary general mentioned above were added to the eleven-member PLO executive committee in June 1974, when the PLO first publicly articulated its support of the phased plan. The inclusion of these relatively more moderate perspectives in the PLO's leadership meant that they would have a stronger impact on future positions.

As Fatah became increasingly dependent on the political support of Palestinians in the territories, actions that might alienate this constituency became more costly. This became evident, for example, in the PLO's response to the 1979 Camp David Accords between Israel and Egypt. While focused on the relationship between Israel and Egypt, this agreement contained a series of (ultimately never implemented) provisions calling for the autonomy of the West Bank and Gaza Strip, a locally elected Palestinian government, and a role for Egypt and Jordan in the ultimate disposition of the territories. Fatah interpreted these provisions as a threat to its position and as another attempt to undermine the Palestinian leadership of the Palestinian cause—this time, by Egypt rather than Jordan.[60] Fatah was thus caught in a bind. On the one hand, they opposed the Camp David Accords because acceptance by the Palestinians in the territories of these provisions would have undermined the PLO's claim to represent all Palestinians (since they were not a party to the talks) and potentially encouraged the replacement of the quest for an independent state with acceptance of autonomy. On the other hand, the autonomy provisions could not be dismissed entirely because they offered the possibility of reducing the burden of living under the occupation for the Palestinian population of the West Bank and Gaza Strip. As a result, even as Fatah allied itself with the rejectionist Arab states, the Fatah-led PLO simultaneously reinforced its demand for an independent state in part of Palestine in order to avoid alienating this increasingly crucial segment of its support base.[61]

Whereas Goddard emphasizes the ways in which mobilization strategies can lock movements into constructing territory as indivisible, the evolution of Fatah's view of partition shows that similar dynamics can aid the withdrawal of homeland territoriality from land to which it was once applied. In this way, territory once constructed as indivisible can be reconstructed as divisible.

This process was also reinforced by the need to respond to external events. The PLO's defeat in the 1982 war with Israel forced its leadership to move from the "state within a state" they had created in Lebanon to Tunisia. The loss of geographical proximity to Palestine by the PLO's leadership enabled West Bankers to increase their relative power within the movement and to move into a position of effective coleadership of the Palestinian national cause.[62] The Palestinian uprising in 1987 also boosted the importance of the Palestinians in the territories relative to the external leadership. This grassroots uprising meant that continuing the ambiguity about their final goals risked not just losing influence in the territories, but losing the leadership of Palestinian nationalism to the activists there who were so evocatively fighting the occupation. Addressing both further reinforced the institutionalization of the once-tactical step as the final goal.[63] Indeed, Arafat was able to use the First Intifada to "secure the acceptance of his [domestic] coalition partners for a two-state solution to the conflict and recognition of Israel."[64] The Oslo process and the 2012 UN General Assembly recognition of Palestine as a state within the borders of the West Bank and Gaza Strip also reinforced the benefits of the acceptance of partition.[65] Maintaining the trappings of statehood and the significant resources that flowed to Fatah as long as it adhered to a rhetorical acceptance of partition made it costly to return to the original application of homeland territoriality to Palestine in its entirety, or even to the open articulation of the phased approach.

Alternative Explanations

The three main categories of alternative explanations—updating based on new realities, the passage of time, and leaders' instrumental considerations on their own—are harder to reconcile with key empirical aspects of the change in Fatah's position.

An argument based on adaptation to information about the location of coethnics would be consistent with the reduced focus on the territory that constitutes Israel proper since the Palestinian *Nakba* (catastrophe) resulted in a significantly smaller population of coethnics there. However, it is difficult to link the timing of the main demographic change that took place—the expulsion, flight, and dispersal of about 750,000 Palestinians from the area which became the state of Israel during the 1948 war—to the shift in the definition of the appropriate extent of the desired Palestinian state. Despite the massive trauma it caused, there is little evidence that the *Nakba* triggered a transformation in the ways in which Palestinian nationalists viewed the appropriate extent of their desired nation-state. With the notable exceptions of the Communist Party and those Palestinians who became Israeli citizens, Palestinian nationalist movements did not accept the de facto partition of Palestine that took place in 1949. If anything, the formative experience of exile had the opposite effect, fostering a more militant and active pursuit of nationalist goals by Palestinian movements and creating a constituency that maintains the dream of returning to their homes—a constituency which continues to uphold the hard line in negotiations with Israel.[66]

Many explanations for the eventual acceptance of partition by the PLO attribute it to a rational adjustment to the reality of Israel's existence—either in response to the 1967 or 1973 war, or to the Palestinian defeat in the Jordanian civil war in 1970–71.[67] Indeed, many Palestinian politicians framed their support of an idea they once vehemently rejected—a Palestinian state in the West Bank and Gaza Strip—as an accommodation to an inescapable reality.[68] Another possibility attributes the change in the Palestinian position to the PLO's weakened international position in the aftermath of the Gulf War and the loss of external support after the collapse of the Soviet Union.

These events did change the political calculus of supporting a phased approach and the political returns to this position. However, as an explanation for the acceptance of partition, rational adaptation to new information about the world generated by the results of the 1967 or 1973 war or by new geopolitical considerations falls short because it cannot explain several features of the empirical record. For instance, there is no doubt that the collapse of the Soviet Union and Arafat's decision to support Saddam Hussein in the first Gulf War severely weakened Fatah. Not only did it lose its most important international patron and its main source of remittances from the Persian Gulf states as a result; Fatah now had to work that much harder to gain the support of (and recognition by) the world's only remaining superpower. However, while the changed geopolitical position of the PLO certainly reinforced the returns to the tactical agreement to partition and likely accelerated its internalization within Fatah, it occurred too late to explain the change in Fatah's view of partition. After all, Fatah had begun advocating a phased approach in 1974 and accepted UN Resolution 242, which recognized Israel's right to exist, in 1988. Since both of these occurred before the geopolitical changes of the early 1990s, on its own, the latter cannot account for the change in Fatah's view of the desirability of a state in part of Palestine.

The refusal to accept partition given the reality of Israel's existence and strength still in the early 1970s—not to mention the very real and tangible barbed wire and minefields that marked the armistice lines between Israel and its neighbors between 1949 and 1967—reinforces the inconsistency of the historical record with the hypothesis that new information would lead to the acceptance of new borders that truncate homelands. After all, if nationalist preferences were automatically updated to new information, Fatah ought to have accepted partition when it emerged since the reality in which it was founded was one of a partitioned Palestine.

The 1967 war was certainly a watershed in the history of the Middle East—literally reshaping the regional map. It is not clear, however, that it provided significant new information about relative Israeli strength to the Palestinians. The consensus among historians that Israel had been objectively stronger in military terms than the Palestinians already in 1948 suggests that little *new* information about Israel's relative capacity was conveyed in 1967.[69] Indeed, Palestinian and Arab observers had been well aware of the power imbalance before 1967.[70] Arafat also dismissed the impact of the June 1967 war as a relevant factor shaping his positions. In 1970 he declared: "We are fighting for the liberation of the whole of this land. . . . Our revolution existed before June 5 [1967]. June 5 was an incidental factor that increased our responsibilities and the burden we have to carry. We are a movement and a revolution for the liberation of the whole of the land, every inch of it."[71]

The 1967 war did reveal information about the relative weakness of the Arab states on whose military support the Palestinian guerrillas' strategy depended. Fatah, however, initially believed that it was in a relatively *better* position after the war. Here, too, the lessons imparted by a changed reality were the product of interpretation by political actors. Israeli control of the territories meant that, for the first time since 1948, most Palestinians were located within a single country and this, they believed, provided a proper base for a successful popular war to liberate the entire country.[72] The 1967 defeat of the Arab states was thus perceived by Fatah as an opportunity to escape Arab control and to create an autonomous Palestinian entity that could spearhead the struggle. As Sayigh recalled, "Borrowing from the Chinese and Vietnamese experiences, they hoped to create a 'revolutionary authority' with a defined territory and international relations, albeit one that would not compromise or negotiate with Israel. The newly occupied West Bank and Gaza Strip offered just such a base: Arab authority had already been removed, and the remaining task was to compel Israel to withdraw."[73] In other words, the results of the 1967 war opened the door for a consideration of establishing a Palestinian entity in the West Bank, but only as an intermediary step toward the complete liberation of the rest of Palestine.

Even if the results of the 1967 war had led some Palestinian leaders to realize that Israel was here to stay and to modify the area to which they sought to apply homeland territoriality accordingly, they were a distinct minority within the movement. This minority included some of Fatah's leaders, like Farouk Kaddoumi and Salah Khalaf (Abu Iyad), who formally introduced the possibility of accepting a ministate as a first phase to the complete liberation of Palestine inside Fatah.[74] It also included Nayaf Hawatmeh, the leader of the Popular Democratic Front for the Liberation of Palestine (PDFLP), who had publicly proposed the establishment of a 'national authority' in the West Bank and Gaza Strip as an interim measure already in 1972.[75] As noted above, the idea of a separate Palestinian state was also raised by a few West Bank notables as early as June 11, 1967.

These reactions, however, were not widespread at the time.[76] The majority within Fatah (and the broader PLO) did not recalibrate their territorial goals and continued to oppose the possibility of settling for partial liberation even as an intermediary step. In fact, Fatah's newspapers attacked the PDFLP for abandoning the commitment to all of Palestine. An article published in Fatah's official paper even argued that the plan for a Palestinian state in the West Bank and Gaza Strip was an Israeli plot aimed at enabling Israel's "swallowing" of these territories.[77] Likewise, the reaction to the proposal by Kaddoumi and Khalaf, including by Arafat, was so negative that their proposal was taken off the table without being put to a vote. As Khalaf euphemistically recalled, at the time he and Kaddoumi "didn't have a wide enough popular base to be able to submit the document to the intermediate cadres of the movement, much less to open a public debate on the issue. So we decided to table [it] . . . while awaiting a more opportune moment."[78] Reflecting the general adherence to their original goals despite the results of the 1967 war, in December 1967 Fatah declared: "Either we agree to surrender and accept humiliation and shame, or we resist with courage and carry on the armed struggle until the new occupation is no more and the old one is liquidated."[79]

As this reaction suggests, the opposition to the idea of what was sometimes called a "national authority," was so strong that proposals for a Palestinian state as an interim solution were routinely described within Fatah as treason aimed at "liquidating" the Palestinian national cause.[80] The proposal for a Palestinian state in the West Bank and Gaza Strip "evoked violently hostile reactions among most Palestinians, whatever organization they belonged to. No terms were sufficiently opprobrious for it. Some Palestinian zealots even appointed themselves the custodians of Palestinian 'patriotism' and vied with each other in their rigorous surveillance of every move in Palestinian circles, lest someone should 'get out of control' and express support for the 'pygmy state' or commit even greater excesses of 'surrenderism' and 'defeatism.'"[81] The rejection of such proposals was not just verbal. In 1968 Fatah even fired a rocket on the home of one of the West Bank proponents of such an idea.[82]

Consistent with the argument that the 1967 war did not lead to an immediate updating of preferences, the resolutions of the Fourth Palestinian National Assembly in Cairo in July 1968 similarly displayed little adaptation to the results of the 1967 war. Their objective was clearly stated as "the liberation of the entire territory of Palestine, over which the Palestinian Arab people shall exercise their sovereignty."[83] The resolutions explicitly rejected the idea of a state in part of Palestine as an attempt to "consolidate Zionist aggression against Palestine" because such a state "would owe its existence to the legitimization and perpetuation of the state of Israel, which is absolutely incompatible with the Palestinian Arab people's right to the whole of Palestine, their homeland."[84] Still, in 1969, the Fatah-dominated executive committee of the PLO declared that "the People of Palestine have an unconditional right to their homeland, which is the whole of Palestine; they have the right to liberate that homeland, to return to it, to terminate and liquidate the Zionist presence in it and to set up a free, democratic Palestinian State in the whole of Palestine."[85] In August of that same year, Arafat argued against a state in part of Palestine. "I believe," he contended, "that if our generation is unable to liberate its homeland, it should not commit the crime of accepting a fait accompli, which will prevent the future generations from carrying on the struggle for liberation."[86] As late as January 1973, the Fatah-dominated PNC identified one of their tasks as the struggle "against the settlement [i.e., compromise] mentality and the projects that it gave rise to, projects directed against our people's cause, which is the liberation of their homeland, or intended to distort this cause by proposing the establishment of entities or a Palestinian state in part of the territory of Palestine, and to resist those projects with armed struggle alongside mass political struggle."[87]

If Fatah did not update its beliefs in response to the 1967 war, the timing of the onset of the acceptance of partition as a tactical step is consistent with the possibility that such updating took place in response to the 1973 war. In this vein, Alain Gresh identified this war as the "great turning point," noting that Fatah's Central Committee declared itself in favor of the idea of a state on any part of territory that was liberated as an interim state in January 1974, very soon after the war ended.[88] Similarly, Ann Lesch concluded that the results of the 1973 war "enabled people to adopt an increasingly realistic approach."[89] Indeed, Abu Iyad claimed that the war and its consequences gave "rise to healthy soul searching in our ranks, to a new awareness which was to help us adapt our objectives to the realities of the situation and make bold decisions bringing to an end the 'all-or-nothing' policy."[90]

However, there is evidence that the turn in Fatah's policy toward an acceptance of a state in the West Bank and Gaza Strip as an interim phase had begun before the results of the October 1973 war were known. Already in May 1973, the PLO had notably failed to reject the call by Habib Bourguiba, Tunisia's president, that they accept partition as they had consistently done on earlier occasions.[91] In fact, Arafat had sent Henry Kissinger a message asserting the PLO's willingness to take part in peace negotiations and, presumably, suggesting a willingness to accept partition on October 10, 1973—that is, in the *middle* of the war, when the Arab forces were still on the offensive.[92]

Moreover, the notable inconsistency with which this new variant was articulated does not match the expectation that change after the creation of the new reality be consistent and relatively uniform. For example, in November 1974, only months after he had argued in the internal debate within Fatah for the acceptance of a phased approach that allowed for a Palestinian state in part of the homeland, Arafat's inaugural speech at the UN did not mention this formula at all, maintaining the goal of a secular, democratic state in all of Palestine—a goal that, as even one sympathetic observer remarked, required the destruction of the Israeli state.[93]

Fatah's leaders continued to reject the possibility of recognizing Israel and routinely spoke of Israel proper as "the territory occupied by Israel since 1948."[94] Still, in 1980, the political program adopted by Fatah's Fourth Convention declared that its "aim [was] the total liberation of Palestine and the liquidation of the Zionist entity economically, militarily, culturally and ideologically."[95]

Throughout the 1970s and early 1980s, the secular democratic state extending over all of Palestine remained their final goal, even as they called for a state in the West Bank and Gaza Strip in the interim.[96] In an especially candid articulation of this stance, Farouk Kaddoumi explained:

> We believe that there is an interim solution with peace and a permanent solution with peace. The permanent peace can only be achieved by the building of a democratic Palestinian state in which Muslims, Christians and Jews coexist on a basis of equality. The permanent peace is in the building of this democratic state—this is the long-term goal. The interim peace lies in the establishment of a Palestinian state in part of our territory, and there will certainly be one of these two peaces in the area. But the Israeli authorities are trying to make the Arabs forget the pre-1967 territories, and to make out that the 1967 war was the start of the conflict. We reject this theory outright, and say that the problem applies from Jaffa to the river, for all these territories are occupied. Tel Aviv is in dispute, Jaffa is in dispute. Our theory on the problem of peace is as follows: An interim peace based on withdrawal and the building of an independent state, and a permanent peace based on the building of the democratic state of Palestine.[97]

Kaddoumi's partner in promoting the tactical acceptance of partition, Abu Iyad, also displayed little evidence that he accepted a partitioned Palestine as the end goal. Had he done so, he might have been willing to accept Israel's right to exist in its 1949 borders. Yet, as late as February 1979, he rejected UN Resolution 242 primarily because it would force the Palestinians to recognize Israel.[98]

While such inconsistencies may have their own guiding logic, it is difficult to make them congruent with an explanation in which the map-image of the desired national state is updated in response to new information because this explanation would predict a more uniform response once change is triggered by external events.

It is also not clear that the 1973 war was perceived by Palestinians as a shock that made the old ideology irrelevant. Rather than a defeat, the Palestinians initially believed themselves to be in a stronger position after the war. The mayor of al-Bireh declared that "for the first time we feel ecstasy, we sense victory. We have achieved a major step towards liberation."[99] As Helena Cobban argued,

> the Palestinians, having contributed to the 1973 war effort, hoped to be able to profit from the diplomatic process which followed it; indeed, in the first flush of Arab self-confidence at the end of 1973 that aim did not seem too far-fetched. The guerrilla movement had come a long way since 1967: it had grown explosively, won a consensus of Palestinian popular support, gained inter-Arab legitimacy, been cut down to size (in Jordan), but nevertheless bounced back with most of its Arab alliances intact. It was therefore with some degree of their own self-confidence that the Fatah/PLO leaders approached the postwar period.[100]

It is also unlikely that Israel's military victory in 1973 conveyed new information about Israel's relative capacity to the Palestinian leadership. The Palestinian nationalist leaders, including those in the PDFLP and the Popular Front for the Liberation of Palestine (PFLP), acknowledged that the military balance of forces had limited the prospects for total liberation even before this war.[101] Finally, such an explanation would have to account for the disjuncture between those Fatah leaders, who promoted an acceptance of partition, and their internal and external opponents, who did not, despite their experience of exactly the same reality.

As Abu Iyad stated, the 1973 war did reshape the political calculus of supporting the phased approach. In its wake, it was widely believed that a Jordanian-Israeli agreement on the future of the territories would be forthcoming. For Fatah's leaders, including those who had previously opposed the phased approach, the goal of ensuring that they, rather than Jordan, would be accepted as the representative of the Palestinians increased the opportunity cost of maintaining the rhetorical opposition to a strategy of phases.

While it is theoretically possible that the leaders of Fatah had fully accepted partition in 1974 but continued to justify it as merely a temporary position in order to mollify the radical flank within Fatah and rejectionist guerrilla organizations outside it, there is little evidence that this was the case. Indeed, as noted above, scholars of Palestinian nationalism agree that the initial acceptance of partition was explicitly understood as a short-term tactical step rather than a foundational ideological change.[102] Empirically, moreover, if it was a deeply rooted ideological change that continued to be masked for tactical political considerations, we might have seen an accompanying change in Fatah's emblem or youth propaganda where such considerations are less likely to apply. There is no evidence, however, that this was the case. There was also a significant cost associated with the articulation of a phased strategy, in that it signaled to Israel that Fatah was not a trustworthy partner for negotiations. It is unclear why the Palestinian leadership would have been willing to bear these costs if the underlying ideological change had already taken place at that time.

If the phased approach masked a sincere acceptance of truncated territorial goals and was intended simply as a way to maintain the loyalty of the more radical elements within the Palestinian national movement, it did not work. The PFLP and other opponents of the phased strategy formed the "Rejection Front" to coordinate their opposition. Paradoxically, however, this also meant that the strongest voices against the institutionalization of the emphasis on the West Bank and Gaza Strip at the expense of the rest of Palestine within the PLO were further removed from whatever sources of power existed within Palestinian nationalism. As a result, their ability to influence the pattern of articulation by Fatah and the PLO was greatly reduced. In fact, by 1977 the PFLP was so weak that it was unable to prevent the PNC from openly articulating the new aim of an independent national state in "any liberated part of Palestine" instead of the claim for the entire homeland.[103]

Explanations based on the impact of time passing have even less purchase in this context. The rise of a territorial integrity norm cannot explain why Fatah decided to accept it only in the 1970s or the initial explicitly temporary portrayal of its acceptance of partition. Likewise, generational arguments are belied by the fact that the adoption of the phased approach was driven by the existing leadership of Fatah and not by a new generation of leaders.

Instrumental considerations, however, likely played an important role. Fatah was under tremendous pressure to accept partition by some of its Arab patrons. By the early 1970s Egypt, especially, sought to reach an agreement with Israel based on partition. Abu Iyad recalled that, in the summer of 1970, Nasser had privately criticized the Palestinians for an "unrealistic" policy and pointed out that a ministate in the West Bank and Gaza Strip was "better than nothing." Nasser sarcastically asked Yasser Arafat: "In your opinion, how many years do you need to destroy the Zionist state and build a new unified and democratic state on the whole of liberated Palestine?"[104]

Yet, as we saw above, it was during this period that Fatah was strongly articulating the goal of a secular democratic state in all of Palestine rather than accepting partition as the end goal. While there is little doubt that the support of the Arab states for partition reinforced the change once it began, it is difficult to attribute the change to any pressure they exerted given the tremendous political energy that Arafat, and Fatah more generally, placed on making Palestinian decision making independent of the influence of the Arab states.[105] Moreover, attributing the change to the Arab states that had already accepted partition ignores the existing influence of other Arab states, such as Syria and Libya, that exerted strong pressure in the opposite direction.

Fatah's leaders also had to accommodate Soviet pressure. The Soviets consistently urged the Palestinians to accept a state in the 1967 borders as their end goal.[106] Indeed, both the timing and the direction of the change are consistent with the onset of serious Soviet support for the Fatah-led PLO. Yet there are a number of factors which suggest caution in adopting Soviet pressure as an explanation of the change in Fatah's position. First, at least initially, the leaders of Fatah openly resisted Soviet pressure to moderate their territorial demands. As Moshe Ma'oz showed, while the Palestinians were happy to accept material aid from the Soviets, they resisted any ideological pressure unless the Soviet directives were already compatible with their own objectives or concerned matters of secondary importance.[107] Second, even if Fatah leaders eventually succumbed to Soviet influence, this argument cannot explain the continued resistance to Soviet entreaties by other Palestinian movements, such as the PFLP, that were, if anything, even more dependent on the Soviets.[108] At the same time, as noted above, the benefits of international recognition and of articulating a territorial claim that was consistent with the Soviet position did reinforce the benefits of the rhetorical modulation, enabling it to become more entrenched within the movement.

Hamas, Politics, and the Possibility of Change

Although Fatah dominated Palestinian politics, the Palestinian political spectrum included a large variety of parties. Increasingly, the most important alternative to Fatah is the Islamic Resistance movement (known by its acronym, Hamas). In 2006 Hamas defeated Fatah in the elections to the Palestinian National Authority (PNA) and ultimately took over governing the Gaza Strip. Unlike Fatah, which is a secular nationalist organization, Hamas promotes a religious version of Palestinian nationalism. Growing out of the Muslim Brotherhood in the Gaza Strip, Hamas was established in 1987 to provide an organizational framework for Palestinian members of the Muslim Brotherhood who wanted to actively participate in the First Palestinian Intifada and to contest Palestinian politics more broadly.

Exploring Hamas's territorial perspective is analytically useful for two main reasons. First, the variation in how Hamas and Fatah delimit the appropriate extent of the nation-state they seek provides additional leverage with which to disentangle alternative explanations of how homeland territoriality is withdrawn from land. Second, Hamas's framing of the conflict with Israel in religious terms and its literal sanctification of Palestine suggests that it is an especially difficult context in which to expect a withdrawal of homeland territoriality from lost land. Yet religious nationalists in other contexts have been shown to be capable of significant ideological transformations, including reshaping the contours of the national homeland.[109] In Hamas's case, the possibility of change in the territorial aspect of their ideology exists because, in addition to the goal of liberating Palestine, the movement seeks to establish Palestine as an Islamic state. Hamas's emphasis of multiple nationalist goals, not to mention its concern with its own institutional autonomy and political success, opens up the possibility that an acceptance of partition could come about if it were seen as aiding the achievement of these other, equally important, goals. Such a tradeoff between the needs of organizational survival and other sacred values on the one hand, and fidelity to the wholeness of the homeland, on the other, may undergird Hamas's increased willingness to endorse a phased approach, much like the one articulated by Fatah in the 1970s.

When it emerged, Hamas strongly rejected the legitimacy of partition. Indeed, its entry into the Palestinian public realm was partly a reaction to Fatah's increased willingness to accept a Palestinian state on part of Palestine. Emphasizing this distinction, a Hamas leaflet on March 13, 1988, declared: "Let any hand be cut off that signs [away] a grain of sand in Palestine in favor of the enemies of God . . . who have seized . . . the blessed land." Another leaflet in August 1988, entitled "Islamic Palestine from the [Mediterranean] Sea to the [Jordan] River," asserted that "the Muslims have had a full—not a partial—right to Palestine for generations, in the past, present, and future. . . . No Palestinian generation has the right to concede the land, steeped in martyrs' blood. . . . You must continue the uprising and stand up against the usurpers wherever they may be, until the complete liberation of every grain of the soil of . . . Palestine, all Palestine, with God's help."[110]

Like all nationalists, Hamas sanctifies the homeland. Its original charter clearly articulated the notion that Palestine "from the sea to the river is Islamic land, and it is impossible to yield one inch of it to the enemy." It further declared that "the homeland is cherished and everything that keeps us from it, including our lives, is cheap. So just think if we are talking about Palestine, the land where Muhammad ascended to Heaven, the land of the prophets and miracles."[111] Hamas's new charter, adopted in 2017, continued to apply homeland territoriality to the entirety of Palestine. Hamas, the new document declares, "rejects any alternative to the full and complete liberation of Palestine, from the river to the sea." Palestine, it emphasizes, "which extends from the River Jordan in the east to the Mediterranean in the west and from Ras al-Naqurah in the north to Umm al-Rashrash in the south, is an integral territorial unit. It is the land and the home of the Palestinian people. The expulsion and banishment of the Palestinian people from their land and the establishment of the Zionist entity therein do not annul the right of the Palestinian people to their entire land and do not entrench any rights therein for the usurping Zionist entity."[112]

As an organization with religious roots, Hamas is also heavily influenced by the significant Islamic jurisprudence that rejects the legitimacy of non-Muslim control of Palestine.[113] Consistent with this position, Hamas's discourse is replete with rejections of the right of Israeli sovereignty over any part of Palestine, even if, at times, it appears to be willing to accept the presence of individual Jews in a Palestinian state.[114]

The sacralization of territory appears to render it indivisible. As one Hamas leader argued while rejecting the possibility of a two-state solution in 1995, "This is not a political issue. It is an Islamic issue. So we are not here representing our views, we are representing our religion."[115] Just before his assassination by Israel, Abdel Aziz Rantisi, one of Hamas's founders, articulated the view that Hamas's strategy is underpinned by the following principles: "1) Our homeland has been usurped in its entirety, but we cannot concede one inch of it. 2) There is an obvious imbalance of power in favor of the Zionist enemy. 3) We do not possess the armaments our enemy possesses, but we have a faith that generates a will that does not recognize defeat or retreat before our goals are accomplished."[116]

At the same time, Hamas has increasingly articulated a willingness to accept a shorter-term arrangement with Israel that holds within it the possibility of subsequent substantive ideological change if it garners sufficient political returns. The existence of this possibility does not mean that Hamas has changed its ideological position, or redefined the appropriate extent of either its homeland or the geographic contours of the Palestinian state that it seeks. It does, however, mean that such a transformation is possible given the presence of sufficient domestic political returns to such an arrangement.

Hamas's phased approach usually involves support for a ceasefire (*hudna*) with Israel and tacit acquiescence to a two-state solution as an intermediate solution, as long as Israel withdraws completely from all the territories it conquered in 1967, dismantles all the settlements, and enables Palestinian refugees to return to their original homes.[117] The offer of a (usually time-limited) ceasefire is nearly always accompanied by an explicit refusal to recognize Israel and therefore grant partition any legitimacy.[118] For example, Khaled Mashal, who took over Hamas's reins in 1996, reversed his previously articulated rejection of the possibility of partition and declared in a 2007 interview that "there will remain a state called Israel. This is a matter of fact. . . . The problem is not that there is an entity called Israel. . . . The problem is that the Palestinian state is non-existent. . . . As a Palestinian today I speak of a Palestinian and Arab demand for a state on 1967 borders. It is true that in reality there will be an entity or state called Israel on the rest of Palestinian land. . . . This is a reality but I won't deal with it in terms of recognizing or admitting it."[119] In 2009 he declared that, "at a minimum, we demand the establishment of a Palestinian state with Jerusalem as its capital with full sovereignty within the 1967 borders, removing all checkpoints and achieving the right of return." In a similar vein, in a 2010 interview with PBS, he argued that "the action is the occupation. And the reaction from the Palestinians is the resistance. So when the occupation comes to an end, the resistance will end. It is as simple as that. If Israel withdraws to the 1967 borders, so that will be the end of the Palestinian resistance."[120]

Hamas leaders explicitly situate this willingness to reach a temporary accommodation with Israel in the context of a phased plan that has unmistakable echoes of Fatah's adaptation of a phased plan in the 1970s. They consistently argue that any implied acquiescence to Israel's existence is temporary and does not reflect any substantive change in their ideological position.[121] Speaking in Teheran in 2011, Khaled Mashal declared that Hamas's strategic objective remains the liberation of Palestine in its entirety and the elimination of the "Zionist project."[122] Sometimes this is phrased less directly, in terms of achieving a state in the 1967 borders in the present, without giving up the right to the rest of the land for future generations.[123] In 2005, for example, Ismael Haniyeh, then the senior spokesman for Hamas in Gaza, stated that in a political sense, Hamas was seeking a state within the 1967 borders, but added that "we will wait until a later date to seek the liberation of other areas" beyond the 1967 boundaries.[124] Likewise, in May 2011, Mahmoud Zahar, one of Hamas's founders and political leaders, explained that Hamas was ready to accept a Palestinian state "on any part of Palestine," but would not recognize Israel because doing so would "cancel the right of the next generations to liberate the [remaining] lands."[125] Hamas intellectuals often legitimate the notion of a ceasefire with Israel as actually the best way to defeat it. In this scenario, lacking an external enemy, either Israel's internal cleavages would lead to its implosion, or "the world situation will change so much that Israel, as a Zionist entity, may not wish, or may not have the ability, to continue to exist."[126]

Hamas's leaders sometimes justify their willingness to establish a state in the West Bank and Gaza Strip by reference to Israel's overwhelming strength.[127] However, Israel's relative power has been a constant over the period since Hamas's emergence and cannot be used to explain the changed approach. If anything, the increase in the relative domestic power of Hamas in the late 1990s and 2000s was accompanied by what might be the beginnings of a more moderate stance on borders and not an expansion of their claims, as one might expect if the application of homeland territoriality tracked relative strength. Moreover, Hamas's leaders were subject to the same set of observable realities as were the leaders of Fatah, but did not change their pattern of articulation when Fatah did, or their ultimate goal. Despite the expectations of the rational adaptation family of mechanisms, Hamas has not updated its ideology to match this reality. In fact, had rational adaptation governed their ideological definition of the homeland, we might have expected both the initial articulation of their goals in 1987 and the reformulated version in 2017 to have reflected an acceptance of partition.[128] The failure of the 2017 version of Hamas's charter to explicitly redefine the homeland in accordance with the international consensus that Israel is a legitimate state is an especially striking indication of the limits of conceptualizing homeland claims as cheap talk since the drive to rewrite their charter was explicitly conceptualized as a public relations move intended to increase their appeal to the outside world.[129]

Rather than an accommodation to reality, Hamas's apparent willingness to settle, in the short term, for a state in the West Bank and Gaza Strip is better explained as a product of Hamas's engagement in Palestinian politics. From the beginning, Hamas understood itself as offering a religiously grounded alternative to the secular PLO. It seeks to lead the Palestinian nationalist project and to create a Palestinian state that comports with its vision of a just society. Hamas's relatively late arrival as an organized actor in Palestinian politics and its exclusion from the PLO meant that, until 2006, it was in a persistent state of relative weakness vis-à-vis Fatah. Its attempt to enter, and then remain, in the mainstream of the Palestinian political spectrum induced Hamas to take the tactical step of signaling a hypothetical willingness to acquiesce to a state in the West Bank and Gaza Strip as a temporary measure.

The periodic offers of a medium-term truce with Israel are one of these steps. There is widespread agreement that these offers do not represent an ideological change in Hamas's position.[130] Hamas's leaders are aware of the possibility that the offers of a ceasefire could provide a mechanism through which the "interim solution" would become *the* solution if the elected Palestinian leadership reached an accommodation with Israel, even if they continued to oppose this outcome. They have occasionally conceded that they would "respect the will of the Palestinian people" if the latter endorsed a two-state solution and the recognition of

Israel after the establishment of an independent Palestinian state in all the territories and the granting of the right of return to the Palestinian refugees.[131] They
have been willing to risk this possibility, however, because the offers of a ceasefire
"served to address the increasing sense of Hamas's marginalization from the centre of gravity of Palestinian popular opinion. Hamas had witnessed the effects on
popular support for the PLO as the latter appeared to enjoy a degree of success
in moving towards the establishment of a Palestinian state and the abandonment
of the strategy of armed struggle."[132]

Since the terms and preconditions of these ceasefire offers make them
extremely unlikely to be taken seriously by Israel, if only because they are often
accompanied by the rejection of Israel's right to exist, it is reasonable to interpret
them as intended as much for a Palestinian audience as for Israeli and international ears. While striving to offer an alternative to Fatah, Hamas's leaders were
well aware that its support by the Palestinian public depended "on its ability to
recognize an aspiration to meet the more immediate demands of ending occupation."[133] Echoing Fatah's rationale in the 1970s, Hamas's declared openness to
considering a two-state solution as a practical matter signals to the Palestinian
population that Hamas also has a plan to end the occupation even as its rejection
of Israel allows Hamas to critique Fatah from the right.[134]

The utility of this approach was reinforced in the aftermath of the 1993 Oslo
Accords. The Oslo Accords recognized the PLO as the sole leader of the Palestinians, undermining in one swoop the meticulous organizational and political
work Hamas had undertaken in the territories since the First Intifada.[135] The
accords were also popular in the West Bank and Gaza Strip because, at least initially, they appeared to offer an end to the Israeli occupation. Hamas's response
to the Oslo Accords was two pronged. On the one hand, they launched a campaign of suicide attacks calculated to undermine the accords by demonstrating
to Israelis that they were unlikely to get the security they wanted.[136] On the other
hand, they simultaneously signaled to the Palestinians in the territories that they
might be willing to accommodate the same practical outcome, as long as it did
not involve the recognition of Israel or legitimating partition. They sought, in
other words, to secure their popularity while arousing public opposition to the
accords, but without being accused of preventing the end of the occupation.[137]

The phased approach and the articulation of a ceasefire, and accommodation, with Israel as an interim phase continued to be politically useful after the
end of the Oslo period (1993–2000). First, Hamas was well attuned to the wea-
riness of the Palestinian public in the early 2000s and their desire to see some
political progress after the long stalemate of the Second Intifada. Second, the
attacks of September 11, 2001, and the resulting war on terror made Hamas's
leadership "keen to distinguish itself to the West from salafi jihadi groups such as

al-Qaeda."[138] Not only did Hamas not want to be caught up in the same net, but they worried that "the Palestinian issue would be lost sight of, subsumed as simply another front in the wider conflict" against the West promoted by al-Qaeda.[139] If until this point the phased approach was largely promoted by the Hamas leadership located inside Palestine, the geostrategic changes of the early 2000s led Hamas's exiled leadership to begin to support this tactical position as well.

Well aware of the Palestinian, Arab, and international coordination around a two-state solution, Hamas has agreed to join this consensus as the minimum that they can all agree on. The new Hamas charter explicitly couches Hamas's apparent willingness to acquiesce to partition (under its terms), as a concession to domestic Palestinian politics. It declares that "without compromising its rejection of the Zionist entity and without relinquishing any Palestinian rights, Hamas considers the establishment of a fully sovereign and independent Palestinian state, with Jerusalem as its capital along the lines of the 4th of June 1967, with the return of the refugees and the displaced to their homes from which they were expelled, to be a formula of national consensus."[140]

True to the expectation that the articulation of the new rhetorical variant would be inconsistent in the period between its introduction and the displacement of the older variants, Hamas's endorsement of even a temporary arrangement with Israel is not steadfast. For example, in a November 2012 interview with CNN, Khaled Mashal expressed positions that seemed to accept partition: "I accept a Palestinian state according [to] the 1967 borders, with Jerusalem as the capital, and with the right to return." Asked about recognizing Israel, he said: "Such a declaration could only be made once a Palestinian state has been created, and after this state is established, it decides its standing towards Israel." However, in a speech before Hamas supporters two weeks later, Mashal sounded a very different note: "The Jewish state will be wiped away through resistance.... Palestine is ours from the river to the sea and from the south to the north. There will be no concession of any inch of land."[141] Such inconsistency suggests that Hamas may be in the midst of a process that, if the relatively moderate perspective yields sufficient political returns, may lead to a growing acceptance of partition. If the implicit acceptance of partition does not yield these returns, we can expect the new variant to be abandoned.

In broad terms, Hamas's tactic has been relatively successful. From a marginal position in Palestinian society, Hamas had risen to the point where it was able to defeat Fatah in the 2006 elections to the Palestinian National Assembly. It was also able to defeat Fatah in a head-to-head armed struggle for control of the Gaza Strip. We might expect, as a result of this success, that as long as Palestinian public opinion remains supportive of an accommodation with Israel, Hamas will continue to leave itself open to the possibility as well.

While the silence about what happens after a two-state solution is achieved opens the door to the possibility that such a solution would become ideologically acceptable as the permanent solution, this has yet to occur.[142] To the extent that a political dynamic has guided the adoption of a phased approach, it also helps explain why this position has not become accepted as the ideological status quo. To begin with, the political returns to this position have been limited. The tactical acceptance of partition as a temporary phase, and the not insignificant differences between Hamas's founding charter and its 2006 election platform, have not led to widespread international recognition like similar changes did for Fatah. This means that some of the main returns which helped reinforce Fatah's tactical change have been absent in the case of Hamas. Second, Hamas has been able to achieve some of its goals without having to recognize Israel. Most prominently, Israel's unilateral disengagement from the interior of the Gaza Strip in 2005 (and the credit Hamas took for it) meant that Hamas was able to achieve an autarkic Palestinian society without having to give Israel anything in return. As a result, paradoxically, the Israeli unilateral withdrawal from the Gaza Strip reduced the incentives to institutionalize the interim solution as *the* solution.

The experience of the Palestinian nationalist movements shows that the view of the homeland's extent articulated by stateless nationalist movements is subject to the same dynamics of change as those with states. Palestinian nationalist movements did not simply update their vision of the appropriate extent of their national state in response to new information about reality or to the demands by its superpower patrons. Rather, the acceptance of new borders in such cases, if it takes place at all, occurs because, like states and the political movements within them, nonstate movements seeking self-determination are fundamentally political organizations. Their pursuit of domestic power, sovereignty, and international recognition mean that it is possible to amend one of their sacred values in the service of another. For Fatah, this was a trade of part of the land of Palestine for the recognition of the PLO as the sole representative of the Palestinian people and of their right to self-determination. For Hamas, such a trade, if it occurs, will likely involve an exchange of territorial goals for Palestinian independence, political power, and the ability to shape the public sphere of the Palestinian state in religious terms.

However, the context of stateless movements does mean that there are important limits to the ability of political returns to foster the acceptance of partition before partitions are implemented. While Fatah has largely accepted that the Palestinian state they seek will be established only in part of Palestine, the extent and durability of this change should not be exaggerated. Consistent with a situation in which the new variant has not been completely eliminated, some within the movement continue to be animated by a vision of Palestine extending from the river to the sea.[143] Even as Fatah's 2009 political program reflected an acceptance of partition, the internal order prepared for the same General Congress maintained the call for "the full liberation of Palestine and the liquidation of the State of the Zionist occupation economically and politically, militarily and culturally."[144] Indeed, Fatah's emblem continues to flag the borders of their desired state as those corresponding to the entire British Mandate. Similarly, while Hamas's tactical modulations open the door to substantive change given sufficient political returns, this has yet to occur.

For both Fatah and Hamas, the political returns to internalizing partition have been driven by the desire of the Palestinian population in the territories to get out from under the occupation. The failure to achieve a Palestinian state limits these political returns. The more disillusioned with the two-state solution Palestinians become, the less political movements wanting to attract their support will articulate territorial formulas that are consistent with withdrawing homeland territoriality from Israel. The spread within Palestinian nationalist movements of a map-image of the Palestinian homeland that is consistent with a peaceful resolution of the conflict with Israel thus depends on the continued accrual of positive political returns to the movements articulating them. To the extent that this does not occur and a two-state solution is not implemented, we can expect the change to stall and expansive visions of the homeland to regain their dominant position.

THE WITHDRAWAL OF HOMELAND TERRITORIALITY IN A CROSS-NATIONAL PERSPECTIVE

The case studies in this book have demonstrated that the application of homeland territoriality to lost lands can vary over time and that evolutionary dynamics rooted in domestic political processes play a significant role in driving these changes. This chapter provides evidence that these findings are broadly generalizable. Using a survival analysis of the application of homeland territoriality to all cases of homeland territory lost between 1945 and 1996, it demonstrates that the withdrawal of homeland territoriality is systematically associated with the presence of the conditions that trigger evolutionary dynamics.

The findings in this chapter reinforce four main conclusions. First, the withdrawal of homeland territoriality from lost parts of the homeland described in the case studies is not idiosyncratic. Consistent with the theory developed in chapter 1, land that was once consecrated as part of the homeland can lose this designation, although there is considerable variation in whether such change occurs and, if it does, how long it takes. Second, such change is not irreversible. Homeland territoriality, even once withdrawn from lost lands, can be reapplied to them at later times. Third, the conditions in which evolutionary dynamics are likely to operate—contexts characterized by meaningful sustained domestic political contestation—increase the likelihood that homeland territoriality would be withdrawn from lost lands. Concretely, the longer states are democratic, the more likely they are to withdraw homeland territoriality from lost homeland territory. Finally, some of the alternative explanations, especially the impact of political mobilization of coethnics in the lost lands, integration into the global economy, the presence of peace treaties to resolve conflict, and Soviet influence, also receive some support.

Identifying the general conditions under which areas once seen as part of the homeland—and therefore worthy of disproportionate, even irrational, sacrifice—no longer merit such devotion has important implications for the use of partitions as a remedy for conflict or failed states. While the material aspects of partitioned territory, the resulting states' ethnic composition, their relative strength, and institutional development have all received important scholarly attention, less systematic attention has been paid to whether or how long it takes for actors to stop desiring the land on the other side of the newly imposed border.[1] Including this component is important because as long as actors believe that parts of their homeland remain under others' sovereignty, conflict is likely to continue and partitions are likely to fail. The concluding chapter will return to the issue of partitions.

The cross-national empirical examination of the conditions under which homeland territoriality is withdrawn from lost lands also bridges the persistent gap between the common operationalization of homelands as static in studies of international conflict and the dominant theoretical understandings of nationalism and territoriality that emphasize their potential mutability. As I noted in chapter 1, the importance of national territory underlies the substantial agreement among scholars that, at least as an empirical matter, contenders in territorial conflict tend to view territory as if it were indivisible.[2] Many scholars rightly make the case that it is the *perception* of indivisibility that is critical and that leaders act *as if* territory is indivisible. However, the implications of these nuanced positions are not often reflected in the ways homelands are operationalized in cross-national studies. Rather than treat homelands as a variable, homelands continue to be commonly operationalized as a time-invariant indicator.[3] Yet, as I argued in chapter 1, and as the case studies have demonstrated, the geographical area to which homeland territoriality is applied is not actually static. The disjuncture between theory and case-based evidence, on the one hand, and empirical practice in cross-national analysis, on the other, limits our ability to investigate the existence, correlates, and consequences of changes in the geographic scope of homelands.

This chapter enables such investigations by providing a way of operationalizing the homeland status of lost territory that allows it to vary over space and time. It then explores the factors that correlate with this variation. In the next chapter, I use this measure to investigate more closely the impact of losing homelands on international conflict.

Where Is the Homeland?

Dear God,
Who draws the lines around the countries?
Nan

Stuart Hample and Eric Marshall, *Children's Letters to God*, 1991[4]

Empirically testing whether and how homeland territoriality is withdrawn from lost lands systematically and cross-nationally requires a way of identifying homelands across space and time. Scholarship that integrates homelands into cross-national studies of international conflict has generally relied on one (or more) of three proxies to do so: territory populated by coethnics, state borders, or a group's history of prior autonomy in a territory. While all of these are reasonable, each comes with a set of drawbacks that ultimately undermines its utility as a measure of the homeland status of territory.

Perhaps the most commonly used measure identifies homeland territory as that populated by coethnics.[5] The rationale for this proxy is captured by Ernest Gellner's "potato principle," whereby territory is claimed as part of the homeland if a group's ancestors once grew potatoes—or, more generally, were physically rooted—in it.[6] This proxy is especially attractive because the historical existence of ancestors on a parcel of land before the onset of any conflict, or even before the creation of nation-states, appears to provide a way of identifying the presence of nationalist sentiment that is exogenous to the strategic and material considerations of states and their leaders.

However, understanding homelands as a nationalist form of territoriality makes this proxy less theoretically appropriate for at least five reasons. First, relying on the prior existence of coethnics in a place as marking that territory as part of the homeland renders homelands necessarily static and domestically undifferentiated. If a group's ancestors grew potatoes in a location, it becomes harder to accommodate either the variation over time or between political movements in the application of homeland territoriality that was evident in the case studies. As both the German and Italian cases suggested, the presence of coethnics matters, but the withdrawal of homeland territoriality depends less on the actual presence or absence of coethnics in lost lands and more on whether movements use ethnic strategies of legitimation to apply homeland territoriality to land.

Second, the use of the past or present existence of coethnics in a space as marking it as part of the homeland assumes an unproblematic and automatic link between ethnicity and nationalism. Yet, as even Gellner noted, the existence of a prior ethnonational community is "inessential" for the creation of nations.[7]

The automatic linkage between ethnicity and nationhood built into this proxy thus introduces a bias into the resulting identification of homelands by systematically excluding the impact of national homelands in the cases of so-called civic nations (whose membership criteria are not based on shared ethnic membership). Analytically, moreover, the assumption that ethnicity and homelands automatically correspond makes it impossible to ask empirically whether ethnicity and homeland territoriality can vary independently or have distinct impacts on outcomes of interest, including conflict.

Used as a rule for coding whether particular land is homeland territory, the assumption that nationalism's membership dimension (say, shared ethnicity) determines its territorial dimension (the homeland), could also lead to systematic errors by counting cases where coethnics sit across borders but in which the land is not part of the homeland. For example, the fact that Israel contains a significant Arab population does not mean that Egyptians consider Israel to be part of their homeland. The inclusion of such irrelevant cases could artificially inflate the likelihood that lost territory would appear to be excluded from the homeland because it would include cases in which the territory was never part of the homeland in the first place.

Third, by prioritizing ideas about national membership over nationalist definitions of the homeland, this proxy assumes that making the nation's territorial and the cultural boundaries congruent has to mean moving the territorial boundaries. However, both the sordid history of ethnic cleansing and the settlement projects carried out by Communist China, Indonesia, Israel, Iraq, Morocco, and the United States, among others (what Brendan O'Leary called "right-peopling" a territory), demonstrate that populations can also be moved to achieve this congruence.[8] In other words, conationals may come to populate a territory because it is seen as part of the homeland rather than the other way around.

Populations can also be recategorized as coethnics in order to legitimate control of a particular territory. As chapter 3 showed, the borders of the Italian homeland were traditionally used to decide who was Italian, not vice versa. Similarly, the concept of natural boundaries deployed by China's nationalist government was accompanied by an assimilationist policy that categorized the various groups living within these boundaries as belonging to a single ethnicity. Han historiography—which considered Tibet, Mongolia, and Eastern Turkestan as integral parts of the Middle Kingdom—thus also held that the "non-Han inhabitants of these regions are just as much 'Chinese' (Zhongguo Ren, that is 'People of the Middle Kingdom') as the Han are."[9]

The interaction between the categorization of coethnics and the nationalist project extends to decisions about which questions are asked by a census and how the information is used. For example, in 1922 an association of German nationalists demanded that the German census ask only about the ability to speak German rather than about respondents' mother tongue in order to enable the state to categorize bilinguals as German and bolster the claim to the territory they inhabited. In a similar vein, at the Versailles negotiations, Germany argued that the 1910 Prussian census should be the source used to determine the border between Poles and Germans. They preferred this source because, unlike the one actually used (a teacher-administered survey of language), the 1910 Prussian census categorized Kaschubes and Masures as distinct ethnicities rather than as bilingual Poles, thereby reducing the proportion of Poles in the region relative to the German population.[10] In Venezia Giulia, too, the attribution of ethnicity through the census was closely tied to the interests of the particular state doing the enumerating.[11] In other words, the set of choices available for the categorization of groups in a region is often shaped by nationalist projects. Since the identification and labeling of a people in a region as belonging to a particular ethnic group are often intimately intertwined with the nationalist desire to control territory, ethnicity and the homeland's borders are often endogenous.[12]

The endogeneity of determinations of ethnicity to the national enterprise is compounded by the reality that, while not infinitely elastic, the selection of a particular group of people as ancestors whose past location justifies a territorial claim is not an empirically neutral task. Indeed, significant scholarship has documented the ways in which historic continuity has been invented in cases around the globe.[13] This is part of the reason why the rampant practice of "peopling the past," in which "specific archaeological cultures are unproblematically seen as ancestral to contemporary ethnic or national groups," is both ahistorical and often misleading.[14] Whether a group belongs to one ethnicity or another is often in the eyes of the beholder. This is not just an academic matter since it means that different analysts can look at the same context and reach different conclusions. For example, a British analysis in 1940 concluded that, according to ethnic criteria, Istria was predominantly Slav and ought to be under Slavic control. Five years later, British analysts concluded that the area was ethnically Italian after all.[15]

Finally, the use of coethnicity to delimit the extent of the homeland also runs into many of the general problems of using ethnicity as a variable identified by Daniel Posner.[16] First, it requires an a priori decision about which kinds of social identity ties are used to delimit coethnicity. Using maps of religious brethren draws a very different picture of the homeland than maps based on linguistic or racial categories (which also differ from each other). For example, if the extent of the ethnic homeland is defined by the presence of coreligionists, then the border between Sudan and Chad truncates a homeland by dividing a Muslim population. If, however, the extent of the ethnic homeland is defined by language, this same border does not divide a homeland since it largely corresponds to the divide between Arabic and Bagirmi speakers.

Second, the use of coethnicity to delimit the extent of the homeland requires a decision about the appropriate level of group aggregation and how to apply it in different contexts. Many people simultaneously belong to multiple, often nested, ethnic groups (for example, there are roughly 250 distinct groups that all speak mutually intelligible versions of Bantu, but that belong to different tribal and religious groups).[17] There is no theoretically coherent way of deciding which of these "levels" of ethnicity is the relevant one across the board. Yet these decisions can have real consequences. For example, the decision at the Versailles Peace Conference to award Pomerania and Silesia to Poland after World War I was based on the categorization of Kaschubes and Masures as Polish (and bilinguals). Had they been coded as distinct ethnic groups, those territories would have been seen as having a majority German population and, perhaps, not stripped from Germany.[18] It may be only a slight exaggeration to say that the history of twentieth-century Europe may have hinged on this arbitrary decision.

As the discussion of the German and Italian cases suggested, the assumption that the presence of coethnics marks the boundary of the homeland also depends on a battery of questions and assumptions that are rarely answered or evaluated. Is it the absolute number of coethnics or their relative share of the population in a particular territory that triggers the designation of homeland? If the former, how many coethnics are required to be present before a previously excluded territory becomes seen as part of the homeland and, conversely, how much emigration or ethnic cleansing would lead us to stop coding a territory that had been identified as a group's homeland in that way? If it is the relative share of coethnics that matters, what is the proportion at which the designation of homeland begins to apply?

It is difficult, if not impossible, to choose the area which serves as the denominator for these calculations without a priori assuming the location of the homeland that the ethnicity proxy is trying to measure. In other words, using the presence of coethnics on a parcel of land as an indicator of its homeland status requires a way of determining which concentrations of coethnics consecrate the land on which they reside and which do not that is independent of any prior assumption about where to look. Unfortunately, the easiest way of addressing this, assuming that all concentrations of coethnics are equally valid, leads to some questionable conclusions, such as the identification of the Pale of Settlement in the Russian Empire as the Jewish homeland in the nineteenth century, present-day Jordan as the Palestinian homeland, and the Upper Midwest of the United States as part of the Norwegian homeland, because all three contain (or once did) significant populations of coethnics.[19] Such remarkable errors raise significant concerns about the utility of this measure.

Indeed, nationalists have long used the squishiness of this measure to their advantage. For example, Italian nationalists openly capitalized on the impossibility of determining the relevant population without first determining the territory whose population is counted. Recognizing that the demographic advantage of Italians over Slavs in the Adriatic region was less impressive if Trieste, Istria, and Dalmatia were considered separately, they argued that "Friuli (Provinces of Gorizia and Gradisca), Trieste, and Istria, which are divided by no natural barrier,... [should] be considered as forming one region, that of Julian Venetia."[20] All these drawbacks should make us skeptical of the use of the location of coethnics as the basis for the definition of the homeland's extent.

A different proxy for identifying homelands uses the borders of the state proper as the homeland to distinguish it from the state's colonial holdings. This is certainly a reasonable distinction since, unlike a nationalist's view of the homeland, colonial possessions are fungible.[21] Indeed, a shift from viewing territory as an inalienable part of the homeland to applying an imperial-like cost-benefit analysis to the land in question may be part of successful processes of state-contraction.[22] However, by equating the current borders of the metropole with those of the homeland, this proxy cannot accommodate the possibility that the definition of the homeland may not correspond to current state borders or the domestic variation in the lands to which homeland territoriality is applied. However, as shown above, not only is domestic variation a real possibility, but states may control some territory that is neither part of the homeland nor a colony (like Israeli rule over the Sinai Peninsula between 1967 and 1982). More commonly, states can have significant parts of the homeland outside their control (as demonstrated by the Hungarian pining for the pre-Trianon borders). Finally, this proxy also risks succumbing to a methodological nationalism in which states' claims to represent nations are taken at face value.[23]

Finally, a third proxy that is sometimes used to identify the status of territory as a homeland is the existence of prior autonomy.[24] Although logical, the use of this proxy requires an arbitrary decision about how far back in time such autonomy could exist and still be relevant. While ICOW's use of prior autonomy as one factor in its index of a territory's intangible value not unreasonably limits this history to the past two hundred years, nationalists commonly go much further back in time to establish the legitimacy and authenticity of their claims.[25] For example, Kwame Nkrumah appealed to a legacy of prior autonomy in the fourteenth century and Zionist movements used the existence of prior autonomy nearly two millennia ago to legitimize their respective nationalist projects.[26] In addition to these measurement concerns, as with the identification of prior

ancestors, it is likely that the identification of prior autonomy is intimately con-
nected to the nationalist project. Indeed, ancient autonomy can be more or less
illusory and the borders in which it was exercised fluid and poorly demarcated.
There is also considerable evidence that, in many cases, ancient polities are better understood as a network of localities rather than as well-bounded territorial
entities.[27] As a result, drawing a line between past autonomy and contemporary
polities often requires significant artistic license. In other words, the identification of the geographical area in which ancient autonomy was practiced is also
subject to concerns about its endogeneity to nationalism. Finally, like the use of
the prior presence of coethnicity as a proxy for the location of the homeland,
relying on a historical legacy for this purpose renders the operationalization of
homelands as static as the legacy.

A New Measure of the Homeland Status of Territory

Given these concerns, this section describes a way of detecting the application
of homeland territoriality to lost parts of the homeland based on the domestic
discourse about land newly located on the other side of international borders.[28]
This measure takes advantage of the fact that, because homelands are a nationalist form of territoriality, their physical contours have to be clearly articulated and
continually demarcated, especially when a state no longer has physical control
of that territory. The need to continually apply homeland territoriality explains
why nationalists are consumed with drawing maps and rhetorically delineating
the territorial boundaries of their homeland. The common nationalist practice
of using familial metaphors to convert mere land into the homeland is one way
of doing so.[29] The resulting depictions of the homeland generate an "instantly
recognizable, everywhere visible" logo that penetrates the popular imagination
and forms a powerful emblem for the nation.[30]

As geographers have long pointed out, such depictions are discursive attempts
to shape the world, to make it congruent with the nationalist vision of where territorial borders should be drawn.[31] They are "a symbolic shorthand for a complex
of nationalist ideas" used as tools of "territorial socialization" by which groups
come to learn which land ought to be theirs.[32] They demonstrate the difference
between inside and outside and signal the territorial shape of the homeland to
the nation. As such, they are a form of "rhetorical action" intended to convince
actors to see the world in a particular way—in this case, to place political boundaries in some places rather than others.[33]

The nationalist discourse used to do so can be used to distinguish between
the areas to which this territoriality is applied (i.e., areas identified as the homeland by a particular nationalism) and areas to which it is not (i.e., nonhomeland

territory).[34] The withdrawal of homeland territoriality, denoting the demotion of territory from homeland to nonhomeland status, is reflected in the elision of homeland claims to that territory from a society's public pattern of articulation about the homeland in general and regarding that territory in particular. Indeed, as has been demonstrated elsewhere and was reinforced by the case studies earlier in this book, even initially short-term elisions of territory from the pattern of articulation defining the extent of the homeland can lead to the eventual exclusion of that territory from the definition of the homeland.[35] As with the process of norm transformation more generally, the persistent absence of lost land from the pattern of articulation about the homeland's extent and debate over this question is equivalent to withdrawing the application of homeland territoriality from that land.[36]

The rhetorical differences between how homeland and nonhomeland territories are spoken of makes it possible to use discourse to identify the homeland status of territory while maintaining greater fidelity to the constructivist foundations of the dominant theories of nationalism. A discourse-based measure of the homeland status of territory is especially helpful because it de-links homeland status from other dimensions of nationalism (most prominently, ethnicity) and allows the homeland status of particular territories to vary over time without making any assumptions about the relationship between the geographic distribution of coethnics and the extent of homeland territory, the length of time beyond which prior autonomy is no longer relevant, or the necessary congruence of homelands and state borders.

This measure does assume that, despite their intersubjective character and distinctiveness in any particular context, the "homeland" means the same thing across cases. That is, it assumes that the Israeli homeland carries similar weight and importance for Israeli nationalists as the Palestinian homeland carries for Palestinian nationalists, or the French homeland for French nationalists. This assumption enables systematic comparison and analysis of the relationship between homelands and conflict.

In order to trace the application of homeland territoriality to lost territory, I examined the domestic discourse about land on the other side of every new international border drawn between 1945 and 1996. A border was defined as new if it separated independent states for the first time or if the location of the border between already independent states changed.[37] Each movement of a line between states was counted as a new border. Borders between colonies of different colonial powers were excluded as preexisting international borders. Borders between former colonies of the same empire were included even if they followed previous subcolonial administrative boundaries. The rationale for doing so is based on the spread of a norm against disrupting state borders since World War II. The spread of this norm implies that international borders are qualitatively different from lower-order administrative ones because they drastically reduce the likelihood of future revisions that could bring lost homeland territory back into the fold.[38] The replacement of one state by another was not counted as a new international border if the line separating the states did not move. For example, the 1991 border between Croatia and Hungary is not counted as a new border because it followed the line that separated Yugoslavia and Hungary. However, the border between Croatia and Slovenia is counted as a new border. Cases where a border revision lasted less than one year were excluded because it is difficult to disentangle their impact from that of the original border change. Cases where the relevant territory on the other side of the border was smaller than 100 square kilometers and cases in which international borders were erased (such as the absorption of Goa into India or the unification of East and West Germany) are also not counted as new borders. The analysis that follows also excludes borders between former colonial powers and their colonies, the transfer of colonies (for example, the transfer of Taiwan from Japan to China), as well as borders between occupying powers and the occupied state (if the state was occupied in its entirety).[39]

There were 162 new international borders between 1945 and 1996 that met these conditions. In 78 of these borders, an application of homeland territoriality to land left on the other side of the border was made in at least one of the states involved.

The main source for detecting the discursive application of homeland territoriality to land across a new international border was the US government's Foreign Broadcast Information Service (FBIS). Originally created as an open-source intelligence-gathering tool, FBIS systematically transcribed news broadcasts from almost every country between 1945 and 1996.[40] The analysis ends in 1996 because the Readex Collection of the FBIS Daily Reports ends then. As a source, FBIS has three main advantages: (1) its scope is nearly global; (2) its records are searchable by keyword; and (3) it translates all foreign news broadcasts into English. The latter is especially important for cross-national analysis because it overcomes the practical challenge posed by the fact that nationalist discourse is everywhere articulated in the vernacular. Because it provides reasonable access to the way in which actors in (nearly) every case where a new border was drawn since 1945 talked about the land on the other side of this new border, discourse about territory captured by FBIS provides a feasible and theoretically consistent proxy for identifying areas that the relevant populations consider to be lost parts of their homeland.

Following the insight that discourse about homeland territory would differ from discourse about nonhomeland territory, I coded an application of homeland territoriality to land on the other side of a new international border as occurring in a particular year if states, state executives, or other nonstate political organizations in the state newly excluded from that territory flagged it as part of their homeland at least once in that year. Specifically, I coded the application of homeland territoriality as occurring if these actors lamented the loss of territory across a new international border as a loss of part of the "homeland," "father-land," or "motherland," if they called for its "unification" or "reunification" with the metropole, if they described the territorial division in invidious terms such as a "partition" or an "amputation," or if they described the presence of another state on that territory as an "occupation." In each case, I conducted a search for the name (often names, along with alternative transliterations) of the territory in question as well as for major cities or significant historical sites in those territo-ries, and for the border itself, to capture as much discourse about that territory as possible. Since any new line on the geopolitical map may be perceived differently by those on either side of it, I coded for the application of homeland territoriality to the land across the border for both sides of every new border.

This measure uses a wider lens to detect the continued application of home-land territoriality to lost lands than the more restrictive focus on the articulations of state executives used in other contexts.[41] This more inclusive view is theoreti-cally appropriate because we are concerned with the continued social resonance of lost territory rather than what the state believes per se. The advantage of this coding rule can be illustrated with the case of Russian views of Crimea during the period of observation. For a variety of reasons, Boris Yeltsin's government was very careful not to explicitly claim Crimea as part of the Russian homeland (dis-tinct from the argument over the fate of the Black Sea Fleet). As a result, looking through a state-executive level lens, one would have concluded that Crimea was no longer seen as part of the Russian homeland. However, Crimea was routinely flagged as part of the Russian homeland by the Liberal Democratic Party (which in 1993 was the largest Russian political party, with nearly 23 percent of the vote) and by Duma members, including those from Yeltsin's party, who were not part of the executive branch.[42] Including such non-state-executive articulations cap-tures the continued Russian application of homeland territoriality to Crimea and places its subsequent annexation in a more appropriate context.

There were four categories of potential claims that were not coded as reflect-ing the homeland status of territory. First, I excluded homeland claims by individuals (for example, op-eds) and generic sentiments that could not be attributed to an existing political organization. This rule was based on the need to provide a minimal threshold (the presence of some identifiable political orga-nization) below which a homeland claim might not be a viable indicator of collective belief. For example, a report that the Polish foreign minister received complaints for saying that Poland has no claims on the Vilnius region was not counted as an application of homeland territoriality to the area Poland lost to the USSR after World War II because these complaints were not attributed to any particular political organization. Since, in the Polish example, there were strong indications that Lvov was considered by many to be part of the Polish homeland—including a still-popular Polish song that included the verse "We will never give up Lvov"—this rule likely undercounts some homeland claims by nonstate actors. Nonetheless, the choice of an organizational cutoff is motivated by the notion that not all individuals are able to affect the content of intersubjective social facts equally, and that those who are organized are better able to do so than atomized individuals.[43]

Applications of homeland territoriality to lost lands in editorials by media outlets that served as the organ of a particular political movement are attributed to that movement. For example, the claim by a 1950 editorial in the Bulgarian *Rabotnichesko Delo* to Macedonia as part of the Bulgarian homeland is counted as a claim by the Bulgarian Communist Party.

Second, I did not count claims to the people on a particular territory or for compensation for lost real estate as an application of homeland territoriality to that land if those claims did not also include a specific reference to the land itself as part of the homeland. For example, the calls by German refugees from Sudeten for compensation are not counted as claims that the Sudeten was part of the German homeland (though these exist elsewhere). Similarly, the concern expressed by the Hungarian state and political organizations for "Hungarians abroad" does not automatically translate into including the territories in which they reside as part of the Hungarian homeland. This decision was driven by a desire to identify the homeland status of territory in a manner that is as independent as possible from the territory's demography or pecuniary value.

Third, arguments by groups seeking to secede from their current state to join another and claiming the land on which they resided was part of the homeland of the state they wished to join were also not counted as applications of homeland territoriality to that territory. For example, the claims by leaders of the Russian Bloc in the Ukraine that the Crimea was part of the Russian homeland were not counted as designating the homeland status of Crimea for Russia because the Russian Bloc party was not part of the domestic Russian political spectrum. However, claims that Crimea was part of the Russian homeland by Russian political organizations, such as the Liberal Democratic Party of Russia, were taken as indicating the homeland status of the Crimea for Russia.

Finally, I did not count potential applications of homeland territoriality that remained implicit. For example, Romania, Pakistan, and Guinea Bissau tended to couch their claims that Moldova, Kashmir, and Cape Verde, respectively, were part of their homeland in terms of demanding the self-determination of the populations residing in those territories. This framing of claims was driven by the belief that, given the choice, these populations would choose to reunite with the homeland. Like in the case of the West German Christian Democratic Party (CDU), while most of the time such claims went hand in hand with more overt applications of homeland territoriality, where the desired territory was not explicitly included as part of the homeland, such implicit claims were not counted as applications of homeland territoriality to the land across the border. Similarly, generic claims for the unity of, for example, the Arab or Slavic homeland, were not counted as applications of homeland territoriality unless they contained a specific reference to land on the other side of a new border.[44] Articulations by Arab states which do not border Israel that Palestine was part of the Arab homeland were also not counted as reflecting the status of Palestine as part of their nation-state.

The Alternative Explanations section later in this chapter addresses potential concerns that these coding decisions shape the results. Overall, however, FBIS provides reasonable access to the way in which actors in (nearly) every case of lost homeland territory since 1945 talked about that territory. By providing a way of accessing the pattern of articulation about lost lands in data that is equivalent across cases and over time it enables cross-national time-series investigations of the application of homeland territoriality to lost lands. As such, the discourse about territory captured by FBIS provides a feasible and theoretically consistent way of tracing the continued application of homeland territoriality to lost lands around the globe.

Explaining Variation in the Application of Homeland Territoriality across New International Borders

The systematic tracing of the application of homeland territoriality to lost lands reveals significant variation. Figure 5.1 shows that the share of territorial divisions in which homeland territoriality was applied to the land on the other side of the border is unevenly distributed over time and across the world.[45] There is considerable variation in how frequently homeland territoriality is applied across new borders depending on the decade in which the border was drawn, with especially notable spikes for borders drawn in the 1940s (as a result of the reordering of territorial borders after World War II) and the 1990s (largely driven by Serbian and Russian claims to the former territories of Yugoslavia and the Soviet Union, respectively). There is also substantial variation across regions. Consistent with the scholarship that has emphasized the general acceptance of borders in Africa,

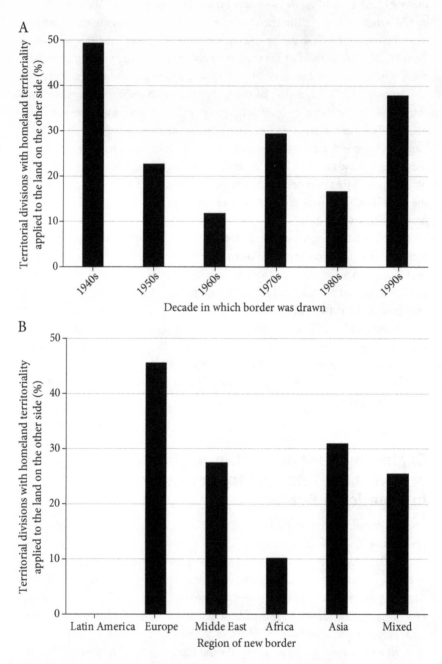

FIGURE 5.1 Percent of post-1945 new borders in which homeland territoriality is applied to lost lands: (A) by decade of the new border; (B) by region

relatively fewer of the post–World War II borders there were characterized by the application of homeland territoriality to lost lands.[46] The apparent absence of applications of homeland territoriality in Latin America is largely a product of how few new borders were drawn in the region during the period of observation. Europe, on the other hand, experienced homeland claims across the border much more commonly than other parts of the world did. This pattern is potentially at odds with the argument that Europe was less prone to nationalist sentiments after World War II than other regions.[47]

There is also substantial variation in how long homeland territoriality continues to be applied to land on the other side of a new international border. Figure 5.2 shows the distribution of the cases according to the percent of years under observation in which they applied homeland territoriality to lands across new borders. A significant proportion of the cases (18 percent) conform to the popular stereotype that homelands are static and apply homeland territoriality to lost lands in every year they are observed (a "1" in figure 5.2). However, a similar proportion of the cases (19 percent) never apply homeland territoriality to land newly located on the other side of new international borders (a "0" in figure 5.2). This bimodal distribution challenges both essentialist arguments that expect homelands to be static and deterministic arguments that expect all countries to

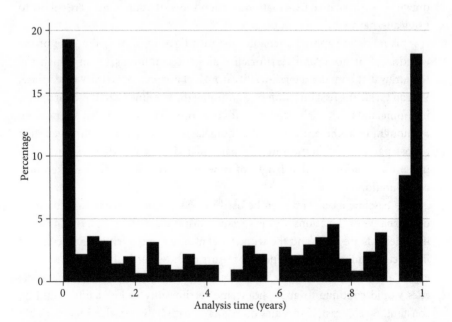

FIGURE 5.2 Proportion of years under observation in which homeland territoriality was applied to lost lands

eventually accommodate themselves to reality and give up lost lands. While there are examples of both, most cases lie somewhere in between.

This variation is investigated further using a Cox conditional shared frailty model, in which a failure is the application of homeland territoriality to land on the other side of a new international border in a particular year. Since we are interested in what accounts for the time until the *last* failure (the last application of homeland territoriality to lost lands), the data is structured as a conditional risk set using time elapsed since the drawing of the international border. This setup assumes that a particular case is not at risk of failing for a second time (or, indeed, a last time) until it has failed for a first time, and so on.[48] The dependent variable is the time elapsed between the drawing of the border and the last observed failure (an application of homeland territoriality to lost lands). The unit of analysis is the state-border because, as we saw in the German case, states can lose homeland territory across more than one border and the continued application of homeland territoriality across multiple borders can vary independently. While using states as stand-ins for societies excludes stateless nations, the nationalizing character of most modern states renders it a reasonable proxy for the society-wide context in which the intersubjective boundaries of the national homeland are forged.[49] The universe of cases includes all new borders across which homeland territoriality was applied at least once after the border was drawn. The Alternative Explanations section shows that the results are robust to using alternative universes of cases.

This modeling approach enables the investigation of both the pace of the withdrawal of homeland territoriality and the conditions under which the withdrawal of homeland territoriality from lost homeland territory takes place. We can tackle the first question by examining the baseline hazard rate of applying homeland territoriality to lost lands over time. The baseline hazard rate can be thought of as the probability that homeland territoriality would be applied to lost parts of the homeland at a particular time, given that a subject was under observation for that length of time, with no other variables taken into consideration.

The baseline hazard rate can be used to evaluate the purchase of a number of alternative explanations for the variation displayed in figure 5.2. For instance, if homelands are static and the withdrawal of homeland territoriality described in the case studies is an idiosyncratic feature of those particular cases, we would expect a relatively flat baseline hazard rate, as the likelihood (hazard) that societies would continue to apply homeland territoriality to lost lands would be constant. By contrast, if societies do regularly withdraw homeland territoriality from lost lands, the baseline hazard rate would decline over time. In this case, a constantly declining baseline hazard rate would be consistent with explanations of the withdrawal of homeland territoriality that point to the impact of new information or to the passage of time.

Figure 5.3 shows the baseline hazard rate (the risk of continuing to apply homeland territoriality to lost lands) since the truncating of the homeland, given that a case was observed for that length of time. It shows that the baseline hazard rate initially experiences a slight (nonsignificant) rise, reflecting a greater likelihood of applying homeland territoriality to lost lands in the first few years after the drawing of the international border. This modest increase is followed by a significant decline in the baseline hazard rate, though the risk of continuing to apply homeland territoriality to lost lands never completely disappears even at its nadir. About a quarter century after the drawing of the border, the likelihood of applying homeland territoriality to lost lands increases again.

The shape of the baseline probability of applying homeland territoriality to lost homeland territory over time has three main implications. First, and most importantly, it is consistent with the case-based findings that the application of homeland territoriality to land varies over time. If the extent of the homeland were static, the baseline hazard rate would be relatively flat. The variation in the baseline hazard rate thus reinforces the empirical traction of constructivist theories that view homelands specifically, and nationalism more generally, as

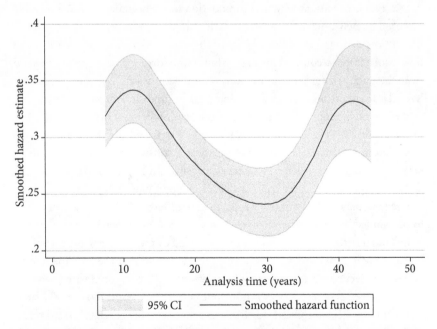

FIGURE 5.3 Baseline hazard rate of claiming lost homeland territory as part of the homeland

mutable. It also underlines the utility of a measure of homeland status that can accommodate this variation.

Second, the increase in the underlying hazard after about a quarter century of observation reinforces the insight that territorial disputes can lie dormant only to re-erupt decades later.[50] This may be the case because expansive visions of the homeland remain available for political entrepreneurs to resuscitate even decades after claims to lost lands fade from a society's pattern of articulation. As chapter 3 showed in the Italian context, despite the de facto losses of Istria and Dalmatia in 1954 and the de jure acceptance of those losses by Italy in 1975, in the early 1990s the neofascist Italian Social Movement (MSI) nonetheless (re)applied homeland territoriality to these lands as part of an effort to cast their party as a conventional nationalist organization. The remaining availability of an expansive vision of the homeland that political entrepreneurs can use decades after the drawing of the border reinforces the purchase of mechanisms of change that expect homeland territoriality to shift gradually (such as evolutionary changes) rather than as abrupt or mechanistic transitions.

Third, the observation of significant variation over time in the baseline hazard rate is inconsistent with either time-invariant explanations of the withdrawal of homeland territoriality from lost lands or explanations that expect time to work on its own to do so. Specifically, although the initial decline in the baseline hazard rate is consistent with accommodation to the boundaries of the possible imposed by new international borders, the subsequent increase in later years is not. If bowing to the inevitable reality of the new border or some other piece of new information accounted for the elision of the former parts of the homeland from the public pattern of articulation about the homeland's extent, the baseline hazard rate would have continued to decline over time rather than increase again.

Arguments that point to the institutionalization of the norm of border fixity since the 1940s or to generational change to explain the acceptance of the loss of homeland territory would also expect a consistent decline in claims of territory across the border, not a later resurgence. As I noted in chapter 1, generational arguments expect cohorts that grow up in new circumstances to have different understandings of the world, to take different things for granted, and to be molded by these differences. As a result, these arguments expect that lost homeland territory would continue to be claimed by the older generation (which presumably has memories of a united homeland) and that the baseline hazard rate would decline as the members of this generation are replaced with individuals whose lived experience does not include control of the lost territory. There is little room in these arguments for the later increase in the baseline hazard rate.

To explore the variation in the continued application of homeland territoriality to lost lands, the statistical model includes proxies for the various potential explanations noted in chapter 1 and whose purchase was explored in the case studies. Since evolutionary dynamics of change cannot be directly observed, the model includes the interaction of regime age and democracy as a (admittedly blunt) proxy for the critical cocktail of variation, differential success, and time that unleash evolutionary dynamics.[51] This is a reasonable proxy because, as I argued in chapter 1, evolutionary dynamics will operate in any context characterized by variation, differential success, and time. Long-lived democracies are likely to be characterized by all three. First, the political contestation that characterizes democracies, by definition, means that there are different political movements that vary according to some dimension. Domestic variation in whether to continue to apply homeland territoriality to lost lands is perhaps especially likely to be one of these dimensions because it is reasonable to expect variation in the perceived costs and benefits of continuing to claim lost territory and in politicians' perceptions of the benefits of accepting the loss or of using it to mobilize popular support.

As Zeev Maoz and Bruce Russett pointed out, the longer a polity is democratic, the greater the institutionalization of democratic norms that enable real variation and competition between different political viewpoints.[52] Democratic regimes are thus more likely to be characterized by real competition for domestic political power than nondemocracies. It is the freedom to contest along multiple political issues that opens the door to strange bedfellows, temporary alliances, and tactical modulations in homeland discourse that can become institutionalized if they succeed. Because the winners in democracies receive real political power, there is a greater likelihood of positive returns to rhetorical modulations about the extent of the homeland made in the name of gaining power. These returns provide the mechanism that selects between variants that succeed and are promoted and those that fail and become less prominent. Without real domestic political benefits accruing as a result of domestic competition, it is less likely that such modulations would be sustained long enough to displace more expansive definitions of the homeland.

Finally, these processes require time in which to unfold and different regime types are likely to have varying effects over time. Initially, the pattern of public articulation about lost lands in democracies may be more likely to include applications of homeland territoriality to lost lands because their more open marketplace of ideas provides more space for the articulation of such claims. Authoritarian regimes, by contrast, might repress any discussion of lost territory if the ruling elite believes that it serves its interests. The passage of time in democracies, however, provides more opportunities for political movements to try out alternative framings of the extent of the homeland, to build alliances with parties that disagree on this issue, to accrue positive returns to more modest definitions of the homeland, and for these variants to displace more expansive ones. Long-lived democracies offer, in other words, more opportunities for evolutionary dynamics to drive change in the definition of the homeland's scope.

To be sure, when an authoritarian regime introduces a new variant of the homeland's map-image or the logic used to claim it, the resulting withdrawal of homeland territoriality from lost lands can still be the product of an evolutionary dynamic. From an evolutionary perspective, the new government-sponsored variant is associated with success in the domestic political game because all the alternatives are repressed. As a result, it can spread in the society and if successful for long enough, become institutionalized.

At the same time, there are good reasons to believe that, even if authoritarian regimes may introduce new variants, they are less likely do so. For instance, the logic of "diversionary peace," identified by Taylor Fravel, in which autocrats seek to eliminate domestic sources of instability by resolving territorial disputes, and which is a key reason authoritarian regimes frequently settle these disputes, does not hold when it comes to homeland territory. Homelands' emotive power means that concessions over them are likely to exacerbate domestic instability by legitimating regime opponents' attacks on the regime on nationalist grounds. This may be why even China, which tends to cede territory in frontier disputes, has never compromised over homeland territory.[53] Variation, in other words, while possible in authoritarian settings, is less likely.

As a result, this analysis makes the conservative assumption that any withdrawal of homeland territoriality that takes place in authoritarian regimes (like those experienced by East Germany) is driven by something other than evolutionary dynamics. The finding that sustained political competition is associated with change thus likely represents a lower bound estimate of the real impact of evolutionary dynamics on the withdrawal of homeland territoriality from lost lands.

The analysis also includes proxies for the other elements that the literature has identified as potentially shaping the likelihood that homeland territoriality would be applied to lost lands. As discussed in chapter 1, these include factors believed to provide relevant new information about some aspect of reality— the geographical distribution of coethnics, prior and current conflict, a state's strength, and a territory's economic and strategic value—as well as factors that shape the instrumental considerations faced by leaders, and ways in which time is hypothesized to matter. Table A.1 in the appendix provides summary statistics for these variables.

The presence of shared ethnic groups across a new international border (Coethnics beyond border) is coded based on the EPR-TEK dataset.[54] The attribution of change to new information arising from shifts in the geographical distribution of coethnics expects homeland territoriality to be withdrawn faster from lost lands that are not populated by coethnics relative to lost lands that are populated by coethnics.

As chapter 1 noted, the changing economic value of territory could also shape the likelihood of continuing to apply homeland territoriality to lost lands through an analogous pathway. Other things being equal, we might expect the withdrawal of homeland territoriality to be less likely where the territory is economically valuable than in cases of less valuable territory. Territory on the other side of a new international border is coded as economically valuable (Econ. valuable) if it contains oil or gas reserves, water resources, diamonds, or ports either in the territory in question if it refers to a discrete territory, or within fifty kilometers of the border.[55]

Changes in the balance of power between states may also shape the likelihood that homeland territoriality would be applied to lost lands or withdrawn from them. Since, ceteris paribus, more territory is better than less, we might expect leaders to expand the definition of the homeland to accommodate what they can get.[56] The possession of nuclear weapons or support by a superpower might also embolden the application of homeland territoriality to lost lands, especially if the state now controlling the territory lacks these sources of relative strength. By the same token, since leaders are strategic actors, the manifest inability to reassert control over lost territory ought to aid the elision of that territory from the homeland's scope. To account for this dynamic, *Capability ratio* captures the relative material and military strength of the states on either side of the new international border.[57]

The model also controls for the (natural log of the) distance between the border and the capital (Capital distance (log)). Distance could be playing at least two analytically distinct roles. First, distance from the capital is a reasonable measure of a territory's strategic significance. Other things being equal, the further away the international border, the less vulnerable a state feels if that border changes. For example, the fact that the 1949 border between Jordan and Israel divided Israel's capital made it strategically very important for Israel. By contrast, since the border between China and Pakistan is more than 3,500 kilometers from Beijing it is relatively less strategically important. This measure also reflects the reality that the strategic value of territory may vary across the members of any particular dyad. Second, this measure also captures other intangible significance territory might have since, other things being equal, state capitals tend to be situated in the core region that a group sees as belonging to it and, therefore, territory that is farther away might be less important than territory that is closer to the capital.[58]

As chapter 1 noted, leaders' instrumental considerations could also shape the application or withdrawal of homeland territoriality to lost lands. Conflict could structure these considerations in especially important ways. For instance, the strategic character of the interaction between the states facing each other across new international borders suggests that information about the other side's willingness to fight could affect the likelihood that societies would apply homeland territoriality to lost lands.[59] Where maintaining the claim to lost homeland territory would be costly (perhaps because the other side has already demonstrated a willingness to fight), we might expect a lower likelihood that homeland territoriality would be applied to lost lands. By the same token, the need to mobilize populations or a desire to signal resolve during a conflict may encourage the application of homeland territoriality to lost lands. The model thus accounts for the existence of conflict during the year in which homeland territoriality is applied as well as for any prior conflict.[60] Finally, the application of homeland territoriality to lost lands across a border could be significantly constrained by the presence of a peace treaty with the cross-border neighbor, as these frequently require the formal renunciation of any territorial claims.[61]

The potential impact of superpower influence in forcing their client states to accept the loss of territory offers another set of instrumental considerations.[62] As shown in the East German context in chapter 2, Soviet pressure likely played a significant role in forcing the East German state to withdraw homeland territoriality from both the lands east of the Oder Neisse, as well as from West Germany. The Soviet position also limited the maneuvering room of the Italian Communist Party (PCI). To explore the possibility that Soviet pressure accounts for the withdrawal of homeland territoriality, the analysis controls for whether a state was a Soviet client in a particular year.[63]

Finally, the analysis also includes measures that account for two additional ways in which the passage of time could matter beyond those already discussed in the context of the baseline hazard rate. The first captures the potential impact of a secular decline in the value of territory as a result of globalization. The delinking of power and territorial control that have resulted from global economic integration implies that states which are highly integrated into the global economy would be relatively less concerned with territory and therefore less likely to continue applying homeland territoriality to lost lands.[64] As a result, *Integration into global economy* controls for the extent to which states are integrated into the global economy (measured as quartile of share of trade to GDP).[65]

The second measure addresses the possibility that the withdrawal of homeland territoriality from lost lands reflects the degree of regime institutionalization. As I noted in chapter 1, from this perspective, the application of homeland territoriality to lost lands may be the product of a new regime's attempt to forge new links between the state and the mass population.[66] Here, the maturing of the regime and the solidification of its social base of support reduces the need to apply homeland territoriality to lost lands in order to consolidate power. As a result, we might expect a corresponding reduction in the risk of applying homeland territoriality to lost lands once regimes are no longer in their early years. Building on Mansfield and Snyder's work, *New regime* captures whether a state is within five years of entering the international system, the end of an occupation, or a transition to democracy.[67]

Table 5.1 presents the results of a Cox conditional shared-frailty model analyzing the effect of these variables on the probability that homeland territoriality continues to be applied to lost parts of the homeland.[68] Coefficients greater than one indicate an increase in the risk of failure (i.e., of continuing to apply homeland territoriality to lost parts of the homeland), conditional on being in a particular risk stratum. Coefficients smaller than one indicate a decrease in the

TABLE 5.1   The risk of applying homeland territoriality to lost parts of the homeland

VARIABLE	EXPONENTIATED COEFFICIENT	STANDARD ERROR	NONPROPORTIONAL HAZARD CORRECTION
Democracy	0.654	(0.259)	^
Regime age	1.001	(0.010)	^
Democracy X regime age	0.881**	(0.034)	^
Coethnics beyond border	5.457***	(1.959)	
Econ. valuable	0.485	(0.309)	^
Capital distance (log)	1.149	(0.141)	^
Current conflict	0.628	(0.152)	^
Prior conflict	1.587	(0.552)	^
Peace Treaty	0.322***	(0.095)	
Capability ratio	2.112	(1.055)	^
Losing state Soviet client	0.278*	(0.178)	^
Integration into global economy	0.734***	(0.065)	
New regime	0.851	(0.138)	
Observations	911		
Failures	854		
θ	1.12		
Log likelihood	−2660		
Wald $\chi2$	251		
Likelihood ratio $\chi2$ for θ	296***		

Notes: Cox conditional shared frailty proportional hazards model. Coefficients with a ^ symbol are corrected for nonproportional hazards. Strata dummies and their nonproportional hazard corrections are also included (not shown).

* $p < 0.05$, ** $p < 0.01$, *** $p < 0.001$

likelihood that homeland territoriality would be applied to land now located on the other side of an international border. Because the data is organized as a conditional risk set, each failure constitutes its own observation and each observation can be interpreted as the opportunity a case has to fail again. This organization of the data leads to the analysis of 101 cases across the 78 borders, and 911 total "observations." The number of failures per case ranges from 1 to 49, with an average of 19 failures (years in which we observe the application of homeland territoriality to lost homeland territory).

The results in table 5.1 provide empirical support for the argument that societies experience lower risk for continuing to apply homeland territoriality to lost lands where the conditions for evolutionary dynamics in the political realm are more likely. The finding that the coefficient of the interaction between the democracy and regime age is less than one indicates that longer-lasting democracies are significantly less likely to continue to claim lost homeland territory.

Figure 5.4 illustrates the impact of being a democracy on the risk of applying homeland territoriality to lost lands over the entire span of regime ages.[69] As it shows, being a democratic state is associated with an increasingly smaller risk of continuing to claim lost homeland territory the longer a state is continuously

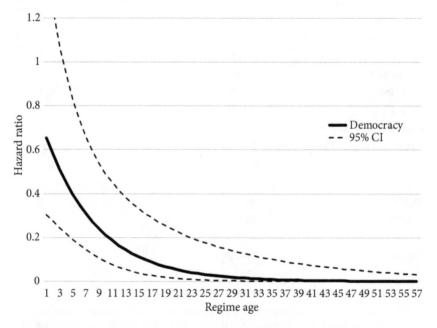

FIGURE 5.4   Effect of democracy on the risk of applying homeland territoriality to lost parts of the homeland the longer a state is continuously democratic

democratic. Because the 95 percent confidence interval is greater than "1" for the first three years of being a democracy, we cannot be certain that democracy actually reduces the risk of claiming lost homeland territory during this period (at that confidence level). After the initial three-year period, however, we can be confident of the negative impact of being a democracy on the risk of applying homeland territoriality to lost lands. Since being a democracy reduces the likelihood of applying homeland territoriality to lost lands by about 12 percent for every additional year a state is democratic, the marginal impact of being a democracy declines the longer a state remains democratic.

While the uncertainty surrounding the estimated impact of being a democracy in the first three years shown in figure 5.4 is consistent with a potential impact of being a new regime, table 5.1 shows that controlling for this factor does not eliminate the impact of the interaction of regime age and democracy. The relationship is also robust to controlling for other circumstances in which we might expect nationalist outbidding to be especially salient, including election years and whether a claim to lost homeland territory is made during the first year of a leader's tenure regardless of regime type.[70] Consistent with leaders' instrumental use of lost lands to mobilize support, election years are significantly associated with an increased risk of applying homeland territoriality to lost lands (not shown). This, however, does not substantively reduce the countervailing impact of being a long-lived democracy. In other words, despite the presence of potential nationalist outbidding in democracies, over time their impact is outweighed by the moderating side effects enabled by the operation of evolutionary dynamics.

Figure 5.5 illustrates the dosage effect of being a democracy for different lengths of time. It shows the smoothed hazard function of applying homeland territoriality to lost lands at various ages of democratic regimes, with all other variables held at their means. The top line graphs the smoothed hazard function for nondemocratic regimes. Each subsequent line shows the smoothed hazard function for regimes that are continuously democratic for ten, twenty, and thirty years, respectively. It shows that, regardless of how many years a case is under observation (analysis time), the risk that democracies would continue to apply homeland territoriality to lost lands declines the longer a state is a democracy. The declining size of the gap between the lines reflects the finding that the marginal impact of being a democracy declines the longer a state is democratic.

Democratic longevity is, as noted above, a blunt proxy for the conditions in which an evolutionary dynamic is likely to operate. As chapter 4 showed, moreover, evolutionary dynamics shape the withdrawal of homeland territoriality even in contexts without sustained democratic procedures and institutions. What matters, then, is less democracy per se than the combination of a vibrant competitive political sphere and meaningful competition sustained over time.

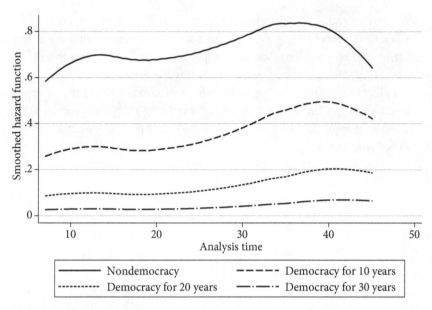

FIGURE 5.5   Effect of democratic longevity at different ages (Cox proportional hazard)

Indeed, the main findings hold when using other proxies for the conditions that unleash evolutionary dynamics (variation, differential success, and time), but that fall short of being democracies. These include the interaction of competitive and factional systems with regime age; the presence of multiple legislative parties over time; the presence of minimally competitive elections over time; and the three-way interaction between having more than one party run for office, minimally competitive elections, and the length of time both continually characterize a society.[71] The main conclusions remain substantively similar (see table A.6 in the appendix); polities likely to be characterized by variation, differential success in the domestic political game, and time, are less likely to continue to apply homeland territoriality to lost lands relative to polities that are not characterized by the conditions that trigger evolutionary dynamics.

Table 5.1 also shows that some of the other alternative explanations for when and why homeland territoriality might be withdrawn are also supported. Figure 5.6 illustrates the results of the significant variables. These figures show the post-estimate smoothed hazard rates of each variable, with the values of all other variables held at their means.

The presence of coethnics across the border is positively associated with continuing to apply homeland territoriality to lost homeland territory for longer. This effect is also substantively large. Societies with coethnics across the border are about five times as likely to continue applying homeland territoriality to lost lands as those without coethnics across the border. As figure 5.6a shows, contexts in which there are no coethnics across the border face a much lower risk of continuing to apply homeland territoriality to lost homelands than contexts in which coethnics continue to inhabit those lands. It is important to note, however, that both the size and significance of this effect are sensitive to the particular measure used to identify the contemporary presence of coethnics across the border.[72] In any case, the impact of the conditions conducive for the operation of evolutionary dynamics remains robust even against the headwind created by the contemporary presence of ethnic kin there.

The presence of coethnics across a border could shape the likelihood of withdrawing homeland territoriality in at least two ways. It could convey information to which actors adapt directly or it could unleash a set of strategic interactions that increase the likelihood of applying homeland territoriality to lost lands. For example, the presence of shared coethnics in other neighboring states may trigger a competition for regional power or for the right to speak for the ethnic group as a whole. In the course of this competition, we might expect political leaders to signal their commitment to the ethnic group as a whole by flagging the lost lands as part of the homeland. Likewise, the agitation for independence, autonomy, or collective minority rights by coethnics in the lost homeland territory (such as, for example, the mobilization of the Russian Bloc party in Crimea) could pressure the society that lost the territory to articulate homeland claims to it in an effort to support the struggle of their coethnics.[73] All these effects may be especially impactful in democracies where politicians are arguably especially susceptible to the outbidding dynamics initiated by these strategic interactions. These contexts may also induce politicians to emphasize ethnic logics of legitimation to apply homeland territoriality to lost lands.

The results are consistent with theories which assume that such triadic relationships have an impact. Sharing coethnics with neighboring states and the presence of a politically mobilized coethnic group in the lost lands are associated with increased likelihood of the application of homeland territoriality to the lost lands.[74] Interestingly, controlling for the presence of a politically mobilized ethnic group renders the impact of coethnics beyond the border no longer significant at conventional levels ($p = 0.14$). This suggests that the impact of coethnics across the border is likely exerted mainly through the way they interact with domestic politics in the state that lost the homeland territory rather than by providing information about the homeland's extent directly.

This conclusion is further reinforced by the supplementary finding that applications of homeland territoriality to lost lands are much more likely in democracies that have coethnics on the other side of the border (see column 3 of table A.7

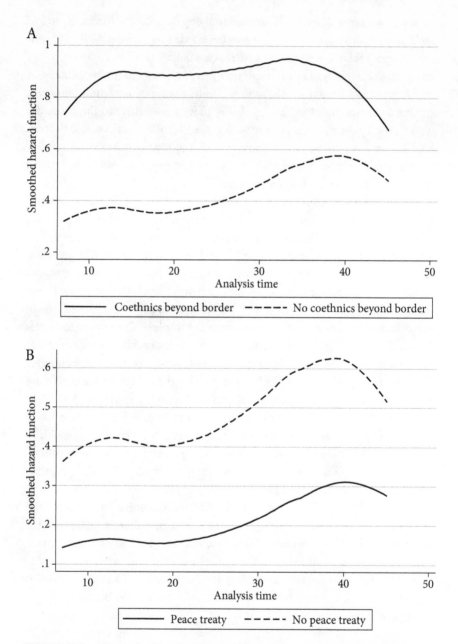

FIGURE 5.6 Effect of other significant factors (Cox proportional hazard): (A) effect of coethnics across border; (B) effect of peace treaty; (C) effect of being a Soviet client; (D) effect of integration into global economy

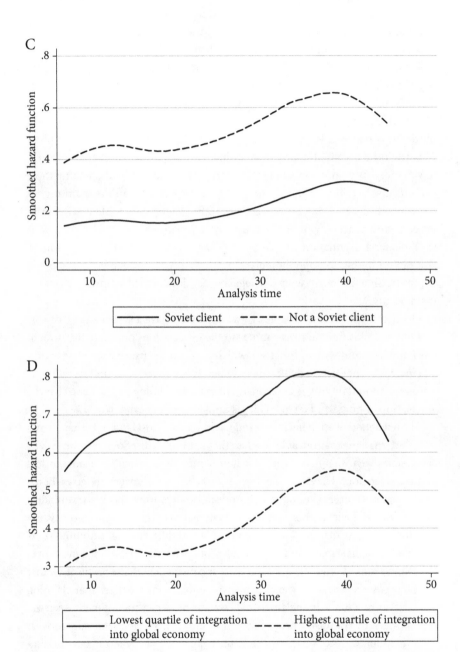

FIGURE 5.6 (Continued)

in the appendix) and by the case-based conclusion that the presence of coethnics in a territory matters more when ethnic strategies of legitimation underlie claims to lost homeland territory. Importantly, in all these permutations, the main finding of a negative relationship between long-lasting democracies and the application of homeland territoriality to lost lands remains robust.[75]

The existence of a peace treaty between the states facing each other across the border also makes it less likely that homeland territoriality would be applied. This could be because the peace treaty increases the domestic political returns to variants that do not apply homeland territoriality to lost lands, helping those variants displace more expansive ones. While not included in the main model, the context in which the border is drawn also matters. Consistent with prior expectations, peacefully drawn borders (by International Court of Justice decision, bilateral negotiations, or colonial powers) are associated with a reduced risk of continuing to apply homeland territoriality to lost lands (not shown). Yet controlling for the drawing of a legal border does not substantively affect the main results.[76]

Other conflict-related variables, however, do not have a systematic or consistent impact. This finding runs counter to the expectations of purely instrumentalist understandings of nationalism, which presume the use of homeland claims will increase as politicians deploy them to justify a conflict or to mobilize support for one. This null finding is also consistent with the finding in chapter 6 that the application of homeland territoriality is unlikely to be cheap talk.

The likelihood of applying homeland territoriality to lost lands was shaped by a state's international patron, at least when that patron was the Soviet Union. Soviet client states were significantly less likely to continue to articulate claims to lost homeland territory. The effect of being a Soviet client was, however, largely a European phenomenon. Excluding new European borders from the analysis renders the behavior of Soviet clients no different than that of US clients. This is consistent with the possibility that the Soviet Union restrained the territorial ambitions of its clients as it sought stability and the avoidance of open territorial conflict in Europe. Overall, the impact of superpower influence is consistent with the proposition that the superpowers restrained their clients where there was a danger that claiming lost lands as part of the homeland could escalate into a confrontation between the superpowers. By contrast, where both states were clients of the same superpower, no such inhibiting force was present and the application of homeland territoriality to lost lands was much more likely. Importantly, the robustness of the impact of long-lived democracy to controlling for the various configurations in which superpower influence could shape the application of homeland territoriality to lost lands helps alleviate the potential concern that the results are driven by the fact that the data is almost entirely from the Cold War period.

Finally, the secular decline in the value of territory in a globalized world also shaped the risk of applying homeland territoriality to lost lands. The more states are integrated into the global economy, the less likely they are to continue to articulate claims to lost homeland territory. This is consistent both with the possibility that globalized states are relatively less concerned with territory per se, and with the possibility that well-developed export sectors are able to promote the withdrawal of homeland territoriality from lost lands in their states. In any case, states that are democratic for longer are still significantly less likely to apply homeland territoriality to lost lands even after controlling for this factor.

Other variables theoretically expected to shape the likelihood of the application of homeland territoriality to lost lands do not have a systematic impact. Neither a territory's economic nor its strategic value have a significant impact on the risk of including lost homeland territory in the homeland's scope. The relative strength of the states facing each other across the new international border also does not significantly affect the likelihood that lost territory would continue to be included in the homeland. As discussed above, this result is robust to also controlling for other factors that could affect the balance of power such as the possession of nuclear weapons (by one or both states) or being under foreign occupation.[77]

Alternative Explanations

The finding of a significant association between the interaction of regime age and democracy and a lower risk of applying homeland territoriality to lost lands is consistent with the argument that the withdrawal of homeland territoriality from lost lands is more likely where the conditions for change as a result of evolutionary dynamics (variation, differential success, and time) are also more likely. This section addresses a number of threats to inference and alternative explanations.

The first potential concern is that the results could be an artifact of particular coding decisions and the limitations inherent in FBIS as a data source. In this regard, both the decision to count any application of homeland territoriality to lost lands in a particular year as reflecting that territory's continued inclusion in the homeland, as well as the wider lens used to designate which articulations count, pose an admittedly high bar for detecting the withdrawal of homeland territoriality. This is especially the case for democracies, whose more open marketplace of ideas means it is more likely that any particular idea would be articulated. This bar, however, biases the analysis in this chapter against both the finding of any withdrawal of homeland territoriality from lost lands and its association with long-lived democracies.

While FBIS provides a way of accessing the pattern of articulation about homelands in data that is equivalent across cases and thereby enables cross-national quantitative investigations of the correlates and consequences of homeland claims, it does have some important limitations. First, FBIS likely overrepresents the views of ruling governments and state leaders as well as cases relevant to US interests. The former is the case because the media outlets that provide the open-source information translated by FBIS have historically been controlled by states. Nonstate actors, perhaps especially opposition movements in authoritarian regimes, may thus get less air time. FBIS also paid greater attention to areas and topics identified as strategically important for the United States. As a result, even if homeland rhetoric was contained in domestic media coverage, news items that are less directly relevant to US interests would be less likely to be selected for translation.

There are, however, two reasons to believe that these potential sources of bias in the data—failure to appear in domestic media or failure by US analysts to detect and translate these claims—are not shaping the results. First, the impact of the US-centric bias is at least partially ameliorated by the fact that homeland claims have long been seen as a trigger for interstate conflict, including by key players in the US foreign policy establishment. As an open-source intelligence-gathering tool, FBIS thus had an incentive to be relatively inclusive as it sought to forecast international conflict that might affect US interests. This was especially important during the Cold War, when even far-flung disputes were potential foci for conflict between the superpowers. Second, because any impact of being excluded from power (and therefore from access to media) on the range of publicly available articulations about the extent of the homeland is likely to be more significant in authoritarian regimes, where, presumably, groups excluded from power have less freedom to create their own media content, we would expect to detect more consistent applications of homeland territoriality to lost lands in democracies. Since the opposite is the case, it is unlikely that this potential bias is driving the results.

The focus on sources that privilege actors associated with the ruling government does mean, however, that FBIS is likely too blunt a source to reliably capture the movement-level variation in the application of homeland territoriality to lost lands consistently across cases. This is the reason that, despite the argument in chapter 1 and the process tracing in the case studies about the utility of focusing analysis at the movement level, the cross-national measure of the application of homeland territoriality to lost lands used in this chapter and the next is aggregated to the state level.

The wider lens used to capture homeland discourse does increase the theoretical possibility of detecting the application of homeland territoriality to lost lands by socially marginal groups. While impossible to discount completely, there are a number of safeguards that help mitigate this concern. First, as noted above, the data do not count homeland claims by individuals or generic sentiments that could not be attributed to a particular political organization as applications of homeland territoriality to lost lands. This coding rule provides a minimal threshold (the presence of an identifiable political organization) below which a homeland claim might not be a viable indicator of collective belief. Second, FBIS's bias toward ruling groups and US interests also helps mitigate the risk of including claims to lost territory by socially irrelevant groups. These biases mean that a group's articulation of a claim to lost homeland territory would have had to be significant enough to merit coverage by domestic media, and then significant enough to be selected for translation by US analysts. These constraints provide reasonable confidence that applications of homeland territoriality to lost lands captured by FBIS are not completely marginal. Finally, even if some claims by marginal groups are included, any bias thus introduced works against the finding of systematic withdrawal of homeland territoriality, especially in democracies, where relatively smaller groups have more freedom to promote their views.[78]

FBIS is also not a sensitive enough source to reliably capture situations where nationalists assign different values to different parts of the homeland. Clearly, an ordinal-level measure of the homeland status of territory would allow for a more nuanced analysis and for the possibility that different mechanisms of change operate in core and peripheral homeland territories. At the same time, since designating territory as part of the homeland is a nationalist strategy of asserting control over that territory, it is possible that the very designation of some homeland territory as peripheral is part of the political process of excluding that territory from the homeland's scope.[79] A nominal measure of the homeland status of territory is thus still useful because it sidesteps the potential endogeneity of the relative centrality of particular pieces of the homeland. In any case, this nominal measurement of the homeland status of territory takes an important step on the way to a better integration of homelands into quantitative scholarship on territory and conflict.

Other potential biases built into FBIS could also theoretically shape the results. For instance, it might be reasonable to assume that the United States was more concerned about authoritarian regimes than about democracies and that, as a result, FBIS paid less attention to gathering open-source intelligence in democracies. If this were the case, the less frequent claims in long-lasting democracies could simply reflect the lower likelihood that FBIS would pick up such claims in the first place.

To be sure, FBIS does not pay equal attention to all states. For example, the mean annual number of articles per state per year in FBIS between 1945 and

1996 is about 664, but the Soviet Union is an extreme outlier, with an average of 9,372 annual articles. Once this outlier is excluded, however, there is nearly no difference in the average number of annual FBIS articles between democracies and nondemocracies ($t = -0.0760$, $df = 6223$, $p = 0.9394$). As a result, we can be relatively confident that the less-frequent nationalist claims in long-lasting democracies is not a product of a systematic bias against democracies in FBIS. Excluding Soviet cases from the analysis also does not substantively change the main results.[80]

A related concern is the possibility that the findings are an artifact of the US's interests in Europe during the Cold War. Indeed, FBIS is characterized by a significant European bias—containing almost 30 percent more articles per year in Europe than in the rest of the world ($t = -8.3487$, $df = 6252$, $p = 0.0000$). The finding in figure 5.1 that the application of homeland territoriality is more common in Europe than in other regions could thus conceivably be an artifact of the overrepresentation of Europe in FBIS. However, the results are broadly consistent even after controlling for the region of the new border or excluding all European borders from the analysis.[81] The impact of long-lived democracies is unlikely, therefore, to be simply a European phenomenon.

A further potential concern revolves around the possibility that the findings are driven by the definition of the universe of truncated homelands. While the use of homeland discourse to identify cases in which homeland territory was lost is consistent with the theoretical understanding of homelands as a nationalist form of territoriality, it does have drawbacks. The temporal limitation of the data tracing this discourse means that cases in which homeland territory was lost before 1945 but in which homeland territoriality was not applied in the post-1945 period would be inappropriately excluded from the analysis because they would falsely appear as if they had not lost homeland territory. This could lead to the systematic undercounting of instances where homeland territoriality was withdrawn from lost lands. The lack of a discourse-based measure prior to 1945 also raises concerns about endogeneity, since it could be the drawing of the border that leads to the presence of homeland discourse in the first place.

To address potential concerns arising from the definition of the universe of cases, the analysis was repeated using two different ways of delimiting the universe of truncated homeland territory. The first defines the universe of truncated homelands on the basis of the presence of coethnics on both sides of the border according to ethnographic maps compiled *before* the border was drawn.[82] While subject to all the conceptual difficulties of using coethnicity as the proxy for the location of homelands noted above, this way of delimiting the universe of cases does have the advantage of being plausibly exogenous to the drawing of the border, if not to the nationalist enterprise in its entirety. A second way of delimiting the universe of truncated homelands simply includes all new post-1945 borders. The finding that the main results hold regardless of how the universe of cases is defined (see table A.5 in the appendix) increases our confidence that they are not a product of the definition of the universe of truncated homelands.

It is also possible that democracies reduce the likelihood of applying homeland territoriality over time through pathways other than providing conditions that facilitate the operation of an evolutionary dynamic. For instance, it may be that populations of democracies are less likely to want to go to war. Expecting the return of lost territory to require conflict, they may prefer to give it up rather than fight. This effect would be expected to be strongest when democracies lose homeland territory to other democracies since this is where the democratic peace theory is most likely to hold.[83] However, controlling for the presence of democratic dyads does not meaningfully shape the main results.[84]

A fourth alternative interpretation could hold that it is not the operation of evolutionary dynamics enabled by democratic longevity, but democratic longevity interacting with some other factor that reduces the risk of claiming lost homeland territory. For example, the presence of coethnics on the other side of the border could have different effects in younger versus older democracies, or coethnics on the other side of the border could play a role in shaping domestic politics differently in younger democracies than in older ones. Likewise, it is possible that powerful mature democracies behave differently than young weak ones. It may be, for example, that politicians in states that are stronger than their neighbors would be more likely to articulate claims to lost homeland territory and that the opportunity to do so increases the longer a state is democratic. Alternatively, politicians in relatively weaker states may articulate claims to territory to distract their domestic constituency from their weakness.

Indeed, there is evidence consistent with an interaction between the presence of coethnics on the other side of the border and regime age as well as between regime age and relative capability. Applications of homeland territoriality to lost land are much more likely in democracies that have coethnics on the other side of the border. Stronger states are also less likely to apply homeland territoriality to lost lands the older the regime is. In any case, controlling for these additional interactions does not substantively affect the impact of the interaction of democracy and regime age.[85]

A final set of potential alternative explanations focuses on the possibility of reverse causality. Scholars have previously concluded that irredentist states tend to be authoritarian because the irredentist issue is used by those in power "to prevent competitive politics and changes in the existing power structure."[86] In a compelling alternative, Doug Gibler argued that territorial disputes create fundamental insecurities for a state's population, and that these insecurities facilitate the centralization of power that is inimical to democracy.[87] From this perspective, it could be the resolution of these disputes and the subsequent elision of homeland claims that alleviate these insecurities and therefore lead to both democracy and democratic longevity.

While an observational study such as this one cannot completely discount the possibility of endogeneity arising from reverse causality, this was clearly not the case in the West German and Italian experience, whose democracy was well rooted long before the territorial question was resolved. In the cross-national, statistical, setting the possibility that nationalist claims either help authoritarian regimes survive or destabilize democratic regimes can be evaluated by incorporating the applications of homeland territoriality into Gibler's model. Both the application of homeland territoriality to lost lands and being a target of such claims plausibly indicate the persistence of unresolved territorial disputes. If these undermine or inhibit democracy, we would expect them to be negatively correlated with democracy. However, this is not the case. Applying homeland territoriality across the border is positively and significantly associated with joint democracy; being the target of homeland claims is also positively, though not significantly, correlated with joint democracy.[88] This finding is inconsistent with the argument that either the presence of claims or being their target destabilizes democratic regimes.

This chapter investigated the empirically observable implications of understanding homelands as a nationalist form of territoriality in a broad, cross-national, perspective. To do so, it presented a measure of the application of homeland territoriality to lost lands which can vary across space and time and that is consistent with its integration into large-N cross-national analysis.

Investigating the correlates of the withdrawal of homeland territoriality from lost lands in a cross-national setting reinforces a number of the arguments made in chapter 1. First, it shows that the case-based findings that domestic political contestation played a significant role in the withdrawal of homeland territoriality from lost lands are broadly generalizable. Conditions likely to trigger evolutionary dynamics (long-lived democracies) are strongly and consistently associated with withdrawing homeland territoriality from lost parts of the homeland, even after controlling for the impact of other factors that also shape the application of homeland territoriality.

Second, the findings provide substantial support to constructivist theories that posit the possibility of change in the meaning of nationalism. Even if actors act as if disputed territory is indivisible in the short term, homeland territoriality can be withdrawn from lost lands. Such change, however, is not monotonic. That is, while homeland territoriality can be withdrawn from lost lands, it can also be reapplied at later times. The findings also bolster the argument that we should treat homelands as a variable rather than a constant. The data deployed in this chapter provide a way of doing so. The chapter thus contributes to synthesizing constructivist understandings of nationalism and the homeland with positivist cross-national investigations of political phenomena and reducing the gap between the theoretical factors understood to shape international conflict and the data used to investigate these phenomena. Chapter 6 takes the next step and integrates homelands as a variable into an investigation of the causes of international conflict and its resolution.

6

LOSING HOMELANDS AND CONFLICT

This chapter continues the cross-national investigation of the implications of the book's theory by evaluating the impact of homeland territoriality on international conflict.[1] Consistent with the argument that discursive definitions of the homeland are meaningful, it demonstrates empirically that losing territory defined as part of the homeland is strongly associated with subsequent international conflict. This relationship holds even after accounting for the other factors that could drive conflict or the application of homeland territoriality to lands. The effect also holds, though more weakly, in the opposite direction. Withdrawing homeland territoriality from lost lands is associated with a lower likelihood of some forms of international conflict.

It might appear obvious that losing homeland territory would lead to conflict. The idea that conflict over homelands is difficult to resolve is certainly not new. More than seventy years ago, Isaiah Bowman argued that the resolution of territorial conflicts often depended on the absence of rival homeland claims.[2] This was also the logic that drove Anthony Eden, the former foreign secretary of the United Kingdom, to object to Germany's partition after World War II.[3] It is nonetheless important to demonstrate this empirically because a significant scholarship continues to minimize the independent role of homelands and homeland territoriality in studies of international conflict.[4] Even some work on the question "What makes territory important?" excluded nationalist attachment to homelands as a potential answer.[5] When they are considered, the possibility that nationalist claims of the homeland could drive territorial conflict is sometimes dismissed as a constant that cannot explain variation in the existence, onset, or severity of conflict.[6]

The omission of ideationally based nationalist attachment to the homeland as a relevant factor also characterizes the logic of many considerations of territorial partition which assume that nationalist conflict is driven fundamentally by the security concerns created by ethnic intermingling.[7] While these arguments acknowledge the importance of a territory's demographic and strategic characteristics, they tend to downplay the importance of nationalists' attachment to homelands. They consider territory to be fungible; any place will do for the location of the national state as long as it has relatively defensible borders and is reasonably ethnically homogeneous. From their perspective, it is not at all obvious that dividing homelands would lead to conflict.

Some studies of conflict do recognize the importance of the ideological value of territory, but are unable to demonstrate the independent impact of the designation of territory as part of the homeland on conflict because of concerns about case selection or about the way homeland territory is operationalized. As discussed in some detail in chapter 5, much of the cross-national scholarship that does pay attention to the impact of homelands uses proxies for the homeland that are either theoretically inconsistent, difficult to systematically apply, or not allowed to vary over time. Other studies have not maximized their analytical leverage on this issue because they restricted their universe of cases to those where conflict takes place.[8] As a result, while these approaches can account for the variation in the level of conflict over territory, they have not addressed the question of why some territory becomes contested at all or whether it was territory that led to the presence of conflict in the first place.

This chapter (re)introduces nationalists' ideational attachment to the homeland into large-N, statistical investigations of international conflict. The measure of the homeland status of lost territory outlined in the previous chapter enables a sincere test of the constructivist expectation that losing homeland territory would lead to more conflict than losing nonhomeland territory. Doing so shows that both the application of homeland territoriality and its withdrawal shape international conflict.

Homelands and Conflict

As I argued in chapter 1, it is difficult to overstate the value of the homeland for nationalists. The homeland's role in constituting the nation itself means that the homeland functions as a sacred value for nationalists. As a result, control of the homeland becomes the sine qua non of national existence. This binding of nation and territory limited the territorial horse-trading that had been the norm until the emergence of nationalism, and transformed the absence of sovereignty over homeland territory into something worth dying for.[9] This attachment is so great that nationalists' willingness to sacrifice for the homeland is sometimes seen as irrational.[10] The loss of homeland territory is, in the words of the former German chancellor Ludwig Erhard, "an unbearable" reality that will be inevitably overturned by a nation's "fundamental" and much stronger urge to recover their homeland territory.[11]

The value nationalists bestow on the homeland has a number of key implications for the role it plays in conflict. First, it implies that reducing nationalist conflicts over homelands to the security concerns arising from ethnic intermingling or attributing territory's role in conflict to its economic utility, strategic location, reputational implications, or demographic characteristics tells only part of the story. Security concerns, for example, can, at least theoretically, be resolved by separating populations and giving each of them any piece of territory. For nationalists, however, homelands are not fungible. As Salah Khalaf (Abu Iyad), one of the founders of the Palestinian Fatah, declared, "The Palestinian . . . can never accept any substitute for Palestine."[12] Nationalists, in other words, seek control of their homeland and are unlikely to accept just any substitute.

Second, the independent value of the homeland means that the delimitation of such hallowed ground is an inevitable part of the nationalist enterprise and may occur independently of prior conflict over that territory. This suggests that the view of the indivisibility of territory as arising from framing processes which occur during conflict, while surely correct, is incomplete.[13] The causal arrow could also point in the other direction. That is, territorial conflict could itself be a product of the ideational designation of an otherwise divisible parcel of land as the homeland. Importantly, this possibility does not require assuming there is anything inherent in the land qua land that is related to conflict—only that lacking national sovereignty over territory ideationally designated as the homeland may make conflict more likely.

The premium nationalism places on controlling a specific territory makes homelands much more salient for international conflict than "the places we are from" because nationalism contains an imperative to maintain sovereignty over that territory which is missing from the latter.[14] As I argued in chapter 1, until nationalism emerged, the places we are from were better thought of in terms of cultural regions rather than homelands per se. Cultural regions are areas with some degree of cultural homogeneity that may evoke strong feelings, but do not necessarily contain an imperative for the group to be sovereign over that space.[15] Thus, a group could be physically separated from its cultural region without being spurred to regain it. This helps explain why the pining of exiles for the places they were from in the eras preceding the rise of nationalism did not usually lead either to attempts to reassert their sovereignty over those places or to significant international conflict. Jews, for example, sought to (and did) return to the land of Israel after the dispersion of the Jewish population by the Romans (132–136 CE) both individually and collectively, but they did not seek sovereignty over it until the emergence of Zionism in the nineteenth century.

The absence of homeland territoriality also helps explain why, until the rise of nationalism, territory could be swapped among states without much trouble. As Lars-Erik Cederman noted, the mere presence of group-based grievances (in this case, about the loss of territory) did not automatically trigger mobilization, let alone violent conflict.[16] Sovereignty over cultural regions can change without triggering conflict. The emergence of nationalism, however, transformed the loss of sovereignty over a particular territory, if it had been designated as part of the homeland, into a grievance worth mobilizing around. The nationalist transformation of land into homeland makes its rule by a foreign power problematic not just because it limits locals' ability to use the land and its resources (which had long been a sufficient reason for conflict), but because it prevents the nation from achieving its full potential. Once the nationalist idea took root, the territorial transfers that characterized international politics in prior eras became insulting rather than routine and losing part of the homeland became a potentially sufficient reason for international conflict. Put another way, after the rise of nationalism, ideas about where the homeland is were added to the list of factors considered by actors when calculating the costs and benefits of territorial conflict.[17]

There are a number of non–mutually exclusive pathways through which the application of homeland territoriality to specific land could increase international conflict. Most directly, the existence of homeland territory outside a nation-state's current borders is likely to increase the domestic appeal of territorially revisionist forces because it provides a substantive issue for conflict. The loss of homeland territoriality also provides a unifying grievance that makes it easier for leaders to initiate international conflict as a way of diverting attention from domestic political challenges.[18] Alternatively, since populations that lost parts of their homeland are more likely to reject the legitimacy of the territorial status quo, they may be more likely to use force to change it if given the ability and opportunity to do so. Their irredentism, in turn, threatens the territorial integrity of their neighbors and intensifies the security dilemma in the region, making violent conflict even more likely.[19] Finally, the centrality of homelands in nationalist thinking also makes homelands a likely focal point for collective action. This means that the loss of homeland territory would lower the barrier to violent collective action by acting as a focal point which leads members of a nation to believe that others would act with them if they seek its return.[20]

These considerations imply that losing homeland territory would be systematically related to international conflict. Specifically, the understanding of homelands developed in this book yields two main hypotheses. First, since homelands have significant ideational value, and this value is endowed through the rhetorical application of homeland territoriality, territorial divisions that are discursively identified as dividing homelands should be systematically related to conflict relative to territorial divisions that are not so identified. Alternatively, if homeland claims play little role, conflict should be equally likely following the loss of homeland and of nonhomeland territory. Second, since homelands are not static, the withdrawal of homeland territoriality from lost lands should be associated with a lower likelihood of subsequent conflict. The remainder of this chapter provides evidence consistent with both propositions. Both the application of homeland territoriality to lost lands and its withdrawal shape the likelihood of international conflict.

Empirical Analysis

Testing the propositions that the application of homeland territoriality and its withdrawal shape conflict requires a comparison of the incidence of dyadic international conflict after losing land to which homeland territoriality is applied with the incidence of conflict after losing land to which homeland territoriality is not applied. As a result, in this section I examine the incidence of dyadic conflict across all new non-decolonization international borders drawn between 1945 and 1996. This universe of cases thus includes all cases in which homelands might have been truncated regardless of how the territorial division was carried out or the existence of prior conflict.[21]

The observations in this analysis are structured as annual directed dyads for each new border with the states on either side of the new border as "state A" in one observation and "state B" in another. Observations enter the data when the new international border is drawn or when states enter the international system, whichever is later. The observations end in 1996, when the data on the application of homeland territoriality to lost lands ends. I use directed dyads because the domestic understanding of whether a new international border truncates the homeland can differ between the members of the dyad.

The main dependent variable is whether a state engaged in international conflict with the state on the other side of a new border in a particular year. The dependent variable is operationalized in three ways, reflecting different levels of conflict: dyadic militarized interstate disputes (MIDs), violent dyadic MIDs, and dyadic wars. Dyadic conflicts are appropriate in this context because we are interested in whether or not states that sit across a new border are more likely to engage in conflict with each other, not if they are more likely to engage in conflict in general.[22] MIDs are disputes ranging in intensity from threats to use force to actual combat that falls short of the threshold for war. Violent MIDs are those disputes in which military force is actually used rather than just displayed or threatened. This variable captures international conflict that is severe enough to be characterized by actual violence, but which still falls short of the standard for war. Wars are operationalized as conflict involving sustained combat and organized armed forces resulting in a minimum of 1,000 battle-related deaths within a twelve-month period.[23]

The basic relationship between the application of homeland territoriality and conflict is illustrated in figure 6.1. It shows the results of a simple t-test (with 95 percent confidence intervals) comparing the average incidence of international conflict following the drawing of new international borders for cases in which homelands were truncated compared to cases in which the new border did not divide homeland territory. The results are consistent with the theoretical expectation that losing homeland territory is more likely to lead to international conflict than losing access to nonhomeland territory. Regardless of the level of international conflict (MID, violent MID, or war), international conflict is more common following the loss of lands to which territoriality is applied.

To more fully explore this relationship, I employ logistic regression including a number of variables that could explain this relationship along with robust standard errors clustered by the dyad.[24] The main independent variable is whether homeland territoriality was applied to the land newly located on the other side of the international border. The application of homeland territoriality to land left on the other side of the border is coded as in chapter 5.

The analysis also controls for the other main factors that scholars have identified as potential confounders.[25] Perhaps most prominently, since prior conflict is strongly associated with future conflict and because conflict can sanctify land, thereby leading to perceptions of the territory over which conflict took place as part of the homeland, the presence of prior conflict could theoretically account for any observed relationship between the application of homeland territoriality and conflict. To account for this possibility, the analysis controls for the impact of prior conflict (*Prior conflict*) using a binary variable for the existence of any dyadic conflict between the two states facing each other across a new border between 1816 and the year of the territorial division, inclusive.[26] The impact of any conflict after the drawing of the border is accounted for by the count of peace years (described below). Similarly, since the existence of a peace treaty has been found to significantly reduce the likelihood of future conflict, *Peace treaty* controls for the existence of any treaty between the states facing each other across a new border.[27]

Given the widespread assumption that borders which divide ethnic groups are more conflict prone than those that do not, the analysis also controls for the presence of coethnics on the other side of a new border.[28] As the previous chapter showed, the agitation for independence, autonomy, or collective minority rights by coethnics in the lost homeland territory is especially important for understanding the continued application of homeland territoriality to lost lands. As such, it may also be implicated in conflict by prodding the state that lost access to the territory to act in support of their coethnics.[29] As a result, the model controls for the existence in the state controlling the lost territory of a self-determination movement (*SDM*) representing an ethnic group that is in the state which lost access to that land.[30]

The desire for economically valuable territory could also trigger both the existence of homeland claims (as a cover for the desire for such territory) and conflict.[31] Territory is considered to be economically valuable (*Econ. valuable*) if it contains oil or gas reserves, water resources, diamonds, or ports in the territory in question or within 50 kilometers of the border. Like a territory's economic value, desire for strategically important territory could also lead to conflict and,

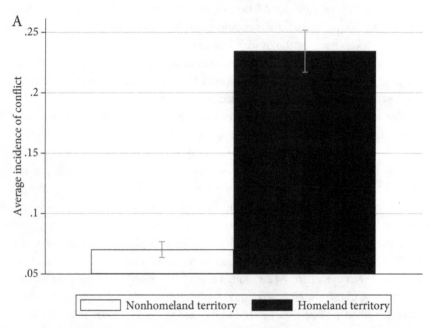

FIGURE 6.1 Probability of international conflict given loss of homeland and nonhomeland territory: (A) Dyadic MID; (B) Dyadic Violent MID; (C) Dyadic War

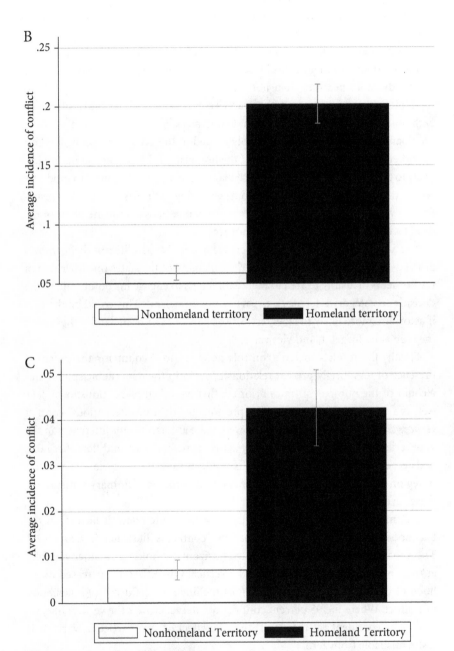

FIGURE 6.1 (Continued)

potentially, to its designation as part of the homeland. As in chapter 5, the strategic value of territory is proxied by the (log) distance of the new international border from the capital city of the states in question.

A large literature has also shown that regime type matters for conflict. The relatively robust finding of this literature is that, while democracies may not be inherently more peaceful than nondemocracies, democracies are less likely to fight one another.[32] As a result, the analysis controls for whether the dyads facing each other across the border are both democracies.[33]

Alliance ties might also be plausibly related to the categorization of land on the other side of the border as part of the homeland if homeland claims are less likely to be articulated against an ally. Alliances have also been found to modestly reduce the chances of a territorial dispute emerging in the first place.[34] As a result, the analysis controls for the presence of any alliance between the members of the dyad facing each other across a new border.[35]

The analysis also controls for the relative material capabilities of the members of the dyad because the relative material capability of the states on either side of the border is plausibly related to their willingness to engage in conflict and to the decision to categorize territory as part of the homeland. This could be the case if actors are more likely to label territory as part of their homeland if they think they can actually get it, and vice versa.[36]

Finally, the models include controls designed to account for the potential presence of temporally present relationships within the data (cubic splines and a count of the number of times prior conflict has taken place [not shown]), as well as a count of the time since the previous incident of international conflict (*Peace years*).[37] Since, as chapter 5 showed, there are significant differences in the application of homeland territoriality across borders drawn in different regions and decades, the models also include fixed effects for every possible combination of region and decade. Table A.2 in the appendix provides summary statistics for these variables.

The marginal impact of each of these theoretically relevant factors on the likelihood of different levels of international conflict is illustrated in figure 6.2.[38] The impact of each variable is illustrated horizontally, holding all other variables at their means. Dots to the right of the vertical line reflect an increased likelihood of conflict, while dots to the left of the line reflect a decreased likelihood of conflict. Where the 95 percent confidence interval crosses the vertical line, we cannot be confident (at that level) that the effect of that particular variable is distinguishable from zero.

Figure 6.2 shows that states which lost homeland territory are significantly more likely to engage in international conflict, including violence and even wars, with the state on the other side of that border than states implicated in territorial divisions which did not involve the loss of homeland territory, even after controlling for other causes of conflict. Substantively, contexts in which a new international border truncates homeland territory are about twice as likely to experience international conflict (including war!) than territorial divisions that do not divide homeland territory.

Figure 6.2 leads to a number of other conclusions as well. First, it reinforces the importance of prior conflict for predicting future conflict. Having experienced a prior conflict renders a state more than twice as likely to engage in dyadic militarized international disputes. Second, consistent with the research on democratic peace, joint democracy is significantly associated with less dyadic conflict. Importantly, the impact of applying homeland territoriality is robust to accounting for these factors.

Interestingly, the presence of coethnics on the other side of the border or their political mobilization for self-determination are not consistently related to the presence of international conflict and do not substantively affect the impact of losing homeland territory on conflict. This finding is consistent with prior research contending that having a majority of one ethnicity in one state and a minority in another is not systematically related to conflict onset and that ethnic homogeneity is not required for territorial partitions to resolve conflict.[39] This result implies that, while interstate conflict may often involve the presence of coethnics on the other side of the border, conflict does not necessarily follow from the presence of coethnics per se. Importantly, the finding that conflict after the drawing of a new border is not systematically related to the present-day presence of coethnics on the other side also reinforces the theoretical weight assigned to territory as a factor in constituting a nation's nationalism distinct from ethnicity in chapter 1. In other words, as I argued there, the violation of a nation's territorial aspirations is enough to trigger the "state-to-nation" incongruence identified by Benjamin Miller as critical for international conflict, regardless of whether coethnics are present on the other side of the border.[40]

Consistent with the intuition that the context in which the border was drawn could shape whether or not subsequent conflict occurs, dyadic international conflict tends to be more likely when borders were the result of war.[41] Controlling for the origin of the border does not, however, substantially influence the relationship between losing homeland territory and conflict, when conflict is defined as MID or Violent MID. The impact of applying homeland territoriality on the likelihood of war is in the expected direction, but no longer significant once the impact of the border origin is accounted for.[42]

To assess the impact of the withdrawal of homeland territoriality from lost lands on the likelihood of conflict, the binary indicator of whether homeland territoriality was applied to land across the border was replaced with a counter

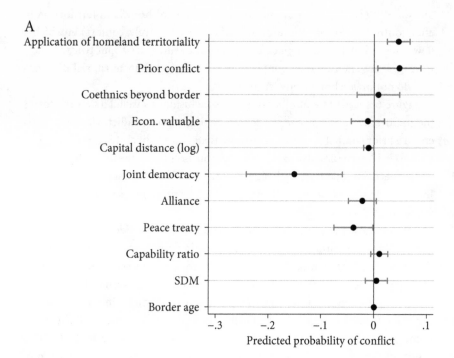

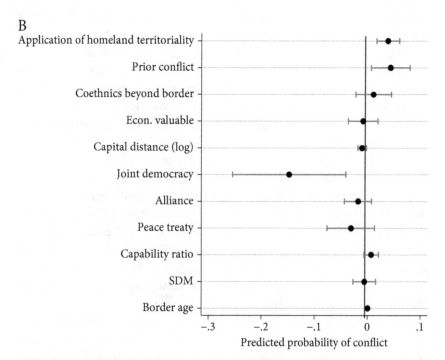

FIGURE 6.2 Marginal impact on the probability of international conflict (95% CI): (A) Dyadic MID; (B) Dyadic Violent MID; (C) Dyadic War

C

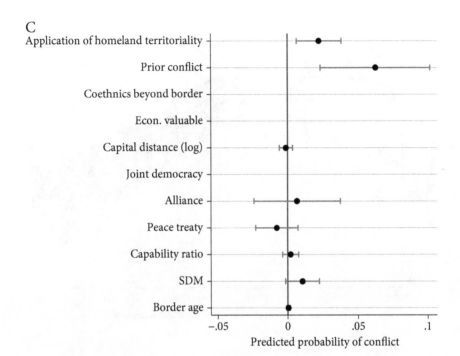

FIGURE 6.2   (Continued)

of the years since homeland territoriality had been applied (*Years since the application of homeland territoriality*). Where homeland territoriality is never applied to the lands on the other side of the border, this counter reflects the age of the border. Combining the implications of work that identifies the absence of debate as a marker of norm internalization with the understanding of homelands as a nationalist form of territoriality that must be continually flagged, allows us to interpret the time since the application of homeland territoriality to lost lands as reflecting a lower chance that the particular territory is still collectively understood as part of the homeland.[43] However, since it is likely that the relationship between the time since the last application of homeland territoriality and conflict is not linear—that is, that longer periods without claiming territory have more of an impact than shorter periods—the model includes the squared term as well.[44]

Figure 6.3 illustrates the predicted probability of international conflict, given the length of time since the application of homeland territoriality (holding all other variables at their means). Consistent with the theoretical expectations developed in chapter 1, it shows that withdrawing homeland territoriality is associated with a reduction in the likelihood of subsequent international conflict. The effect, however, is not linear. For MIDs, the effect is indeterminate for

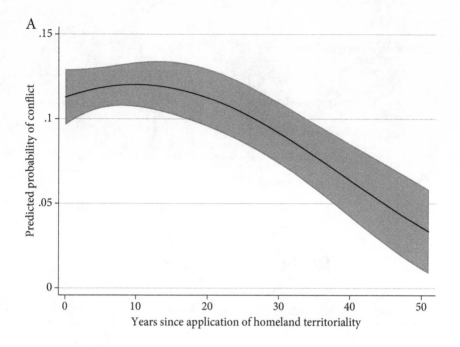

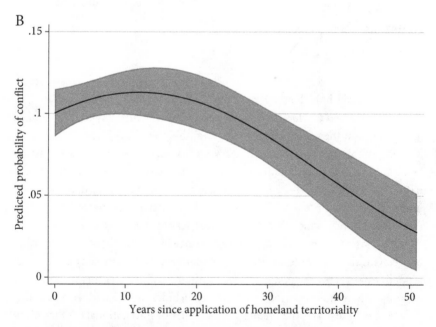

FIGURE 6.3 Effect of years since application of homeland territoriality on the predicted probability of international conflict (95% CI): (A) Dyadic MID; (B) Dyadic Violent MID; (C) Dyadic War

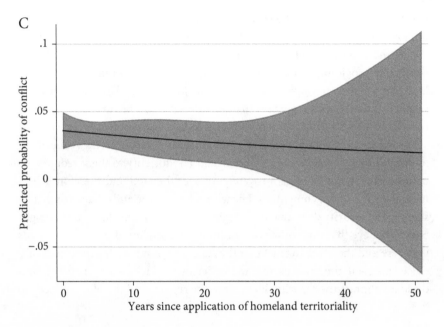

FIGURE 6.3 (Continued)

the first twenty-six years, while for violent MIDs the effect is indeterminate for twenty-nine years. After that length of time, however, neglecting to apply homeland territoriality for longer leads to a significant decline in the probability of conflict. For wars, the direction of the effect is consistent, but likely because wars are so infrequent, the result is not statistically significant. In fact, relaxing the very restrictive imposition of fixed effects for every combination of region and decade renders the impact of the time since the last application of homeland territoriality on war significant as well. This is also the case in many of the robustness tests. Nonetheless, I present the figures and results with the most restrictive set of modeling choices to maintain comparability with the analyses that use other conflict levels as the relevant outcome of interest. All told, while the results suggest that there could very well be a meaningful impact of the time since the last application of homeland territoriality on the probability of war, more caution is warranted in interpreting the results in this way.

Overall, the preceding analysis shows that both the application of homeland territoriality and its withdrawal shape international conflict. The application of homeland territoriality is associated with about a doubling of the likelihood of international conflict, including war, in a particular year. Consistent with the importance of the application of homeland territoriality, the more time that passes after homeland territoriality is applied to lost homeland territory, the lower the likelihood of conflict. This relationship, however, is not linear. Where the application of homeland territoriality increases the probability of conflict by providing a substantive issue for conflict, the withdrawal of homeland territoriality may take time to drain the loss of homeland territory of its salience. Robert Sack's argument that territoriality "can be turned on and off" notwithstanding, the attachment to homelands is not simply switched off.[45] If sustained for long enough, however, excluding lost lands from the scope of the homeland by neglecting to apply homeland territoriality to them reduces the nationalist imperative to gain sovereignty over the land and therefore eliminates the issue under contention. Likewise, where homelands shape conflict by shaping the security dilemma in the region, it may take time for a state's neighbors to believe that this withdrawal of homeland territoriality from lost lands is sincere and therefore to trust that the state does not have hostile intentions. Once sufficient time has passed, the belief in the lack of irredentist desires could ameliorate the security dilemma in the region, and therefore reduce the likelihood of conflict.

Alternative Explanations

This section addresses three types of potential challenges to interpreting the findings in this chapter as showing that homelands shape international conflict: potential problems arising from the measure used to detect the application of homeland territoriality to lost lands, potential endogeneity to either the drawing of new borders or conflict, and omitted variable bias.

There are two main potential issues that arise from the measure used to detect the application of homeland territoriality to lost lands that could undermine the results. The first of these stems from the built-in biases in FBIS. The second is derived from the possibility that the application of homeland territoriality reflects either cheap talk by political elites or contestation over the border rather than capturing the socially resonant definition of the homeland. Each of these will be addressed in turn.

As I discussed in chapter 5, although the FBIS-based measure of the application of homeland territoriality to land across new international borders enables systematic cross-national analysis, it does have some drawbacks. FBIS's overemphasis of European cases is especially concerning in this context because it raises the possibility that the association between the application of homeland territoriality and its withdrawal and conflict could simply reflect the decline of irredentism in Europe.[46]

FBIS's European bias, however, is not likely to be driving the results. To begin with, the main analysis includes region fixed effects, meaning that the results are driven by variation within regions rather than by any particular region. Going even further, and excluding all European states that lose territory does not substantively change the results of the impact of applying homeland territoriality on the likelihood of conflict. The results for the impact of the withdrawal of homeland territoriality are consistent but statistically weaker for violent MIDs, likely because the exclusion of European cases eliminates a third of the observations and therefore dramatically reduces the power of the analysis.[47]

FBIS's privileging of articulations by states and ruling parties and the significant role elites play in shaping nationalism raises the possibility that the application of homeland territoriality it captures simply reflects cheap talk used to mobilize domestic populations.[48] There are, however, a number of reasons, both theoretical and empirical, that help alleviate this concern.

First, the argument that applications of homeland territoriality are merely cheap talk depends on the assumption that the nationalist commitments of political leaders differ fundamentally from those of the populations they lead.[49] At the very least, this assumption has not been systematically verified, and there is mounting evidence that elites are not fundamentally different from general populations.[50] Second, even if politicians are less-committed nationalists than their followers, their application of homeland territoriality to lost lands as part of a mobilizational strategy must reflect the belief that doing so will resonate with their audience and, therefore, that the notion of the homeland exists for the audience in more than simply instrumental terms.[51] Third, even if they are deployed by politicians for purely instrumental reasons, homeland claims could still have significant real-world consequences. As Martha Finnemore and Kathryn Sikkink remind us, "mere" speech "can change people's minds about what goals are valuable and about the roles they play (or should play) in social life."[52] Such public speech fosters the sense that people see those territories as part of the homeland. The more individuals believe that everybody else believes these territories are part of the homeland, the less likely they are to challenge those notions even if they privately disagree.[53] Since the application of homeland territoriality to lost lands is a rhetorical act, the public designation of the lost lands as part of the homeland reinforces the continued homeland status of these lands regardless of any private belief.

The possibility that homeland rhetoric is cheap talk also has a number of observable implications that can be explored empirically. For instance, if the application of homeland territoriality to lost lands was merely cheap talk, we would expect that leaders would usually choose to do so given the opportunity. After all, from this perspective, applying homeland territoriality to land on the other side of the border carries potential benefits—in terms of mobilizing domestic support, undermining domestic opponents, improving one's bargaining position by demonstrating resolve, and so on—at little cost. Moreover, since this logic applies equally to the states on both sides of all new borders, we would expect reciprocal applications of homeland territoriality to also be the norm as both sides seek to take advantage of this useful tool.

Neither of these implications is supported by the patterns of application of homeland territoriality to land on the other side of new international borders. Although claims to land on the other side of the border as part of the homeland are common, they are far from universal. As figure 5.2 showed, there are many new borders in which homeland territoriality is never or rarely applied to land on the other side of the border. Even in years when states experience conflict and when, if homeland territoriality were cheap talk we would expect it to be deployed, homeland territoriality is applied only about one-third of the time. If the application of homeland territoriality were so cheap, we might have expected to see it applied much more frequently and consistently. The less-frequent application of homeland territoriality to lost lands implies that such articulations should not be dismissed as simply cheap talk either because they are sincere reflections of the socially resonant definition of the homeland, or because there is a meaningful price paid for claiming territory as part of the homeland. The latter could be the case, for instance, if there were audience costs to claiming territory as the homeland and not including it within the state. Either would render applications of homeland territoriality costly talk.

Reciprocal applications of homeland territoriality are also less common than we would expect to be the case if these rhetorical territorial claims were cheap talk. Of the non-decolonization dyads that experienced at least one new border, only fifteen (about 10 percent) are characterized by reciprocal claims, meaning that domestic actors in both states applied homeland territoriality to the land on the other side of the border. Restricting our examination to cases where we know that there are disputes about the border (as identified by Paul Huth and Todd Allee) and therefore actors face clear incentives to claim the territory on the other side of the border as homeland territory, it still takes place in only 35 percent of the cases.[54] On average, the empirically detectable application of homeland territoriality to land across the border is not consistent with it being cheap talk.

This is not to say that the application of homeland territoriality to land on the other side of the border is never instrumental. This is clearly sometimes the case. For example, the occasional claims by Morocco's Istiqlal Party to Bechar and Tindouf in Algeria are barely disguised reactions to the Algerian support for Western Sahara. Similarly, Idi Amin's sudden declaration that Uganda's "natural borders" extend all the way to the Kagera River clearly fits this category as well.

To ensure that such instrumental applications of homeland territoriality are not driving the results, the analysis was repeated excluding applications of homeland territoriality that are especially likely to be instrumental. Since applications of homeland territoriality to lost lands that are infrequent or appear for the first time long after the border is drawn are especially suspect, I recoded as not reflecting the application of homeland territoriality two kinds of claims: (1) instances in which homeland claims were made only in a single calendar year and never again; and (2) instances in which claims first appeared more than five years after the territorial division or the entry of the state in which these claims are articulated into the international system. This recoding treats these applications of homeland territoriality as not reflecting the homeland status of territory on the other side of the border. Not counting such potentially instrumental cases, or even excluding those cases entirely from the analysis, does not substantively affect the impact of either applying homeland territoriality to lost lands or withdrawing it.[55]

A final measurement concern is posed by the possibility that the application of homeland territoriality to land on the other side of the border functions as a measure of the contestation over a border rather than the homeland status of the lost territory per se. This could be the case because MIDs are much more likely between states that disagree about some aspect of where the border ought to be.[56] To check this possibility, the models were reestimated in a sample restricted to those states with new international borders that Huth and Allee identified as having a territorial dispute.[57] The substantive relationship between the application of homeland territoriality and international conflict remains the same.[58] This lessens the possibility that the effects of applying homeland territoriality on international conflict simply reflect disagreement about the location of the borders per se.

A second set of concerns stems from the possibility that the application of homeland territoriality to lost lands is endogenous to prior conflict or to the act of drawing a border. The shedding of blood in particular locations and the sacrifices expended to defend them (for whatever reason) could sanctify those locations, perhaps leading to their inclusion in the homeland and to the presence of homeland claims. It could also be the case that the act of territorial division itself could lead to the eruption of homeland claims—perhaps by making once-marginal claims salient or by undercutting dominant understandings of the homeland.

Observational statistical analysis such as that conducted in this chapter is limited in its ability to definitively disentangle such questions of endogeneity. However, the case studies in the first part of the book show that the application of homeland territory to lost lands can predate the drawing of the border or conflict over the lost territory. Indeed, the application of homeland territoriality to those lands was part of the nation-building project from its inception. The fact that the designation of a homeland through the application of homeland territoriality to land is a critical part of *every* nationalist enterprise but that not every nationalism is born out of international conflict also means that homeland territoriality is not necessarily endogenous to conflict. While conflict over territory could certainly lead to the emergence of nationalism in some cases, most theories of nationalism point to other factors—such as industrialization, domestic exclusion from power, or blocked economic mobility—as the main reasons nationalism emerges.[59] To the extent that these factors, and not international conflict, drove the emergence of nationalism, the application of homeland territoriality would necessarily predate international conflict and could not be caused by it.

One way of addressing concerns about endogeneity empirically is to repeat the analysis in a subset of cases in which the definition of the homeland is based on information that predates the drawing of the border. In these cases, therefore, the drawing of the border could not have caused the application of homeland territoriality. To do so, the analysis relies on the operationalization of homelands based on the presence of members of ruling ethnic groups on the other side of (what would later become) the border *before* the border was drawn. This measure of ethnic (rather than discursive) national homelands codes lost territory as part of the homeland if an ethnographic map, based on data compiled before the border was drawn, noted the presence of members of a ruling ethnic group on the other side of what would eventually become the border. I focused on the presence of ruling ethnic groups in this context because those are the groups most likely to be in a position to drive international conflict.[60] As noted above, such a measure is somewhat problematic because it is inconsistent with key aspects of the dominant theories of nationalism which lead us to expect that homelands matter. Nonetheless, because the identification of the homeland status of lost territory by this measure took place before the border was drawn and prior to any machinations of contemporary politicians, it cannot be caused by either thereby mitigating concerns about endogeneity.

Limiting the analysis only to this subset of cases in which the extent of homeland territory was plausibly defined before the drawing of the international border does not substantively change the results. The application of homeland territoriality to land on the other side of the border remains positively and significantly related to the incidence of international conflict. The impact of the withdrawal of homeland territoriality in this context is of a similar magnitude but, likely because it takes place in the context of about 30 percent fewer observations, is no longer statistically significant.[61] As a whole, even if the worry about endogeneity cannot be fully discounted, the subgroup analysis does reduce the concern that the impact of applying homeland territoriality on international conflict is endogenous to the drawing of the border.

Potential issues of the endogeneity of applying homeland territoriality to conflict can be addressed empirically by restricting the analysis to the sample of cases that never experienced conflict before the new border was drawn and in which, therefore, endogeneity to prior conflict is not a concern. Here, too, the results, at least for MIDs and violent MIDs, are not substantively affected.[62] These results provide suggestive, though not conclusive, evidence that the impact of the articulation of homeland territoriality and its withdrawal on conflict is not endogenous to the latter, at least when conflict is defined in terms of militarized disputes.

We might also be concerned that a particular subsample of cases is driving the results. Those most likely to do so are cases in which both sides of the dyad make reciprocal homeland claims to areas on the other side of the border. These are also cases that might be especially violent and may account for a disproportionate number of homeland claims. However, this subset of cases is not driving the results since the relationship between homeland status and international conflict remains substantively similar, at least for MIDs and violent MIDs, even when they are excluded.[63] The results are also robust to a more general exclusion of outliers, defined as covariates with a predicted dfbeta > 1 (not shown).

A final set of alternative explanations could point to potential omitted variables. One such possibility could build on the research showing that young regimes, especially democracies, are more likely to engage in conflict.[64] From this perspective, the negative relationship between the withdrawal of homeland territoriality and conflict could be a product of the maturing and institutionalization of regimes rather than of the withdrawal of homeland territoriality per se. However, controlling for the age of the regime in general, as well as for the regime age of democracies does not substantively affect the results.[65]

A final potential concern is posed by the fact that the bulk of the investigation covers the period of the Cold War. The Cold War era could be shaping the relationship between the withdrawal of homeland territoriality and conflict because it is conceivable that superpower influence could shape both the application of homeland territoriality to lost lands and, more directly, the existence of conflict.[66] This scenario is especially likely if the states facing each other across a new border are clients of opposing superpowers. In this context, conflict could have been rendered either more likely as proxy wars or less likely as the superpowers sought to avoid the spiraling of proxy contests into direct superpower confrontation. In either case, superpower influence could account for the outcome. Indeed, if the members of the dyad were clients of opposing superpowers, international conflict (at the level of MIDs and violent MIDs) was much less likely. The main results, however, are not substantively affected.[67]

States fight over territory for many reasons. A territory's economic value, its strategic location, the presence of groups with cultural or ethnic ties to those who might fight for it, the political behavior and influence of these kin groups, as well as the reputational and strategic concerns and regime type of the state in question, among other variables, have been found to contribute to conflict over land. This chapter adds to the list. It demonstrates that a territory's discursively maintained status as part of the homeland is also a reason for territorial conflict.

The view of homelands as a nationalist form of territoriality has two main implications for how homelands are likely to affect international conflict. First, the rhetorical designation of territory as part of the homeland endows it with great and disproportionate value. As a result, the loss of homeland territory ought to lead to more conflict than the loss of nonhomeland territory. Second, homeland territory can be withdrawn from lost lands. As a result, we would expect that the more time that passes after a territory is flagged as part of the homeland, the less that territory would be implicated in conflict. This chapter provides support for both of these observable implications of the theory. The rhetorical designation of some territory as part of the homeland renders its loss more likely to lead to international conflict than the loss of nonhomeland territory. Conversely, the more time that passes after a territory is designated as part of the homeland, the less likely states are to engage in militarized disputes and even violent conflict (though there is weaker support for its impact on wars).

These findings also reinforce the empirical traction of constructivist understandings of the homeland and the importance of integrating homelands and changes in their contours into studies of international conflict. Despite some skepticism of "discourse effects,"[68] the discursive definition of the homeland shapes international conflict. These results raise the possibility that the relationship between territory and conflict may be driven by a subset of territorial disputes—those that involve homelands—rather than by territory per se.

This relationship between intersubjectively defined homelands and conflict suggests that territorial divisions are more likely to successfully resolve conflict to the extent that both sides do not claim the same territory as their homeland (as may be the case in strictly ethnic rather than nationalist conflicts). While dividing territory in the context of nationalist struggles may be the best possible option in some cases, it is unlikely to bring peace on its own. The concluding chapter turns to applying the lessons from the foregoing analyses to the question of territorial partitions in greater depth.

CONCLUSION

This book brings homelands back into contemporary political science. Along the way, it makes three interrelated arguments. First, synthesizing scholarship from geography, comparative politics, and international relations, I argue that homelands should be understood as a nationalist form of territoriality. Territoriality is a strategy with which to assert control over space, and nationalist territoriality does so in the name of a particular nation and as part of its nationalist project. The application of homeland territoriality intimately links a people with the territory to which it is applied and delimits the geographical area in which a nation is to assert control of its political destiny. Designating territory as part of the homeland endows that territory with the power to constitute the nation itself and makes it an equal partner in the nationalist project. It is this designation of land as part of the homeland as much as any material characteristic that mobilizes nationalists to kill and die in its name. As a result, the ideational value of homeland territory should be included in studies of international conflict in general, and of territorial conflict in particular, alongside other factors commonly understood to shape conflict.

The value ascribed to homelands and the important role played by their loss was demonstrated in the German, Italian, and Palestinian cases. After World War II, Germany lost the Saar to France, East Prussia to Russia, and Pomerania and Silesia to Poland. The German rump was also divided into two different states. Italy, for its part, lost most of the Istrian Peninsula to Yugoslavia and faced the prospect of losing even more to the (eventually stillborn) Free Territory of

Trieste. In the Palestinian case, it was the absence of sovereignty over the homeland that drove their nationalist aspirations. In all of these cases, the absence of sovereignty over homeland territory fundamentally structured the axes around which politics revolved. While the case studies focused on accounting for the withdrawal of homeland territoriality from lost parts of the homeland, the different ways in which the loss of homeland and nonhomeland territory were dealt with was notable as well. In both the German and Italian cases, the loss of nonhomeland territory, such as their colonial holdings, was bemoaned as a marker of their reduced international status but was accommodated relatively easily. Unlike lost homeland territory, the recovery of nonhomeland territory did not serve as the primary political axis around which politics was organized; its recovery was not enshrined in their constitutions nor did it become the guiding principle of domestic political movements. Not all territory, in other words, is equal ground. There is something especially meaningful about land categorized as part of the homeland.

This distinction also shapes international politics. Chapter 6 demonstrated that the difference between homeland and nonhomeland territory helps explain why some territory becomes the focal point of international conflict. As it showed, the loss of territory discursively defined as part of the homeland is significantly more likely to lead to international conflict, even war, than the loss of nonhomeland territory. The implications of the findings in both the case studies and the cross-national comparison is that homelands matter and their value should not be dismissed as simply cheap talk.

Understanding homelands as a nationalist form of territoriality also implies that there may be meaningful domestic variation in whether particular territories are categorized as part of the homeland and in the legitimating logics with which homeland territoriality is applied. Homelands are ideational constructs. They are a product of the nationalist project and are called into being through the rhetorical application of homeland territoriality to particular parcels of land. Territoriality, moreover, is a technique used to assert control over space, not a reflection of natural geographical features. Homeland territoriality is no exception. The lines it draws on the globe are attempts to get us to understand our geographical world in ways consistent with the particular nationalist project deploying it.

As with any political project, multiple competing versions can coexist in a particular nation. These alternative projects are equally nationalist and their adherents equally committed even as they disagree about who should be part of the nation, what kind of society is just, and, as this book has demonstrated, where the boundaries of the homeland ought to be located, or the legitimating logic used to claim them. As the case studies showed, the domestic understandings of the homeland's extent and why some land is part of the homeland are not necessarily unitary.

While I have focused in the book on the role of this domestic variation in enabling the withdrawal of homeland territoriality through an evolutionary dynamic, such variation is also likely to shape the existence of conflict and its resolution. Domestic variation in the application of homeland territoriality to particular territories could be thought of as reflecting the assignment of different values to the same piece of land by different political movements, or as meaning that the belief that a parcel of territory is sacred because it is part of the homeland is not shared by everyone. Such variation would reasonably lead these political movements to arrive at different policy preferences (say, about continuing to fight after a partition). This was evident, for example, in the acceptance by the Likud of the Israeli withdrawal from the Sinai Peninsula in 1982 and the vocal opposition to the same step by the Religious Zionists. For the Religious Zionists, the withdrawal from the Sinai Peninsula was an amputation of part of the homeland. For the Likud, however, it was a strategic move that did not involve withdrawing from homeland territory.[1] Successful conflict resolution in cases characterized by domestic variation in the definition of the homeland could thus depend as much on who wins the domestic political battle between movements with different visions of the homeland as on broader security, demographic, and resource factors.

The second main argument of the book is that, the value of homeland territory notwithstanding, its geographic scope can change over time. Built into the understanding of homelands as a nationalist form of territoriality is the possibility that this territoriality can be withdrawn from land to which it was once applied. The very same foundation that grants homelands their power also renders them divisible.[2]

This foundational lesson emerges from the case studies and is validated by the cross-national analysis in chapter 5. In the German, Italian, and (to a less certain extent) Palestinian cases, the geographical area to which homeland territoriality was applied has changed over time. In the German case, homeland territoriality was eventually withdrawn from the lands east of the Oder-Neisse boundary. As a result, the absence of German sovereignty over areas that had been a cardinal part of the homeland only a short time before and that contributed to the outbreak of World War II became accepted as natural. In Italy, the loss of the territory that had spurred the country to jump into the First World War and which was so important that the desire to redeem it still shapes the very way we speak of territorially expansive projects, was eventually so noncontroversial that almost no one bothered to participate in the parliamentary session approving the formal renunciation of Italy's claim to the Istrian Peninsula. Even in the Palestinian context, where the main mechanism of the withdrawal of homeland territoriality faces an uphill battle, the dominant Palestinian political movement was in a clear process of reshaping the scope of the area of its desired national state until the second decade of the twenty-first century.

The experience in these particular cases carries a broader lesson for the integration of homelands into political science scholarship: the inclusion of particular territory in the geographical scope of the homeland is a variable, not a constant. We cannot assume that because land had once been categorized as part of the homeland it necessarily continues to be part of it. The dismissal of homelands as a constant that cannot explain variation in conflict is thus misplaced. The observed and consequential variation in the homeland status of territory over time also reinforces the drawbacks of using time-invariant proxies to identify the homeland status of territory. To address this drawback, chapter 5 developed a measure of the homeland status of lost lands which enables the integration of the basic idea that homelands matter into quantitative scholarship in international relations in a way that also captures its ability to vary over time. Using this measure of the homeland status of territory, I demonstrated that contractions in the scope of the homeland are a regular feature of our world and not an idiosyncratic feature of particular cases.

Developing such data helps bridge the nagging gap between constructivist theories of nationalism and quantitative empirical analyses of international relations. Much of the constructivist-inspired scholarship on nationalism rightly emphasizes the importance of ideas and meaning, but fails to address real questions about generalizability. Quantitative cross-national scholarship about territorial conflict usefully identifies general trends and average effects, but rarely integrates key constructivist insights about the importance of ideas, meaning, and change into either explanations of these trends or into the data used to identify them. The result has been a persistent gulf between the widely accepted theoretical understanding of nationalism and of why territory matters, and the data used to evaluate its impact cross-nationally. Reducing this gap contributes to synthesizing constructivist understandings of nationalism and the homeland with positivist cross-national investigations of political phenomena. In this way, this book joins the growing efforts to create data that enables systematic and cross-national tests of the empirically observable implications of constructivist theories.[3]

The third main argument made in the book is that these transformations in the shape of the homeland can be the product of the combined presence of variation, differential success in the domestic political struggle, and time. Mechanisms of change categorized as evolutionary dynamics expect change to occur whenever and wherever we find the combination of variation, differential success, and time. Homelands are no exception. In the German, Italian, and Palestinian contexts, homeland territoriality was withdrawn from lost lands when the, often initially implicit or even unintended idiosyncratic, withdrawal of homeland territoriality embedded in a more modest variant of the articulated map-image of the homeland or in a logic used to apply homeland territoriality to a particular parcel, were associated with domestic political success for long enough to become institutionalized. This politically embedded mechanism of change is better able to account for the empirical features of the withdrawal of homeland territoriality from lost lands in the case studies than alternative explanations based on updating to new information about reality, the passage of time, or leaders' instrumental considerations.

The role of evolutionary dynamics means that while the withdrawal of homeland territoriality from lost lands may be rational and intentional, it does not have to be. Sometimes, it can even take place against the wishes of the actors who promote particular variants of the homeland's map-image or logic of legitimation. In both the German and Italian cases, logics of legitimation initially pursued with the explicit intent of preserving the homeland status of lost lands eventually facilitated the withdrawal of homeland territoriality from them. Likewise, in all three cases, the political success of rhetorical variants introduced as solutions to local political problems locked the movements articulating them into accepting their far-reaching, and initially undesired, territorial implications. While expansionist movements may seek to temporarily narrow their territorial claims in order to gain short-term benefits and intend to expand their ideas about the homeland in the future, this second step can be harder than it seems.

Broader Implications

This constellation of arguments—that homelands are a nationalist form of territoriality and therefore both matter and can change, and that such change can be driven by an evolutionary dynamic rooted in domestic politics—has implications for a number of outstanding questions in international relations and comparative politics beyond the immediate concern with homelands per se. These include the apparently inconsistent impact of ethnic geography, the sources of democratic peace, how the end of conflict is conceptualized, and how we think about partition as a potential solution to nationalist conflicts.

The variation in the strategies of legitimation employed by different nationalist movements and its consequences helps explain why changes in ethnic geography sometimes reduce and sometimes increase claims to particular territories. While the deep dive into the actual cases tells a more nuanced story, in the aggregate the expulsion of coethnics in the German and Italian cases reinforced the eventual withdrawal of homeland territoriality from those lands. In other cases, however, ethnic cleansing seems to have had the opposite effect. For example, the Roman expulsion of the Jews from Judea and the Israeli expulsion of Palestinians from the area that became Israel in 1948 did little to diminish either the Jewish pining for the land of Israel or the Palestinian dream of establishing their state in place of Israel. Indeed, in both cases, the massive changes in the geographical distribution of coethnics became the basis for the continued claim to the territory.[4]

Both outcomes exist because, in the context of determining the homeland's scope, whether ethnicity is the foundation for the logic used to apply homeland territoriality to land matters as much as the reality of the geographical distribution of coethnics. Like all of us, nationalists see the world that their prior beliefs predispose them to see.[5] For this reason, as Ronald Krebs noted, realities, including of the actual geographic distribution of coethnics, do not speak for themselves. Rather, the lessons derived from new realities are filtered through political actors' interpretations—interpretations that are fundamentally shaped by their prior beliefs.[6] The filtering of reality through different logics of legitimation explains why the same reality can lead to different conclusions. For the Italian Christian Democrats and the German Social Democratic Party (SPD) after the 1960s, shared ethnicity was increasingly used to legitimate the application of homeland territoriality to lost lands. As a result, for them, ethnic geography mattered; homeland territoriality was more easily withdrawn from lands that were not densely populated by coethnics. For the German Christian Democratic Party (CDU) as well as for Fatah (and the early Zionists), ethnic logics of legitimation played a much smaller role relative to legal and historical logics for applying homeland territoriality. As a result, for them, the real geographic distribution of coethnics was less relevant. To understand the role that ethnic geography plays in contestation over the homeland, we thus need to look not just at the distribution of coethnics but at the way it interacts with how homeland territoriality is applied to land.

The role of evolutionary dynamics in driving the withdrawal of homeland territoriality from lost lands also offers another reason for the existence of democratic peace. A significant scholarship has identified a number of plausible reasons for the general findings that democracies are less likely to fight other democracies. These range from cultural explanations, to ideas about the restraining role of publics who have to pay and shed blood for conflict, to the argument that it is the lack of conflict that leads to democracy in the first place.[7]

The findings in this book suggest another way through which democratic peace may operate. Democracies may be less likely to fight because they are less

likely to apply homeland territoriality to lost lands as they age. Political movements in democracies can, and often do, disagree about a wide range of fundamental political questions. These include the appropriate role of religion in the
public realm, what language should be spoken in a multilingual society, what is
the rule for determining who can be fully part of the political community, and
the like. The positions movements hold on these and other nonterritorial issues
restrict the range of logics of legitimation that they can use to apply homeland
territoriality to lost lands. Thus, even if there were no initial variation in the map-
image of the homeland, over time, whichever logic of legitimation is associated
with domestic political success is likely to displace the alternatives. On average,
logics of legitimation used to apply homeland territoriality that correspond more
closely to actual reality are easier to sustain and are more likely to be associated with policy success. To the extent that policy success is politically beneficial,
movements articulating more modest claims are thus more likely to win over
time and homeland territoriality less likely to be applied to lost lands. Democracies, then, because they provide conditions conducive for the operation of an
evolutionary dynamic, are less likely to continue to claim lost homeland territory. In other words, despite the risk of outbidding in the short term, over time,
democracies are more likely to withdraw homeland territoriality from lost lands.
The resulting removal of one of the most refractory reasons for international
conflict may thus account for why democracies are less likely to fight.

The argument in this book also challenges the way scholarship on international relations conventionally thinks of the end of conflict. Studies of territorial
conflict often operationalize the end of conflict as either two or five years without
war recurrence. The assumption behind these benchmarks is that violence which
ends for a time and then restarts is probably caused by something unrelated to
the previous round of violence. While this may be a generally reasonable assumption, the high value nationalists place on their homelands makes it untenable in
conflicts that implicate homelands. The value of homelands can help explain
why, as John Vasquez and Brandon Valeriano noted, territorial disputes can fester
for decades without leading to violence, only to suddenly erupt into war.[8] While
this can be partially addressed by the selection of a longer time horizon—Paul
Hensel, for example, argued for the use of a benchmark of fifteen years without
war—the particular time frame chosen still reflects an arbitrary measure of absolute time rather than the expectations of a particular theory of conflict development and resolution.[9]

Just how challenging it can be to decide whether an episode of violence is
related to prior episodes is reflected in the ways studies of partition treat the
drawing of the border in Palestine and the conflict that followed. In this context,
the conventional benchmark of two or five years without war leads some scholars

to reach the curious conclusion that the division of the British Mandate of Palestine in 1949 ended the conflict over that territory because there was no war between 1949 and 1954.[10] A similar problem characterizes studies that identify this conflict has having ended with the 1993 Oslo Accords.[11] This decision would not only be contested by participants on either side, but the level of violence between Israelis and Palestinians (the measure of war recurrence and survival of peace that are their respective dependent variables) is, if anything, actually higher for much of the post-1994 period than before it.[12]

The difficulty of determining the end of a conflict is not a unique feature of the Israeli-Palestinian case. For example, scholars also disagree about whether the partition of Cyprus in 1974 ended conflict or not. Some identify the partition of Cyprus as a case in which partition ended conflict and reduced suffering, while others point to it as a paragon of failure, in which partition led to further conflict.[13] More broadly, as opponents of partition frequently point out, territorial division can replace intrastate conflict with interstate war (as in the case of India and Pakistan) and there is generally little basis for judging these to be unrelated.[14]

The findings in this book suggest that, at least when it comes to territorial conflict, the determination of the end of conflict is more appropriately pegged to the withdrawal of homeland territoriality from lost lands. Doing so builds on the recurring calls for including the resolution of the underlying issues of conflict into measures of when rivalries end.[15] This way of operationalizing the end of conflict is also consistent with Vasquez's identification of the acceptance of borders as the key for peace, Doug Gibler's emphasis on the importance of removing territorial issues between neighbors as a factor accounting for the emergence of democratic peace, and Markus Kornprobst's suggestion that we look at the end of a formal state claim to once-desired land as the end of irredentist projects.[16] The underlying logic is that, once the main political movements within a state no longer claim a particular territory as part of their homeland, the nationalist (and most refractory) dimension of the territorial conflict would be resolved. While this poses a high bar for identifying the end of a conflict, a change in the definition of the homeland offers a theoretically grounded measure of success rather than one linked to an arbitrary length of time.

Understanding Partitions from the Inside Out

Perhaps the more far-reaching implication of the constellations of arguments presented in this book is for how we understand territorial partitions and their potential use as a policy of conflict resolution. The use of partitions to resolve conflict is deeply contested. Supporters of implementing territorial partition present it as a necessary evil needed to achieve the separation of peoples which, they argue, is required to end conflict.[17] Opponents of partition argue that the ethnic cleansing required to achieve homogeneous populations and the likely replacement of intrastate violence with interstate war mean that partitions do little to ameliorate conflict.[18]

Many of the competing evaluations of the ability of partitions to resolve conflict attempt to adjudicate the question on an ad hoc, case-by-case, basis. This has had at least two unfortunate consequences. First, the focus on individual cases has led to inconsistent arguments and policy recommendations. For example, given the bitter legacy of ethnic violence in the former Yugoslavia, partition was proposed as the only reasonable way to resolve the conflict there. However, in other cases that by all accounts share a similar legacy of bitterness, like the Israeli-Palestinian conflict, an analogous partition is sometimes seen as impossible by the same observers.[19] Second, the focus on individual cases in the absence of a global overview may inadvertently underestimate the systemic security risks posed by partition. In this view, if partitions signal potential secessionist groups that they may be able to get an internationally recognized state if they fight long and hard enough, they may unintentionally provide those groups with an incentive to do so rather than work within the framework of the existing state. This could be a problem if it unleashed what one scholar called a "matrioshka process," in which, like the Russian nesting dolls, groups within groups continually emerged to demand their independent state after seeing one granted to others.[20]

Over the last two decades, an impressive scholarship has turned to systematically testing the relationship between partition and conflict.[21] Their emphasis on cross-national research represents a significant step forward in the inferences we can draw about partitions. This turn, however, has done little to resolve disagreements about what partitions are and the relationship between partitions, conflict, and its resolution. Reflecting the continued disagreement about what partitions are and what, if anything, distinguishes them from other related kinds of territorial divisions, especially secession and de-colonization, comparative studies of partition use different rules for what counts as a partition—different rules that result in the identification of anywhere between five and fifty-four partitions as having taken place between 1945 and 1996.[22] Perhaps unsurprisingly, this scholarship continues to be divided about the relationship between partition and conflict. Some conclude that, in certain circumstances, partitions can help ameliorate conflict.[23] Others, however, argue that partitions do little to resolve ethnic civil wars.[24]

Understanding homelands as a nationalist form of territoriality offers a theoretically grounded approach to resolving these disagreements. This perspective implies that partitions should be understood as the drawing of international borders that leave lands to which homeland territoriality had been applied outside the nation's control. Partitions, in other words, are best identified from the inside out.[25] The emphasis of the subjective sense of loss of parts of the homeland (usefully characterized by Brendan O'Leary as a "fresh cut") accounts for the ideational value of homeland territory.[26] Few observers would place the redrawing of the border between Argentina and Paraguay in the late 1980s in the same category as the drawing of a border in Mandatory Palestine. The intuition behind this judgment reflects the reality that not every new border is implicated in nationalist claims of homeland. As the nationalist slogans emblazoned on buildings across the Balkans declare in the name of all nationalists, "What belongs to others we don't want, what is ours we will never surrender."

While this definition of partition shares O'Leary's attention to the intersubjective element in determining whether a homeland was truncated, it goes further by applying the same nuance to the understanding of what makes a new border fresh. In other words, the freshness or novelty of a border cannot be determined independently of the way actors communally understand it. For instance, cutting through the Balkans along the old lines of the Ottoman vilayets or dividing the United States along the Mississippi River are likely to be perceived as partitions by nationalists in these contexts despite the fact that these lines would follow the contours of preexisting administrative boundaries and would, therefore, not be objectively novel. Conversely, the line dividing the Korean Peninsula is more than seventy years old but is still rejected by the governments of North and South Korea, as well as by significant segments of their populations. In other words, integrating homeland territoriality into the analysis of partitions means that there is no unit of time independent of the local understanding of the territorial division that can be used as a measure of novelty.

Focusing on the intersubjective belief that one's homeland has been truncated provides a theoretically grounded way to resolve the debate over whether secessions ought to count as partitions.[27] Some, for example, argue that secessions are not helpful for understanding "whether international intervention reduces or increases the cost of ethnic conflict" and that, therefore, such internally motivated territorial divisions should be excluded from analyses of partition.[28] Others reject the distinction between partitions and secessions because "the far-reaching implications of partition theory affect secessions and partitions equally" and because "who imposes partition is relatively unimportant: the critical factor is whether dividing warring groups into separate entities can prevent war recurrence."[29] While O'Leary distinguishes between partitions and secessions in his more recent work (2007), the taxonomy of ethnic conflict regulation he developed with John McGarry in 1993 had listed "partition and/or secession" as a single method for eliminating ethnic difference, suggesting that they are functionally equivalent.[30]

The definition of partition enabled by viewing homelands as nationalist territoriality—as the loss of land to which homeland territoriality had been applied—helps us move beyond this debate because it holds that the key is whether a nation loses control of land to which it applied homeland territoriality, not whether a group seeks to secede from an existing state or who draws the new border. Thus, a secessionist movement that gets all the territory it claims as its homeland does not experience a partition.[31] For example, to the extent that the Eritreans (or more specifically the Eritrean People's Liberation Front [EPLF]) received the entire area that they claimed as their homeland, they did not experience a partition when Eritrea gained its independence from Ethiopia. The rump states, and the movements in them, on the other hand, do experience a partition if they considered the newly lost territory to be part of their homeland.

In other words, the drawing of an international border may be a partition for those on one side of the new border, but not for those on the other. Indeed, as chapter 6 showed, about two-thirds of partitions (that is, of the divisions of territory to which domestic actors applied homeland territoriality) between 1945 and 1996 involved the perception that a homeland was truncated by only one side of the dyad. A useful analogy here is to a custody battle, where partition is analogous to losing custody of a child. In the event that one parent is awarded full custody, only one member of the conflict dyad experiences the loss of custody.

Allowing for the presence of domestic variation in the application of homeland territoriality means that there may also be domestic variation on this score as well. Remaining with the example of Ethiopia and Eritrea, the Derg who governed Ethiopia from 1974 to 1991, as well as the Amhara and monarchist rebel movements that fought against it, certainly included Eritrea in their conceptualization of the Ethiopian homeland (see figure 1.1). For them, the loss of Eritrea was a partition. However, as was noted in chapter 1, the same is not equally true of the Tigray People's Liberation Front (TPLF). This movement, which eventually defeated the Derg and governed Ethiopia during the period in which Eritrea seceded, did not claim that Eritrea was appropriately part of Ethiopia. In fact, the TPLF advocated for Eritrean *independence* and excluded Eritreans from the scope of the "Ethiopian problem" they sought to address. In 1985 the TPLF even honored the prospective liberation of Eritrea as a heroic, just, and valiant goal. They pledged "today, as in the past, [to] go as far as paying with the lives of [our] heroic fighters for the cause of the Eritrean struggle."[32] This was graphically illustrated in figure 1.2 by the exclusion of the area of Eritrea from the map-image of the homeland it sought to liberate. Since the TPLF did not see Eritrea as appropriately part of Ethiopia, it is difficult to justify identifying them as having lost homeland territory when Eritrea became independent; for them, the division between Ethiopia and Eritrea should not be understood as a partition.

This difference is more than semantic. The fine-grained identification and categorization of partitions matters for how we understand the causes of international conflict in cases of territorial division. Since neither of the movements that ruled Ethiopia and Eritrea in 1993 believed that they lost homeland territory as a result of the new international border drawn at that time, attributing the 1998 war between Eritrea and Ethiopia to nationalist territorial concerns would represent a type 1 error.

Using the loss of land to which homeland territoriality was applied to define partitions also helps address the conceptual problems posed by the territorial divisions between colonial powers and their former colonies. While most studies, including the cross-national work in this book, distinguish between homelands and colonial possessions and exclude cases of decolonization from their analyses of partition, the rule for making this decision is rarely clear. For example, all the recent cross-national studies of partition include the division of Ireland from the United Kingdom as a case of partition but exclude the division of Algeria from France, despite the fact that both can be usefully characterized as cases of state contraction and both Algeria and Ireland were once considered to be part of their respective metropoles.[33] The difficulty of distinguishing between partition and decolonization is a broader phenomenon. Would an Israeli withdrawal from the West Bank count as a partition or as a case of decolonization? What about an Indonesian withdrawal from Aceh? If we accept the Palestinian and Achenese nationalist perspective that these would be cases of decolonization, then such territorial divisions ought to be excluded from studies of partition. However, the use of the loss of land to which homeland territoriality had been applied as the defining feature of partition leads to the opposite categorization. Because, for many in Israel and Indonesia, drawing these borders would involve the loss of national control over homeland territory, such territorial divisions ought to count as partitions for them. The implosions of the Soviet Union and Yugoslavia raise similar questions. Should the new international borders drawn in the wake of their collapse be understood as partitions? If so, are they a single partition (of the collapsed state) or multiple partitions (leading to multiple new states)?

Emphasizing the loss of land to which homeland territoriality had been applied as the distinguishing marker of a partition provides a theoretically grounded rubric for answering these questions and for disentangling the differences between partition and decolonization. The imperial view of colonies as fungible is fundamentally different from the nationalist view of homelands as constitutive of the nation. This helps explain why it is appropriate to identify the split between the United Kingdom and Ireland as a case of partition, but not the split between the United Kingdom and India. When the border was drawn, many in Britain applied homeland territoriality to Ireland while India, however important, never rose to this status.[34] When it comes to the breakup of states (like the USSR and Yugoslavia), they are partitions for the movements that see their homeland truncated, but not for those who do not.

Viewing partitions from the inside out also helps analytically disentangle territorial divisions and their impact from related demographic changes.[35] Incorporating demographic change into considerations of partitions certainly captures something important. At a minimum, territorial borders have concrete implications for who can play the political game. More broadly, it is certainly appropriate to consider the demographic implications of partitions in considerations of their consequences.

However, making the identification of partition dependent on demographic change assumes that the real problem in these cases is the mixing of populations rather than anything about the territory itself. This is certainly a pervasive and consequential belief. It guided, for example, Churchill's support for "the total expulsion" of the Germans from the area awarded to Poland after World War II.[36] Following this logic, Chaim Kaufmann argued that restoring civil politics in multiethnic states shattered by war is nearly impossible because "intermingled population settlement patterns create real security dilemmas that intensify violence, motivate ethnic 'cleansing,' and prevent de-escalation unless the groups are separated." From this perspective, separating populations by a "well defined demographic front" that is defended by organized military forces removes "the strongest motive for attack . . . since there are few or no endangered co-ethnics behind enemy lines."[37]

Emphasizing ethnic intermingling as the real crux of the conflict, however, flattens nationalism into a one-dimensional ideology and overlooks the independent importance of the homeland to actors involved in nationalist conflicts. This can sometimes lead to unsustainable conclusions. For example, one prominent analysis concludes that, in the Irish case, "appeals to their membership to die for mere land would have been much less compelling than a call to rescue fellow Catholics from pillage and murder."[38] This assumption may be appropriate in some cases, but it is less plausible in cases where the conflict is a nationalist one. Since, for nationalists, the homeland is important in its own right, they may fight for it regardless of its demographic profile. Unlike *trans*national actors, like Al Qaeda or Doctors Without Borders, who are mobilized for a cause around the world, the attentions of nationalists are more focused. It is thus likely that Irish nationalists, unlike, say Catholic Charities, were mobilized in defense of Eire and not just for fellow Catholics elsewhere.

Viewing partitions from the inside out also allows an analysis of partitions to move beyond the common limitation of the universe of cases to the aftermath of civil wars.[39] Limiting the scope of investigation to those territorial divisions that take place in the context of civil wars (ethnic or otherwise) is certainly reasonable. The terrible cost and high visibility of ethnic civil wars make these cases precisely those in which we would care most about the ability of partition to end conflict.

However, this excludes many relevant cases since about half of all partitions have taken place in contexts in which there was no civil war. Limiting the universe of cases to civil wars also implicitly assumes that territory and attachment to it function differently in this context than in others. While this may be the case, viewing partitions from the inside out suggests that a more useful distinction is between borders that divide homelands and those that do not, regardless of the context in which the division takes place. Broadening the view to include partition after civil wars, interstate wars, as well as partitions that do not follow violence, allows the analysis to focus more solidly on the impact of dividing homelands and to explore empirically the potential impact of the context in which this division takes place.

The conceptual brush clearing enabled by integrating homeland territoriality into considerations of partitions enables the use of the findings from this book to evaluate the conditions under which partitions are likely to succeed in resolving conflict. Partitions are indeed, as some critics have argued, a "nationalist solution to a nationalist problem."[40] This same critique, however, points the way to understanding the conditions under which partitions may work to resolve conflict.

On the one hand, the results in chapter 6 support arguments, made by critics of partition, that partitions are likely to lead to more violence.[41] Partitions are strongly and consistently linked to more international conflict. While dividing territory may be the best possible option in some cases, it is unlikely to bring peace on its own. This, however, does not mean that partitions cannot contribute to conflict resolution. As chapter 6 also showed, albeit more tentatively, the withdrawal of homeland territoriality from lost homeland territory is associated with a reduction in the likelihood of international conflict. Taken together, these findings imply that partitions are likely to fail as long as actors continue to believe that parts of their homeland remain under others' sovereignty.

Partitions can (and sometimes do) work because homelands are not static. Partitions can succeed in resolving nationalist conflicts where beliefs about the homeland's extent change. While drawing a new border is usually not enough on its own, contexts in which evolutionary dynamics operate on homelands are more likely to experience such transformations. Partitions may therefore be more likely to contribute to peace where the society that lost access to part of its homeland is characterized by long-lasting domestic political contestation. To be successful, in other words, policy makers advocating partitions need to pay as much attention to creating or maintaining domestic political institutions that foster such contestation within the states on either side of the border as to where the particular line is drawn.

The role of domestic politics in general, and unguided change in particular, however, also means that the influence of external actors is more limited than is sometimes believed. Yet, even if their direct impact may be limited, external actors who are interested in conflict resolution can help foster democratic institutions that enable a vibrant and competitive domestic political environment. While this may provide space for extremist voices and those arguing for expansive territorial positions in the short term, over time, it is likely to contribute to their marginalization. External actors can also attempt to help the domestic political fortunes of political movements articulating more modest map-images of the homeland or legitimating logics more consistent with the peaceful resolution of the conflict. Such interventions, however, are quite risky. As Arjun Chowdhury and Ronald Krebs noted, moderates can be mobilized, but cannot be seen as having been mobilized lest they lose their legitimacy.[42]

This book has shown that homelands matter for domestic and international politics, that they can change, and that evolutionary dynamics can account for these transformations. Much more remains to be done to fully understand the ways in which homelands shape domestic and international politics. A need remains for the tracing of the particular ways in which homelands have changed in a wider variety of cases and at the level of the relevant political movement, and the development of even more nuanced data both about map-images of the homeland and the logics used to apply homeland territoriality to contested lands. As long as nationalism continues to be the primary organizing principle for societies around the globe, homelands will continue to play a starring role in politics and conflict worldwide. Our analyses of international politics will thus be richer and more accurate to the extent that we account both for the value of homelands and for their variation.

Appendix

This appendix contains supplementary material for chapters 5 and 6, including the additional tables referred to in the text.

The main survival model of the continued application of homeland territoriality to lost territory used in chapter 5 is formulated in elapsed time so that parameter estimates are interpreted as an estimate of the risk for the kth event since entry into the data (for right-censored failures only). The equation for the underlying model, based on Box-Steffensmeier, De Boef, and Joyce, is as follows:[1]

$$\lambda_{ik}(t) = \lambda_{0k}(t - t_0) e^{X_{ik}\beta + \omega I},$$

Where k denotes the event number, λ_{0k} is the baseline hazard rate and varies by event number, $(t - t_0)$ incorporates the elapsed time structure so that the hazard gives the risk for event k since entry into the data, X is a vector of independent variables (which may be time varying), and β gives the effect parameters. The remaining portion of the hazard incorporates random effects. Each subject i has a random effect that is shared across events (i.e., constant over time) and ω is a vector containing the unknown random effects or frailties. The data is structured to allow the implementation of the counting process approach of Andersen and Gill, which assumes that all failure types are indistinguishable. The risk set at time t for event k is thus all subjects under observation at time t.[2]

Cox models are especially appropriate where, as in this book, the data are both right and left censored. Since the FBIS-based observation of cases ends in 1996, any later application of homeland territoriality to lost lands would be missed. At the same time, because cases are observed for differing lengths of time, the interpretation of the absence of applications of homeland territoriality to lost lands in a case that is observed for five years should not be the same as in a case observed for fifty years. Cox models address both of these concerns.

Regular Cox models assume that failure times are independent. This assumption is unproblematic in most applications of Cox models in political science because these usually analyze the duration until a single event (e.g., the outbreak of disputes, the breakdown of treaties, the end of a leader's tenure, or the adoption of a particular policy) after which the analysis ends.[3] Chapter 5, however, explored an event (the application of homeland territoriality to lost lands) that can, and does, recur. Allowing for the presence of repeated events is critical.

Indeed, excluding the possibility of repeated events would obscure the finding in figure 5.3 that change is not monotonic.

Including repeated events, however, creates two sources of potential correlation between failure times that violate the underlying assumption that failure times are independent and therefore could produce biased results. The first is the potential presence of unobserved heterogeneity—meaning that there may be some unobserved factor (a shared 'frailty') that makes some cases more prone to fail (more likely to apply homeland territoriality to land across the border). This captures the real possibility that, for example, there may be fundamental differences between the India-Pakistan border and the United States–Canada border that make failures in the former more likely to occur. The second is the presence of event dependence caused by the fact that a second homeland claim depends on the prior existence of a first claim, and so on. Indeed, the different strata in the model display different cumulative hazard function curves (not shown), thus meeting the test for event dependence. Therefore, in order to account for within-subject correlation arising from both event dependence and heterogeneity, the analysis uses Cox conditional shared frailty models.[4]

To correct for the different baseline hazard rates for each stratum, the model includes dummy variables for the various strata (not shown). Specifically, the model includes controls for the second and third failures, and for all higher failure strata aggregated together. Above the fourth failure, all the strata experience failures less than 5 percent of the time. The results remain essentially the same if the cutoffs for individual strata are varied to all those above the third or all those above the fifth (not shown).

The remainder of the appendix describes the supplementary tables it includes. Tables A.1 and A.2 provide descriptive statistics for the variables used in chapters 5 and 6, respectively.

Table A.3 shows that chapter 5's main finding, that the conditions conducive for the operation of evolutionary dynamics are negatively associated with continuing to apply homeland territoriality to lost lands, is robust to a number of alternative ways of measuring the contemporary presence of coethnics on the other side of the border. These alternatives included measures based on the EPR Core dataset, the ethnicity measure developed by Alesina et al., and the "cultural similarity" measure based on the combination of ethnic, religious, and linguistic similarities between states developed by Gartzke and Gleditsch.[5] Column 1 shows the analysis using a strict application of the EPR-TEK data without the modifications discussed in chapter 5. Columns 2–3 use a modified and strict version of the coding of coethnics across the border as reflected in the EPR Core 2014 dataset. The strict version of the data (column 3) is

TABLE A.1 Summary statistics for chapter 5

VARIABLE	OBS.	MEAN	STD. DEV.	MIN.	MAX.
Democracy	911	0.346	0.476	0	1
Regime age	911	23.559	17.36	1	56
Democracy X regime age	911	5.685	11.655	0	56
Coethnics beyond border	911	0.953	0.212	0	1
Econ. valuable	911	0.953	0.212	0	1
Capital distance (log)	911	0.5709	1.392	0	9.17
Current conflict	911	0.361	0.481	0	1
Prior conflict	911	0.374	0.484	0	1
Peace Treaty	911	0.041	0.198	0	1
Capability ratio	911	0.516	0.324	0.001	0.998
Losing state Soviet client	911	0.049	0.217	0	1
Integration into global economy	911	3.205	0.997	1	4
New regime	911	1.92	0.394	0	1

TABLE A.2 Summary statistics for chapter 6

VARIABLE	OBS.	MEAN	STD. DEV.	MIN.	MAX.
Dyadic MID	8102	0.117	0.321	0	1
Dyadic violent MID	8102	0.099	0.299	0	1
Dyadic war	8102	0.017	0.13	0	1
Apply homeland territoriality to lost land	8102	0.1	0.3	0	1
Years since application of homeland territoriality	8102	15.509	12.84	0	51
Prior conflict	8102	0.365	0.482	0	1
Coethnics beyond border	8102	0.779	0.415	0	1
Economically valuable territory	8102	0.838	0.368	0	1
Distance to capital	8102	5.817	1.287	0	9.181
Joint democracy	8102	0.082	0.275	0	1
Alliance	8102	0.368	0.482	0	1
Capability ratio	8102	0.503	0.3	0.001	1
SDM	8102	0.217	0.412	0	1
Border age	8102	20.244	12.7	1	51

coded "1" if both states contain the same named group as per the EPR Core data. The modified version of the data (column 2) fills in cases missing from EPR Core as well as updating cases where groups shared a coethnicity despite being called different things in different countries.[6] Column 4 uses the coding of coethnicity developed by Alesina et al. Missing data for the presence of coethnics and cases in which the ethnic categories used in one state were incongruent with the categories used in the neighboring state (for example, ethnic groups in one state were coded by tribe while the ethnic groups in the other state were coded by broader racial or ethnic categories [e.g., "blacks" or "other Slavs"]) were filled in from census and reference data for the particular

TABLE A.3   Robustness to alternative ways of coding coethnics across the border

	(1)	(2)	(3)	(4)	(5)
	EPR TEK STRICT	EPR CORE BROAD	EPR CORE STRICT	COETHNICS (ALESINA ET AL.)	ANY CULTURAL LINK (GARTZKE AND GLEDITSCH)
Democracy X regime age	0.886***^	0.882***^	0.873***^	0.871***^	0.901***^
	(0.036)	(0.034)	(0.035)	(0.038)	(0.036)
Coethnics beyond border	3.327^	5.202***	3.150***	3.389***	0.566*^
	(2.446)	(1.915)	(0.868)	(0.868)	(0.179)
Components of interaction	YES	YES	YES	YES	YES
Control variables from main model	YES	YES	YES	YES	YES
Observations	885	911	907	911	903
Failures	832	854	851	854	847
θ	.996	1.14	1.09	1.08	.836
Log likelihood	−2528	−2661	−2639	−2659	−2632
Wald χ^2	255	249	246	239	236
Likelihood ratio χ^2 for θ	253***	295***	274***	303***	252***

Notes: Cox conditional shared frailty proportional hazards model. Exponentiated coefficients; standard errors in parentheses. Coefficients with a ^ symbol are corrected for nonproportional hazards. Strata dummies and their nonproportional hazard corrections are also included (not shown).

* $p < 0.10$, ** $p < 0.05$, *** $p < 0.01$

cases where possible. Column 5 codes coethnics as present across the border if Gartzke and Gleditsch noted a shared religion, language, or ethnicity between the neighboring states.[7] While the main results are robust across these different ways of coding for the contemporary presence of coethnics across the border, the relationship between this presence and the risk of applying homeland territoriality to lost lands is not.

Table A.4 shows that the findings presented in chapter 5 are robust to accounting for other factors besides relative capability that could also influence relative strength, including nuclear weapons and superpower-client status. Table A.5 shows that the results in chapter 5 are robust to alternative ways of identifying the universe of truncated homelands, based on various ways of defining ethnic homelands or all post–World War II borders. Table A.6 shows that proxies for the conditions that would, other than long-lived democracy, also yield substantively similar results.

Table A.7 presents a number of additional robustness tests for the analysis in chapter 5. Column 1 shows the results excluding all European cases. As noted in the text, the results are consistent, but perhaps due to the drop in the number of cases, appear as no longer statistically significant. Further analysis following Braumoeller and Brambor, Clark, and Golder, however, shows that the

TABLE A.4 Robustness to additional components of relative strength

	(1)	(2)	(3)	(4)	(5)	(6)	(7)
Democracy X regime age	0.885***^ (0.036)	0.854****^ (0.034)	0.881****^ (0.034)	0.869****^ (0.033)	0.882***^ (0.034)	0.870****^ (0.035)	0.889***^ (0.033)
Components of interaction	YES	YES	YES	YES	YES	YES	YES
Control variables from main model	YES	YES	YES	YES	YES	YES	YES
Losing state nuclear	1.724* (0.420)						
Gaining state nuclear		0.860^ (0.319)					
Both nuclear			2.384^ (1.407)				
Losing state US client				3.009***^ (1.283)			
Clients of same superpower					8.627****^ (5.576)		
Clients of opposing superpower						0.618* (0.128)	
Losing state occupied							0.560^ (0.355)
Observations	911	911	911	911	911	911	911
Failures	854	854	854	854	854	854	854
θ	1.16	1.19	1.08	1.25	1.3	1.25	1.06
Log likelihood	−2665	−2652	−2658	−2660	−2655	−2661	−2657
Wald $\chi 2$	242	257	257	251	249	248	259
Likelihood ratio $\chi 2$ for θ	300***	278***	283***	309***	282***	320***	289***

Notes: Exponentiated coefficients; standard errors in parentheses. Cox conditional shared frailty proportional hazards model. Coefficients with a ^ symbol are corrected for nonproportional hazards.

* p < 0.05, ** p < 0.01, *** p < 0.001

interaction is very likely still present.[8] A joint F-test of the interaction term and its component parts shows that it is very unlikely that there is no interaction effect of democracy and regime age (Wald $\chi 2$ of interaction & components = 37.05, $p < 0.0000$).

To investigate the possibility of an omitted interaction between the presence of coethnics on the other side of the border, democracy, and regime age, column 2 of table A.7 repeats the analysis, but only in a subsample in which all the cases contain coethnics on the other side of the border.[9] If the effect of the interaction of democracy and regime age was conditional on an additional

TABLE A.5 Robustness to alternative universes of cases

	(1)	(2)	(3)	(4)
	ETHNIC HOMELANDS	ETHNIC HOMELAND OF DOMINANT GROUPS	ETHNIC HOMELAND, STRICT EPR	ALL NEW BORDERS
Democracy X regime age	0.972**	0.882***^	0.874***^	0.863****^
	(0.010)	(0.035)	(0.035)	(0.034)
Components of interaction	YES	YES	YES	YES
Control variables from main model	YES	YES	YES	YES
Observations	1053	1005	1027	1322
Failures	805	791	804	859
θ	4.82	5.16	4.19	5.33
Log likelihood	−2635	−2535	−2606	−2877
Wald χ2	272	233	245	416
Likelihood ratio χ2 for θ	293***	271***	278***	297***

Notes: Exponentiated coefficients; standard errors in parentheses. Cox conditional shared frailty proportional hazards model. Coefficients with a ^ symbol are corrected for nonproportional hazards.

* p < 0.05, ** p < 0.01, *** p < 0.001

TABLE A.6 Alternative ways of identifying conditions producing evolutionary dynamics

	COMPETITIVE AND FACTIONAL POLITIES X REGIME AGE	MULTIPLE LEGISLATIVE PARTIES X REGIME AGE	MINIMALLY COMPETITIVE ELECTIONS X REGIME AGE	MULTIPLE LISTS X MINIMALLY COMPETITIVE ELECTIONS X REGIME AGE
Conditions for evolution	0.984***	0.912***^	0.947***^	0.943***^
	(0.006)	(0.02)	(0.020)	(0.021)
Components of interaction	YES	YES	YES	YES
Control variables from main model	YES	YES	YES	YES
Observations	886	858	907	825
Failures	831	803	851	770
θ	1.08	.983	1.25	1.26
Log likelihood	−2551	−2505	−2649	−2297
Wald χ2	189	192	237	255
Likelihood ratio χ2 for θ	336***	334***	327***	271***

Notes: Exponentiated coefficients; standard errors in parentheses. Cox conditional shared frailty proportional hazards model. Coefficients with a ^ symbol are corrected for nonproportional hazards.

* p < 0.05, ** p < 0.01, *** p < 0.001

TABLE A.7   Additional robustness tests for chapter 5

	(1)	(2)	(3)	(4)
	EXCLUDING EURO-PEAN CASES	ONLY CASES WITH COETHNICS ACROSS BORDER	CONTROLLING FOR INTERACTIONS WITH COETHNICITY	CONTROLLING FOR INTERACTIONS WITH RELATIVE CAPABILITY
Democracy X regime age	0.942 $^{\dagger\wedge}$ (0.057)	0.900*** $^{\wedge}$ (0.034)	0.872*** $^{\wedge}$ (0.039)	0.904*** $^{\wedge}$ (0.034)
Coethnics beyond border X democracy			138.8** $^{\wedge}$ (344.809)	
Coethnics beyond border X regime age			1.166*** (0.045)	
Capability ratio X democracy				2.560 $^{\wedge}$ (2.482)
Capability ratio X regime age				1.190*** (0.042)
Components of interactions	YES	YES	YES	YES
Control variables from main model	YES	YES	YES	YES
Observations	579	868	911	911
Failures	549	819	854	854
θ	1.24	1.02	1.13	.845
Log likelihood	−1375	−2466	−2648	−2635
Wald χ2	181	201	225	284
Likelihood ratio χ2 for θ	219***	295***	296***	209***

Notes: Exponentiated coefficients; standard errors in parentheses. Coefficients with a ^ symbol are corrected for nonproportional hazards. † A joint F-test of the interaction term and its components shows that it is very likely ($p < 0.0000$) that there is an interaction effect of democracy and regime age.

* $p < 0.10$, ** $p < 0.05$, *** $p < 0.01$

interaction with the presence of coethnics on the other side of the border, this effect should dissipate in the subsample analyses. As column 2 of table A.7 shows, the effect of the interaction of democracy and regime age holds even under this condition.

As an additional test of the possibility that the impact of the interaction of democracy and regime age is due to an omitted interaction with the presence of coethnics on the other side of the border, column 3 of table A.7 includes these interactions as controls. Although there is evidence consistent with an interaction between the presence of coethnics on the other side of the border and regime age, the interaction of regime age and democracy continues to have a significant and negative impact on the risk of claiming lost homeland territory even against this

TABLE A.8   Testing for reverse causality

	(1)	(2)
Capability ratio	−8.404***	−1.777***
	(0.154)	(0.238)
Allied	−.236***	−0.01844
	(0.084)	(0.106)
Peace years	0.1943***	.06255***
	(0.002)	(0.004)
Natural log of dyad duration	−.3016***	−.6846***
	(0.038)	(0.060)
Same colonial master	−1.237***	−1.692***
	(0.090)	(0.165)
Peaceful territorial transfer	.7662***	1.116***
	(0.096)	(0.149)
Violent territorial transfer	.4196***	1.225***
	(0.128)	(0.169)
Defense pact with all neighbors	.6753***	1.103***
	(0.117)	(0.168)
Intrastate war in either state	−.61***	−.5537***
	(0.104)	0.136
Highest neighbor militarization	−20.65***	−29.19***
	(3.214)	(4.472)
Either targeted in territorial MID	−.7745***	−.3681***
	(0.096)	(0.124)
Making homeland claim	.6318***	
	(0.177)	
Target of homeland claim		0.008857
		(0.335)
Constant	−.4778***	−0.2004
	(0.111)	(0.152)
Observations	9687	7338

Notes: Dependent variable is the observation of joint democracy in the dyad. Analyses include all contiguous dyads, 1945–1995, estimated using logistic regression with robust standard errors.

* p < 0.10, ** p < 0.05, *** p < 0.01

headwind. This suggests that, even if there are meaningful interactions between the presence of coethnics beyond the border, regime age, and regime type, they do not account for the observed relationship between regime age and democracy.

Column 4 of table A.7 explores the possible effect of an omitted interaction with relative capability. Here, too, there is evidence consistent with a significant interaction between regime age and relative capability. Although including this interaction in the model slightly attenuates the impact of the interaction of democracy and regime age, that effect nonetheless persists.

Table A.8 reproduces table 7.1 in Gibler (2012) in which the dependent variable is joint democracy.[10] This table adds, in column 1, the presence of the application of homeland territoriality to land across the border by a state in a particular year. Column 2 uses being the target of such a claim as the added measure of territorial

TABLE A.9   Losing homelands and conflict, full table

	MIDs		VIOLENT MIDs		WARs	
Apply homeland territoriality to lost land	2.103*** (.369)		2.021*** (.409)		3.039** (1.33)	
Years since application of homeland territoriality		1.025 (.019)		1.041* (.0233)		.984 (.076)
Years since application of homeland territoriality^2		.9991** (.000467)		.9986** (.000616)		1 (.00242)
Prior conflict	2.154** (.76)	1.9* (.662)	2.212** (.79)	1.883* (.686)	22.77*** (21.5)	24.82*** (24.1)
Coethnics beyond border	1.137 (.381)	1.215 (.393)	1.217 (.393)	1.294 (.407)	.	.
Economically valuable territory	.8237 (.212)	.8253 (.221)	.8456 (.224)	.8402 (.231)	.	.
Distance to capital	.8463** (.0697)	.8691* (.0693)	.8166** (.0645)	.8419** (.0657)	.9419 (.115)	.9507 (.104)
Joint democracy	.08655*** (.0644)	.09295*** (.0701)	.06343*** (.0642)	.07168*** (.0709)	.	.
Alliance	.7014* (.15)	.697* (.151)	.7128 (.173)	.711 (.173)	1.388 (1.09)	1.472 (1.12)
Peace treaty	.5358** (.161)	.4355*** (.119)	.5555 (.235)	.4706* (.185)	.6748 (.256)	.7881 (.416)
Capability ratio	1.182 (.16)	1.171 (.158)	1.14 (.15)	1.121 (.149)	1.106 (.164)	1.107 (.126)
SDM	1.086 (.188)	1.016 (.166)	.8968 (.183)	.8375 (.16)	1.679* (.496)	1.336 (.476)
Border age	1.004 (.00806)		1.006 (.00916)		1.017 (.0298)	
Time since last dyadic MID	.4599*** (.0358)	.4553*** (.0351)				
No. of prior MIDS	1.013 (.0226)	1.03 (.0213)				
Time since last dyadic violent MID			.4527*** (.0366)	.4504*** (.0354)		
No. of prior violent MIDS			1 (.0221)	1.016 (.0213)		
Time since last dyadic war					.3785*** (.0589)	.3853*** (.0641)
No. of prior wars					1.063 (.1)	1.145 (.101)
N	7984	7984	7969	7969	4186	4186

Notes: Exponentiated coefficients; robust standard errors clustered by dyad in parentheses. All models contain fixed effects for every pair of region and decade and cubic splines of time since conflict.

* p < 0.10, ** p < 0.05, *** p < 0.01

TABLE A.10 Losing homelands and conflict, robustness

	EFFECT OF APPLYING HOMELAND TERRITORIALITY ON MID			EFFECT OF APPLYING HOMELAND TERRITORIALITY ON VIOLENT MID			EFFECT OF APPLYING HOMELAND TERRITORIALITY ON WAR		
	EXPONEN-TIATED COEFFICIENT	SE	N	EXPONEN-TIATED COEFFICIENT	SE	N	EXPONEN-TIATED COEFFICIENT	SE	N
Robust SE clustered by border	2.103**	(.346)	7984	2.021***	(.384)	7969	3.039**	(1.35)	4186
Control for prior civil war	2.168***	(.37)	7984	2.066***	(.399)	7969	2.782**	(1.14)	4186
Control for prior territorial change	2.062***	(.364)	7984	1.968***	(.392)	7969	2.805**	(1.16)	4186
Control for prior violent territorial transfer	2.068***	(.34)	7984	1.957***	(.361)	7969	2.147**	(.832)	4186
Control for border origin war	1.645***	(.267)	7984	1.44*	(.271)	7969	1.7	(.721)	4186
Control for losing state nuclear	2.126***	(.371)	7984	2.065***	(.416)	7969	3.088**	(1.36)	4186
Control for gaining state nuclear	2.179***	(.383)	7984	2.071***	(.43)	7969	3.37***	(1.48)	4186
Control for both nuclear	2.101***	(.37)	7984	2.015***	(.41)	7969	2.978**	(1.35)	4186
Control for clients of same superpower	1.943***	(.334)	7984	1.872***	(.381)	7969	2.922**	(1.3)	4186
Control for clients of opposing superpowers	1.874***	(.314)	7984	1.759***	(.33)	7969	2.478**	(1.03)	4186
Excluding Europe	2.221***	(.553)	5365	2.239***	(.629)	5350	3.24**	(1.54)	2932
Control for instrumental cases	2.504***	(.423)	7984	2.43***	(.456)	7969	3.671***	(1.61)	4186
Excluding instrumental cases	2.734***	(.487)	6959	2.695***	(.525)	6925	5.208***	(2.66)	3467
Only in known territorial disputes	2.236***	(.373)	4006	2.024***	(.425)	3991	2.58**	(1.03)	2339
Only ethnic homelands	2.572***	(.475)	5784	2.467***	(.546)	5811	3.089**	(1.37)	2591
Only no prior conflict	2.849**	(.759)	4861	3.432***	(.884)	4861			
Excluding reciprocal claims	2.105***	(.345)	7360	2.018***	(.349)	7345	1.059	(.317)	3700
Control for regime age	2.104***	(.371)	7984	2.02***	(.41)	7969	2.966**	(1.31)	4186
Control for regime age of democracies	2.088***	(.372)	7984	2.009***	(.42)	7969	3.139**	(1.45)	4186

Notes: Other than in first row, robust standard errors clustered by dyad in parentheses. All models contain all control variables in the main analysis.

* $p < 0.10$, ** $p < 0.05$, *** $p < 0.01$

TABLE A.11 Withdrawing homeland territoriality and conflict, robustness

	EFFECT OF YEARS² OF WITHDRAWING HOMELAND TERRITORIALITY ON MID PROBABILITY			EFFECT OF YEARS² OF WITHDRAWING HOMELAND TERRITORIALITY ON VIOLENT MID PROBABILITY			EFFECT OF YEARS² OF WITHDRAWING HOMELAND TERRITORIALITY ON WAR PROBABILITY		
	EXPONENTIATED COEFFICIENT	SE	N	EXPONENTIATED COEFFICIENT	SE	N	EXPONENTIATED COEFFICIENT	SE	N
Robust SE clustered by border	.9991**	(.0005)	7984	.9986**	(.0006)	7969	1	(.00222)	4186
Control for prior civil war	.9989**	(.000468)	7984	.9985***	(.000594)	7969	.9992	(.00219)	4186
Control for prior territorial change	.9989**	(.000472)	7984	.9984***	(.000599)	7969	.9991	(.00218)	4186
Control for prior violent territorial transfer	.9989**	(.00218)	7984	.9985**	(.000601)	7969	.9988	(.0023)	4186
Control for border origin war	.9986***	(.000473)	7984	.998***	(.00063)	7969	.9982	(.0024)	4186
Control for losing state nuclear	.9991**	(.000467)	7984	.9986***	(.000617)	7969	1	(.00248)	4186
Control for gaining state nuclear	.9991*	(.000475)	7984	.9986**	(.000621)	7969	1	(.00256)	4186
Control for both nuclear	.999**	(.000467)	7984	.9986**	(.000619)	7969	.9986	(.00258)	4186
Control for clients of same superpower	.9989**	(.000444)	7984	.9985**	(.000592)	7969	.9998	(.0024)	4186
Control for clients of opposing superpowers	.9991**	(.000425)	7984	.9986**	(.000537)	7969	1	(.00214)	4186
Excluding Europe	.9987*	(.000702)	5365	.9988	(.000828)	5350	1	(.00246)	2932
Control for instrumental cases	.9991*	(.000481)	7984	.9986**	(.000562)	7969	.9998	(.00163)	4186
Excluding instrumental cases	.9992*	(.000485)	6959	.9988*	(.000645)	6925	.9987	(.0027)	3467
Only in known territorial disputes	1	(.00053)	4006	.9998	(.00067)	3991	1	(.00237)	2339
Only ethnic homelands	.9993	(.000627)	5784	.9988	(.00082)	5811	1	(.00238)	2591
Only no prior conflict	.9983*	(.000867)	4861	.9979*	(.00118)	4861			
Excluding reciprocal claims	.999**	(.000492)	7360	.9985**	(.000634)	7345	.9989	(.00242)	3700
Control for regime age	.9991**	(.000462)	7984	.9986**	(.000611)	7969	1	(.00245)	4186
Control for regime age of democracies	.999**	(.000451)	7984	.9986**	(.000603)	7969	1	(.00261)	4186

Notes: Other than in first row, robust standard errors clustered by dyad in parentheses. All models contain all control variables in the main analysis.

* p < 0.10, ** p < 0.05, *** p < 0.01

threat. If unresolved territorial conflicts—proxied by applying homeland territoriality to land across a border or being the target of such claims—undermined or inhibited democracy, we would expect them to be negatively correlated with democracy. However, this is not the case. Applying homeland territoriality across the border is positively and significantly associated with joint democracy; being the target of homeland claims is also positively, though not significantly, correlated with joint democracy.

Table A.9 reports the results of the logit regressions on which figures 6.2 and 6.3 are based. In the context of wars, the presence of coethnics on the other side of the border, democratic dyads, and economically valuable territory are dropped from the analysis because they are perfectly correlated with war. Tables A.10 and A.11 show the main results for each of the robustness tests and alternative explanations discussed in chapter 6.

Notes

INTRODUCTION

1. For some of the prominent work in this area, see Myron Weiner, "The Macedonian Syndrome: An Historical Model of International Relations and Political Development," *World Politics* 23, no. 4 (1971): 665–83; Naomi Chazan, ed., *Irredentism and International Politics*, Boulder, CO: Lynne Rienner, 1991; Gary Goertz and Paul F. Diehl, *Territorial Change and International Conflict*, New York: Routledge, 1992; Paul K. Huth, *Standing Your Ground: Territorial Disputes and International Conflict*, Ann Arbor: University of Michigan Press, 1996; John A. Vasquez, *The War Puzzle*, Cambridge: Cambridge University Press, 1993; Stephen M. Saideman and R. William Ayers, "Determining the Causes of Irredentism: Logit Analyses of Minorities at Risk Data from the 1980s and 1990s," *Journal of Politics* 62, no. 4 (2000): 1126–44; Paul D. Senese and John A. Vasquez, *The Steps to War: An Empirical Study*, Princeton, NJ: Princeton University Press, 2008; Thomas Ambrosio, *Irredentism: Ethnic Conflict and International Politics*, Westport, CT: Praeger, 2001; Paul R. Hensel, "Contentious Issues and World Politics: Territorial Claims in the Americas, 1816–1992," *International Studies Quarterly* 45, no. 1 (2001): 81–109; Halvard Buhaug and Scott Gates, "The Geography of Civil War," *Journal of Peace Research* 39, no. 4 (2002): 417–33; Paul K. Huth and Todd Allee, *The Democratic Peace and Territorial Conflict in the Twentieth Century*, Cambridge: Cambridge University Press, 2002; Douglas M. Gibler, *The Territorial Peace: Borders, State Development, and International Conflict*, Cambridge, Cambridge University Press, 2012; and David S. Siroky and Christopher W. Hale, "Inside Irredentism: A Global Empirical Analysis," *American Journal of Political Science* 61, no. 1 (2017): 117–28.

2. Ian S. Lustick, "Taking Evolution Seriously: Historical Institutionalism and Evolutionary Theory," *Polity* 43, no. 2 (2011): 179–209; Orion A. Lewis and Sven Steinmo, "How Institutions Evolve: Evolutionary Theory and Institutional Change," *Polity* 44, no. 3 (2012): 314–39; Daniel C. Dennett, *Darwin's Dangerous Idea: Evolution and the Meaning of Life*, New York: Simon and Schuster, 1995.

3. See, for example, Lars-Erik Cederman, *Emergent Actors in World Politics: How States and Nations Develop and Dissolve*, Princeton, NJ: Princeton University Press, 1997; and Susan Blackmore, *The Meme Machine*, Oxford: Oxford University Press, 2000.

4. Nadav G. Shelef, *Evolving Nationalism: Homeland, Religion, and National Identity in Israel, 1925–2005*, Ithaca, NY: Cornell University Press, 2010.

5. United States, War Department General Staff, Military Intelligence Division, "Feature Section: The Security Council and Trieste," *Intelligence Review* 59 (April 3, 1947): 17–24; United States, Central Intelligence Agency, "The Current Situation in the Free Territory of Trieste," ORE 23-48 (April 15, 1948); Feliks Gross, *Ethnics in a Borderland: An Inquiry into the Nature of Ethnicity and Reduction of Ethnic Tensions in a One-Time Genocide Area*, Westport, CT: Greenwood Press, 1978.

6. See Shelef, *Evolving Nationalism*.

7. Evan S. Lieberman, "Nested Analysis as a Mixed-Method Strategy for Comparative Research," *American Political Science Review* 99, no. 3 (2005): 435–52.

8. Harris Mylonas and Nadav G. Shelef, "Which Land Is Our Land?: Domestic Politics and Change in the Territorial Claims of Stateless Nationalist Movements," *Security Studies* 23, no. 4 (2014): 754–86.

1. UNDERSTANDING HOMELANDS

1. See, for example, Dominic D. P. Johnson and Monica Duffy Toft, "Grounds for War: The Evolution of Territorial Conflict," *International Security* 38, no. 3 (2014): 7–38.

2. Robert David Sack, *Human Territoriality: Its Theory and History*, Cambridge: Cambridge University Press, 1986, 19.

3. See also Sack, *Human Territoriality*, 2, 30–31; Jean Gottmann, *The Significance of Territory*, Charlottesville: University Press of Virginia, 1973; John A. Agnew, *Reinventing Geopolitics: Geographies of Modern Statehood*, Heidelberg: Department of Geography, University of Heidelberg, 2001; Richard L. Nostrand and Lawrence E. Estaville Jr., "Introduction: The Homeland Concept," *Journal of Cultural Geography* 13 (Spring/Summer 1993): 1–4; Anssi Paasi, *Territories, Boundaries, and Consciousness: The Changing Geographies of the Finnish-Russian Border*, New York: John Wiley and Sons, 1996; Thongchai Winichakul, *Siam Mapped: A History of the Geo-Body of a Nation*, Honolulu: University of Hawai'i Press, 1994.

4. Michael Biggs, "Putting the State on the Map: Cartography, Territory, and European State Formation," *Comparative Studies in Society and History* 41, no. 2 (1999): 374–405; Jordan Branch, *The Cartographic State: Maps, Territory, and the Origins of Sovereignty*, Cambridge: Cambridge University Press, 2013; Jeremy Black, *Maps and History: Constructing Images of the Past*, New Haven, CT: Yale University Press, 2000; Winichakul, *Siam Mapped*. See also the discussion of the impact of changing access to space in Jean Gottmann, "The Political Partitioning of Our World: An Attempt at Analysis," *World Politics* 4, no. 4 (1952): 512–19.

5. Seokwoo Lee, *Boundary and Territory Briefing: Territorial Disputes among Japan, China and Taiwan concerning the Senkaku Islands*, Durham: International Boundaries Research Unit, 2002; Krista Eileen Wiegand, *Enduring Territorial Disputes: Strategies of Bargaining, Coercive Diplomacy, and Settlement*, Athens: University of Georgia Press, 2011.

6. Gottmann, *Significance of Territory*; Andrew F. Burghardt, "Boundaries: Setting Limits to Political Areas," in *Concepts in Human Geography*, ed. Carville Earle, Kent Mathewson, and Martin S. Kenzer, Lanham, MD: Rowman and Littlefield, 1996, 213–30; Paasi, *Territories, Boundaries, and Consciousness*; Malcolm Anderson, *Frontiers: Territory and State Formation in the Modern World*, Cambridge: Polity Press, 1996; Shmuel Sandler, "Territoriality and Nation-State Formation: The Yishuv and the Making of the State of Israel," *Nations and Nationalism* 3, no. 4 (1997): 667–88; George W. White, *Nation, State, and Territory: Origins, Evolution, and Relationships*, Lanham, MD: Rowman and Littlefield, 2004; Guntram Henrik Herb, "Double Vision: Territorial Strategies in the Construction of National Identities in Germany, 1949–1979," *Annals of the Association of American Geographers* 94, no. 1 (2004): 140–64; Stuart Elden, *The Birth of Territory*, Chicago: University of Chicago Press, 2013; Linda S. Bishai, *Forgetting Ourselves: Secession and the (Im)possibility of Territorial Identity*, Lanham, MD: Lexington Books, 2004, 3–4.

7. For a complementary critique, see Paasi, *Territories, Boundaries, and Consciousness*, 51.

8. Hans Kohn, "The Nature of Nationalism," *American Political Science Review* 33, no. 6 (1939): 1001–21, 1002.

9. Ernest Gellner, *Nations and Nationalism*, Ithaca, NY: Cornell University Press, 1983, 1.

10. Benedict Anderson, *Imagined Communities: Reflections on the Origin and Spread of Nationalism*, New York: Verso, 1991, 6. See also John A. Agnew, "The Territorial Trap: The Geographical Assumptions of International Relations Theory," *Review of International*

Political Economy 1, no. 1. (1994): 53–80, 71; and Sandler, "Territoriality and Nation-State Formation." The importance of a geographical location holds for all kinds of sovereignty. Even international legal sovereignty, which does not always require a particular territory, is much easier to secure given control of such a territory. See Stephen D. Krasner, *Sovereignty: Organized Hypocrisy*, Princeton, NJ: Princeton University Press, 1999.

11. John A. Agnew, "No Borders, No Nations: Making Greece in Macedonia," *Annals of the Association of American Geographers* 97, no. 2 (2007): 398–422, 403. For similar conclusions, see also James Anderson, "Nationalist Ideology and Territory," in Johnston, Knight, and Kofman, *Nationalism, Self-Determination, and Political Geography*, 18–39; Peter J. Taylor, "The State as Container: Territoriality in the Modern World-System," *Progress in Human Geography* 18, no. 2 (1994): 151–62; Lowell W. Barrington, "'Nation' and 'Nationalism': The Misuse of Key Concepts in Political Science," *PS: Political Science and Politics* 30, no. 4 (1997): 712–16; Oren Yiftachel, "The Homeland and Nationalism," in *Encyclopedia of Nationalism*, ed. A. J. Motyl, London: Academic Press, 2001, 359–83; Jan Penrose, "Nations, States and Homelands: Territory and Territoriality in Nationalist Thought," *Nations and Nationalisms* 8, no. 3 (2002): 277–97; Paasi, *Territories, Boundaries, and Consciousness*, 51; and David Miller, "In Defence of Nationality," *Journal of Applied Philosophy* 10, no. 1 (1993): 3–16.

12. Michael P. Conzen, "Culture Regions, Homelands, and Ethnic Archipelagos in the United States: Methodological Considerations," *Journal of Cultural Geography* 13 (Spring/ Summer 1993): 13–29.

13. Gottmann, *Significance of Territory*, 48–49; Taylor, "State as Container," 155–56. See also Andrew F. Burghardt, "The Bases of Territorial Claims," *Geographical Review* 63, no. 2 (1973): 225–45; Alexander B. Murphy, "National Claims to Territory in the Modern State System," *Geopolitics* 7, no. 2 (2002): 193–241; Milton J. Esman, *Ethnic Politics*, Ithaca, NY: Cornell University Press, 1994, 6–7; Isaiah Bowman, "The Strategy of Territorial Decisions," *Foreign Affairs* 24, no. 2 (1946): 177–94, 177; D. Miller, "In Defence of Nationality"; and Ronald John Johnston, David B. Knight, and Eleonore Kofman, "Nationalism, Self-Determination, and the World Political Map: An Introduction," in Johnston, Knight, and Kofman, *Nationalism, Self-Determination and Political Geography*, 1–17.

14. Herb, "Double Vision," 156.

15. Rodney Bruce Hall, *National Collective Identity: Social Constructs and International Systems*, New York: Columbia University Press, 1999.

16. See, for example, Walker Connor, *Ethnonationalism: The Quest for Understanding*, Princeton, NJ: Princeton University Press, 1994; and Weiner, "Macedonian Syndrome," 677–78.

17. For examples of the use of this dichotomy, see Louis Dumont, *German Ideology: From France to Germany and Back*, Chicago: University of Chicago Press, 1994; Elie Kedourie, *Nationalism*, New York: Praeger, 1961; Anthony D. Smith, *Theories of Nationalism*, London: Duckworth, 1971; Rogers Brubaker, *Citizenship and Nationhood in France and Germany*, Cambridge: Cambridge University Press, 1992; and Michael Ignatieff, *Blood and Belonging: Journeys into the New Nationalism*, New York: Farrar, Straus and Giroux, 1993.

18. Connor, *Ethnonationalism*, 205, original emphasis.

19. B. Anderson, *Imagined Communities*, 175. See also Michael Billig, *Banal Nationalism*, London: Sage, 1995; Shelef, *Evolving Nationalism*; and M. Anderson, *Frontiers*, 3.

20. Quoted in Connor, *Ethnonationalism*, 205.

21. Quoted in Colin Legum, "Somali Liberation Songs," *Journal of Modern African Studies* 1, no. 4 (1963): 515.

22. Bowman, "Strategy of Territorial Decisions."

23. Quoted in Penrose, "Nations, States and Homelands," 286.

24. For other examples, see the Croatian national anthem, "Our Beautiful Home-land," and the entire genre of Somali liberation songs. Christopher Kelen and Aleksandar Pavković, "Of Love and National Borders: The Croatian Anthem 'Our Beautiful Home-land,'" *Nations and Nationalism* 18, no. 2 (April 1, 2012): 247–66; Legum, "Somali Libera-tion Songs."

25. Walker Connor, "Homelands in a World of States," in *Understanding National-ism*, ed. Montserrat Guibernau and John Hutchinson, Malden, MA: Polity Press, 2001, 53–73, 53.

26. Hensel, "Contentious Issues and World Politics"; see also Paul R. Hensel, "Terri-tory: Theory and Evidence on Geography and Conflict," in Vasquez, *What Do We Know About War?*, 57–84.

27. Paul K. Huth, "Territory: Why are Territorial Disputes between States a Central Cause of International Conflict," in Vasquez, *What Do We Know About War?*, 85–110; John A. Vasquez and Brandon Valeriano, "Territory as a Source of Conflict and a Road to Peace," in *The Sage Handbook of Conflict Resolution*, ed. Jacob Bercovitch, Viktor A. Kremeniuk, and William I. Zartman, Thousand Oaks, CA: Sage, 2009, 193–209; Jack L. Snyder, *From Voting to Violence: Democratization and Nationalist Conflict*, New York: W. W. Norton, 2000; Benjamin Miller, *States, Nations, and the Great Powers: The Sources of Regional War and Peace*, Cambridge: Cambridge University Press, 2007; Monica Duffy Toft, *The Geog-raphy of Ethnic Violence: Identity, Interests, and the Indivisibility of Territory*, Princeton, NJ: Princeton University Press, 2003; Edward D. Mansfield and Jack L. Snyder, *Electing to Fight: Why Emerging Democracies Go to War*, Cambridge, MA: MIT Press, 2007.

28. For an exception which nonetheless does not seek to integrate ideational features into large-N analysis, see Tuomas Forsberg, "Explaining Territorial Disputes: From Power Politics to Normative Reasons," *Journal of Peace Research* 33, no. 4 (1996): 433–49.

29. Goertz and Diehl, *Territorial Change*, 132. Other studies of conflict omit such variables entirely. See, for example, Stuart A. Bremer, "Dangerous Dyads: Conditions Affecting the Likelihood of Interstate War, 1816–1965," *Journal of Conflict Resolution* 36, no. 2 (1992): 309–41.

30. Paul F. Diehl, "What Are They Fighting For?: The Importance of Issues in Interna-tional Conflict Research," *Journal of Peace Research* 29, no. 3 (1992): 333–44, 333.

31. Huth, *Standing Your Ground*.

32. Mark W. Zacher, "The Territorial Integrity Norm: International Boundaries and the Use of Force," *International Organization* 55, no. 2 (2001): 215–50.

33. Wiegand, *Enduring Territorial Disputes*, 39.

34. See, for example, Barbara F. Walter, *Reputation and Civil War: Why Separatist Conflicts Are So Violent*, Cambridge: Cambridge University Press, 2009.

35. Daniel J. Dzurek, "What Makes Territory Important: Tangible and Intangible Dimensions," *GeoJournal* 64 (2005): 263–74.

36. See, for example, Weiner, "Macedonian Syndrome"; Chazan, *Irredentism and International Politics*; Saideman and Ayers, "Determining the Causes of Irredentism"; Ambrosio, *Irredentism*; Markus Kornprobst, *Irredentism in European Politics: Argumen-tation, Compromise and Norms*, Cambridge: Cambridge University Press, 2008, 67; and Siroky and Hale, "Inside Irredentism."

37. For a notable exception, see Hedva Ben-Israel, "Irredentism: Nationalism Reex-amined," in *Irredentism and International Politics*, ed. Naomi Chazan, Boulder, CO: Lynne Rienner, 1991, 9–22.

38. See, for example, Stephen Van Evera, "Hypotheses on Nationalism and War," *International Security* 18, no. 4 (1994): 5–39; Chaim Kaufmann, "Possible and Impossible Solutions to Ethnic Civil Wars," *International Security* 20, no. 4 (1996): 136–75; Edward P. Joseph and Michael E. O'Hanlon, "The Case for Soft Partition in Iraq," *Saban Center*

for *Middle East Policy at the Brookings Institution* 12 (2007): 1–45; Saideman and Ayers, "Determining the Causes of Irredentism"; John J. Mearsheimer, "Back to the Future: Instability in Europe after the Cold War," *International Security* 15, no. 1 (1990): 5–56; Chaim Kaufmann, "When All Else Fails: Ethnic Population Transfers and Partitions in the Twentieth Century," *International Security* 23, no. 2 (1998): 120–56; John J. Mearsheimer, "The Case for Partitioning Kosovo," in *NATO's Empty Victory: A Postmortem on the Balkan War*, ed. T. G. Carpenter, Washington, DC: CATO Institute, 2000, 133–38; Alexander B. Downes, "The Holy Land Divided: Defending Partition as a Solution to Ethnic Wars," *Security Studies* 10, no. 4 (2001): 58–116; Jaroslav Tir, "Dividing Countries to Promote Peace: Prospects for Long-Term Success of Partitions," *Journal of Peace Research* 42, no. 5 (2005): 545–62; Thomas Chapman and Philip G. Roeder, "Partition as a Solution to Wars of Nationalism: The Importance of Institutions," *American Political Science Review* 101, no. 4 (2007): 677–91; and Carter Johnson, "Partitioning to Peace: Sovereignty, Demography, and Ethnic Civil Wars," *International Security* 32, no. 4 (2008): 140–70.

39. Jeremy Ginges et al., "Sacred Bounds on the Rational Resolution of Violent Political Conflict," *Proceedings of the National Academy of Sciences* 104, no. 18 (2007): 7357–60.

40. Burghardt, "Bases of Territorial Claims"; Anthony D. Smith, "The 'Sacred' Dimension of Nationalism," *Millennium: Journal of International Studies* 29, no. 3 (2000): 791–814; Murphy, "National Claims to Territory." On literal sacred ground, see Ron E. Hassner, *War on Sacred Grounds*, Ithaca, NY: Cornell University Press, 2009.

41. See, for example, Alan Page Fiske and Philip E. Tetlock, "Taboo Trade-Offs: Reactions to Transactions That Transgress the Spheres of Justice," *Political Psychology* 18, no. 2 (1997): 255–97; Philip E. Tetlock et al., "The Psychology of the Unthinkable: Taboo Trade-Offs, Forbidden Base Rates, and Heretical Counterfactuals," *Journal of Personality and Social Psychology* 78, no. 5 (2000): 853–70; Philip E. Tetlock, "Thinking the Unthinkable: Sacred Values and Taboo Cognitions," *Trends in Cognitive Sciences* 7, no. 7 (2003): 320–24; A. Peter McGraw, Philip E. Tetlock, and Orie V. Kristel, "The Limits of Fungibility: Relational Schemata and the Value of Things," *Journal of Consumer Research* 30, no. 2 (2003): 219–29; A. Peter McGraw and Philip Tetlock, "Taboo Trade-Offs, Relational Framing, and the Acceptability of Exchanges," *Journal of Consumer Psychology* 15, no. 12 (2005): 2–15; and Jeremy Ginges and Scott Atran, "Noninstrumental Reasoning over Sacred Values: An Indonesian Case Study," *Psychology of Learning and Motivation* 50 (2009): 193–206.

42. Quoted in Hans Kohn, *The Mind of Germany: The Education of a Nation*, New York: Charles Scribner's Sons, 1960, 76.

43. Quoted in Mahmoud Darwish, ed., *Palestinian Leaders Discuss the New Challenges for the Resistance*, Beirut: Palestine Research Center, 1974, 52–53.

44. For an analogous argument about the difficulty of observing audience costs, see Kenneth A. Schultz, "Looking for Audience Costs," *Journal of Conflict Resolution* 45, no. 1 (2001): 32–60.

45. Martha Finnemore and Kathryn Sikkink, "Taking Stock: The Constructivist Research Program in International Relations and Comparative Politics," *Annual Review of Political Science* 4, no. 1 (2001): 391–416, 402. See also Stacie E. Goddard and Ronald R. Krebs, "Rhetoric, Legitimation, and Grand Strategy," *Security Studies* 24, no. 1 (2015): 5–36; Ronald R. Krebs and Patrick Thaddeus Jackson, "Twisting Tongues and Twisting Arms: The Power of Political Rhetoric," *European Journal of International Relations* 13, no. 1 (2007): 35–66; Dustin H. Tingley and Barbara F. Walter, "Can Cheap Talk Deter?: An Experimental Analysis," *Journal of Conflict Resolution* 55, no. 6 (2011): 996–1020; and Stacie E. Goddard, *Indivisible Territory and the Politics of Legitimacy: Jerusalem and Northern Ireland*, Cambridge: Cambridge University Press, 2010, 28, 31.

46. Timur Kuran, *Private Truths, Public Lies: The Social Consequences of Preference Falsification*, Cambridge, MA: Harvard University Press, 1995.

47. Crawford Young, *The Politics of Cultural Pluralism*, Madison: University of Wisconsin Press, 1976, 72. See also Montserrat Guibernau, "Nationalism and Intellectuals in Nations without States: The Catalan Case," *Political Studies* 48, no. 5 (2000): 989–1005; Billig, *Banal Nationalism*, 74, 85; Roger Brubaker, *Nationalism Reframed: Nationhood and the National Question in the New Europe*, Cambridge: Cambridge University Press, 1996; Craig Calhoun, "Nationalism and Ethnicity," *Annual Review of Sociology* 19 (1993): 211–39; Craig Calhoun, *Nationalism*, Minneapolis: University of Minnesota Press, 1997; and Shelef, *Evolving Nationalism*.

48. Rawi Abdelal et al., "Identity as a Variable," *Perspectives on Politics* 4, no. 4 (2006): 695–711; Jennifer Todd, "Partitioned Identities?: Everyday National Distinctions in Northern Ireland and the Irish State," *Nations and Nationalism* 21, no. 1 (2015): 21–42; Glynis M. Breakwell, "Identity Processes and Social Changes," in *Changing European Identities: Social Psychological Analyses of Social Change*, ed. Glynis M. Breakwell and Evanthia Lyons, Oxford: Butterworth Heinemann, 1996, 13–27, 22.

49. See, for example, Stephen M. Saideman and R. William Ayers, *For Kin or Country: Xenophobia, Nationalism, and War*, New York: Columbia University Press, 2008; Goddard, *Indivisible Territory*; Shelef, *Evolving Nationalism*; Mylonas and Shelef, "Which Land Is Our Land?"; and Ladis K. D. Kristof, "The Image and the Vision of the Fatherland: The Case of Poland in Comparative Perspective," in Hooson, *Geography and National Identity*, 221–32.

50. Joya Chatterji, *Bengal Divided: Hindu Communalism and Partition, 1932–1947*, Cambridge: Cambridge University Press, 1994, 226.

51. Medhane Tadesse, *The Eritrean-Ethiopian War: Retrospect and Prospects; Reflections on the Making of Conflicts in the Horn of Africa, 1991–1998*, Addis Ababa: Mega, 1999; Aregawi Berhe, *A Political History of the Tigray People's Liberation Front (1975–1991): Revolt, Ideology and Mobilisation in Ethiopia*, Los Angeles: Tsehai, 2009.

52. For representative examples of the uses of these, see the Italian claims to Istria, the Zionist Memorandum to the Peel Commission, or the claims of German expellees to the lands east of the Oder-Neisse boundaries. *Dalmatia, Fiume and the Other Unreedemed* [*sic*] *Lands of the Adriatic: A Historical and Statistical Study . . . with a Map of the Eastern Frontier of Italy*, Rome: L'Universelle, 1916; Government of Italy, *Trieste: The Italian Viewpoint*, Rome: Government of Italy, 1946; Great Britain, *Palestine Royal Commission: Minutes of Evidence Heard at Public Sessions*, London: H.M.S.O., 1937; Karl Pagel, ed., *The German East*, Berlin: K. Lemmer, 1954; Ernst Giese, *Ostdeutschland, unvergessenes Land: Pommern, Schlesien, Ostpreussen*, Frankfurt: Wochenschau Verlag, 1957; Friedrich von Wilpert, *The Oder-Neisse Problem: Towards Fair Play in Central Europe*, Bonn: Atlantic Forum, 1964.

53. Shelef, *Evolving Nationalism*.

54. Goddard, *Indivisible Territory*.

55. Hein E. Goemans, "Bounded Communities: Territoriality, Territorial Attachment, and Conflict," in *Territoriality and Conflict in an Era of Globalization*, ed. Miles Kahler and Barbara F. Walter, Cambridge: Cambridge University Press, 2006, 25–61; Philip G. Roeder, *Where Nation-States Come from: Institutional Change in the Age of Nationalism*, Princeton, NJ: Princeton University Press, 2007; David B. Carter and Hein E. Goemans, "The Making of the Territorial Order: New Borders and the Emergence of Interstate Conflict," *International Organization* 55, no. 2 (2011): 275–309.

56. See, for example, Weiner, "Macedonian Syndrome"; Chazan, *Irredentism and International Politics*; Ian S. Lustick, *Unsettled States, Disputed Lands: Britain and Ireland, France and Algeria, Israel and the West Bank–Gaza*, Ithaca, NY: Cornell University Press, 1993; Brendan O'Leary, Ian S. Lustick, and Thomas Callaghy, eds., *Right-Sizing the State: The Politics of Moving Borders*, Oxford: Oxford University Press, 2001; Saideman and Ayers,

For Kin or Country; and Ambrosio, *Irredentism*. For more on the role of external powers in state-minority relations, see Erin Jenne, "A Bargaining Theory of Minority Demands: Explaining the Dog That Did Not Bite in 1990s Yugoslavia," *International Studies Quarterly* 48, no. 4 (2004): 729–54; and Harris Mylonas, *The Politics of Nation-Building: Making Co-Nationals, Refugees, and Minorities*, Cambridge: Cambridge University Press, 2013.

57. Shelef, *Evolving Nationalism*.

58. Doing so builds on work that disaggregates actors in conflict more generally. See, for example, Halvard Buhaug, Lars-Erik Cederman, and Jan Ketil Rød, "Disaggregating Ethno-Nationalist Civil Wars: A Dyadic Test of Exclusion Theory," *International Organization* 62, no. 3 (2008): 531–51; Kathleen Gallagher Cunningham, *Inside the Politics of Self-Determination*, Oxford: Oxford University Press, 2014; Nils Petter Gleditsch et al., "Armed Conflict, 1946–2001: A New Dataset," *Journal of Peace Research* 39, no. 5 (2002): 615–37; Andrew Kydd and Barbara F. Walter, "Sabotaging the Peace: The Politics of Extremist Violence," *International Organization* 56, no. 2 (2002): 263–96; Wendy Pearlman, "Spoiling Inside and Out: Internal Political Contestation and the Middle East Peace Process," *International Security* 33, no. 3 (2009): 79–109; Shelef, *Evolving Nationalism*; Fotini Christia, *Alliance Formation in Civil Wars*, Cambridge: Cambridge University Press, 2012; Kathleen Gallagher Cunningham, Kristin M. Bakke, and Lee J. M. Seymour, "Shirts Today, Skins Tomorrow: Dual Contests and the Effects of Fragmentation in Self-Determination Disputes," *Journal of Conflict Resolution* 56, no. 1 (2012): 67–93; Paul Staniland, "Between a Rock and a Hard Place: Insurgent Fratricide, Ethnic Defection, and the Rise of Pro-State Paramilitaries," *Journal of Conflict Resolution* 56, no. 1 (2012): 16–40; Peter Krause, "The Structure of Success: How the Internal Distribution of Power Drives Armed Group Behavior and National Movement Effectiveness," *Security Studies* 38, no. 3 (2014): 72–116; and Kathleen Gallagher Cunningham, Marianne Dahl, and Anne Frugé, "Strategies of Resistance: Diversification and Diffusion," *American Journal of Political Science* 61, no. 3 (2017): 591–605. The Minorities at Risk Organizational Behavior (MAROB) project is also a notable addition in this vein. See Victor Asal, Amy Pate, and Jonathan Wilkenfeld, *Minorities at Risk Organizational Behavior Data and Codebook Version 9/2008*, http://www.cidcm.umd.edu/mar/data.asp.

59. Zsuzsa Csergo and James M. Goldgeier, "Nationalist Strategies and European Integration," *Perspectives on Politics* 2, no. 1 (2004): 21–37; Goddard, *Indivisible Territory*; Shelef, *Evolving Nationalism*.

60. On the importance of the perceived authority of the producers of rhetoric or particular narratives, see Ronald R. Krebs, "How Dominant Narratives Rise and Fall: Military Conflict, Politics, and the Cold War Consensus," *International Organization* 69, no. 4 (2015): 809–45; Neta Crawford, *Argument and Change in World Politics: Ethics, Decolonization, and Humanitarian Intervention*, Cambridge: Cambridge University Press, 2002; Hassner, *War on Sacred Grounds*; Goddard and Krebs, "Rhetoric, Legitimation, and Grand Strategy"; and Achim Hurrelmann, "Empirical Legitimation Analysis in International Relations: How to Learn from the Insights—and Avoid the Mistakes—of Research in EU Studies," *Contemporary Politics* 23, no. 1 (2017): 63–80.

61. For other critiques of the use of the state as the unit of analysis, see Agnew, "Territorial Trap"; David Newman and Anssi Paasi, "Fences and Neighbours in the Postmodern World: Boundary Narratives in Political Geography," *Progress in Human Geography* 22, no. 2 (1998): 186–207; Jouni Häkli, "In the Territory of Knowledge: State-Centred Discourses and the Construction of Society," *Progress in Human Geography* 25, no. 3 (2001): 403–22; and Sidney Tarrow, "Inside Insurgencies: Politics and Violence in an Age of Civil War," *Perspectives on Politics* 5, no. 3 (2007): 587–600.

62. See, for example, Burghardt, "Bases of Territorial Claims"; Anthony D. Smith, *The Ethnic Origins of Nations*, New York: Basil Blackwell, 1987; Esman, *Ethnic Politics*;

Connor, *Ethnonationalism*; Taylor, "State as Container"; Connor, "Homelands in a World of States"; James D. Fearon, "Rationalist Explanations for War," *International Organization* 49 (1995): 379–414; Murphy, "National Claims to Territory"; Toft, *Geography of Ethnic Violence*; Ron E. Hassner, "'To Halve and to Hold': Conflicts over Sacred Space and the Problem of Indivisibility," *Security Studies* 12, no. 4 (2003): 1–33; Vasquez and Valeriano, "Territory as a Source of Conflict"; Stacie E. Goddard, "Uncommon Ground: Indivisible Territory and the Politics of Legitimacy," *International Organization* 60, no. 1 (2006): 35–68; and Barbara F. Walter, "Bargaining Failures and Civil War," *Annual Review of Political Science* 12 (2009): 243–61.

63. Ahmad Shukeiri, *Liberation—Not Negotiation*, Beirut: Palestine Liberation Organization Research Centre, 1966, 20.

64. Winichakul, *Siam Mapped*. See also Kohn, *Mind of Germany*.

65. Rogers Brubaker, "Ethnicity, Race, and Nationalism," *Annual Review of Sociology* 35 (2009): 21–42; Yiftachel, "Homeland and Nationalism"; Sack, *Human Territoriality*; Anssi Paasi, "Deconstructing Regions: Notes on Scales of Spatial Life," *Environment and Planning A* 23 (1991): 239–56; Shelef, *Evolving Nationalism*; Paasi, *Territories, Boundaries, and Consciousness*; Eric Hobsbawm and Terence Ranger, eds., *The Invention of Tradition*, Cambridge: Cambridge University Press, 1983; Lustick, *Unsettled States, Disputed Lands*; Newman and Paasi, "Fences and Neighbours"; O'Leary, Lustick, and Callaghy, *Right-Sizing the State*; M. Anderson, *Frontiers*.

66. Donald H. Akenson, *God's People: Covenant and Land in South Africa, Israel, and Ulster*, Ithaca, NY: Cornell University Press, 1992. This is not as unusual as it may seem at first blush. Cultural geographers contend that the development of "emotional feelings of attachment, desires to possess, and compulsions to defend" territory can occur within one or two generations, enabling nationalist territoriality to piggyback on these attachments. See Nostrand and Estaville, introduction, 2; Thomas D. Boswell, "The Cuban-American Homeland in Miami," *Journal of Cultural Geography* 13, no. 2 (1993): 133–48; and Ary J. Lamme III and Douglas B. McDonald, "The 'North Country' Amish Homeland," *Journal of Cultural Geography* 13, no. 2 (1993): 107–18.

67. Eugen Weber, *Peasants into Frenchmen: The Modernization of Rural France, 1870–1914*, Stanford, CA: Stanford University Press, 1976; Branch, *Cartographic State*.

68. Quoted in Connor, *Ethnonationalism*, 205. On the consolidation of Uzbek identity, see Olivier Roy, *The New Central Asia: Geopolitics and the Birth of Nations*, New York: I. B. Tauris, 2007.

69. Guntram Henrik Herb, *Under the Map of Germany: Nationalism and Propaganda, 1918–1945*, London: Routledge, 1997.

70. Goemans, "Bounded Communities."

71. Sack, *Human Territoriality*, 75, also 20.

72. Lustick, *Unsettled States, Disputed Lands*; Martha Finnemore and Kathryn Sikkink, "International Norm Dynamics and Political Change," *International Organization* 52, no. 4 (1998): 887–917, 895; Ronald R. Krebs, *Narrative and the Making of US National Security*, Cambridge: Cambridge University Press, 2015.

73. For examples of these Italian claims, see Duke of Litta-Visconti-Arese, "Unredeemed Italy," *North American Review* 206, no. 743 (1917): 561–74; and chapter 3 in this volume.

74. Shelef, *Evolving Nationalism*.

75. Oto Luthar, *The Land Between: A History of Slovenia*, Brussels: Peter Lang, 2008. The Slovenian National Party departs from this consensus. See the expansive territorial claims implied by the emblem displayed on their webpage (https://web.archive.org/web/20110429024046/http://www.sns.si/) as late as 2011, accessed April 29, 2011.

76. Mylonas and Shelef, "Which Land Is Our Land?"

77. B. R. Nanda, "Nehru, the Indian National Congress and the Partition of India, 1937–1947," in *The Partition of India: Policies and Perspectives, 1935–1947*, ed. C. H. Philips and Mary Doreen Wainwright, London: George Allen and Unwin, 1970, 148–87.

78. See, for example, Lustick, "Taking Evolution Seriously"; Shelef, *Evolving Nationalism*; Lewis and Steinmo, "How Institutions Evolve"; Dennett, *Darwin's Dangerous Idea*; and Blackmore, *Meme Machine*. Technically, evolution also requires the retention of the information conveyed by the variant over time. Nationalist educational systems, both formal and informal, help nationalist ideology meet this criterion as well.

79. Crawford, *Argument and Change in World Politics*, 104–5, 37. See also Finnemore and Sikkink, "Taking Stock"; and Shelef, *Evolving Nationalism*.

80. Shelef, *Evolving Nationalism*; Goddard and Krebs, "Rhetoric, Legitimation, and Grand Strategy," 11.

81. For an example of the importance of political failure in a different ideational context, see Jack L. Snyder, "Dueling Security Stories: Wilson and Lodge Talk Strategy," *Security Studies* 24, no. 1 (2015): 171–97.

82. Importantly, modest territorial demands are not a feature of communist parties per se. The East German SED, for example, continued to apply homeland territoriality to the area of West Germany for a long time after the border was drawn. Similarly, the Chinese Communist Party continues to apply homeland territoriality to Taiwan to this day. On Chinese homeland claims, see M. Taylor Fravel, "Regime Insecurity and International Cooperation: Explaining China's Compromises in Territorial Disputes," *International Security* 20, no. 2 (2005): 46–83.

83. Goddard, *Indivisible Territory*.

84. Ann Swidler, "Culture in Action: Symbols and Strategies," *American Sociological Review* 51, no. 2 (1986): 273–86, 277.

85. J. L. Snyder, "Dueling Security Stories," 180. See also Mlada Bukovansky, *Legitimacy and Power Politics: The American and French Revolutions in International Political Culture*, Princeton, NJ: Princeton University Press, 2002; and Martin B. Carstensen, "Ideas are Not as Stable as Political Scientists Want Them to Be: A Theory of Incremental Ideational Change," *Political Studies* 59 (2011): 596–615.

86. On the importance of visibility, see Goddard and Krebs, "Rhetoric, Legitimation, and Grand Strategy."

87. See also, for example, Saul B. Cohen and Nurit Kliot, "Place-Names in Israel's Ideological Struggle over the Administered Territories," *Annals of the Association of American Geographers* 82, no. 4 (1992): 653–80.

88. Weiner, "Macedonian Syndrome," 681; Lustick, *Unsettled States, Disputed Lands*.

89. Shelef, *Evolving Nationalism*.

90. Krebs, "How Dominant Narratives Rise and Fall," 835; Markus Kornprobst and Martin Senn, "Arguing Deep Ideational Change," *Contemporary Politics* 23, no. 1 (2017): 100–119, 101; Carstensen, "Ideas Are Not as Stable."

91. Frank Schimmelfennig, "The Community Trap: Liberal Norms, Rhetorical Action, and the Eastern Enlargement of the European Union," *International Organization* 55, no. 1 (2001): 47–80. See also Crawford, *Argument and Change in World Politics*, 113–17; Krebs and Jackson, "Twisting Tongues and Twisting Arms," 36; Ronald R. Krebs and Jennifer Lobasz, "The Sound of Silence: Rhetorical Coercion, Democratic Acquiescence, and the Iraq War," in *American Foreign Policy and the Politics of Fear: Threat Inflation since 9/11*, ed. A. Trevor Thrall and Jane K. Cramer, New York: Routledge Taylor and Francis Group, 2009, 117–34; James Martin, "Situating Speech: A Rhetorical Approach to Political Strategy," *Political Studies* 63, no. 1 (2015): 25–42; and Thomas Risse, "'Let's Argue!': Communicative Action in World Politics," *International Organization* 54, no. 1 (2000): 1–39.

92. Lustick, *Unsettled States, Disputed Lands*.

93. Ginges and Atran, "Noninstrumental Reasoning." For examples of assumptions that the utility of homelands is nearly infinite, see Toft, *Geography of Ethnic Violence*, 20; and Vasquez and Valeriano, "Territory as a Source of Conflict."

94. Tetlock et al., "Psychology of the Unthinkable," 853.

95.Scott Atran et al., "Sacred Barriers to Conflict Resolution," *Science* 317 (2007): 1039–40; Ginges et al., "Sacred Bounds."

96. Saideman and Ayers, *For Kin or Country*.

97. Shelef, *Evolving Nationalism*.

98. See, for example, Stuart J. Kaufman, *Nationalist Passions*, Ithaca, NY: Cornell University Press, 2015.

99. See, for example, Anthony D. Smith, "Gastronomy or Geology?: The Role of Nationalism in the Reconstruction of Nations," *Nations and Nationalism* 1, no. 1 (1995): 3–23; Howard Schuman and Cheryl Rieger, "Historical Analogies, Generational Effects, and Attitudes toward War," *American Sociological Review* 57, no. 3 (1992): 315–26; and Jack Citrin et al., "Is American Nationalism Changing?: Implications for Foreign Policy," *International Studies Quarterly* 38, no. 1 (1994): 1–31. On generational change more broadly, see Karl Mannheim, "The Problem of Generations," in *Essays on the Sociology of Knowledge*, ed. Karl Mannheim, London: Routledge and Kegan Paul, 1952, 276–320.

100. Boaz Atzili, *Good Fences, Bad Neighbors: Border Fixity and International Conflict*, Chicago: University of Chicago Press, 2011; Boaz Atzili and Anne Kantel, "Accepting the Unacceptable: Lessons from West Germany's Changing Border Politics," *International Studies Review* 17, no. 4 (2015): 588–616; Zacher, "Territorial Integrity Norm"; Tanisha M. Fazal, *State Death: The Politics and Geography of Conquest, Occupation, and Annexation*, Princeton, NJ: Princeton University Press, 2007.

101. Ambrosio, *Irredentism*.

102. For example, Susan Strange, *States and Markets*, 2nd ed., New York: Continuum, 1994, 136; Yan Wang, "Globalization and Territorial Identification: A Multilevel Analysis across 50 Countries," *International Journal of Public Opinion Research* 28, no. 3 (2016): 401–14; Jean-Marie Guehenno, *The End of the Nation-State*, Minneapolis: University of Minnesota Press, 1995; and Jessica Mathews, "Power Shift," *Foreign Affairs* 76, no. 1 (1997): 50–66.

103. J. L. Snyder, *From Voting to Violence*; Mansfield and Snyder, *Electing to Fight*.

104. Dennis Kennedy, *Widening Gulf: Northern Attitudes to the Independent Irish State, 1919–49*, Belfast: Blackstaff Press, 1988. See also Gertjan Dijink, *National Identity and Geopolitical Visions: Maps of Pride and Pain*, London: Routledge, 2002.

105. For studies that assume a relationship between the location of coethnics and the extent of the homeland, see Weiner, "Macedonian Syndrome"; Ernest Gellner, "Nationalism in the Vacuum," in *Thinking Theoretically about Soviet Nationalities: History and Comparison in the Study of the USSR*, ed. Alexander J. Motyl, New York: Columbia University Press, 1992, 243–54; Anthony D. Smith, "Culture, Community and Territory: The Politics of Ethnicity and Nationalism," *International Affairs* 72, no. 3 (1996): 445–58; Saideman and Ayers, *For Kin or Country*; Alberto Alesina and Enrico Spolaore, *The Size of Nations*, Cambridge, MA: MIT Press, 2003; Toft, *Geography of Ethnic Violence*; Ambrosio, *Irredentism*; and Chazan, *Irredentism and International Politics*.

106. Kaufmann, "When All Else Fails"; Mearsheimer, "Case for Partitioning Kosovo"; C. Johnson, "Partitioning to Peace"; Max-Stephan Schulze and Nikolaus Wolf, "On the Origins of Border Effects: Insights from the Habsburg Empire," *Journal of Economic Geography* 9, no. 1 (2009): 117–36.

107. See, for example, Peter Krause and Ehud Eiran, "How Human Boundaries Become State Borders: Radical Flanks and Territorial Control in the Modern Era," *Comparative Politics* 40, no. 4 (2018): 479–99.

108. For explorations of the more general impact of these considerations on conflict, see Huth, *Standing Your Ground*; Huth and Allee, *Democratic Peace*; and Paul R. Hensel and Sara McLaughlin Mitchell, "Issue Indivisibility and Territorial Claims," *GeoJournal* 64 (2005): 275–85.

109. A prominent example is the Biafra movement. See John Boye Ejobowah, "Who Owns the Oil?: The Politics of Ethnicity in the Niger Delta of Nigeria," *Africa Today* 47, no. 1 (2000): 28–47.

110. Krebs, "How Dominant Narratives Rise and Fall," 810–11; Emanuel Adler, "Seizing the Middle Ground: Constructivism in World Politics," *European Journal of International Relations* 3, no. 3 (1997): 319–63; Kornprobst, *Irredentism in European Politics*. The observation that people act against their observable interests has bedeviled philosophers and social scientists alike. See, for example, Jonathan Haidt, *The Righteous Mind: Why Good People Are Divided by Politics and Religion*, New York: Pantheon Books, 2012; and Antonio Gramsci, *Selections from the Prison Notebooks of Antonio Gramsci*, ed. Quintin Hoare and Geoffrey Nowell Smith, New York: International, 1971.

111. While this works most openly in democracies, there is no reason it cannot apply to selectorates as well. Bruce Bueno de Mesquita et al., *The Logic of Political Survival*, Cambridge, MA: MIT Press, 2003.

112. Alvin Rabushka and Kenneth A. Shepsle, *Politics in Plural Societies: A Theory of Democratic Instability*, Columbus, OH: Merrill, 1972, 66–88; Donald L. Horowitz, *Ethnic Groups in Conflict*, Berkeley: University of California Press, 1985, 349–64; Saideman and Ayers, *For Kin or Country*; Paul R. Brass, *Ethnicity and Nationalism: Theory and Comparison*, London: Sage, 1991, 21.

113. Stephen M. Saideman, "Inconsistent Irredentism?: Political Competition, Ethnic Ties, and the Foreign Policies of Somalia and Serbia," *Security Studies* 7, no. 3 (1998): 51–93; Kanchan Chandra, "Ethnic Parties and Democratic Stability," *Perspectives on Politics* 3, no. 2 (2005): 235–52; Paul Mitchell, Geoffrey Evans, and Brendan O'Leary, "Extremist Outbidding in Ethnic Party Systems Is Not Inevitable: Tribune Parties in Northern Ireland," *Political Studies* 57, no. 2 (2009): 397–421.

114. On these settlement projects, see, for example, Brendan O'Leary, "The Elements of Right-Sizing and Right-Peopling the State," in O'Leary, Lustick, and Callaghy, *Right-Sizing the State*, 15–73; Lustick, *Unsettled States, Disputed Lands*; Stephen Zunes and Jacob Mundy, *Western Sahara: War, Nationalism, and Conflict Irresolution*, Syracuse, NY: Syracuse University Press, 2010; Oded Haklai and Neophytos Loizides, eds., *Settlers in Contested Lands: Territorial Disputes and Ethnic Conflicts*, Stanford, CA: Stanford University Press, 2015; Ehud Eiran, *Post-Colonial Settlement Strategy*, Edinburgh: Edinburgh University Press, 2019.

115. See, for example, Stanley Waterman, "Partitioned States," *Political Geography Quarterly* 6, no. 2 (1987): 151–70, 159; Gregory Henderson and Richard Ned Lebow, "Conclusions," in Henderson, Lebow, and Stoessinger, *Divided Nations*, 433–56; and Weiner, "Macedonian Syndrome."

116. Weiner, "Macedonian Syndrome"; Chazan, *Irredentism and International Politics*; Brubaker, *Nationalism Reframed*; Saideman and Ayers, "Determining the Causes of Irredentism"; Erin K. Jenne, *Ethnic Bargaining: The Paradox of Minority Rights*, Ithaca, NY: Cornell University Press, 2006; Mylonas, *Politics of Nation-Building*; Wiegand, *Enduring Territorial Disputes*; Siroky and Hale, "Inside Irredentism."

117. Harris Mylonas and Nadav G. Shelef, "Methodological Challenges in the Study of Stateless Nationalist Territorial Claims," *Territory, Politics, Governance* 5, no. 2 (2017): 145–57.

118. Mylonas and Shelef, "Methodological Challenges."

119. See also Shelef, *Evolving Nationalism*; Mylonas and Shelef, "Which Land Is Our Land?"; and Mylonas and Shelef, "Methodological Challenges." On the role of time more

generally, see Anna Grzymala-Busse, "Time Will Tell?: Temporality and the Analysis of Causal Mechanisms and Processes," *Comparative Political Studies* 44, no. 9 (2011): 1267–97, 1272.

2. THE SHIFTING CONTOURS OF THE GERMAN HOMELAND

1. Quoted in Günter Grass, *Two States—One Nation?*, New York: Harcourt Brace Jovanovich, 1990, 53.

2. Quoted in Louis Leo Snyder, *Roots of German Nationalism*, Bloomington: Indiana University Press, 1978, 60–61. See also Kohn, *Mind of Germany*, 78.

3. Helmut Walser Smith, *The Continuities of German History: Nation, Religion, and Race across the Long Nineteenth Century*, Cambridge: Cambridge University Press, 2008, 44. See also the similar depictions of the extent of the German homeland by Johann Fichte, Friedrich List, and Friedrich Ratzel, in H. W. Smith, *Continuities of German History*, 65; L. L. Snyder, *Roots of German Nationalism*, 15; and Dijink, *National Identity and Geopolitical Visions*, 19.

4. For examples of the emotional, archaeological, historical, ethnic, and religious claims to these territories, see, for example, Pagel, *German East*; Giese, *Ostdeutschland*; and Wilpert, *Oder-Neisse Problem*.

5. See, for example, Z. Michael Szaz, *Germany's Eastern Frontiers: The Problem of the Oder-Neisse Line*, Chicago: Regnery, 1960, 15.

6. L. L. Snyder, *Roots of German Nationalism*; Herb, *Under the Map of Germany*; Kohn, *Mind of Germany*.

7. Quoted in Peter Alter, "Nationalism and German Politics after 1945," in Breuilly, *State of Germany*, 154–76, 165.

8. "The Real German Question," *Time* 78, no. 16 (1961): 21.

9. See, for example, Dijink, *National Identity and Geopolitical Visions*, 26; L. L. Snyder, *Roots of German Nationalism*, 172; and Herb, *Under the Map of Germany*, 1.

10. Alter, "Nationalism and German Politics," 154.

11. For an example of this argument, see Alter, "Nationalism and German Politics."

12. Hans Mommsen, "History and National Identity: The Case of Germany," *German Studies Review* 6, no. 3 (1983): 559–82; Anna J. Merritt and Richard L. Merritt, *Public Opinion in Semisovereign Germany: The HICOG Surveys, 1949–1955*, Urbana: University of Illinois Press, 1980, 28.

13. Elizabeth Wiskemann, *Germany's Eastern Neighbours: Problems Relating to the Oder-Neisse Line and the Czech Frontier Regions*, Oxford: Oxford University Press, 1956, 197; Timothy Garton Ash, *In Europe's Name: Germany and the Divided Continent*, New York: Random House, 1993, 227; Henry J. Kellerman, "Party Leaders and Foreign Policy," in *West German Leadership and Foreign Policy*, ed. Hans Speier and W. Phillips Davison, Evanston, IL: Row, Peterson, 1957, 57-95; Pertti Ahonen, "Domestic Constraints on West German Ostpolitik: The Role of the Expellee Organizations," *Central European History* 31, no. 1/2 (1998): 31–63.

14. Association of Expellee Landsmannschaften, *The European Significance of the Oder-Neisse Territories*, Bonn: Association of Expellee Landsmannschaften, 1955, 7.

15. Herb, "Double Vision," 149–50.

16. Peter H. Merkl, "The Role of Public Opinion in West German Foreign Policy," in Hanrieder, *West German Foreign Policy, 1949–1979*, 157–80.

17. Dietrich Orlow, "Delayed Reaction: Democracy, Nationalism, and the SPD, 1945–1966," *German Studies Review* 16, no. 1 (1993): 77–102, 86.

18. Quoted in Harold Kent Schellenger, *The SPD in the Bonn Republic: A Socialist Party Modernizes*, The Hague: Martinus Nijhoff, 1968, 74. See also Orlow, "Delayed Reaction," 89.

19. Schellenger, *SPD in the Bonn Republic*; Diane L. Parness, *The SPD and the Challenge of Mass Politics: The Dilemma of the German Volkspartei*, Boulder, CO: Westview Press, 1991, 54; Orlow, "Delayed Reaction," 86; Heinrich Potthoff and Susanne Miller, *The Social Democratic Party of Germany, 1848–2005*, Bonn: Dietz, 2006; Kellerman, "Party Leaders and Foreign Policy"; William E. Paterson, *The SPD and European Integration*, Farnborough: Saxon House, 1974, 7, 98–99. At the same time, their strident anti-communism also meant that, although reunification was their primary goal, they were unwilling to support unification under Soviet tutelage. See Schellenger, *SPD in the Bonn Republic*, 74.

20. Quoted in Schellenger, *SPD in the Bonn Republic*, 52–53.

21. The most prominent of these was Stalin's 1952 note which, at least theoretically, would have allowed the unification of the FRG and GDR, though not the reclamation of the Eastern Territories. On the Stalin note, see Rolf Steininger, *The German Question: The Stalin Note of 1952 and the Problem of Reunification*, New York: Columbia University Press, 1990, 26; and Wolfram F. Hanrieder, "West German Foreign Policy, 1949–1979: Necessities and Choices," in Hanrieder, *West German Foreign Policy, 1949–1979*, 15–36. For scholars who conclude that the rejection of Stalin's note did not reflect an abandonment of the goal of reunification, see, for example, Ash, *In Europe's Name*; Ronald J. Granieri, *The Ambivalent Alliance: Konrad Adenauer, the CDU/CSU, and the West, 1949–1966*, New York: Berghahn Books, 2003, 9–10, 51, 114; and Clay Clemens, *Reluctant Realists: The Christian Democrats and West German Ostpolitik*, Durham, NC: Duke University Press, 1989.

22. Clemens, *Reluctant Realists*; A. James McAdams, *Germany Divided: From the Wall to Reunification*, Princeton, NJ: Princeton University Press 1994; Thomas F. Banchoff, *The German Problem Transformed: Institutions, Politics, and Foreign Policy, 1945–1995*, Ann Arbor: University of Michigan Press, 1999; Hanrieder, "West German Foreign Policy, 1949–1979"; Hans-Peter Schwarz, "Adenauer's Ostpolitik," in Hanrieder, *West German Foreign Policy, 1949–1979*, 127–43; Thomas Paul Koppel, "Sources of Change in West German Ostpolitik: The Grand Coalition, 1966–1969," PhD diss., University of Wisconsin, 1972.

23. Quoted in Granieri, *Ambivalent Alliance*, 114.

24. Clemens, *Reluctant Realists*; Ash, *In Europe's Name*, 51; Imanuel Geiss, *The Question of German Unification, 1806–1996*, New York: Routledge, 1997; McAdams, *Germany Divided*; Kellerman, "Party Leaders and Foreign Policy," 93; Granieri, *Ambivalent Alliance*, 9; Julia von Dannenberg, *The Foundations of Ostpolitik: The Making of the Moscow Treaty between West Germany and the USSR*, Oxford: Oxford University Press, 2008, 19; Paterson, *SPD and European Integration*, 22; Mommsen, "History and National Identity".

25. Quoted in McAdams, *Germany Divided*, 20n8.

26. Clemens, *Reluctant Realists*, 33; Granieri, *Ambivalent Alliance*.

27. The Christian Democratic Union of Germany, *The CDU: History, Idea, Program, Constitution*, Bonn: Christian Democratic Union of Germany, 1961, 44–45. See also Wolfram F. Hanrieder, "The Foreign Policies of the Federal Republic of Germany, 1949–1989," *German Studies Review* 12, no. 2 (1989): 311–32; Granieri, *Ambivalent Alliance*; Ash, *In Europe's Name*; Schwarz, "Adenauer's Ostpolitik"; and McAdams, *Germany Divided*, 20.

28. Granieri, *Ambivalent Alliance*, 9. See also Clemens, *Reluctant Realists*, 30.

29. United States, Department of State, *Documents on Germany, 1944–1985*, Washington, DC: Office of the Historian, Bureau of Public Affairs, US Department of State, 1985, 1042–43.

30. Clemens, *Reluctant Realists*, 29–30; Schwarz, "Adenauer's Ostpolitik." Both the legal and self-determination logics permeated the discourse of the expellee associations as well. See Ahonen, "Domestic Constraints on West German Ostpolitik," 37.

31. McAdams, *Germany Divided*. There were some indications that, at least sometimes and in private, CDU leaders realized that at least the Eastern Territories would not return to German sovereignty. In 1955, for example, Adenauer reportedly told Ollenhauer

that the "Oder-Neisse, Eastern provinces—they're gone! They don't exist anymore!" Ash, *In Europe's Name*, 225. See also Ahonen, "Domestic Constraints on West German Ostpolitik," 48. In fact, Brandt would later criticize Adenauer for saying one thing in private and another in public. Willy Brandt, *My Life in Politics*, London: Hamish Hamilton, 1992, 35. Helmut Kohl also privately considered declaring that the FRG should accept the Oder-Neisse Line as early as 1970. Ash, *In Europe's Name*, 225–28.

32. See, for example, the reaction to a 1957 suggestion by the CDU foreign minister that the FRG might consider renouncing the claim to the Oder-Neisse territories in exchange for reunification with the GDR. Ahonen, "Domestic Constraints on West German Ostpolitik," 44.

33. Quoted in Clemens, *Reluctant Realists*, 34–35.

34. United States, Department of State, *Documents on Germany*, 503.

35. United States, Department of State, *Documents on Germany*, 752.

36. Quoted in Christian Democratic Union of Germany, *CDU*, 43.

37. Quoted in Christian Democratic Union of Germany, *CDU*, 46.

38. Christian Democratic Union of Germany, *CDU*, 15, 58.

39. For a detailed treatment of the German legal case, see *Phillip A. Bühler, The Oder-Neisse Line: A Reappraisal under International Law, Boulder, CO: East European Monographs, 1990.*

40. Quoted in Wilpert, *Oder-Neisse Problem*, 109.

41. Quoted in Wilpert, *Oder-Neisse Problem,* 122. Ludwig Erhard, who replaced Adenauer as chancellor on behalf of the CDU in 1963, continued his predecessor's approach. See, for example, Wilpert, *Oder-Neisse Problem*, 123; and United States, Department of State, *Documents on Germany*, 867.

42. United States, Department of State, *Documents on Germany*, 914.

43. See, for example, the Polish request for the US position on the issue in 1960 and the address by Adam Rapacki, the Polish foreign minister, at the United Nations General Assembly, December 14, 1964, quoted in United States, Department of State, *Documents on Germany*, 712, 886–89.

44. See the letter "Concerning a German Peace Treaty and the Right of Self- Determination, on July 12, 1961" sent to the USSR, reproduced in United States, Department of State, *Documents on Germany*, 751–52. For other examples, see Adenauer's 1950 and 1953 statements and Erhard's speech to the Council on Foreign Relations in 1964, in United States, Department of State, *Documents on Germany*, 313–14, 398, 866.

45. Klaus von Beyme, "National Consciousness and Nationalism: The Case of the Two Germanies," *Canadian Review of Studies in Nationalism* 8, no. 2 (1986): 227–48. On the continuities in the German conceptions of membership in the nation, see Brubaker, *Citizenship and Nationhood*.

46. Jacques Freymond, *The Saar Conflict, 1945–1955*, London: Stevens, 1960, 229; Merritt and Merritt, *Public Opinion in Semisovereign Germany*, Report No. 124.

47. Freymond, *Saar Conflict, 1945–1955*, 314; Schellenger, *SPD in the Bonn Republic*, 70; Potthoff and Miller, *Social Democratic Party of Germany*, 193; Paterson, *SPD and European Integration*, 22, 34–35; Orlow, "Delayed Reaction."

48. Süddeutsche Zeitung, "Das deutsche Weißbuch zur Saarfrage," March 10, 1950, accessed July 30, 2018, http://www.cvce.eu/obj/the_german_white_paper_on_the_saar_question_from_the_suddeutsche_zeitung_10_march_1950-en-94e43ff0-ac8b-4cc5–85a3–22651f37ecd7.html. See also Freymond, *Saar Conflict, 1945–1955*, 79.

49. Freymond, *Saar Conflict, 1945–1955*, 65, 212, 238; Arnold J. Heidenheimer, *Adenauer and the CDU: The Rise of the Leader and the Integration of the Party*, The Hague: Martinus Nijhoff, 1960, 209, 213.

50. Granieri, *Ambivalent Alliance*, 93.

51. Clemens, *Reluctant Realists*, 48; Ash, *In Europe's Name*, 54–55; McAdams, *Germany Divided*, 69–70; Dannenberg, *Foundations of Ostpolitik*, 28.

52. Clemens, *Reluctant Realists*, 51.

53. Parness, *SPD and the Challenge of Mass Politics*; Potthoff and Miller, *Social Democratic Party of Germany*; Paterson, *SPD and European Integration*, 135; Harold James, *A German Identity, 1770–1990*, New York: Weidenfeld and Nicolson, 1989, 191; Schellenger, *SPD in the Bonn Republic*.

54. Parness, *SPD and the Challenge of Mass Politics*, 72; Volker Berghahn and Uta Poiger, eds., "Occupation and the Emergence of Two States (1945–1961)," 2018, accessed August 1, 2018, http://germanhistorydocs.ghi-dc.org/section.cfm?section_id=14; Andreas Wilkens, "New Ostpolitik and European Integration: Concepts and Policies in the Brandt Era," in *European Integration and the Cold War: Ostpolitik-Westpolitik, 1965–1973*, ed. Piers Ludlow, New York: Routledge, 2007, 67–80.

55. See, for example, Social Democratic Party, *Das Regierungsprogramm der SPD, 1961*; and Social Democratic Party, *A Programme for Government: Presented by Willy Brandt, Governing Mayor of Berlin and Chancellor-Candidate, April 28, 1961*, Bonn: Social Democratic Party of Germany, 1961.

56. Willy Brandt, *People and Politics: The Years 1960–1975*, New York: Harper Collins, 1978, 20.

57. See, for example, Willy Brandt, *A Peace Policy for Europe*, London: Weidenfeld and Nicolson, 1969, 129.

58. Social Democratic Party, *SPD Party Conference 1966: The State of the Nation*, Bonn: Social Democratic Party of Germany, 1966, 27, my emphasis. At this point, their resolutions, rather than openly renouncing the claim to the Eastern Territories, call on the "Polish People to have understanding for our people's desire for reunification in peace and lasting freedom." This contrasts with their treatment of the border with Czechoslovakia, in which they explicitly declare that they have "no territorial claims against Czechoslovakia" (38). See also Brandt, quoted in Koppel, "Sources of Change in West German Ostpolitik," 99–100.

59. Ash, *In Europe's Name*, 224, also 68–69.

60. See, for example, Social Democratic Party, *Das Regierungsprogramm der SPD, 1961*.

61. See, for example, Social Democratic Party, *SPD Party Conference 1966*; and Brandt, *Peace Policy for Europe*, 98, 117, 129. There is evidence that this had already begun earlier. See Social Democratic Party, *Programme for Government*.

62. See, for example, Michael Kreile, "Ostpolitik Reconsidered," in *The Foreign Policy of West Germany: Formation and Contents*, ed. Ekkehart Krippendorff and Volker Rittberger, London: Sage, 1980, 123–46; Gebhard Schweigler, *National Consciousness in Divided Germany*, Beverly Hills, CA: Sage, 1975, 275n34; David Curtis Geyer and Bernd Schaefer, eds., *American Détente and German Ostpolitik, 1969–1972*, Washington, DC: German Historical Institute, 2004, 80–97; Roger Tilford, introduction to Tilford, *Ostpolitik and Political Change in Germany*, 1–22; Josef Korbel, *Detente in Europe: Real or Imaginary*, Princeton, NJ: Princeton University Press, 1972; Barbara Marshall, *Willy Brandt: A Political Biography*, New York: St. Martin's Press, 1997; and Gottfried Niedhart, "Ostpolitik: Phases, Short-Term Objectives, and Grand Design," in Geyer and Schaefer, *American Détente and German Ostpolitik, 1969–1972*, 118–36.

63. There was a faction within the SPD that was openly willing to abandon reunification entirely. Until at least the 1980s, however, they remained secondary to Brandt's approach. Dannenberg, *Foundations of Ostpolitik*, 119.

64. Ash, *In Europe's Name*, 74; Karl Cordell, "The Basic Treaty between the Two German States in Retrospect," *Political Quarterly* 61, no. 1 (1990): 36–50; Ernest D. Plock, *The Basic Treaty and the Evolution of East-West German Relations*, Boulder, CO: Westview Press, 1986.

65. Geyer and Schaefer, *American Détente and German Ostpolitik, 1969–1972*, 139, my emphasis. See also John H. Herz, "Germany," in Henderson, Lebow, and Stoessinger, *Divided Nations*, 31; Juliet Lodge, *The European Policy of the SPD*, Beverly Hills, CA: Sage, 1976; Kenneth A. Myers, *Ostpolitik and American Security Interests in Europe*, Washington, DC: Center for Strategic and International Studies, Georgetown University, 1972; Carsten Tessmer, "'Thinking the Unthinkable' to 'Make the Impossible Possible': Ostpolitik, Intra-German Policy, and the Moscow Treaty, 1969–1970," in Geyer and Schaefer, *American Détente and German Ostpolitik, 1969–1972*, 53–66, 53; Ash, *In Europe's Name*, 65–66, 292; Dannenberg, *Foundations of Ostpolitik*; Kristina Spohr Readman, "National Interests and the Power of 'Language': West German Diplomacy and the Conference on Security and Cooperation in Europe, 1972–1975," *Journal of Strategic Studies* 29, no. 6 (2006): 1077–1120; and Cordell, "Basic Treaty between the Two German States in Retrospect."

66. Social Democratic Party, *SPD Party Conference 1966*, 24, my emphasis. See also Renata Fritsch-Bournazel, *Confronting the German Question: Germans on the East-West Divide*, New York: Berg, 1988, 96–97.

67. Niedhart, "Ostpolitik," 119.

68. Schweigler, *National Consciousness in Divided Germany*; Dannenberg, *Foundations of Ostpolitik*; Sebastian Gehrig, "Cold War Identities: Citizenship, Constitutional Reform, and International Law between East and West Germany, 1967–1975," *Journal of Contemporary History* 49, no. 4 (2014): 794–814.

69. Quoted in Ash, *In Europe's Name*, 68.

70. Quoted in Niedhart, "Ostpolitik," 129.

71. Herz, "Germany," 20.

72. Tessmer, "'Thinking the Unthinkable,'" 60.

73. Brandt, *My Life in Politics*, 220.

74. Geyer and Schaefer, *American Détente and German Ostpolitik, 1969–1972*, 138.

75. Ash, *In Europe's Name*, 75.

76. Quoted in Ash, *In Europe's Name*, 78, see also 75; Dannenberg, *Foundations of Ostpolitik*, 52.

77. Niedhart, "Ostpolitik," 130; Ash, *In Europe's Name*, 77–78; McAdams, *Germany Divided*, 101; Jan Palmowski, *Inventing a Socialist Nation: Heimat and the Politics of Everyday Life in the GDR, 1945–1990*, Cambridge: Cambridge University Press, 2009.

78. Quoted in Niedhart, "Ostpolitik," 121–22.

79. Ash, *In Europe's Name*, 44, 64, 130.

80. Brandt, *Peace Policy for Europe*, 117.

81. Geyer and Schaefer, *American Détente and German Ostpolitik, 1969–1972*, 139.

82. Ash, *In Europe's Name*, 134.

83. United States, Department of State, *Documents on Germany*, 1307.

84. For the importance of being recognized as a state in other contexts, see Mikulas Fabry, *Recognizing States: International Society and the Establishment of New States since 1776*, Oxford: Oxford University Press, 2010; Bridget Coggins, "Friends in High Places: International Politics and the Emergence of States from Secessionism," *International Organization* 65, no. 3 (2011): 433–67; and Nadav G. Shelef and Yael Zeira, "Recognition Matters!: UN State Status and Attitudes towards Territorial Compromise," *Journal of Conflict Resolution* 61, no. 3 (2017): 537–63.

85. Compare Social Democratic Party, *Programme for Government*; and United States, Department of State, *Documents on Germany*, 1049.

86. Quoted in United States, *Documents on Germany*, 1059–64, my emphasis.

87. United States, Department of State, *Documents on Germany*, 1207.

88. United States, Department of State, *Documents on Germany*, 1307.

89. See, for example, Social Democratic Party, *Weiter arbeiten am Modell Deutschland: Regierungsprogramm 1976–1980, 1976*; and Social Democratic Party, *Sicherheit für Deutchland: Leistungen für Deutschland ein Leistunsbericht zum Whalprogramm 1980*, 1980.

90. See Imanuel Geiss, "The Federal Republic of Germany in International Politics before and after Unification," in Larres and Panayi, *Federal Republic of Germany since 1949*, 137–68, 154.

91. B. Marshall, *Willy Brandt*, 135–36. See also McAdams, *Germany Divided*, 168; Stephen Padgett, "The SPD: The Decline of the Social Democratic *Volkspartei*," in Larres and Panayi, *Federal Republic of Germany since 1949*, 230–53, 244; and Ash, *In Europe's Name*, 134.

92. Social Democratic Party, *Das Regierungsprogramm der SPD, 1983–1987*, 1983; Johannes Rau, *Zunkunft für alle: Arbeiten für soziale Gerechtigkeit und Frieden*, Bonn: Social Democratic Party Press and Information Department, 1987.

93. Ash, *In Europe's Name*, 333.

94. McAdams, *Germany Divided*, 137, 157.

95. Elizabeth Pond, *Beyond the Wall: Germany's Road to Unification*, Washington, DC: Brookings Institution Press, 1993, 137; McAdams, *Germany Divided*; B. Marshall, *Willy Brandt*.

96. Clemens, *Reluctant Realists*. See also Dannenberg, *Foundations of Ostpolitik*; McAdams, *Germany Divided*; and Geoffrey Pridham, *Christian Democracy in Western Germany: The CDU/CSU in Government and Opposition, 1945–1976*, New York: St. Martin's Press, 1977, 202.

97. The CSU (Christian Social Union) is the Bavarian wing of the CDU. It is technically a different party but functions as part of the CDU in national politics. On the role of the expellees in West German politics more broadly, see Ahonen, "Domestic Constraints on West German Ostpolitik"; and Pertti Ahonen, *After the Expulsion: West Germany and Eastern Europe, 1945–1990*, Oxford: Oxford University Press, 2003.

98. Clemens, *Reluctant Realists*, 62–63.

99. Clemens, *Reluctant Realists*, 65, 254; Kornprobst, *Irredentism in European Politics*, 4–6. For another view of the growing apparent acceptance of the partition among Germans, see Schweigler, *National Consciousness in Divided Germany*; and Mommsen, "History and National Identity."

100. Clemens, *Reluctant Realists*, 65.

101. Clemens, *Reluctant Realists*, 274; Clay Clemens, *CDU Deutschlandpolitik and Reunification, 1985–1989*, Washington, DC: German Historical Institute, 1992; McAdams, *Germany Divided*, 13, 119; Dannenberg, *Foundations of Ostpolitik*; Karl-Rudolf Korte, "The Art of Power: The 'Kohl System,' Leadership and *Deutschlandpolitik*," in *The Kohl Chancellorship*, ed. Clay Clemens and William E. Paterson, London: Frank Cass, 1998, 64–90; Plock, *Basic Treaty and the Evolution of East-West German Relations*; Ash, *In Europe's Name*.

102. Cordell, "Basic Treaty between the Two German States in Retrospect."

103. Bühler, *Oder-Neisse Line*, 85.

104. United States, Department of State, *Documents on Germany*, 1189.

105. Bühler, *Oder-Neisse Line*, 77; Ash, *In Europe's Name*.

106. Ash, *In Europe's Name*; Clemens, *Reluctant Realists*, 33, 224–28.

107. CDU Federal Office, *The Election Program of the CDU and CSU, 1976*.

108. McAdams, *Germany Divided*, 121.

109. Ash, *In Europe's Name*, 32, 100–102; William D. Zuckerman, "The Germans: What's the Question?," *International Affairs* 61, no. 3 (1985): 465–70.

110. Korte, "Art of Power," 65; Fritsch-Bournazel, *Confronting the German Question*, 97.

111. Quoted in Ash, *In Europe's Name*, 100.

112. United States, Department of State, *Documents on Germany*, 1365.

113. United States, Department of State, *Documents on Germany*, 1365–72.

114. Ash, *In Europe's Name*; Korte, "Art of Power"; Clemens, *CDU Deutschlandpolitik*.

115. Korte, "Art of Power"; McAdams, *Germany Divided*, 154, 170.

116. United States, Department of State, *Documents on Germany*, 1388–89.

117. Ash, *In Europe's Name*, 171.

118. Quoted in Clemens, *CDU Deutschlandpolitik*, 9–10.

119. Clemens, *CDU Deutschlandpolitik*, 15, 22.

120. Clemens, *Reluctant Realists*, 167; McAdams, *Germany Divided*, 152–53; Kreile, "Ostpolitik Reconsidered."

121. Clemens, *Reluctant Realists*.

122. Peter Radunski, "The Christian Democratic Union," in Livingston, *West German Political Parties*, 16–28.

123. Quoted in Ash, *In Europe's Name*, 125. See also Horst Teltschik, "Gorbachev's Reform Policy and the Outlook for East-West Relations," *Aussenpolitik*, no. 3 (1989): 201–14; and McAdams, *Germany Divided*, 172.

124. Quoted in McAdams, *Germany Divided*, 191–92.

125. Clemens, *CDU Deutschlandpolitik*, 13.

126. Clemens, *CDU Deutschlandpolitik*, 13–14.

127. Quoted in Helga Haftendorn, *Coming of Age: German Foreign Policy since 1945*, Lanham, MD: Rowman and Littlefield, 2006, 278–79.

128. Clemens, *CDU Deutschlandpolitik*.

129. Breuilly, *State of Germany*, 229.

130. McAdams, *Germany Divided*, 171.

131. McAdams, *Germany Divided*, 205–6.

132. Quoted in Richard T. Gray and Sabine Wilke, eds., *German Unification and Its Discontents: Documents from the Peaceful Revolution*, Seattle: University of Washington Press, 1996, 85.

133. Clemens, *Reluctant Realists*, 181, also 33, 224–28; Ash, *In Europe's Name*.

134. Foreign Broadcast Information Service (FBIS), "Kohl on 'European' Dimension of Unification," *Düsseldorf Handelsblatt*, *Foreign Radio Broadcasts*, Daily Report, West Europe, FBIS-WEU-90-195, October 9, 1990.

135. Ash, *In Europe's Name*, 230; see also Pond, *Beyond the Wall*, 194–95.

136. For examples of scholarship that points to the impact of Germany's defeat in World War II, see Schellenger, *SPD in the Bonn Republic*; L. L. Snyder, *Roots of German Nationalism*; Pond, *Beyond the Wall*; Peter K. Breit, "Case Studies of West German Views on Reunification," PhD diss., University of Massachusetts, 1967; William Sheridan Allen, "The Collapse of Nationalism in Nazi Germany," in Breuilly, *State of Germany*, 141–53; and Alter, "Nationalism and German Politics." For examples of scholarship highlighting the impact of the Berlin Wall, see William E. Griffith, *The Ostpolitik of the Federal Republic of Germany*, Cambridge, MA: MIT Press, 1978; Michael Wolffsohn, *West-Germany's Foreign Policy in the Era of Brandt and Schmidt, 1969–1982: An Introduction*, Frankfurt: Peter Lang Gmbh Internationaler Verlag der Wissenschaften, 1986; Jean Edward Smith, "The Berlin Wall in Retrospect," *Dalhousie Review* 47, no. 2 (1967): 173–84; Geiss, "Federal Republic of Germany in International Politics," 152; Wolfram F. Hanrieder, *Germany, America, Europe: Forty Years of German Foreign Policy*, New Haven, CT: Yale University Press, 1989; William G. Gray, "West Germany and the Lost German East: Two Narratives," in *The Germans and the East*, ed. Charles W. Ingrao and Franz A. J. Szabo, West Lafayette, IN: Purdue University Press, 2008, 402–20; and Kornprobst, *Irredentism in European Politics*.

137. Fritsch-Bournazel, *Confronting the German Question*, 11; Koppel, "Sources of Change in West German Ostpolitik," 221; Ash, *In Europe's Name*, 228.

138. A Student of Central Europe, "The Polish-German Frontier," *International Relations* 1, no. 1 (1954): 23–28; Ralph Hall Pickett, *Germany and the Oder-Neisse Line,* Clarkson, ON: Canadian Peace Research Institute, 1968. As in many cases, the figures and motivations for the demographic change, and even its existence, are (or were) hotly contested between Polish and German partisans. In 1953 West Germany claimed that roughly 1.5 million Germans (of the almost 12 million who lived there before the war) remained east of the Oder-Neisse Line. See Pickett, *Germany and the Oder-Neisse Line.* For a summary of the Polish view, including a rebuttal of the numbers used by the Germans about how many refugees there were, and attributing population movements to wartime changes rather than postwar events, see Józef Kokot, *The Logic of the Oder-Neisse Frontier,* Warsaw: Wydawn Zachodnie, 1959.

139. Haftendorn, *Coming of Age,* 124; Dietrich Orlow, "The GDR's Failed Search for a National Identity, 1945–1989," *German Studies Review* 29, no. 3 (2006): 537–58; Herb, "Double Vision," 147. For an example of the withdrawal of homeland territoriality from the Eastern Territories by the GDR, see its framing of the Oder-Neisse boundary as justifiably ending the partition of Poland in *GDR and Poland—Friends and Battle Comrades Forever,* Dresden: Panorma DDR, 1975.

140. McAdams, *Germany Divided,* 6, 26, 37–38, 40. See also Schweigler, *National Consciousness in Divided Germany,* 95.

141. Orlow, "GDR's Failed Search for a National Identity," 543.

142. McAdams, *Germany Divided,* 40.

143. Quoted in McAdams, *Germany Divided,* 77. See also Orlow, "GDR's Failed Search for a National Identity"; and United States, Department of State, *Documents on Germany,* 494–95, 505. For a differing assessment of Ulbricht's commitment to reunification, see Cordell, "Basic Treaty between the Two German States in Retrospect."

144. Kohn, *Mind of Germany,* 17–18.

145. For early public opinion on the topic, see, for example, Merritt and Merritt, *Public Opinion in Semisovereign Germany,* 28, 47, 174; and Schweigler, *National Consciousness in Divided Germany,* 148. For later views, see, for example, Clemens, *Reluctant Realists,* 266; Fritsch-Bournazel, *Confronting the German Question,* 111; Mommsen, "History and National Identity," 568–69; Klaus von Beyme, "The Legitimation of German Unification between National and Democratic Principles," *German Politics and Society,* no. 22 (1991): 1–17, 3; and Beyme, "National Consciousness and Nationalism," 244.

146. Brandt, *People and Politics,* 20. See also Ash, *In Europe's Name,* 60; Koppel, "Sources of Change in West German Ostpolitik"; and Hope M. Harrison, "The Berlin Wall, Ostpolitik, and Détente," in Geyer and Schaefer, *American Détente and German Ostpolitik, 1969–1972,* 5–18, 5.

147. Quoted in Koppel, "Sources of Change in West German Ostpolitik," 90.

148. Dannenberg, *Foundations of Ostpolitik,* 22.

149. Schweigler, *National Consciousness in Divided Germany,* 168; Herz, "Germany," 16.

150. Schweigler, *National Consciousness in Divided Germany.* See also Herz, "Germany"; David Schoenbaum and Elizabeth Pond, *The German Question and Other German Questions,* New York: St. Martin's Press, 1996, 54; Tilford, introduction; and W. E. Paterson, "The Ostpolitik and Regime Stability in West Germany," in Tilford, *Ostpolitik and Political Change in Germany,* 23–44.

151. Herb, "Double Vision," 158.

152. Schweigler, *National Consciousness in Divided Germany,* tables 4.8–4.10.

153. Clemens, *Reluctant Realists,* 247.

154. Pond, *Beyond the Wall,* 193; Ash, *In Europe's Name,* 30, 133; Geiss, *Question of German Unification,* 97; Schoenbaum and Pond, *German Question,* 19; McAdams, *Germany Divided*; Mommsen, "History and National Identity"; Mary Fulbrook, "Nation, State and

Political Culture in Divided Germany, 1945–90," in Breuilly, *State of Germany*, 177–200; Alter, "Nationalism and German Politics"; John Bornemann, *Belonging in the Two Berlins: Kin, State, Nation*, Cambridge: Cambridge University Press, 1992.

155. Atzili and Kantel, "Accepting the Unacceptable."

156. McAdams, *Germany Divided*, 17.

157. Herb, "Double Vision," 150.

158. Koppel, "Sources of Change in West German Ostpolitik," 385; McAdams, *Germany Divided*, 52–55.

159. Herb, "Double Vision," 150.

160. Merkl, "Role of Public Opinion." See also McAdams, *Germany Divided*, xiii.

161. James, *German Identity, 1770–1990*, 203. See also W. D. Zuckerman, "Germans"; and Hanrieder, "Foreign Policies of the Federal Republic of Germany, 1949–1989," 311.

162. McAdams, *Germany Divided*, 22–23. For Dulles's comments, see United States, Senate Committee on Foreign Relations, *Documents on Germany, 1944–1959: Background Documents on Germany, 1944–1959, and a Chronology of Political Developments Affecting Berlin, 1945–1956*, Washington, DC: United States Government Printing Office, 1959, 308. A few years later, Kennedy would repeat the emphasis on the Western part of Berlin, effectively ceding control over East Berlin to the GDR. McAdams, *Germany Divided*, 51.

163. Quoted in Dannenberg, *Foundations of Ostpolitik*, 21.

164. Quoted in McAdams, *Germany Divided*, 23, see also 44–45.

165. McAdams, *Germany Divided*, 54; Granieri, *Ambivalent Alliance*.

166. Ahonen, "Domestic Constraints on West German Ostpolitik," 49.

167. Quoted in Ash, *In Europe's Name*, 66.

168. Ash, *In Europe's Name*, 237. See, for example, Student of Central Europe, "Polish-German Frontier"; Pickett, *Germany and the Oder-Neisse Line*; and Herz, "Germany."

169. G. W. White, *Nation, State, and Territory*, 55.

170. Student of Central Europe, "Polish-German Frontier," 23; Wiskemann, *Germany's Eastern Neighbours*.

171. Kreile, "Ostpolitik Reconsidered," 135; Dannenberg, *Foundations of Ostpolitik*, 214–15.

172. Freymond, *Saar Conflict, 1945–1955*, 201, 313–14.

173. Willi Leibfritz, "Economic Consequences of German Unification," *Business Economics* 25, no. 4 (1990): 5–9.

174. Reuters, "Study Shows High Cost of German Reunification: Report," 2009, accessed August 1, 2018, https://www.reuters.com/article/us-germany-wall/study-shows-high-cost-of-german-reunification-report-idUSTRE5A613B20091107.

175. Cited in Jennifer Hunt, "The Economics of German Reunification," National Bureau of Economic Research working paper, 2006, accessed August 1, 2018, http://www.rci.rutgers.edu/jah357/Hunt/Transition_files/german_unification.pdf.

176. R. T. Gray and Wilke, *German Unification and Its Discontents*.

177. Pew Research Center, *End of Communism Cheered but Now with More Reservations*, Pew Research Center, 2009, accessed August 1, 2018, http://www.pewglobal.org/2009/11/02/chapter-5-views-of-german-reunification/#standard-of-living-in-east-germany. See also Beyme, "Legitimation of German Unification," 3.

178. See, for example, Schweigler, *National Consciousness in Divided Germany*, 249. See also Banchoff, *German Problem Transformed*, 84; Clemens, *Reluctant Realists*, 236–43; Schoenbaum and Pond, *German Question*, 48; Konrad H. Jarausch, Hinrich C. Seeba, and David P. Conradt, "The Presence of the Past: Culture, Opinion, and Identity in Germany," in *After Unity: Reconfiguring German Identities*, ed. Konrad H. Jarausch, Providence, RI: Berghahn Books, 1997, 25–60; Fritsch-Bournazel, *Confronting the German Question*, 111; Haftendorn, *Coming of Age*, 170; David P. Conradt, "Changing German Political Culture,"

in *The Civic Culture Revisited*, ed. Gabriel Almond and Sidney Verba, Boston, MA: Little, Brown, 1980, 212–72; and Mommsen, "History and National Identity." For an argument that generational change was also implicated in changing conceptions of the homeland in East Germany, see Mary Fulbrook, *German National Identity after the Holocaust*, Cambridge: Polity Press, 1999, 195.

179. Clemens, *Reluctant Realists*, 247.

180. Beyme, "National Consciousness and Nationalism," 244, 235.

181. Atzili and Kantel, "Accepting the Unacceptable."

182. Stefan Wolff, *The German Question since 1919: An Analysis with Key Documents*, Westport, CT: Greenwood, 2003, 105.

183. Quoted in Haftendorn, *Coming of Age*, 140.

184. Dannenberg, *Foundations of Ostpolitik*, 9–10; Jerzy Hauptmann, "The Problem of Partition," in Collier and Glaser, *Conditions for Peace in Europe*, 87–93; Atzili and Kantel, "Accepting the Unacceptable"; McAdams, *Germany Divided*, 46, 65.

185. McAdams, *Germany Divided*, 6.

186. Granieri, *Ambivalent Alliance*.

187. Hanrieder, *Germany, America, Europe*, 319, 172. See also Debra J. Allen, *The Oder-Neisse Line: The United States, Poland, and Germany in the Cold War*, Westport, CT: Praeger, 2003; Pickett, *Germany and the Oder-Neisse Line*; and McAdams, *Germany Divided*.

188. Granieri, *Ambivalent Alliance*, 49; McAdams, *Germany Divided*, 60.

189. Gottfried Niedhart, "The Federal Republic's Ostpolitik and the United States: Initiatives and Constraints," in *The United States and the European Alliance since 1945*, ed. Kathleen Burke and Melvyn Stokes, Oxford: Berg, 1999, chap. 11, 289–312; Wilkens, "New Ostpolitik"; Haftendorn, *Coming of Age*; Atzili and Kantel, "Accepting the Unacceptable."

190. Indeed, Kissinger considered the German-Soviet negotiations over the Moscow Treaty to be disruptive. He told Undersecretary Paul Frank: "I'll tell you one thing for sure, if any détente policy is to be pursued with the Soviet Union, then we'll be the ones doing it." Quoted in Haftendorn, *Coming of Age*, 189.

191. Quoted in Wilkens, "New Ostpolitik," 77. See also Brandt, *My Life in Politics*, 174–75; and Niedhart, "Federal Republic's Ostpolitik."

192. Melvin Croan, "Dilemmas of Ostpolitik," in *West German Foreign Policy: Dilemmas and Directions*, ed. Peter Merkl, Chicago: Chicago Council on Foreign Relations, 1982, 35–52.

193. McAdams, *Germany Divided*; Haftendorn, *Coming of Age*, 29, 41, 55; Orlow, "GDR's Failed Search for a National Identity"; James, *German Identity, 1770–1990*, 170.

194. Gehrig, "Cold War Identities"; Palmowski, *Inventing a Socialist Nation*; Schweigler, *National Consciousness in Divided Germany*, 33; Jarausnch, Seeba, and Conradt, "Presence of the Past," 43; Orlow, "GDR's Failed Search for a National Identity"; Fritsch-Bournazel, *Confronting the German Question*, 99; Ash, *In Europe's Name*, 189; Herb, "Double Vision," 146.

195. McAdams, *Germany Divided*, 91.

196. Ash, *In Europe's Name*, 189.

197. McAdams, *Germany Divided*; Orlow, "GDR's Failed Search for a National Identity"; Ash, *In Europe's Name*, 77; Cordell, "Basic Treaty between the Two German States in Retrospect"; Fritsch-Bournazel, *Confronting the German Question*, 97–98; Jarausnch, Seeba, and Conradt, "Presence of the Past," 42. Palmowski, *Inventing a Socialist Nation*, 19, however, argues that the attempt to create an East Germany national identity did not require the East German state to openly accept the territorial division as permanent.

3. ITALY'S FORGOTTEN PARTITION

1. For reviews of Italian claims to Venezia Giulia, see Bogdan C. Novak, *Trieste, 1941–1954: The Ethnic, Political, and Ideological Struggle*, Chicago: University of Chicago Press, 1970, 14–17; Glenda Sluga, *The Problem of Trieste and the Italo-Yugoslav Border: Difference*,

Identity, and Sovereignty in Twentieth-Century Europe, Albany: SUNY Press, 2001; Gerald Stourzh, *From Vienna to Chicago and Back: Essays on Intellectual History and Political Thought in Europe and America,* Chicago: University of Chicago Press, 2010, chap. 6; René Albrecht-Carrié, *Italy at the Paris Peace Conference,* Hamden, CT: Archon Books, 1966; Maura Elise Hametz, *Making Trieste Italian, 1918–1954,* Woodbridge: Boydell and Brewer, 2005; Alessandra Miklavcic, "Border of Memories, Memories of Borders: An Ethnographic Investigation of Border Practices in the Julian Region (Italy, Slovenia)," PhD thesis, University of Toronto, 2006; Gross, *Ethnics in a Borderland; Trieste e la Venezia Giula,* Rome: Istituto Editoriale Julia Romana, 1951; *Italy and the Free Territory of Trieste,* special supplement of *Esteri: Quindicinale di politica estera,* May 1953; Carlo Schiffrer, *Historic Glance at the Relations between Italians and Slavs in Venezia Giulia,* Trieste: Istituto di storia dell'Università di Trieste, 1946; Committee for the Defense of the Italian Character of Trieste and Istria, *Trieste—November 1953: Facts and Documents,* Trieste, 1953; Fabio Capano, "Between the Local and the National: The Free Territory of Trieste," PhD diss., West Virginia University, 2014; Giorgio Federico Siboni, *Il confine orientale: Da campoformio all'approdo europeo,* Sestri Levante: Oltre Edizioni, 2012; Francesco L. Pullé, *Italia genti e favelle (disegno antropologico-linguistico) atlante,* Turin: Fratelli Bocca Editori, 1927; and Marina Cattaruzza, *L'Italia e il confine orientale,* Bologna: Il Mulino, 2007. For Slav claims to the same territory, see Joseph Velikonja, "The Quest for Slovene National Identity," in Hooson, *Geography and National Identity,* 249–56; Jože Pirjevec, "Slovene Nationalism in Trieste, 1848–1982," *Nationalities Papers* 11, no. 2 (1983): 152–61; and Eric R. Terzuolo, *Red Adriatic: The Communist Parties of Italy and Yugoslavia,* Boulder, CO: Westview, 1985.

2. There are some minor variations in what each label includes. See Novak, *Trieste,* 4; Miklavcic, "Border of Memories, Memories of Borders"; and Siboni, *Il confine orientale,* 5.

3. Gross, *Ethnics in a Borderland,* 75, 79.

4. Quoted in Emilio Gentile, *La Grande Italia: The Myth of the Nation in the Twentieth Century,* Madison: University of Wisconsin Press, 1997, 22. See also Lucy Riall, *Garibaldi: Invention of a Hero,* New Haven, CT: Yale University Press, 2007, 21.

5. See also Schiffrer, *Historic Glance at the Relations between Italians and Slavs,* 15; and Cattaruzza, *L'Italia e il confine orientale,* 50.

6. Miklavcic, "Border of Memories, Memories of Borders," 112.

7. Miklavcic, "Border of Memories, Memories of Borders," 115; Terzuolo, *Red Adriatic,* 4. As a result, as many as 100,000 Slavs left the ethnically mixed towns in the region. See Čermelj, cited in Milan Bufon, "The Changeable Political Map of the Upper Adriatic Region: From Conflict to Harmony," *Revija za geografijo* 1, no. 3 (2008): 9–23.

8. Dennison I. Rusinow, *What Ever Happened to the "Trieste Question"?: De-Fusing a Threat to World Peace,* Hanover, NJ: American Universities Field Staff, 1969, 2.

9. It is not counted as a partition by, for example, Kaufmann, "When All Else Fails"; Nicholas Sambanis, "Partition as a Solution to Ethnic War: An Empirical Critique of the Theoretical Literature," *World Politics* 52, no. 4 (2000): 437–83; Tir, "Dividing Countries to Promote Peace"; Chapman and Roeder, "Partition as a Solution"; C. Johnson, "Partitioning to Peace"; or Nicholas Sambanis and Jonah Schulhofer-Wohl, "What's in a Line?: Is Partition a Solution to Civil War?," *International Security* 34, no. 2 (2009): 82–118.

10. See, for example, the combination of historical, nationalist, and ethnic reasons used to legitimate Italian control of the territory earlier in the twentieth century. *Dalmatia, Fiume and the Other Unreedemed [sic] Lands of the Adriatic.* See also Albrecht-Carrié, *Italy at the Paris Peace Conference;* and John E. Ashbrook, " 'Istria Is Ours, and We Can Prove It': An Examination of Istrian Historiography in the Nineteenth and Twentieth Centuries," *Carl Beck Papers in Russian and East European Studies,* no. 1707 (2006): 1–43.

11. Ronald S. Cunsolo, *Italian Nationalism: From Its Origins to World War II*, Malabar, FL: Krieger, 1990, 6, 23; Charles L. Killinger, *The History of Italy*, Westport, CT: Greenwood, 2002, 1.

12. On nationalizing states more broadly, see Brubaker, *Nationalism Reframed*.

13. See Hametz, *Making Trieste Italian*; and Gentile, *La Grande Italia*, 31.

14. Manlio Graziano, *The Failure of Italian Nationhood: The Geopolitics of a Troubled Identity*, New York: Springer, 2010, 60–64. See also Cunsolo, *Italian Nationalism*, 6–7; and Lucy Riall, *The Italian Risorgimento: State, Society, and National Unification*, New York: Routledge, 1994, 63, 74.

15. John Creighton Campbell, *Successful Negotiation, Trieste 1954: An Appraisal by the Five Participants*, Princeton, NJ: Princeton University Press, 1976, 5; Novak, *Trieste*, 11.

16. Ashbrook, "'Istria Is Ours, and We Can Prove It'"; Albrecht-Carrié, *Italy at the Paris Peace Conference*; Novak, *Trieste*, 14.

17. Government of Italy, *Trieste*, 67. See also Novak, *Trieste*, 123, 382; and Osvaldo Croci, "The Trieste Crisis, 1953," PhD thesis, McGill University, 1991, 75.

18. Government of Italy, *Trieste*, 82.

19. Novak, *Trieste*, 128, 245; Antonio Giulio M. de Robertis, *La frontiera orientale italiana nella diplomazia della seconda guerra mondiale*, Naples: Edizioni scientifiche italiane, 1981, 217.

20. Corrado Belci, *Quel confine mancato: La linea Wilson, 1919–1945*, Brescia: Morcelliana, 1996.

21. Diego De Castro, *La questione di Trieste: L'azione politica e diplomatica italiana dal 1943 al 1954*, Trieste: LINT, 1981, 112–13.

22. Graziano, *Failure of Italian Nationhood*, 153. See also Gentile, *La Grande Italia*, 297–99; Antonio Varsori, "De Gasperi, Nenni, Sforza and Their Role in Post-War Italian Foreign Policy," in Becker and Knipping, *Power in Europe?*, 89–116; and Ennio Di Nolfo, "The Shaping of Italian Foreign Policy during the Formation of the East-West Blocs: Italy between the Superpowers," in Becker and Knipping, *Power in Europe?*, 485–502.

23. Goddard and Krebs, "Rhetoric, Legitimation, and Grand Strategy."

24. Kornprobst, *Irredentism in European Politics*.

25. Raphael Zariski, "Intra-Party Conflict in a Dominant Party: The Experience of Italian Christian Democracy," *Journal of Politics* 27, no. 1 (1965): 3–34; Robert Leonardi and Douglas A. Wertman, *Italian Christian Democracy: The Politics of Dominance*, New York: Macmillan, 1989.

26. Quoted in Gentile, *La Grande Italia*, 324.

27. Giulia Prati, *Italian Foreign Policy, 1947–1951: Alcide De Gasperi and Carlo Sforza between Atlanticism and Europeanism*, Göttingen: Vandenhoeck and Ruprecht, 2006, 64. See also Croci, "Trieste Crisis," 135–38; and Novak, *Trieste*.

28. Osvaldo Croci, "Search for Parity: Italian and Yugoslav Attitudes toward the Question of Trieste," *Slovene Studies* 12, no. 2 (1992): 141–55, 147; United States, Central Intelligence Agency, "Current Situation in the Free Territory of Trieste."

29. Capano, "Between the Local and the National." See also Sluga, *Problem of Trieste*, 76; Elizabeth Wiskemann, *Italy since 1945*, New York: MacMillan, 1971, 2; and Gentile, La Grande Italia, chap. 17, also 215, 219.

30. Jean Baptiste Duroselle, *Le conflit de Trieste: 1943–1954*, Brussels: Éditions de l'Institut de sociologie de l'Université libre de Bruxelles, 1966, 254–56; Capano, "Between the Local and the National"; Christopher Seton-Watson, "Italy's Imperial Hangover," *Journal of Contemporary History* 15, no. 1 (1980): 169–79, 174.

31. See, respectively, Raimondo Strassoldo, "Perspectives on Frontiers: The Case of Alpe Adria," in *The Frontiers of Europe*, ed. Malcolm Anderson and Eberhard Bort, London: Pinter, 75–90, 77; Leopoldo Nuti, "Italian Foreign Policy in the Cold War: A Constant

Search for Status," in *Italy in the Post–Cold War Order: Adaptation, Bipartisanship, Visibility*, ed. Maurizio Carbone, Lanham, MD: Lexington Books, 2011, 25–47, 42n1; and Croci, "Trieste Crisis," 125–26. See also Alberto Tarchiani, who was the Italian ambassador to the United States, in Croci, "Trieste Crisis," 125; Ennio Di Nolfo, "'Power Politics': The Italian Pattern (1951–1957)," in Nolfo, *Power in Europe?*, 530–45; De Castro, La questione di Trieste, 285–86; and Diego D'Amelio, "Frontiere in transizione: Il lungo dopoguerra dei confini Italiani fra ereditá, emergenze e distensioni," in Diego, Di Michele, and Mezzalira, *La Difesa dell'Italianitá*, 539–94, 560.

32. Both quoted in Croci, "Trieste Crisis," 126. A similar (sacrifice-based) argument was made to the Allied Powers by Ivanoe Bonomi, the Italian representative to the Political and Territorial Commission for Italy. See Government of Italy, *Trieste*, 82.

33. Quoted in Sluga, *Problem of Trieste*, 144. See also Duroselle, *Le conflit de Trieste*, 255; and Novak, *Trieste*, 277.

34. Ivanoe Bonomi, "Abbiamo firmato: Chiediamo giustiza per l'Italia," *Nuovo Corriere della Sera*, February 11, 1947.

35. Seton-Watson, "Italy's Imperial Hangover," 174.

36. Maurice Edelman, "Italy's Foreign Policy," *Political Quarterly* 21, no. 4 (1950): 374–84, 375.

37. Fabio Capano, "Cold-War Trieste: Metamorphosing Ideas of Italian Nationhood, 1945–1975," *Modern Italy* 21, no. 1 (2016): 51–66; Foreign Broadcast Information Service (FBIS), "Trieste Labor Rejoices at Allied Action," Daily Report, *Foreign Radio Broadcasts*, FBIS-FRB-48-275, March 25, 1948; Capano, "Between the Local and the National."

38. Arnalso Cortesi, "De Gasperi, Sforza Leave for London: Italians Will Meet Tomorrow with British on Relations between Two Nations," *New York Times*, March 12, 1951, 12.

39. Campbell, *Successful Negotiation*, 13.

40. Brunello Vigezzi, "Italy: The End of a 'Great Power' and the Birth of a 'Democratic Power,'" in Becker and Knipping, *Power in Europe?*, 67–88.

41. Quoted in Vigezzi, "Italy," 71.

42. Croci, "Trieste Crisis," 123. For more on the Italian drive to regain full sovereignty, see David W. Ellwood, "Italy, Europe and the Cold War: The Politics and Economics of Limited Sovereignty," in *Italy in the Cold War: Politics, Culture and Society 1948–1958*, ed. Christopher Duggan and Christopher Wagstaff, Oxford: Berg, 1995, 25–46.

43. Novak, *Trieste*, 279.

44. Edvard Kardelj, *Trieste and Yugoslav-Italian Relations*, New York: Yugoslav Information Center, 1953, 20. See also Capano, "Between the Local and the National," 66, 73.

45. Croci, "Search for Parity," 145. See also Camille M. Cianfarra, "Italy Will Defer Action on Trieste: Government Circles Declare U.S. and Britain Must Take the Initiative for Solution, Return of Area Is Aim, Rome Amenable to Proposal," *New York Times*, March 4, 1951, 29; Capano, "Between the Local and the National"; Prati, *Italian Foreign Policy*; Jože Pirjevec, "Italian Policy toward the Slovenes from 1915 to 1994," *Slovene Studies* 12, nos. 1–2 (1993): 63–73; Campbell, *Successful Negotiation*, 68; Severino Galante, "The Genesis of Political Impotence: Italy's Mass Political Parties in the Years between the Great Alliance and the Cold War," in Becker and Knipping, *Power in Europe?*, 185–206; and Nolfo, "Shaping of Italian Foreign Policy."

46. Bogdan C. Novak, "American Policy toward the Slovenes in Trieste, 1941–1974," *Slovene Studies*, no. 1 (1978): 1–25. This declaration was the product of Italian lobbying and represented an explicit and self-aware attempt by the US government to aid the DC in the upcoming Italian elections. See James E. Miller, "Taking Off the Gloves: The United States and the Italian Elections of 1948," *Diplomatic History* 7, no. 1 (1983): 35–56; Campbell, *Successful Negotiation*, 10; and United States, Central Intelligence Agency, "Current Situation in the Free Territory of Trieste."

47. Capano, "Between the Local and the National," 86.

48. Croci, "Trieste Crisis," 437.

49. Raymond S. Nickerson, "Confirmation Bias: A Ubiquitous Phenomenon in Many Guises," *Review of General Psychology* 2, no. 2 (1998): 175.

50. Quoted in Croci, "Trieste Crisis," 165, 173n37.

51. "De Gasperi, Home, Faces New Crisis: Right-Wing Socialists Threaten to Quit Italian Cabinet and He Is Scored on Trieste," *New York Times*, March 18, 1951, 33.

52. Donald Sassoon, *The Strategy of the Italian Communist Party: From the Resistance to the Historic Compromise*, London: Pinter, 1981, 88.

53. Novak, *Trieste*, 257, 333, 394.

54. Both quoted in Croci, "Trieste Crisis," 135. See also Novak, *Trieste*.

55. Croci, "Trieste Crisis," 173–74n38, 432.

56. Kim Eric Bettcher, "Factionalism and the Adaptation of Dominant Parties: Japan's Liberal Democratic Party and Italy's Christian Democracy," PhD diss., Johns Hopkins University, 2001.

57. Jane Perry Clark Carey and Andrew Galbraith Carey, "The Italian Elections of 1958: Unstable Stability in an Unstable World," *Political Science Quarterly* 74, no. 4 (1958): 566–89; Wiskemann, *Italy since 1945*, 22–23.

58. Croci, "Search for Parity," 148.

59. Croci, "Trieste Crisis," 122–23, 151, 165. See also Novak, *Trieste*, 416–17; and Capano, "Between the Local and the National," 100.

60. Croci, "Trieste Crisis," 138, 155–56.

61. Quoted in Croci, "Trieste Crisis," 190. See also Mainardo Benardelli, *La questione di Trieste: Storia di un conflitto diplomatico (1945–1975)*, Udine: Del Bianco, 2006, 94.

62. Croci, "Search for Parity," 148–49; Croci, "Trieste Crisis," 157, 190–91, 242.

63. Campbell, *Successful Negotiation*, 61; Novak, *Trieste*, 463.

64. Pierpaolo Luzzatto Fegiz, *Il volto sconosciuto dell'Italia: Dieci anni di sondaggi Doxa*, Milan: Giuffrè, 1966, 779.

65. Giovanni Bognetti, "The Role of Italian Parliament in the Treaty-Making Process—Europe," *Chicago-Kent Law Review* 67, no. 2 (1991): 391–412.

66 Novak, *Trieste*, 462, 469; "Italian House OK's Trieste Pact in Brawl," *Chicago Tribune*, October 20, 1954, 1.

67. Jane Perry Clark Carey and Andrew Galbraith Carey, "The Varying Seasons of Italian Politics, 1956–57," *Political Science Quarterly* 72, no. 2 (1957): 200–223, 201; Carey and Carey, "Italian Elections of 1958."

68. Raoul Pupo, "A Mistaken History?: A Survey of the Short Century of Italian-Yugoslav Relations," in Bucarelli et al., *Italy and Tito's Yugoslavia*, 152. See also, for example, Nuti, "Italian Foreign Policy," 42n1; Nolfo, "'Power Politics'"; Novak, *Trieste*; and Wiskemann, *Italy since 1945*, 26.

69. John P. Glennon, ed., *Foreign Relations of the United States, 1955–1957*, vol. 27, *Western Europe and Canada*, Washington, DC: United States Government Printing Office, 1992, 244.

70. Novak, *Trieste*, 463. See also Pupo, "Mistaken History?," 152.

71. Quoted in Croci, "Trieste Crisis," 231. See also Novak, *Trieste*, 429.

72. Capano, "Between the Local and the National," 143, 155.

73. Capano, "Between the Local and the National," 132; Fabio Capano, "Resisting Détente: The Associative Network and the Osimo Treaty," in Bucarelli et al., *Italy and Tito's Yugoslavia*, 367–96.

74. Quoted in Saša Mišić, "A Difficult Reconciliation on the Adriatic: The Yugoslav Road to the Osimo Agreements of 1975," in Bucarelli et al., *Italy and Tito's Yugoslavia*, 257.

75. Benedetto Zaccaria, *The EEC's Yugoslav Policy in Cold War Europe, 1968–1980,* London: Palgrave MacMillan, 2016, 106.

76. See, for example, Leonardi and Wertman, *Italian Christian Democracy,* 162–63; and Paolo Farnetti, *The Italian Party System,* London: Pinter, 1985, 80, 85.

77. Capano, "Between the Local and the National," 200. See also Roberto Fornasier, *The Dove and the Eagle,* Newcastle: Cambridge Scholars, 2012, 22; Frank P. Belloni, "Dislocation in the Italian Political System: An Analysis of the 1968 Parliamentary Elections," *Western Political Quarterly* 24, no. 1 (1971): 114–35; Leonardi and Wertman, *Italian Christian Democracy*; and Capano, "Cold-War Trieste."

78. On the Continental Shelf Boundary Treaty, see United States, Office of the Geographer, Bureau of Intelligence and Research, *Limits in the Seas, No. 9, Continental Shelf Boundary: Italy-Yugoslavia,* US Department of State, 1970.

79. Capano, "Between the Local and the National," 261–63, also 256, 259, 286; Capano, "Resisting Détente"; Bucarelli, "Détente in the Adriatic: Italian Foreign Policy and the Road to the Osimo Treaty," in Bucarelli et al., *Italy and Tito's Yugoslavia,* 11.

80. Pupo, "Mistaken History?," 153.

81. Novak, *Trieste,* 470–71.

82. Simona Colarizi and Guido Panvini, "From Enemy to Opponent: The Politics of Delegitimation in the Italian Christian Democratic Party (1945–1992)," *Journal of Modern Italian Studies* 22, no. 1 (2017): 57–70, 60–61.

83. Capano, "Between the Local and the National," 289, also 165, 265.

84. Milan Bufon and Julian Minghi, "The Upper Adriatic Borderland: From Conflict to Harmony," *GeoJournal* 52, no. 2 (2000): 119–27.

85. Richard West, *Tito and the Rise and Fall of Yugoslavia,* New York: Carroll and Graf, 1994.

86. Quoted in Capano, "Cold-War Trieste," 58.

87. See, for example, Gross, *Ethnics in a Borderland*; Rusinow, *What Ever Happened to the "Trieste Question"?,* 36–37; Bufon and Minghi, "Upper Adriatic Borderland"; Miklavcic, "Border of Memories, Memories of Borders," 292; Capano, "Between the Local and the National"; Capano, "Cold-War Trieste"; Wiskemann, *Italy since 1945,* 26; Strassoldo, "Perspectives on Frontiers"; and Bufon, "Changeable Political Map."

88. Capano, "Between the Local and the National," 243.

89. Severino Galante, "In Search of Lost Power: The International Policies of the Italian Christian Democrat and Communist Parties in the Fifties," in Nolfo, *Power in Europe?,* 407–34.

90. Massimo Bucarelli et al., eds., *Italy and Tito's Yugoslavia in the Age of International Détente,* Brussels: Peter Lang, 2016; Capano, "Cold-War Trieste."

91. Capano, "Between the Local and the National," 279. Italy had long been concerned with its northeast corner as a corridor through which the Warsaw Pact might attack. These concerns were mitigated by the Osimo Treaty, after which Italy switched its security concerns to perceived dangers coming from the south. Yannis Valinakis, "Italian Security Concerns and Policy," *International Spectator* 19, no. 2 (1984): 110–14; Umberto Cappuzzo, "The New Italian Perception of Security," *International Spectator* 19, nos. 3–4 (1984): 133–36.

92. Luciano Monzali, "Aldo Moro, Italian *Ostpolitik* and Relations with Yugoslavia," in Bucarelli et al., *Italy and Tito's Yugoslavia,* 199–216; Bucarelli et al., *Italy and Tito's Yugoslavia.*

93. Capano, "Cold-War Trieste," 57.

94. Quoted in Capano, "Between the Local and the National," 242.

95. Altiero Spinelli, "Remarks on Italian Foreign Policy," in Calzini, *Italo-Yugoslav Relations,* 24; see also Alfonso Sterpellone, "Italy and Yugoslavia," in Calzini, *Italo-Yugoslav Relations,* 42–61.

96. Capano, "Between the Local and the National," 260.

97. Bucarelli, "Détente in the Adriatic."

98. Capano, "Between the Local and the National," 153, 212, 271–72.

99. Diego D'Amelio, "Imperfect Normalization: The Political Repercussions of the Treaty of Osimo," in Bucarelli et al., *Italy and Tito's Yugoslavia*, 343–66, 345, 347; Capano, "Between the Local and the National," 292, 296; and Monzali, "Aldo Moro."

100. Pamela Ballinger, *History in Exile: Memory and Identity at the Borders of the Balkans*, Princeton, NJ: Princeton University Press, 2003, 52.

101. John W. Holmes, "Italian Foreign Policy in a Changing Europe," in *Italian Politics: A Review*, vol. 8, ed. Stephen Hellman and Gianfranco Pasquino, New York: Pinter, 1993, 165–77; Roberto Aliboni and Ettore Greco, "Foreign Policy Re-Nationalization and Internationalism in the Italian Debate," *International Affairs* (Royal Institute of International Affairs 1944) 72, no. 1 (1996): 43–51; Strassoldo, "Perspectives on Frontiers"; Stefano Fella and Carlo Ruzza, *Re-Inventing the Italian Right: Territorial Politics, Populism and 'Post-Fascism,'* New York: Routledge, 2009, 162; Ettore Greco, "Italy, the Yugoslav Crisis and the Osimo Agreements," *International Spectator* 29, no. 1 (1994): 13–31.

102. See, for example, Graziano, *Failure of Italian Nationhood*; and Gentile, *La Grande Italia*. For a critique of this literature, see Christopher Duggan, *The Force of Destiny: A History of Italy since 1796*, Boston, MA: Houghton Mifflin Harcourt, 2008, 549–51.

103. Rusinow, *What Ever Happened to the "Trieste Question"?*, 19.

104. The actual number of Italians who left areas under Yugoslav control is highly contested. Jože Pirjevec and Dennison Rusinow, for example, argue that about 200,000 Italians left Istria after 1945. See Pirjevec, "Italian Policy toward the Slovenes"; and Rusinow, *What Ever Happened to the "Trieste Question"?* Alessandra Miklavcic and Gustavo Corni put it at 250,000. See Miklavcic, "Border of Memories, Memories of Borders," 256; and Gustavo Corni, "The Exodus of Italians from Istria and Dalmatia, 1945–56," in Reinisch and White, *Disentanglement of Populations*, 71–90. Pamela Ballinger and Giorgio Federico Siboni put the total number of refugees, including both Slavs and Italians at between 200,000 and 350,000. See Ballinger, *History in Exile*; and Siboni, *Il confine orientale*. Paul Myers and Arthur Campbell argue that, between 1939 and 1948, within its postwar boundaries, Yugoslavia lost about 100,000 Italians. See Paul F. Myers and Arthur A. Campbell, *The Population of Yugoslavia*, International Population Statistics Report P-90, No. 5, Washington, DC: US Government Printing Office, 1954. See also Bufon and Minghi, "Upper Adriatic Borderland"; Sluga, *Problem of Trieste*, 144–45; Miklavcic, "Border of Memories, Memories of Borders"; Corni, "Exodus of Italians from Istria and Dalmatia," 71–90; Pupo, "Mistaken History?"; and Raoul Pupo, "Gli esodi e la realtá politica dal dopoguerra a oggi," in *Storia d'Italia: Le regioni dall'Unitá a oggi; Il Friuli-Venezia Giulia*, 2002, 663–758.

105. Demographic Research Center Institute of Social Sciences, *The Population of Yugoslavia: 1974 World Population Year*, Belgrade: Demographic Research Center Institute of Social Sciences, 1975. While the Yugoslav census may have an incentive to undercount the number of Italians, this figure is consistent with other estimates. See, for example, Paul Shoup, "Yugoslavia's National Minorities under Communism," *Slavic Review* 22, no. 1 (1963): 64–81; and Bufon, "Changeable Political Map."

106. Novak, *Trieste*. The vast majority of these Italian speakers were along the Dalmatian coast. P. Myers and Campbell, *Population of Yugoslavia*, 21, 53.

107. See the 'l'orgoglio di essere italiano la forza della gioventù' [the pride of being Italian the strength of youth] pamphlet, http://www.cnj.it/immagini/meniafini.jpg; Roberto Bianchin, "Trieste si ribella il MSI è pronto a 'sconfinare,'" *La Repubblica*, November 8, 1992. See also Fella and Ruzza, *Re-Inventing the Italian Right*, 162; and Ballinger, *History in Exile*, 52, 91–96.

108. See Irne Bolzon, "Da Roma alla Zona B: Il Comitato di liberazione nazionale dell'Istria, l'Ufficio per le zone de confine e le comunitá istriane tra informazioni, propaganda e assistenza," in Diego, Di Michele, and Mezzalira, *La difesa dell'Italianitá*, 487–509, 497.

109. Capano, "Cold-War Trieste"; Anna Millo, "Il 'filo nero': Violenza, lotta politica, apparti dello stato al confine orientale (1945–1954)," in Diego, Di Michele, and Mezzalira, *La difesa dell'Italianitá*, 415–38; Bolzon, "Da Roma alla Zona B."

110. Pupo, "Mistaken History?"; Novak, *Trieste*, 463.

111. Croci, "Trieste Crisis," 437.

112. Capano, "Between the Local and the National," 121.

113. Capano, "Between the Local and the National," 105. Survey evidence supports Taviani's claim. In November 1953, only about a quarter of Italians surveyed could name a city or town in Zone B. Fegiz, *Il volto sconosciuto dell'Italia*, 778.

114. De Castro lamented this development. See De Castro, *La questione di Trieste*, 283–84. For a similar process in another context, see Shelef, "From 'Both Banks of the Jordan' to the 'Whole Land of Israel.'"

115. D'Amelio, "Frontiere in transizione."

116. Miklavcic, "Border of Memories, Memories of Borders," 243. See also Strassoldo, "Perspectives on Frontiers," 86.

117. Prati, *Italian Foreign Policy*.

118. See, for example, Graziano, *Failure of Italian Nationhood*. Ballinger also charts the course of Italian irredentist demands as following the geopolitical needs of the Italian state. See Ballinger, *History in Exile*, 8.

119. See, for example, Pietro Quaroni in Croci, "Search for Parity," 143.

120. Novak, *Trieste*, 360; Croci, "Trieste Crisis," 87.

121. When he did appear to acquiesce to negotiate with Yugoslavia in response to American pressure, he did so with no intention of retreating from his previous position. Rather, he saw entering into negotiations as the price to be paid for US agreement to postponing the administrative elections in Trieste, which he sought because he feared that the Independence Front would win. See Croci, "Trieste Crisis," 139–41.

122. Capano, "Between the Local and the National"; Croci, "Search for Parity," 149.

123. Donald L. M. Blackmer, "The International Strategy of the Italian Communist Party," in *The International Role of the Communist Parties of Italy and France*, ed. Donald L. M. Blackmer and Annie Kriegel, Cambridge, MA: Center for International Affairs, Harvard University, 1975, 19–25; Terzuolo, *Red Adriatic*; Anna Maria Gentili and Angelo Panebianco, "The PCI and International Relations, 1945–1975: The Politics of Accommodation," in *The Italian Communist Party: Yesterday, Today, and Tomorrow*, ed. Simon Serfaty and Lawrence Gray, Westport, CT: Greenwood Press, 1980, 109–27; Capano, "Between the Local and the National," 52–53; Josef L. Kunz, "The Free Territory of Trieste," *Western Political Quarterly* 1, no. 2 (1948): 99–112; Aldo Agosti, *Palmiro Togliatti: A Biography*. New York: I. B. Tauris, 2008. On the national impulses of the PCI after 1945 more generally, see Gentile, *La Grande Italia*, chaps. 17–18.

124. Patrick Karlsen, "La 'terra di mezzo' del comunismo adriatico alla vigilia della rottura fra Tito e Stalin," *Qualestoria: Rivista di storia contemporanea* 45, no. 1 (2017): 19–41; Karlo Ruzicic-Kessler, "Comunismi di frontiera: L'Alto Adige e la Venezia Giulia in una prospettiva transnazionale," *Qualestoria: Rivista di storia contemporanea* 45, no. 1 (2017): 123–38. Indeed, the attitudes of PCI supporters about what should be done regarding Trieste in 1958 were not significantly different from those of DC supporters. See Instituto per le Recerche Statistiche e l'Analisi dell'Opinione Pubblica, *DOXA Survey 1958–5801: Political and Social Research*, Ithaca, NY: Roper Center for Public Opinion Research, 1958.

125. Novak, *Trieste*, 233.

NOTES TO PAGES 106–112   253

126. The Diocese border was only brought into congruence with the international border in 1975. Capano, "Between the Local and the National," 171, 290.

127. Capano, "Resisting Détente."

128. On the role of the Catholic Church in Italian politics, see Douglas A. Wertman, "The Catholic Church and Italian Politics: The Impact of Secularisation," *West European Politics* 5, no. 2 (1982): 87–107; Carolyn M. Warner, *Confessions of an Interest Group: The Catholic Church and Political Parties in Europe*, Princeton, NJ: Princeton University Press, 2000; and Ilvo Diamanti and Luigi Ceccarini, "Catholics and Politics after the Christian Democrats: The Influential Minority," *Journal of Modern Italian Studies* 12, no. 1 (2007): 37–59.

4. HOMELANDS AND CHANGE IN A STATELESS NATION

1. Parts of this chapter were previously published as Mylonas and Shelef, "Which Land Is Our Land?"

2. Walter, *Reputation and Civil War*; Tanisha Fazal and Ryan Griffiths, "A State of One's Own: The Rise of Secession since World War II," *Brown Journal of World Affairs* 15 (2008): 199; K. G. Cunningham, *Inside the Politics of Self-Determination*.

3. Rashid Khalidi, *Palestinian Identity: The Formation of National Consciousness*, New York: Columbia University Press, 1998; Baruch Kimmerling and Joel S. Migdal, *The Palestinian People: A History*, Cambridge, MA: Harvard University Press, 2003.

4. Fuad A. Jabber, ed., *International Documents on Palestine, 1967*, Beirut: Institute for Palestine Studies, 1970, 570–71, originally on June 1, 1967; Shukeiri, *Liberation—Not Negotiation*, 81, originally on November 1963, see also 37, 57, 134.

5. Issa Al-Shuaibi, "The Development of Palestinian Entity-Consciousness: Part I," *Journal of Palestine Studies* 9, no. 1 (1979): 67–84, 72.

6. Helga Baumgarten, "The Three Faces/Phases of Palestinian Nationalism, 1948–2005," *Journal of Palestine Studies* 34, no. 4 (2005): 25–48, 32, original emphasis. See also, Alain Gresh, *The PLO: The Struggle within: Towards an Independent Palestinian State*, London: Zed Books, 1985; Ehud Yaari, "Al Fath's Political Thinking," *New Outlook* 11, no. 9 (102) (November–December 1968): 20–33; Yezid Sayigh, *Armed Struggle and the Search for State: The Palestinian National Movement, 1949–1993*, Oxford: Oxford University Press, 1997; and Helena Lindholm Schulz, *The Reconstruction of Palestinian Nationalism: Between Revolution and Statehood*, Manchester: Manchester University Press, 1999.

7. See Abu Iyad, *My Home, My Land: A Narrative of the Palestinian Struggle*, New York: Times Books, 1980, 45, originally on January 28, 1965.

8. S ee Zuhair Diab, ed., *International Documents on Palestine, 1968*, Beirut: Institute for Palestine Studies, 1971, 304, Press Release No. 1 by Fatah, January 1968.

9. Jabber, *International Documents on Palestine, 1967*, 721, "Statement of Policy Issued by the 'Fatah' Movement declaring its rejection of the Security Council resolution of 22 November," originally published in *Al-Jumhuriyah*, Baghdad, December 12, 1967. See also Walid Khadduri, ed., *International Documents on Palestine, 1970*, Beirut: Institute for Palestine Studies, 1973, 754; Farouk Kaddoumi in IPS Research and Documents Staff, ed., *International Documents on Palestine, 1977*, Beirut: Institute for Palestine Studies, 1979, 337. Arafat tried as early as the summer of 1977 to win PLO backing for UN Resolution 242, but was unable to overcome the opposition to doing so from both outside and inside Fatah. Sayigh, *Armed Struggle and the Search for State*, 685–86.

10. Diab, *International Documents*, 402, Resolutions of the Fourth Palestinian National Assembly, Cairo, July 17, 1968.

11. Quoted in Gresh, *PLO*, 105.

12. For an English translation of Bourguiba's Jericho speech, see http://www.bour-guiba.com/uploads/docs/ pdf/en/Jercho-speech-template-gb.pdf, accessed August 28, 2013.

13. Gresh, *PLO*, 106.

14. Khadduri, *International Documents on Palestine, 1970,* 749, originally on January 14, 1970.

15. Said K. Aburish, *Arafat: From Defender to Dictator,* New York: Bloomsbury, 1999, 120.

16. See Palestinian National Council, "Political Programme for the Present Stage of the Palestine Liberation Organization Drawn Up by the Palestinian National Council, Cairo, June 9, 1974," *Journal of Palestine Studies* 3, no. 4 (1974): 224. Unfortunately, as Gresh notes, there are no available internal Fatah documents that allow for an examination of the evolution of Fatah's position on a separate Palestinian state in the West Bank and Gaza Strip before October 1973. He argues that "some cadres," presumably led by Kaddoumi and Khalaf (see below), appeared willing to accept a state in the West Bank and Gaza Strip during the debate that took place in the movement between 1970 and 1973, but that this willingness was not widespread. See Gresh, *PLO,* 120.

17. Abu Iyad, *My Home, My Land*; Helena Cobban, *The Palestinian Liberation Organisation: People, Power and Politics,* Cambridge: Cambridge University Press, 1984, 60–62; H. L. Schulz, *Reconstruction of Palestinian Nationalism,* 107–8; Gresh, *PLO,* 139.

18. David Anable, "Israelis, Palestinians Move Closer to Negotiating," *Christian Science Monitor,* October 17, 1974.

19. Abu Iyad, *My Home, My Land,* 135–36. See also Darwish, *Palestinian Leaders,* 31.

20. IPS Research and Documents Staff, ed., *International Documents on Palestine, 1977,* 393, originally published in *Al-Ba'ath,* August 29, 1977.

21. IPS Research and Documents Staff, ed., *International Documents on Palestine, 1977,* 365–66, originally in an interview with *Sh'un Filastiyuna,* June 1977.

22. Farouk Kaddoumi, "Kaddumi [sic]: Confidence in Armed Struggle," *Free Palestine* 4, nos. 1–2 (January–February 1976): 7. See also "Editorial: The Struggle Continues," *Free Palestine* 5, nos. 3–4 (April 1977): 1.

23. H. L. Schulz, *Reconstruction of Palestinian Nationalism.*

24. PLO, "Executive Committee Statement, Tunis, 7 March 1986," *Journal of Palestine Studies* 15, no. 4 (1986): 232–41, 239.

25. Yehoshafat Harkabi and Matti Steinberg, *The Palestinian Covenant: In the Test of Time and Reality; Explanations and Implications,* Jerusalem: Leonard Davis Center, Hebrew University, 1987, 11.

26. PLO Central Committee, "Statement, Baghdad, 9 January 1988," *Journal of Palestine Studies* 17, no. 3 (1988): 181–84, 182, my emphasis.

27. See, for example, PLO, "Executive Committee Statement, Tunis, 7 March 1986."

28. Palestine National Council, "Political Communique, Algiers, 15 November 1988," *Journal of Palestine Studies* 18, no. 2 (1989): 216–23, 216–17.

29. Fateh Revolutionary Council, "Political Statement, Tunis, 15 November 1993," *Journal of Palestine Studies* 23, no. 2 (1994): 134.

30. Political platform of Fatah, ratified by the Sixth General Congress, August 2009, in *The Politics of Change in Palestine: State-Building and Non-Violent Resistance,* by Michael Bröning, New York: Pluto Press, 2011, 204.

31. Bröning, *Politics of Change in Palestine,* 220.

32. Dan Williams, "Abbas Hints Has No 'Right of Return' to Home in Israel," *Reuters,* November 1, 2012.

33. Joost R. Hiltermann, *Behind the Intifada: Labor and Women's Movements in the Occupied Territories,* Princeton, NJ: Princeton University Press, 1991, 40–41; Jamil Hamad, "Palestinian Future: New Directions," *New Middle East* (August 1971): 20–22.

34. Hiltermann, *Behind the Intifada*, 45; Bernd Schoch, *The Islamic Movement: A Challenge for Palestinian State-Building*, Jerusalem: PASSIA (Palestinian Academic Society for the Study of International Affairs), 1999, 36-37; Hillel Frisch, "From Armed Struggle over State Borders to Political Mobilization and Intifada within It: The Transformation of PLO Strategy in the Territories," *Plural Societies* 19, nos. 2–3 (1990): 92–115; Hamad, "Palestinian Future"; Aziz Shihadeh, "The Palestinian Demand Is for Peace, Justice and an End to Bitterness—the Initiative Is with Israel—the Time to Negotiate Is Now," *New Middle East* (August 1971): 16–19.

35. Sayigh, *Armed Struggle and the Search for State*, 207, 286, 345–46.

36. Francis Ofner, "Al-Fatah Guerilla Group Are Big Losers in West Bank Council Elections," *Christian Science Monitor*, April 3, 1972.

37. Hiltermann, *Behind the Intifada*, 43, 12; Frisch, "From Armed Struggle over State Borders to Political Mobilization"; Amal Jamal, "The Palestinian Media: An Obedient Servant or a Vanguard of Democracy?," *Journal of Palestine Studies* 29 (Spring 2000): 2.

38. Sayigh, *Armed Struggle and the Search for State*, 447–48; Hiltermann, *Behind the Intifada*, 45.

39. H. L. Schulz, *Reconstruction of Palestinian Nationalism*, 57; Cobban, *Palestinian Liberation Organisation*, 171–73; Muhammad Muslih, "A Study of PLO Peace Initiatives, 1974–1988," in Sela and Ma'oz, *PLO and Israel*, 40. See also IPS Research and Documents Staff, ed., *International Documents on Palestine, 1978*, Beirut: Institute for Palestine Studies, 1980, 537; and Ann Mosely Lesch, *Political Perceptions of the Palestinians on the West Bank and the Gaza Strip*, Washington, DC: Middle East Institute, 1980.

40. Gresh, *PLO*, 89. For the text of the appeal, see "Documents and Source Material: Arab Documents on Palestine, June 1–September 1, 1973," *Journal of Palestine Studies* 3 (Autumn 1973): 187–89.

41. The Israeli Communist Party accepted partition in 1947. The Jordanian Communist Party accepted it in 1969. See Gresh, *PLO*, 72–73, 133. On the competition between the PLO and the JCP, see Hiltermann, *Behind the Intifada*, 46–49.

42. Gresh, *PLO*, 81–86.

43. Sayigh, *Armed Struggle and the Search for State*, 148, 307–8; Meir Litvak, "Inside versus Outside: The Challenge of the Local Leadership, 1967–1994," in Sela and Ma'oz, *PLO and Israel*, 176; Gresh, *PLO*, 114–18. This was especially the case for Fatah, but the other guerrilla movements were also worried about this possibility. See, for example, Nayef Hawatmeh, the secretary general of the PDFLP, in Darwish, *Palestinian Leaders*, 52–53.

44. Abu Iyad, *My Home, My Land*, 91.

45. Quoted in Sayigh, *Armed Struggle and the Search for State*, 307–8.

46. Quoted in Gresh, *PLO*, 116–17.

47. Quoted in Sayigh, *Armed Struggle and the Search for State*, 338, also 334.

48. Originally published in George D. Moffet III, "PLO Chief Seeks US Acceptance," *Christian Science Monitor*, November 15, 1988.

49. Sayigh, *Armed Struggle and the Search for State*, 336.

50. Abu Iyad, *My Home, My Land*, 135–36.

51. Abu Iyad in Darwish, *Palestinian Leaders*; see also Sayigh, *Armed Struggle and the Search for State*, 361.

52. Sayigh, *Armed Struggle and the Search for State*, 349.

53. Sabri Jiryis, "On Political Settlement in the Middle East: The Palestinian Dimension," *Journal of Palestine Studies* 7, no. 1 (1977): 3–25, 5.

54. Jiryis, "On Political Settlement in the Middle East," 5.

55. Sayigh, *Armed Struggle and the Search for State*, 284.

56. Muhammad Muslih, "Towards Coexistence: An Analysis of the Resolutions of the Palestine National Council," *Journal of Palestine Studies* 19, no. 4 (1990): 3–29.

57. Fatah's ability to win this battle was reinforced by the increased influx of Arab funds after 1978, which enabled the Fatah leadership to dispense patronage on a widening scale, construct deep clientelist networks in the territories, and promote its (still contested) vision of a Palestinian entity as a phase to total liberation. Sayigh, *Armed Struggle and the Search for State*, 354.

58. Goddard, *Indivisible Territory*.

59. For more on the rise of the West Bank Palestinians in Palestinian politics, see Hiltermann, *Behind the Intifada*; Sayigh, *Armed Struggle and the Search for State*; and Gresh, *PLO*, 134–35.

60. Sayigh, *Armed Struggle and the Search for State*; Lesch, *Political Perceptions of the Palestinians on the West Bank and the Gaza Strip*.

61. Cobban, *Palestinian Liberation Organisation*, 94. Abu Sharif goes further and claims that "although Arafat continued collaborating with the Steadfastness and Collaboration Front [the Arab states that rejected the Camp David Accords], he in fact was ready to join Sadat should he succeed in negotiating an end to the occupation of any part of Palestine." Bassam Abu Sharif, *Arafat and the Dream of Palestine: An Insider's Account*, New York: Macmillan, 2009, 56.

62. H. L. Schulz, *Reconstruction of Palestinian Nationalism*, 52; Cobban, *Palestinian Liberation Organisation*, 178; Hiltermann, *Behind the Intifada*, 13–14.

63. Muslih, "Study of PLO Peace Initiatives, 1974–1988," 46–47; As'ad Ghanem, "Palestinian Nationalism: An Overview," *Israel Studies* 18, no. 2 (2013): 11–29, 22.

64. Sayigh, *Armed Struggle and the Search for State*, 688–89.

65. For the additional impacts of the UN recognition of Palestine, see Shelef and Zeira, "Recognition Matters!"

66. Khalil Shikaki, "Refugees and the Legitimacy of Palestinian-Israeli Peace Making," in *Arab-Jewish Relations: From Conflict to Resolution?; Essays in Honour of Professor Moshe Ma'oz*, ed. Elie Podeh and Asher Kaufman, Brighton: Sussex Academic Press, 2006, 363–74.

67. See, for example, Rashid Khalidi, *The Iron Cage: The Story of the Palestinian Struggle for Statehood*, Boston, MA: Beacon Press, 2006, 169, 194; Darwish, *Palestinian Leaders*; Jiryis, "On Political Settlement in the Middle East"; Cobban, *Palestinian Liberation Organisation*; and Abu Sharif, *Arafat and the Dream of Palestine*, 173. See also the Palestinian participants in "Operation Charlie," in Joseph Alpher, *Ve-gar ze'ev 'im ze'ev: Ha-mitnahalim veha-Palestinim*, Tel Aviv: Hakibbutz Hameuchad, 2001; and Issa Al-Shuaibi, "The Development of Palestinian Entity-Consciousness: Part III," *Journal of Palestine Studies* 9, no. 3 (1980): 99–124, 105.

68. See, for example, Arafat in IPS Research and Documents Staff, ed., *International Documents on Palestine, 1978*, 565–66. Later, Arafat pegged the rational adaptation as taking place, not to the reality of Israel's existence, but to Israel's rejection of the idea of a secular democratic state. See his speech to the UN General Assembly in 1988 (United Nations Archive, AM/3 A/43/PV.78, 8–10). See also Hanan Ashrawi, *This Side of Peace: A Personal Account*, New York: Simon and Schuster, 1996; and Abu Iyad, *My Home, My Land*, 139.

69. Benny Morris, *Righteous Victims: A History of the Zionist-Arab Conflict, 1881–1998*, New York: Vantage Books, 2001, 191–96; Avi Shlaim, "Israel and the Arab Coalition in 1948," in *The War for Palestine: Rewriting the History of 1948*, ed. Eugene L. Rogan and Avi Shlaim, Cambridge: Cambridge University Press, 2001, 79–103.

70. See, for example, Musa Alami, "The Lesson of Palestine," *Middle East Journal* 3, no. 4 (1949): 373–405; and Constantine K. Zurayk, *The Meaning of the Disaster*, Beirut: Khayat's College Book Cooperative, 1956.

71. Khadduri, *International Documents on Palestine, 1970*, 877, originally published in *Fatah*, July 26, 1970.

72. Yaari, "Al Fath's Political Thinking," 29.

73. Sayigh, *Armed Struggle and the Search for State*, 155.

74. Gresh, *PLO*; Abu Iyad, *My Home, My Land*.

75. Gresh, *PLO*, 125. Hawatmeh was open about the tactical character of this step. Reinforcing the character of this change as falling short of an ideological acceptance of partition, the DFLP's emblem (the successor to the PDFLP) continues to include a map of Palestine in its entirety. See, for example, http://www.dflp-palestine.net/, accessed August 26, 2013.

76. Gresh, *PLO*, 68–72.

77. Quoted in Aziz Shihadeh, "Must History Repeat Itself?: The Palestinian Entity and Its Enemies," *New Middle East* (January 1971): 36–37.

78. Abu Iyad, *My Home, My Land*, 138. On the initial weakness of the proponents of the phased strategy, see also Al-Shuaibi, "Development of Palestinian Entity-Consciousness: Part I"; and Gresh, *PLO*.

79. Jabber, *International Documents on Palestine, 1967*, 721, "Statement of Policy Issued by the 'Fatah' Movement."

80. Sayigh, *Armed Struggle and the Search for State*, 223, 282–83, 341, 351.

81. Jiryis, "On Political Settlement in the Middle East," 4.

82. Sayigh, *Armed Struggle and the Search for State*, 173.

83. Diab, *International Documents*, 399.

84. Diab, *International Documents*, 401.

85. Walid Khadduri, ed., *International Documents on Palestine, 1969*, Beirut: Institute for Palestine Studies, 1972, 666, originally published in April 1969.

86. Khadduri, *International Documents on Palestine, 1969*, 774.

87. Al-Shuaibi, "Development of Palestinian Entity-Consciousness: Part III," 105.

88. Gresh, *PLO*, 130, 141–43.

89. Lesch, *Political Perceptions of the Palestinians on the West Bank and the Gaza Strip*, 55, although, importantly, she notes that the PLO had not yet changed its view (68).

90. Abu Iyad, *My Home, My Land*, 133.

91. Gresh, *PLO*, 121.

92. Henry A. Kissinger, *Years of Upheaval*, Boston: Little, Brown, 1979, 503.

93. Walter Laqueur and Barry Rubin, eds., *The Israeli-Arab Reader: A Documentary History of the Middle East Conflict*, New York: Penguin Books, 2001, 171–82. See Irene L. Gendzier, "The Palestinian Revolution, the Jews, and Other Matters," *New Middle East* (January 1971): 38–41. For more on the adoption of this framing of their objective, see William B. Quandt, Paul Jabber, and Ann Mosely Lesch, *The Politics of Palestinian Nationalism*, Berkeley: University of California Press, 1973, 101–6. As the "Internal Circular Concerning Debates and Results of the Sixth National Council," produced by the Popular Democratic Front for the Liberation of Palestine, noted, the rhetoric of a secular democratic state was largely tactical, propagated because "it has been well received internationally." Yehoshafat Harkabi, "The Meaning of 'A Democratic Palestinian State,'" *Wiener Library Bulletin* 24, no. 2 (1970): 1–6, 2.

94. IPS Research and Documents Staff, ed., *International Documents on Palestine, 1981*, Beirut: Institute for Palestine Studies, 1983, 108. For additional examples, see also IPS Research and Documents Staff, ed., *International Documents on Palestine, 1981*, 95; Arafat's 1978 interview in IPS Research and Documents Staff, ed., *International Documents on Palestine, 1978*, 215; Muslih, "Study of PLO Peace Initiatives, 1974–1988," 40; Arafat in IPS Research and Documents Staff, ed., *International Documents on Palestine, 1977*, 426–27; Arafat's speech at the opening of the third conference of the Steadfastness and Confrontation states in Damascus, September 20, 1978, in which he refers to northern Israel as "northern Palestine"; IPS Research and Documents Staff, ed., *International Documents on Palestine, 1978*, 511; IPS Research and Documents Staff, ed., *International*

Documents on Palestine, 1979, Beirut: Institute for Palestine Studies, 1981, 81, originally on March 21, 1979; Khaled Hasan in IPS Research and Documents Staff, ed., *International Documents on Palestine, 1980*, Beirut: Institute for Palestine Studies, 1983, 137–38; Kaddoumi in IPS Research and Documents Staff, ed., *International Documents on Palestine, 1981*, 4, originally in 1981; the 1981 and 1983 PNC statements reproduced in Lukacs, *Israeli-Palestinian Conflict*, 352, 358; and IPS Research and Documents Staff, ed., *International Documents on Palestine, 1981*, 427.

95. Cobban, *Palestinian Liberation Organisation*, 63, 107.

96. See, for example, Arafat, originally in 1977 in IPS Research and Documents Staff, ed., *International Documents on Palestine, 1977*, 331, 347; IPS Research and Documents Staff, ed., *International Documents on Palestine, 1980*, 347; and Arafat in an interview with CBS's *Face the Nation* in December 1978, IPS Research and Documents Staff, ed., *International Documents on Palestine, 1978*, 612–15; Arafat in an interview with *Der Spiegel* on March 19, 1979, in IPS Research and Documents Staff, ed., *International Documents on Palestine, 1979*, 52; Arafat, originally on January 1, 1980, in IPS Research and Documents Staff, eds., *International Documents on Palestine, 1980*, 5; Khalid Hasan, a Fatah Central Committee member who headed a PLO delegation to the European Parliament, in an interview on May 20, 1980, in IPS Research and Documents Staff, ed., *International Documents on Palestine, 1980*, 137–38; and Abu Iyad, *My Home, My Land*, 199.

97. IPS Research and Documents Staff, ed., *International Documents on Palestine, 1977*, 364, originally published in an interview with *Sh'un Filastiyuna*, June 1977.

98. Abu Iyad, "Abu Iyad on the PNC Session and Other Topics," *Journal of Palestine Studies* 8, no. 3 (1979): 137–48.

99. Quoted in Lesch, *Political Perceptions of the Palestinians on the West Bank and the Gaza Strip*, 55.

100. Cobban, *Palestinian Liberation Organisation*, 57.

101. Gresh, *PLO*, 123–24.

102. Sayigh, *Armed Struggle and the Search for State*, 335, 343; Muslih, "Study of PLO Peace Initiatives, 1974–1988," 48–49; Harkabi and Steinberg, *Palestinian Covenant*, 64–65; Jiryis, "On Political Settlement in the Middle East," 5; Al-Shuaibi, "Development of Palestinian Entity-Consciousness: Part III," 106.

103. Cobban, *Palestinian Liberation Organisation*, 78–81.

104. Abu Iyad, *My Home, My Land*, 79.

105. The limited ability of the Arab states to pressure Fatah into accepting partition was displayed again in 1977 when it resisted Sadat's pressure to do so. Abu Sharif, *Arafat and the Dream of Palestine*, 44.

106. Moshe Ma'oz, "The Palestinian Guerrilla Organizations and the Soviet Union," in *Palestinian Arab Politics*, ed. Moshe Ma'oz, Jerusalem: Academic Press, 1975, 96; Galia Golan, "Moscow and the PLO: The Ups and Downs of a Complex Relationship, 1964–1994," in Sela and Ma'oz, *PLO and Israel*, 121, 126–27; Sayigh, *Armed Struggle and the Search for State*, 342.

107. Ma'oz, "Palestinian Guerrilla Organizations," 100. For other skeptical assessments of the role of Soviet influence in this regard, see Golan, "Moscow and the PLO."

108. See, for example, the explicit arguments by George Habash, the secretary general of the PFLP, for resisting Soviet pressure, in Darwish, *Palestinian Leaders*, 23.

109. For a proof of principle that the territorial aspirations of a religious nationalist movement can change, see Shelef, *Evolving Nationalism*; see also Hassner, *War on Sacred Grounds*.

110. Both quoted in Shaul Mishal and Avraham Sela, *The Palestinian Hamas: Vision, Violence and Coexistence*, New York: Columbia University Press, 2000, 51.

111. Cited in H. L. Schulz, *Reconstruction of Palestinian Nationalism*, 80.

112. For an English language version of the document, see "Charters of Hamas," *Contemporary Review of the Middle East* 4, no. 4 (2017): 393–418.

113. For a review of some of this jurisprudence, see Yitzhak Reiter, "Islam and the Question of Peace with Israel," in *Muslim Attitudes to Jews and Israel: The Ambivalences of Rejection, Antagonism, Tolerance and Cooperation*, ed. Moshe Ma'oz, Brighton: Sussex Academic Press, 2010, 90–112; Azzam Tamimi, *Hamas: A History from Within*, Northhampton, MA: Olive Branch Books, 2007, 157; and Uri M. Kupferschmidt, *The Supreme Muslim Council: Islam under the British Mandate for Palestine*, Leiden: Brill, 1987, 245. Technically, this jurisprudence could be consistent with partition as long as all of Palestine was under the sovereignty of a Muslim ruler. There is also, it should be noted, a strain of Islamic jurisprudence that does accept Israel's existence and is consistent with partition. See Reiter, "Islam and the Question of Peace."

114. See, for example, Mark Juergensmeyer, *Terror in the Mind of God: The Global Rise of Religious Violence*, Berkeley: University of California Press, 2003, 238–39.

115. H. L. Schulz, *Reconstruction of Palestinian Nationalism*, 112.

116. Tamimi, *Hamas*, 148, originally in March 2004.

117. H. L. Schulz, *Reconstruction of Palestinian Nationalism*, 113; Beverley Milton-Edwards and Alastair Crooke, "Waving, Not Drowning: Strategic Dimensions of Ceasefires and Islamic Movements," *Security Dialogue* 35, no. 3 (2004): 295–310.

118. Joshua L. Gleis and Benedetta Berti, *Hezbollah and Hamas: A Comparative Study*, Baltimore: Johns Hopkins University Press, 2012; Tamimi, *Hamas*, 102. The length of time of this truce varies, sometimes ranging from ten to twenty years, and in other times left undefined.

119. Richard Beeston, "Hamas Leader Accepts the 'Reality' of Israel," *Times* (London), January 11, 2011. See also AFP, "Hamas Implies Tacit Acceptance of Israel," *Ma'an News Agency*, May 8, 2011.

120. Quoted in Bröning, *Politics of Change in Palestine*, 17.

121. Mishal and Sela, *Palestinian Hamas*, 110; Bröning, *Politics of Change in Palestine*, 22; Tamimi, *Hamas*, 156.

122. "Teheran: Mashaal Calls on Abbas for a Comprehensive National Dialogue and Affirms the Option of Resistance," *Palestine Today*, October 1, 2011.

123. See Adnan Asfour in "West Bank Hamas Official: The Destruction of Israel Is Not the Job of Hamas," *Ma'an News Agency*, January, 30, 2006. BBC Monitoring Middle East—Political Supplied by BBC Worldwide Monitoring, "Hamas Official Offers Truce for Israeli Withdrawal to 1967 Lines—Israel Radio," January 26, 2006, *LexisNexis Academic*. Khaled Mashal in "Khaled Mash'al: All Factions Agree—a Palestinian State on the 1967 Borders," *Ma'an News Agency*, December 9, 2006; Haniyeh in "Haniyeh Says Hamas Won't Obstruct State on '67 Borders," *Ma'an News Agency*, July 24, 2009; Khaled Abu Toameh, "Hamas Downplays Yassin 'Peace Offer,'" *Jerusalem Post*, January, 9, 2004; Rantisi in Justin Huggler, "Israel Summarily Rejects Hamas Offer of 10-Year Truce," *Independent* (London), January, 27, 2004.

124. "Hamas Spokesman Briefs Journalists in Gaza," *Ma'an News Agency*, July 14, 2005. See also Haniyeh AFP, "Haniyeh: Hamas Will Not Back UN Bid, Support Statehood," *Ma'an News Agency*, September 18, 2011; and "Khalid Mash'al: All Factions Agree." Muhammad Nazzal, a member of the Hamas Political Bureau, in BBC Monitoring Middle East—Political Supplied by BBC Worldwide Monitoring, "Hamas Official Offers Truce for Israeli Withdrawal to 1967 Lines—Israel Radio," January 26, 2006, *LexisNexis Academic*; "Palestinian Hamas Figure Discusses Demands on Israeli Withdrawal, Russian Moves," February 13, 2006, *LexisNexis Academic*.

125. "Hamas: Recognizing Israel Jeopardizes Rights," *Ma'an News Agency*, May 11, 2011. He also called, in 2010, for an armed struggle to liberate all of historic Palestine. "Zahhar: Armed Struggle Will Free Palestine," *Ma'an News Agency*, September, 9, 2010.

126. Tamimi, *Hamas*, 169.

127. See, for example, Rantisi quoted in Tamimi, *Hamas*, 148, originally on March 7, 2004. See also Ismail H. Abu-Shanab, "An Islamic Approach of the Resistance against Israeli Occupation in Palestine: The Strategy of 'Hamas' in the Present and in the Future," in *Palestinian Perspectives*, ed. Wolfgang Freund, Frankfurt: Peter Lang, 1999, 165–73; Beeston, "Hamas Leader Accepts the 'Reality' of Israel"; and AFP, "Hamas Implies Tacit Acceptance of Israel."

128. There are some indications that at least some within the movement were willing to accommodate partition as a practical matter as early as 1988. For example, Mahmoud Zahhar, then the spokesman for Hamas in Gaza, indicated a readiness to agree to a two-state solution. In 1989 Yassin expressed his willingness to join a Palestinian delegation in negotiations with Israel. Nonetheless, these overtures were drowned out by the vocal rejections by Hamas of Israel's right to exist. H. L. Schulz, *Reconstruction of Palestinian Nationalism*, 84. Moreover, Yassin, while frequently articulating his support for a temporary truce with Israel, was relatively consistent in rejecting the possibility of actual reconciliation with, and recognition of, Israel. See "Palestinian Hamas Rejects International Control over Jerusalem," Agence France Presse—English, September 22, 2000, accessed September 10, 2013, *LexisNexis Academic*; and "Hamas Leader Speaks Out against Mideast Peace Negotiations," Agence France Presse—English, October 15, 2000, accessed September 10, 2013, *LexisNexis Academic*. Milton-Edwards and Crooke conclude, moreover, that when it emerged Hamas was uncomfortable with the idea of a ceasefire "because that clashed with the central concept of a historic struggle in which Islam and its forces were pitched against a political entity constructed as the Jewish state. The early covenant epitomized a hatred of the Jewish presence in historic Palestine and distinguished Hamas from other Palestinian groups by addressing the strategic presence of Israel as an entirely religious issue." Milton-Edwards and Crooke, "Waving, Not Drowning," 298–99. For a similar assessment, see International Crisis Group, *Dealing with Hamas*, 2004, accessed July 30, 2018, https://www.crisisgroup.org/middle-east-north-africa/eastern-mediterranean/israelpalestine/dealing-hamas.

129. Tamimi, *Hamas*.

130. Bröning, *Politics of Change in Palestine*, 22; Tamimi, *Hamas*, 156; Mishal and Sela, *Palestinian Hamas*; Nathan Brown, *Is Hamas Mellowing?*, January 17, 2012, Carnegie Endowment for International Peace, accessed July 27, 2017, http://carnegieendowment.org/2012/01/17/is-hamas-mellowing-pub-46488.

131. See, for example, Khaled Mashal in "Report: Mash'al Says Ready to Accept 2 States," *Ma'an News Agency*, October 22, 2010.

132. Milton-Edwards and Crooke, "Waving, Not Drowning," 300. See also Menachem Klein, "Against the Consensus: Oppositionist Voices in Hamas," *Middle Eastern Studies* 45, no. 6 (2009): 881–92.

133. Milton-Edwards and Crooke, "Waving, Not Drowning," 299. As others have found, by the 1990s, the Palestinian public largely supported making do with a Palestinian state in the West Bank and Gaza Strip. See Hillel Frisch, "Ethnicity, Territorial Integrity, and Regional Order: Palestinian Identity in Jordan and Israel," *Journal of Peace Research* 34, no. 3 (1997): 257–69, 259.

134. Bröning, *Politics of Change in Palestine*, 19.

135. Schoch, *Islamic Movement*, 48. See also Pearlman, "Spoiling Inside and Out."

136. Kydd and Walter, "Sabotaging the Peace."

137. Mishal and Sela, *Palestinian Hamas*, 81–82.

138. Milton-Edwards and Crooke, "Waving, Not Drowning," 303.

139. Milton-Edwards and Crooke, "Waving, Not Drowning," 304.

140. See "Charters of Hamas," 397.

141. Both are quoted in Basem Ezbidi, "'Arab Spring': Weather Forecast for Palestine," *Middle East Policy* 20, no. 3 (2013): 99–110, 103.

142. For an opposing view, see Khaled Hroub, "A 'New Hamas' through Its New Documents," *Journal of Palestine Studies* 35, no. 4 (2006): 6–27.

143. See, for example, Amira Hass, "Senior Fatah Officials Call for Single Democratic State, Not Two-State Solution," *Haaretz.com*, May 17, 2013, accessed July 24, 2013, https://www.haaretz.com/.premium-fatah-officials-2-states-unrealistic-1.5243139.

144. Fatah, 2009 Political Program, accessed July 24, 2013, http://web.archive.org/web/20090805005319/http://www.e-fateh.org/paper_full_3.aspx.

5. THE WITHDRAWAL OF HOMELAND TERRITORIALITY IN A CROSS-NATIONAL PERSPECTIVE

1. See, for example, Kaufmann, "When All Else Fails"; Sambanis, "Partition as a Solution to Ethnic War"; Tir, "Dividing Countries to Promote Peace"; Chapman and Roeder, "Partition as a Solution"; C. Johnson, "Partitioning to Peace"; and Sambanis and Schulhofer-Wohl, "What's in a Line."

2. See, for example, Burghardt, "Bases of Territorial Claims"; A. D. Smith, *Ethnic Origins of Nations*; Esman, *Ethnic Politics*; Connor, *Ethnonationalism*; Connor, "Homelands in a World of States"; Fearon, "Rationalist Explanations for War"; Murphy, "National Claims to Territory"; Hassner, "'To Halve and to Hold'"; Vasquez and Valeriano, "Territory as a Source of Conflict"; Goddard, "Uncommon Ground"; and Walter, "Bargaining Failures and Civil War."

3. See, for example, Toft, *Geography of Ethnic Violence*; Goertz and Diehl, *Territorial Change*; Hensel, "Contentious Issues and World Politics"; Hensel and Mitchell, "Issue Indivisibility"; Walter, *Reputation and Civil War*; Nadav G. Shelef, "Unequal Ground: Homelands and Conflict," *International Organization* 70, no. 1 (2016): 33–63; and Minorities at Risk Project, Minorities at Risk Dataset, 2009 (2003 release). This is even the case for Ambrosio's nuanced study of irredentism. In that work, the irredentist desire remains constant and is tempered only by the degree of international intolerance of irredentist projects. Ambrosio, *Irredentism*. ICOW does allow for variation in the intangible salience of a territorial claim, but this variation is a product of the time since sovereignty in a territory, not its status as a homeland or in the identity claims of a territory. For a similar critique, see Juliet J. Fall, "Artificial States?: On the Enduring Geographical Myth of Natural Borders," *Political Geography* 29, no. 3 (2010): 140–47.

4. Quoted in Agnew, "No Borders, No Nations," 399.

5. See, for example, Huth, *Standing Your Ground*; Toft, *Geography of Ethnic Violence*; Kaufmann, "When All Else Fails"; C. Johnson, "Partitioning to Peace"; Saideman and Ayers, *For Kin or Country*; Nils B. Weidmann, "Geography as Motivation and Opportunity: Group Concentration and Ethnic Conflict," *Journal of Conflict Resolution* 53, no. 4 (2009): 526–43; and B. Miller, *States, Nations, and the Great Powers*.

6. Gellner, "Nationalism in the Vacuum," 251.

7. Ernest Gellner, "Do Nations Have Navels?," *Nations and Nationalism* 3, no. 2 (1996): 366–70, 367.

8. O'Leary, "Elements of Right-Sizing and Right-Peopling the State." See also Lustick, *Unsettled States, Disputed Lands*; Zunes and Mundy, *Western Sahara*; Ehud Eiran, "Explaining the Settlement Project: We Know More but What More Should We Know?," *Israel Studies Forum* 25, no. 2 (2010): 102–15; Haklai and Loizides, *Settlers in Contested Lands*; and Eiran, *Post-Colonial Settlement Strategy*.

9. Lisa E. Husmann, "'National Unity' and National Identities in the People's Republic of China," in Hooson, *Geography and National Identity*, 141–57, 146–47.

10. Herb, *Under the Map of Germany*, 68 and chap. 3.

11. See Stourzh, *From Vienna to Chicago*, chap. 6, "Ethnic Attribution in Late Imperial Austria: Good Intentions, Evil Consequences"; Bufon and Minghi, "Upper Adriatic Borderland"; Bufon, "Changeable Political Map"; and Sluga, *Problem of Trieste*. For a broader discussion of the nationalist politics of attributing ethnicity in censuses, see David I. Kertzer and Dominique Arel, eds., *Census and Identity: The Politics of Race, Ethnicity, and Language in National Censuses*, Cambridge: Cambridge University Press, 2002.

12. These biases have been widely discussed by geographers and scholars of cartography. See, for example, Black, *Maps and History*, 78–80; Jeremy Black, *Maps and Politics*, Chicago: University of Chicago Press, 2002; Agnew, "Territorial Trap"; Denis Wood and John Fels, *The Power of Maps*, New York: Guilford Press, 1992; and Edoardo Boria, "Violence beyond Trenches: Ethnographical Maps from Science to Propaganda and the Case of the Julian March," in *The First World War: Analysis and Interpretation*, ed. Antonello Biagini and Giovanna Motta, Newcastle: Cambridge Scholars, 2015, 199–212. See also Bufon, "Changeable Political Map"; Jordan Branch, "Mapping the Sovereign State: Technology, Authority, and Systemic Change," *International Organization* 65, no. 1 (2011): 1–36; and Charles S. Maier, *Once within Borders: Territories of Power, Wealth, and Belonging since 1500*, Cambridge, MA: Harvard University Press, 2016.

13. See, for example, Hobsbawm and Ranger, *Invention of Tradition*, and the studies they inspired.

14. Philip L. Kohl, "Nationalism and Archaeology: On the Constructions of Nations and the Reconstructions of the Remote Past," *Annual Review of Anthropology* 27 (1998): 223–46, 231. For a discussion of this process in the Sri Lankan context, see Margo Kleinfeld, "Destabilizing the Identity-Territory Nexus: Rights-Based Discourse in Sri Lanka's New Political Geography," *GeoJournal* 64, no. 4 (2005): 287–95, 290.

15. Robertis, *La frontiera orientale italiana*, 19, 186–87.

16. Daniel N. Posner, "Measuring Ethnic Fractionalization in Africa," *American Journal of Political Science* 48, no. 4 (2004): 849–63. See also Kanchan Chandra, ed., *Constructivist Theories of Ethnic Politics*, Oxford: Oxford University Press, 2012.

17. Young, *Politics of Cultural Pluralism*.

18. Herb, *Under the Map of Germany*, chap. 3.

19. The Russian Pale of Settlement contained more than one-third of the global Jewish population and was the single largest territorial concentration of Jews at the turn of the twentieth century. Herbert Friedenwald and H. G. Friedman, eds., *The American Jewish Year Book*, Philadelphia: Jewish Publication Society of America, 1913. Jordan contains nearly as many Palestinians as does the West Bank. United States, Central Intelligence Agency, *The CIA World Factbook: Jordan*, 2012; Central Intelligence Agency, *The CIA World Factbook: West Bank*, May 2012. There were more than 1.6 million people claiming Norwegian ancestry in Minnesota, the Dakotas, and Wisconsin in 2006. This is more than a third of Norway's population. See American Community Survey, *S0201—Selected Population Profile in the United States*, May 2012.

20. *Dalmatia, Fiume and the Other Unreedemed [sic] Lands of the Adriatic*, 11.

21. Michael W. Doyle, *Empires*, Ithaca, NY: Cornell University Press, 1986, 30–45.

22. Lustick, *Unsettled States, Disputed Lands*.

23. Andreas Wimmer and Nina Glick Schiller, "Methodological Nationalism and Beyond: Nation-State Building, Migration and the Social Sciences," *Global Networks* 2, no. 4 (2002): 301–34.

24. Walter, *Reputation and Civil War*; Hensel, "Contentious Issues and World Politics"; Hensel and Mitchell, "Issue Indivisibility"; B. Miller, *States, Nations, and the Great Powers*.

25. Paul R. Hensel, "Charting a Course to Conflict: Territorial Issues and Interstate Conflict, 1816–1992," *Conflict Management and Peace Science* 15, no. 1 (1996): 43–73.

26. Kwame Nkrumah, *Ghana: The Autobiography of Kwame Nkrumah*, New York: International, 1957; Yael Zerubavel, *Recovered Roots: Collective Memory and the Making of Israeli National Tradition*, Chicago: Chicago University Press, 1995, 185.

27. A. D. Smith, "Culture, Community and Territory," 454. See also Winichakul, *Siam Mapped*; and Monica L. Smith, "Networks, Territories, and the Cartography of Ancient States," *Annals of the Association of American Geographers* 95, no. 4 (2005): 832–49.

28. A static version of this measure was originally described in Shelef, "Unequal Ground."

29. Connor, *Ethnonationalism*, 205.

30. B. Anderson, *Imagined Communities*, 175. See also Billig, *Banal Nationalism*; Shelef, *Evolving Nationalism*; and M. Anderson, *Frontiers*, 3.

31. Hans Speier, "Magic Geography," *Social Research* 8, no. 3 (1941): 310–30; Louis B. Thomas, "Maps as Instruments of Propaganda," *Surveying and Mapping* 9, no. 2 (1949): 75–81; Winichakul, *Siam Mapped*; J. B. Harley, "Maps, Knowledge, and Power" in *The Iconography of Landscape: Essays on the Symbolic Representation, Design and Use of Past Environments*, ed. Denis Cosgrove and Stephen Daniels, Cambridge: Cambridge University Press, 1988; Wood and Fels, *Power of Maps*; David Newman, "Boundaries, Borders, and Barriers: Changing Geographic Perspectives on Territorial Lines," in *Identities, Borders, Orders: Rethinking International Relations Theory*, ed. M. Albert, D. Jacobson, and Y. Lapid, Minneapolis: University of Minnesota Press, 2001, 137–52; Black, *Maps and History*; Black, *Maps and Politics*; Agnew, "No Borders, No Nations"; John Agnew, "Borders on the Mind: Reframing Border Thinking," *Ethics and Global Politics* 1, no. 4 (2008): 175–91; Herb, "Double Vision"; Denis Wood, *Rethinking the Power of Maps*, New York: Guilford Press, 2010; Harvey Starr, *On Geopolitics: Space, Place, and International Relations*, New York: Routledge, 2015; Paasi, *Territories, Boundaries, and Consciousness*; Arthur Jay Klinghoffer, *The Power of Projections: How Maps Reflect Global Politics and History*, Westport, CT: Praeger, 2006. For a more extreme view which posits that maps constitute reality itself, see Geoff King, *Mapping Reality: An Exploration of Cultural Cartographies*, New York: St. Martin's Press, 1996.

32. Harley, "Maps, Knowledge, and Power," 300; David Newman, "From National to Post-National Territorial Identities in Israel-Palestine," in *Israelis in Conflict: Hegemonies, Identities and Challenges*, ed. Adriana Kemp et al., Brighton: Sussex Academic Press, 2004, 30–31.

33. On rhetorical action, see Risse, "'Let's Argue!'"; Schimmelfennig, "Community Trap"; Krebs and Jackson, "Twisting Tongues and Twisting Arms"; and Goddard and Krebs, "Rhetoric, Legitimation, and Grand Strategy."

34. This approach follows a well-established tradition in case studies of nationalism of using both official and unofficial discourse as data about nationalism in general, and about territory in particular. See, for example, Billig, *Banal Nationalism*; Liah Greenfeld, *Nationalism: Five Roads to Modernity*, Cambridge, MA: Harvard University Press, 1992; Lustick, *Unsettled States, Disputed Lands*; G. W. White, *Nation, State, and Territory*; Goddard, *Indivisible Territory*; Shelef, *Evolving Nationalism*; Paasi, *Territories, Boundaries, and Consciousness*; Jon E. Fox and Cynthia Miller-Idriss, "Everyday Nationhood," *Ethnicities* 8, no. 4 (2008): 536–63; and Hensel, "Contentious Issues and World Politics." For a complementary perspective on the use of discourse to sanctify territory, see Richard Sosis, "Why Sacred Lands Are Not Indivisible: The Cognitive Foundations of Sacralising Land," *Journal of Terrorism Research* 2, no. 1 (2011): 1.

35. Shelef, *Evolving Nationalism*; Mylonas and Shelef, "Which Land Is Our Land?"

36. Lustick, *Unsettled States, Disputed Lands*; Finnemore and Sikkink, "International Norm Dynamics," 895; Krebs, *Narrative and the Making of US National Security*.

37. In identifying the new borders I relied on a number of reference works and datasets, including Gideon Biger, ed., *The Encyclopedia of International Boundaries*, New York:

Facts on File, 1995; Jaroslav Tir et al., "Territorial Changes, 1816–1996: Procedures and Data," *Conflict Management and Peace Science* 16, no. 1 (1998): 89–97; The Correlates of War Territorial Change Dataset, version 4.01; Jacob Berkovitch and Richard Jackson, *International Conflict: A Chronological Encyclopedia of Conflicts and Their Management, 1945–1995*, Washington, DC: CQ Press, 1997; and John B. Allcock et al., eds., *Borders and Territorial Disputes*, 3rd ed., Essex: Longman Current Affairs, 1992.

38. Zacher, "Territorial Integrity Norm"; Fazal, *State Death*; and Atzili, *Good Fences, Bad Neighbors*.

39. Subsequent border changes between colonial powers and former colonies (for example, the Spanish withdrawal from Spanish Sahara after 1956, the Dutch withdrawal from Western New Guinea after Indonesian independence, the phased British withdrawal from Malaysia, the two-step withdrawal of South Africa from Namibia, the partial French withdrawal from Comoros, and the phased French withdrawal from Tunisia) are included. The results are robust to including all new borders, including those drawn as a result of decolonization (see column 4 of table A.5 in the appendix).

40. FBIS excludes coverage for Canada, the United States, Eritrea, Zanzibar, Tanganyika, and the Seychelles. As a result, borders involving these cases are excluded from the analysis in this and the following chapter.

41. For example, Hensel, "Contentious Issues and World Politics."

42. For more on this case and the contestation between the Russian executive and legislative branches of government on this issue, see Saideman and Ayers, *For Kin or Country*, 180.

43. On the importance of possessing the social standing to modify such narratives, see Goddard and Krebs, "Rhetoric, Legitimation, and Grand Strategy."

44. The exception to this treatment of the Arab homeland was the claims by Arab nationalists in Egypt and Syria to the combined United Arab Republic as the Arab homeland.

45. Region definitions are based on UN and World Bank definitions. The "mixed" category includes neighboring states across regional lines. Malta and Russia are defined as part of Europe, and Sudan and Turkey are defined as part of the Middle East and North Africa.

46. A. I. Asiwaju, "The Conceptual Framework," in Asiwaju, *Partitioned Africans*, 14; Saadia Touval, "Partitioned Groups and Inter-State Relations," in Asiwaju, *Partitioned Africans*, 228; Jeffrey Herbst, "The Creation and Maintenance of National Boundaries in Africa," *International Organization* 43, no. 4 (1989): 673–92; Benyamin Neuberger, "Irredentism and Politics in Africa," in Chazan, *Irredentism and International Politics*, 97–109; Hein E. Goemans and Kenneth A. Schultz, "The Politics of Territorial Claims: A Geospatial Approach Applied to Africa," *International Organization* 71, no. 1 (2017): 31–64.

47. Kornprobst, *Irredentism in European Politics*.

48. More technically, the data are set up as for Andersen and Gill's counting processes method and then stratified by failure order. P. K. Andersen and R. D. Gill, "Cox's Regression Model for Counting Processes: A Large Sample Study," *Annals of Statistics* 10, no. 4 (1982): 1100–1120; Mario Cleves, "Stata: Analysis of Multiple Failure-Time Survival Data," *Stata Technical Bulletin* 49 (1999): 30–39. See the appendix for additional details and discussion of modeling choices.

49. On nationalizing states, see Brubaker, *Nationalism Reframed*.

50. Vasquez and Valeriano, "Territory as a Source of Conflict." See also the discussions of German claims to Alsace and Turkish irredentism by Emanuel Gutmann "Concealed or Conjured Irredentism: The Case of Alsace" and Jacob Landau, "The Ups and Downs of Irredentism: The Case of Turkey" respectively, in Chazan, *Irredentism and International Politics*, 37–50 and 81–96. The timing of the increase in the baseline hazard rate about a quarter century after the drawing of the new border (given that a case was observed for

that long) means that it cannot be the direct product of the entry of states into the world system in the early 1990s. Since the new states that emerged after the end of the Cold War are only observed for a maximum of six years before the pattern of articulation in their societies is right-censored, they cannot account for developments that take place after a quarter century of analysis time.

51. Both regime type and age are based on V-Dem's "Electoral democracy index ordinal" measure, Michael Coppedge et al., *V-Dem Dataset version 7.1*, 2017. A score of "1" on this measure is understood as reflecting a "minimally democratic" polity, while both "electoral authoritarian" and "autocratic" polities are coded as "0", or nondemocracies, in a particular year. Missing data was updated as follows: colonies and occupied states are coded as nondemocracies. In addition, the following cases were coded as nondemocracies based on case-specific research: Bahrain 1971; Brunei 1984; Burkina Faso 1966 and 1979; Burundi 1995; Cameroon 1960–1963; Czechoslovakia 1945; Bosnia 1992; Georgia 1993–1994; Macedonia 1993; Mozambique 1973–1977; Oman 1960 and 1992; and Yemen Arab Republic (all years). The following states were coded as democratic: Belgium 1945; Czechoslovakia 1990–1992; Estonia 1991; German Federal Republic 1949–1953; Latvia 1991–1992; Lithuania 1991; and Slovakia 1993. Regime age is counted with 1940 as the first year.

52. Zeev Maoz and Bruce Russett, "Normative and Structural Causes of Democratic Peace, 1946–1986," *American Political Science Review* 87, no. 3 (1993): 624–38.

53. Fravel, "Regime Insecurity and International Cooperation."

54. Manuel Vogt et al., "Integrating Data on Ethnicity, Geography, and Conflict: The Ethnic Power Relations Dataset Family," *Journal of Conflict Resolution* 59, no. 7 (2015): 1327–42. My coding of this variable diverges from the EPR-TEK data in the following ways: Cases where decolonization occurred in phases (France-Comoros, France-Tunisia, Netherlands-Indonesia, United Kingdom-Malaysia, Spain-Morocco, South Africa–Namibia), are coded as having coethnics across the border until the completion of the decolonization process. (Technically, the decolonization of Mauritius by the United Kingdom ought to also follow this rule. However, the remaining atolls claimed by Mauritius are populated solely by British and American military personnel.) Mauritania and Senegal are coded as sharing coethnics because Mauritania has a "Black Africans" group in TEK. Tanzania is coded as sharing coethnics with all its neighbors because it has a category "Mainland Africans." United Kingdom and Zimbabwe are coded as sharing coethnics because of "Europeans" in Zimbabwe. Missing data was updated based on the *CIA World Factbook* and other sources. Where a new state is faced on the other side by its former colonial power which still controls that territory (for example, Tunisia and France, which still controlled Algeria), this variable is coded according to the presence of coethnics in the state that would eventually emerge rather than in the colonial power. Table A.3 in the appendix shows that the main results are robust to coding this variable based on a strict application of the EPR-TEK data as well as other sources, including codings of coethnicity created by Alesina et al. and by Gartzke and Gleditsch, both of whom use a different conceptualization of ethnicity than the EPR project. Alberto Alesina et al., "Fractionalization," *Journal of Economic Growth* 8, no. 2 (2003): 155–94; Erik Gartzke and Kristian Skrede Gleditsch, "Identity and Conflict: Ties That Bind and Differences That Divide," *European Journal of International Relations* 12, no. 1 (2006): 53–87.

55. Oil or natural gas reserves are based on Ewan W. Anderson's identification of the presence of oil or gas reserves in the border region or if the PRIO Petroleum Dataset (version 1.2) identified the presence of petroleum reserves within 50 kilometers of the border. See Ewan W. Anderson, *International Boundaries: A Geopolitical Atlas*, New York: Psychology Press, 2003; and Paivi Lujala, Jan Ketil Rød, and Nadja Thieme, "Fighting over Oil: Introducing a New Dataset," *Conflict Management and Peace Science* 24, no.

3 (2007): 239–56. Water resources are operationalized in terms of a shared river (of any type) between states. See Hans Petter Wollebæk Toset, Nils Petter Gleditsch, and Håvard Hegre, "Shared Rivers and Interstate Conflict," *Political Geography* 19, no. 8 (2000): 971–96. Data on the location of diamond resources and ports are taken from PRIO diamond resources dataset, and the GIS ports data of the Natural Earth dataset. See Elisabeth Gilmore et al., "Conflict Diamonds: A New Dataset," *Conflict Management and Peace Science* 22, no. 3 (2005): 257–72; and the Natural Earth website, http://www.naturalearthdata.com/downloads/10m-cultural-vectors/ports/, respectively.

56. See, for example, Weiner, "Macedonian Syndrome"; Waterman, "Partitioned States," 159; Henderson and Lebow, "Conclusions"; and Ambrosio, *Irredentism*.

57. Relative material capabilities were calculated from the CINC scores (composite capabilities score, ranging from 0 to 1) as calculated by the Correlates of War database, version 4.0. J. David Singer, "Reconstructing the Correlates of War Dataset on Material Capabilities of States, 1816–1985," *International Interactions* 14 (1987): 115–32. The variable is defined as the ratio of the capabilities of "State A" to the total capabilities in the dyad, where power parity is 0.5 and the most unequal dyad is 1.0. This source, while relatively comprehensive, is still characterized by a significant amount of nonrandom missing data. Specifically, data is often missing for the year in which new borders are drawn as well as for all cases in which a new state faced across a new international border a (would-be) state that was still under the rule of a colonial power. These cases with missing capability data would account for about one-third of the observations. As a result, missing data was updated using two alternative strategies. The first, based on the assumption that national material capabilities rarely change drastically from year to year, filled in the missing data using the closest available year. A second strategy modified the first by using the capability of the colonial power or occupier for a year in which a state was not independent. The models used in this chapter employ the second strategy, but the main results are robust to using either method (and to not filling in the missing data at all) (not shown). Table A.4 shows that the main results are also robust to controlling for other factors that could also shape the balance of power, including the possession of nuclear weapons, the status of either or both sides as a client of a superpower (or opposing ones), and being under foreign occupation. The possession of nuclear weapons was coded based on Sonali Singh and Christopher R. Way, "The Correlates of Nuclear Proliferation: A Quantitative Test," *Journal of Conflict Resolution* 48, no. 6 (2004): 859–85. Membership in the Soviet Bloc is based on Thad Dunning's identification of Soviet clients. Thad Dunning, "Conditioning the Effects of Aid: Cold War Politics, Donor Credibility, and Democracy in Africa," *International Organization* 58, no. 2 (2004): 409–23. Missing data was supplemented from other sources, including Mark J. Gasiorowski, *US Foreign Policy and the Shah: Building a Client State in Iran*, Ithaca, NY: Cornell University Press, 1991; and David E. Albright, "Soviet Economic Development and the Third World," *Soviet Studies* 43, no. 1 (1991): 27–59. US clients are coded according to David J. Sylvan and Stephen J. Majeski, "What Choices Do US Foreign Policy Makers Actually Face?," 2011. Paper presented at the Annual Conference of the American Political Science Association, available at SSRN: https://ssrn.com/abstract=1902551.

58. Distance between the capital city and the border was measured from the capital's coordinates to the nearest point of the international border.

59. Fearon, "Rationalist Explanations for War."

60. *Current conflict* is operationalized as a binary variable coded as "1" if either of the states across the new border were involved in a dyadic MID in a particular year. *Prior conflict* accounts for whether or not the states on either side of a new international border experienced any prior dyadic MID before the border was drawn. The results are robust to coding prior conflict as any dyadic MID prior to the year of observation, violent dyadic

MIDs, and dyadic wars (not shown). All conflict variables are based on Zeev Maoz's Dyadic Militarized Interstate Disputes Dataset, version 2.0.

61. Peace treaties are coded as the existence of a renunciation of the use of force, restoration of diplomatic relations, or a full-fledged peace treaty based on Virginia Page Fortna, "Scraps of Paper?: Agreements and the Durability of Peace," *International Organization* 57, no. 2 (2003): 337–72.

62. See, for example, Hauptmann, "Problem of Partition."

63. Table A.4 in the appendix also controls for the impact of being a client of the United States, whether the two states are clients of the same superpower, and whether the states facing each other across a new border are clients of opposing superpowers.

64. For example, Strange, *States and Markets*, 136; Wang, "Globalization and Territorial Identification"; and John M. Stopford, Susan Strange, and John Henley, *Rival Firms, Rival States: Competition for World Market Shares*, Cambridge: Cambridge University Press, 1991.

65. Kristian Skrede Gleditsch, "Expanded Trade and GDP Data," *Journal of Conflict Resolution* 46, no. 5 (2002): 712–24, version 4.1. Both are measured in current-year US dollars. Missing data was updated based on the closest available year.

66. J. L. Snyder, *From Voting to Violence*; Mansfield and Snyder, *Electing to Fight*.

67. Following Mansfield and Snyder, the threshold for democracy used for this variable is a Polity2 threshold of 7. Mansfield and Snyder, *Electing to Fight*.

68. Following Park and Hendry, the Grambsch-Therneau scaled Schoenfeld residual test employing a rank transformation of time is used to test for violations of the proportionality assumption. Sunhee Park and David J. Hendry, "Reassessing Schoenfeld Residual Tests of Proportional Hazards in Political Science Event History Analyses," *American Journal of Political Science* 59, no. 4 (2015): 1072–87. Where variables violate this assumption, the models include an interaction term with the natural log of time (not shown) as a correction. Following Royston and Lambert, these time-varying interaction terms are also included for the strata dummies (not shown) in all analyses. Patrick Royston and Paul C. Lambert, *Flexible Parametric Survival Analysis Using Stata: Beyond the Cox Model*, College Station, TX: Statacorp, 2011.

69. This approach to illustrating the impact of interaction effects follows Bear F. Braumoeller, "Hypothesis Testing and Multiplicative Interaction Terms," *International Organization* 58, no. 4 (2004): 807–20.

70. The exponentiated coefficients of the risk of failure for the interaction of democracy and regime age are 0.884 when controlling for the first year of a new leader (both in a democracy and in general), and 0.891 when controlling for election years. All significant at the $p \leq 0.01$ level. Data on leader tenure is taken from the Archigos Dataset. Henk E. Goemans, Kristian Skrede Gleditsch, and Giacomo Chiozza. "Introducing Archigos: A Dataset of Political Leaders." *Journal of Peace Research* 46, no. 2 (March 1, 2009): 269–83.

71. The categorization of polities as either competitive or factional follows Polity IV's *PARCOMP* variable, and distinguishes these from polities that are either repressed, suppressed, or transitional (Monty G. Marshall, Keith Jaggers, and Ted Robert Gurr, *Polity IV Dataset*, 2004). The existence of multiple parties in a legislature and the continuous time this was the case are coded using a binary version of the Democracy and Dictatorship's *lparty* variable, which codes legislatures with multiple parties as "1", and those with no parties or only regime parties as "0" (José Antonio Cheibub, Jennifer Gandhi, and James Raymond Vreeland, "Democracy and Dictatorship Revisited," *Public Choice* 143, nos. 1–2 [2010]: 67–101). Minimally competitive elections (in which the chief executive and legislature are filled by elections sufficiently free to (theoretically) enable the opposition to gain power), the length of time a polity was characterized by them, and the presence of more than one list presented to voters in an election are coded based on V-DEM's

e_competiton and *e_elecparty_leg* variables (Coppedge et al., *V-Dem Dataset Version 7.1*). These alternative operationalizations cover slightly different time spans and have more missing data than the main operationalizations. As a result, these analyses contain delayed entries or gaps and their interpretation is subject to the restrictive assumption that the frailty distribution is independent of the covariates and the truncation points.

72. See table A.3 in the appendix. The main finding linking long-lived democracies to a reduced risk of claiming lost homeland territory remains robust to all these alternatives.

73. Chazan, *Irredentism and International Politics*; Brubaker, *Nationalism Reframed*; Jenne, *Ethnic Bargaining*; Mylonas, *Politics of Nation-Building*.

74. Shared coethnicity with neighbors is coded using the same EPR Trans-Ethnic Kin (TEK) based measure discussed above. The political mobilization of coethnics in lost lands is captured using the presence in the state controlling the lost homeland territory of a self-determination movement (SDM) representing an ethnic group which is in the state that lost access to those lands based on Nicholas Sambanis, Micha Germann, and Andreas Schädel, "SDM: A New Data Set on Self-Determination Movements with an Application to the Reputational Theory of Conflict," *Journal of Conflict Resolution* 62, no. 3 (2017): 656–86. This variable was coded "1" if a group that the EPR-CORE 2014 dataset identified as being in the state that lost homeland territory was identified as having an SDM in the state that controlled the territory. Vogt et al., "Integrating Data on Ethnicity, Geography, and Conflict."

75. The exponentiated coefficient of the risk of failure for the interaction of democracy and regime age when controlling for sharing coethnics with neighbors and the political mobilization of coethnics across the border are 0.878 and 0.852, respectively—all significant at the $p \leq 0.001$ level.

76. The exponentiated coefficient of the risk of failure for the interaction of democracy and regime age when controlling for legal border origin or borders drawn as a result of war are 0.890 and 0.976, respectively. Both significant at the $p \leq 0.01$ level. For work on the impact of these contexts, see Carter and Goemans, "Making of the Territorial Order"; and Stephen A. Kocs, "Territorial Disputes and Interstate War, 1945–1987," *Journal of Politics* 57, no. 1 (1995): 159–75.

77. See table A.4 in the appendix.

78. For a list of groups included as making claims in cases where the state executive does not, see Nadav G. Shelef, "How Homelands Change," *Journal of Conflict Resolution* 64, no. 2–3 (2020): 490–517.

79. Lustick, *Unsettled States, Disputed Lands*.

80. The exponentiated coefficient on the interaction of democracy and regime age is 0.908 and is significant at the $p \leq 0.05$ level. The results of the other variables are also largely consistent with the results in table 5.1 (not shown).

81. Controlling for the region in which the border was drawn, the exponentiated coefficient of the interaction of democracy and regime age is 0.886 and is significant at the $p < 0.01$ level. Since many post–World War II borders were also in Europe, the very stringent test of excluding all European borders also results in a large reduction in the cases under observation and in statistical power. As a result, while the exponentiated coefficient on the interaction of democracy and regime age is consistent (0.915), it initially appears to be no longer significant at conventional levels ($p \leq 0.14$). However, a joint F-test of the interaction term and its component parts shows that it is very likely that there is interaction of democracy and regime age (Wald $\chi 2$ of interaction & components = 37.05, $p < 0.0000$). Braumoeller, "Hypothesis Testing and Multiplicative Interaction Terms"; Thomas Brambor, William Roberts Clark, and Matt Golder, "Understanding Interaction Models: Improving Empirical Analyses," *Political Analysis* 14, no. 1 (2005): 63–82.

82. The list of ethnic groups used to construct this universe of cases was based on the Ethnic Power Relations (EPR) Core Dataset 2014. Vogt et al., "Integrating Data on Ethnicity, Geography, and Conflict." I depart from the EPR when there are connections between coethnic groups that EPR-2014 does not strictly recognize (such as between different Arab groups and between "mainland Africans" in Tanzania and more specific groups in its neighbors) and to update states missing from EPR. The results are robust to using a strict application of the EPR Core Dataset 2014 (see column 3 of table A.5 in the appendix). The use of the truncation of any ethnic group as the delimiter of truncated ethnic homelands could raise a potential concern that the sample is biased by the inclusion of irrelevant cases (such as the truncating of the Roma in Europe). As a result, column 2 of table A.5 shows the results when only ethnic groups that are ever part of a ruling coalition at the level of junior partner or higher according to the EPR Core Dataset 2014 are divided by a new international border. The primary source for ethnographic maps for most of the cases was the *Atlas Narodov Mira* (ANM). While published in the early 1960s, it was based on the work of Soviet ethnographers in the late 1950s. Coethnics were coded as being on the other side of the border if the geocoding of the ANM by the Geo-Referencing of Ethnic Groups (GREG) dataset listed both groups in adjacent polygons that were on either side of what would be the border. Solomon I. Bruk and V. S. Apenchenko, eds., *Atlas Narodov Mira* [Atlas of the peoples of the world], Moscow: Glavnoe Upravlenie Geodezii i Kartografi, 1964; Nils B. Weidmann, Jan Ketil Rød, and Lars-Erik Cederman, "Representing Ethnic Groups in Space: A New Dataset," *Journal of Peace Research* 47, no. 4 (2010): 491–99. The ANM is, unsurprisingly, particularly problematic in identifying the presence and location of ethnic groups within the Soviet Union as these were influenced by a variety of political factors. As a result, some cases were recoded based on case-specific research. Other sources included De Agostini's Geographical Institute, ed., *L'Europe ethnique et linguistique*, Novara, Italy: De Agostini's Geographical Institute, 1917; Andras Ronai, ed., *Atlas of Central Europe*, Budapest: Society of St. Steven-Puski, 1993; United States, Office of Strategic Services (OSS), *Indochina Linguistic Groups: Adapted from L'Indochine, Carte Linguistique, Paris 1929*, 1945; George Peter Murdock, *Africa: Its Peoples and Their Culture History*, New York: McGraw-Hill, 1959; United States, Office of Strategic Services (OSS), *Borneo: Indonesian Peoples and Christian Missions*, 1945; Service Geographique de l'Indochine, *L'Indochine, Carte Linguistique*, 1928; Jovan Cvijic, *Ethnographic Map of the Balkan Peninsula*, 1918; and United States, Central Intelligence Agency, *Peoples of Yugoslavia: Distribution by Opstina 1981 Census*, 1983.

83. Allan Dafoe, John R. Oneal, and Bruce Russett, "The Democratic Peace: Weighing the Evidence and Cautious Inference," *International Studies Quarterly* 57, no. 1 (2013): 201–14.

84. Democratic dyads are coded using the V-Dem democracy measure described above. Controlling for democratic dyads, the exponentiated coefficient of the risk of failure for the interaction of democracy and regime age is 0.882, significant at the $p \le .01$ level. The impact of democratic dyads themselves is not significant (not shown).

85. See able A.7, columns 3 and 4.

86. Weiner, "Macedonian Syndrome," 676. See also Ranabir Samaddar, "Introduction: The Infamous Event," in Bianchini et al., *Partitions*, 4.

87. Gibler, *Territorial Peace*.

88. Table A.8 replicates table 7.1 in Gibler, *Territorial Peace*, 126, with the addition in column 1 of the presence of the application of homeland territoriality to land across the border by state. Column 2 uses being the target of such a claim as the added measure of territorial threat.

6. LOSING HOMELANDS AND CONFLICT

1. Parts of this chapter are based on Shelef, "Unequal Ground."

2. Bowman, "Strategy of Territorial Decisions," 180.

3. Alter, "Nationalism and German Politics," 165.

4. See, for example, Goertz and Diehl, *Territorial Change*, 132; Diehl, "What Are They Fighting For?," 333; Bremer, "Dangerous Dyads"; Huth, *Standing Your Ground*; Zacher, "Territorial Integrity Norm"; Saideman and Ayers, "Determining the Causes of Irredentism"; and Joslyn Barnhart, "Humiliation and Third-Party Aggression," *World Politics* 69, no. 3 (2017): 532–68.

5. Dzurek, "What Makes Territory Important."

6. See, for example, Walter, *Reputation and Civil War*; and Wiegand, *Enduring Territorial Disputes*.

7. See, for example, Van Evera, "Hypotheses on Nationalism and War"; Kaufmann, "Possible and Impossible Solutions"; Joseph and O'Hanlon, "Case for Soft Partition in Iraq"; Saideman and Ayers, "Determining the Causes of Irredentism"; Mearsheimer, "Back to the Future"; Kaufmann, "When All Else Fails"; Mearsheimer, "Case for Partitioning Kosovo"; Downes, "Holy Land Divided"; Leslie H. Gelb, "The Three-State Solution," *New York Times*, November 25, 2003; Tir, "Dividing Countries to Promote Peace"; Chapman and Roeder, "Partition as a Solution"; and C. Johnson, "Partitioning to Peace."

8. See, for example, John A. Vasquez, "Why Do Neighbors Fight?: Proximity, Interaction, or Territoriality," *Journal of Peace Research* 32, no. 3 (1995): 277–93; Hensel, "Territory"; Hensel, "Contentious Issues and World Politics"; John Vasquez and Marie T. Henehan, "Territorial Disputes and the Probability of War, 1816–1992," *Journal of Peace Research* 38, no. 2 (2001): 123–38; Huth and Allee, *Democratic Peace*; and Paul D. Senese and John Vasquez, "Assessing the Steps to War," *British Journal of Political Science* 35, no. 4 (2005): 607.

9. Hall, *National Collective Identity*.

10. See, for example, Connor, *Ethnonationalism*; and Weiner, "Macedonian Syndrome."

11. Quoted in Wilpert, *Oder-Neisse Problem*, 24.

12. IPS Research and Documents Staff, *International Documents on Palestine, 1977*, 392.

13. Fearon, "Rationalist Explanations for War"; Senese and Vasquez, *Steps to War*.

14. D. Miller, "In Defence of Nationality."

15. Conzen, "Culture Regions, Homelands, and Ethnic Archipelagos in the United States."

16. Lars-Erik Cederman, "Nationalism and Ethnicity in International Relations," in *Handbook of International Relations*, ed. Walter Carlsnaes, Thomas Risse, and Beth A. Simmons, Los Angeles: Sage, 2013, chap. 21, 530–54, 538.

17. See also Hauptmann, "Problem of Partition."

18. Huth, "Territory."

19. B. Miller, *States, Nations, and the Great Powers*, 57, 88–100.

20. Jack A. Goldstone, "Toward a Fourth Generation of Revolutionary Theory," *Annual Review of Political Science* 4, no. 1 (2001): 139–87, 164.

21. New international borders are defined as in chapter 5. As in that chapter, the analysis here excludes new borders that involved Canada, the United States, Eritrea, Zanzibar, Tanganyika, and the Seychelles since these cases are missing from FBIS. Some of these borders did involve the loss of homeland territory, as in the US control of the Panama Canal (a loss of homeland territory for Panama) and the US occupation of a number of Japanese islands after World War II (a loss of homeland territory for Japan).

22. The coding for all three is based on Zeev Maoz's Dyadic Militarized Interstate Disputes Dataset, Version 2.0. Violent MIDs are those in which the MID intensity is coded as

either a "4" or a "5". States are coded as having experienced conflict regardless of whether they are coded as State A or State B in Maoz's data.

23. Daniel M. Jones, Stuart A. Bremer, and J. David Singer, "Militarized Interstate Disputes, 1816–1992: Rationale, Coding Rules, and Empirical Patterns," *Conflict Management and Peace Science* 15, no. 2 (1996): 163–213; Meredith Reid Sarkees and Frank Whelon Wayman, *Resort to War: A Data Guide to Inter-State, Extra-State, Intra-State, and Non-State Wars, 1816–2007*, Thousand Oaks, CA: CQ Press, 2010.

24. The results are clustered by dyad because the observation of conflict for each member of the dyad is not independent of the observations for the other member of the dyad. The main results in this chapter, with the exception of the impact of the withdrawal of homeland territoriality on war, are robust to clustering by the border. See tables A.10 and A.11 in the appendix.

25. Unless otherwise noted, all variables are coded as in chapter 5.

26. Because we are interested in the presence of conflict, successor states with contiguous borders are coded as having experienced conflict even if they did not technically exist prior to 1945. For example, the GDR and Poland are coded as having experienced conflict before 1945 despite the fact that the GDR did not exist until 1954, but the GDR and France are not. Similarly, Poland and Lithuania are coded as having prior conflict, despite the fact that this conflict took place between Poland and the USSR. The results are also generally robust to four alternative definitions of prior conflict: (1) as a state's experience of any territorial change between 1816 and 1944 (as coded by the Correlates of War Territorial Change dataset in Tir et al., "Territorial Changes 1816–1996," version 4.01); (2) the existence of a violent territorial transfer between the states in the dyad between 1900 and 1944 (as coded by Carter and Goemans, "Making of the Territorial Order"); (3) involvement in a civil war before 1945 (as coded by version 4.0 of the Correlates of War Intra-State War data set, Sarkees and Wayman, *Resort to War*); and (4) having the border drawn as the result of a war (the latter based on E. W. Anderson, *International Boundaries*; and the International Boundary Studies produced by the US State Department, Office of the Geographer, Bureau of Intelligence and Research). See tables A.10 and A.11 in the appendix.

27. Fortna, "Scraps of Paper?"

28. Douglas M. Gibler, "Bordering on Peace: Democracy, Territorial Issues, and Conflict," *International Studies Quarterly* 51, no. 3 (2007): 509–32.

29. Brubaker, *Nationalism Reframed*; Saideman and Ayers, "Determining the Causes of Irredentism"; Jenne, *Ethnic Bargaining*; Mylonas, *Politics of Nation-Building*.

30. This measure relies on Sambanis, Germann, and Schädel, "New Data Set on Self-Determination Movements."

31. On the economic value of territory and conflict, see Robert Gilpin, *War and Change in World Politics*, Cambridge: Cambridge University Press, 1981. For a summary of the contrasting view, see Wiegand, *Enduring Territorial Disputes*.

32. Dafoe, Oneal, and Russett, "Democratic Peace"; Maoz and Russett, "Normative and Structural Causes of Democratic Peace, 1946–1986"; Bruce M. Russett, *Grasping the Democratic Peace: Principles for a Post–Cold War World*, Princeton, NJ: Princeton University Press, 1995; Bruce Bueno de Mesquita et al., "An Institutional Explanation of the Democratic Peace," *American Political Science Review* 93, no. 4 (1999): 791–807; Huth and Allee, *Democratic Peace*.

33. Joint democracy is coded based on a binary version of V-DEM's "Electoral democracy index" ordinal measure, as in chapter 5. Colonies and occupied states are coded as nondemocracies.

34. Huth, *Standing Your Ground*.

35. Alliances are coded as a binary variable where any alliance is "1" and no alliance is "0" based on the Correlates of War Formal Alliance data in Douglas M. Gibler, *International Military Alliances, 1648–2008*, Thousand Oaks, CA: CQ Press, 2009, version 4.1.

36. The results are robust to also controlling for whether one or both states in the dyad possessed nuclear weapons and whether the members of the dyad were clients of the same or opposite superpowers. See tables A.10 and A.11 in the appendix.

37. The splines for each dependent variable were generated using the Binary Time Series Cross Section (BTSCS) command in Stata. Peace years tracks the number of years between MIDs, violent MIDS, or wars, as appropriate. The inclusion of these variables in the logistic regression framework creates the equivalent of hazard analysis. Nathaniel Beck, Jonathan N. Katz, and Richard Tucker, "Taking Time Seriously: Time-Series-Cross-Section Analysis with a Binary Dependent Variable," *American Journal of Political Science* 42, no. 4 (1998): 1260–88; David B. Carter and Curtis S. Signorino, "Back to the Future: Modeling Time Dependence in Binary Data," *Political Analysis* 18, no. 3 (2010): 271–92.

38. Table A.9 in the appendix reports the results of the logit regressions on which figures 6.2 and 6.3 are based. In the context of wars, the presence of coethnics on the other side of the border, democratic dyads, and economically valuable territory are dropped from the analysis because they are perfectly correlated with war.

39. James D. Fearon and David D. Laitin, "Explaining Interethnic Cooperation," *American Political Science Review* 90, no. 4 (1996): 715–35; Huth, *Standing Your Ground*; Gartzke and Gleditsch, "Identity and Conflict"; Tir, "Dividing Countries to Promote Peace."

40. B. Miller, *States, Nations, and the Great Powers*.

41. See, for example, Kocs, "Territorial Disputes and Interstate War"; and Tir, "Dividing Countries to Promote Peace."

42. See tables A.10 and A.11 in the appendix.

43. Lustick, *Unsettled States, Disputed Lands*; Finnemore and Sikkink, "International Norm Dynamics"; Krebs, *Narrative and the Making of US National Security*.

44. Following Osborne, graphing the predicted probabilities of the observed relationship against the linear and quadratic relationship demonstrates that the latter is a better fit (not shown). See Jason Osborne, *Best Practices in Logistic Regression*, London: Sage, 2015, 208–9.

45. Sack, *Human Territoriality*, 75.

46. Kornprobst, *Irredentism in European Politics*.

47. See tables A.10 and A.11 in the appendix.

48. See, for example, Wiegand, *Enduring Territorial Disputes*.

49. For arguments that this assumption may be unwarranted, see Tadashi Anno, "Collective Identity as an 'Emotional Investment Portfolio': An Economic Analogy to Psychological Process," in *Beyond Boundaries?: Disciplines, Paradigms, and Theoretical Integration in International Studies*, ed. Rudra Sil and Eileen M. Doherty, Albany: SUNY Press, 2000, 117–41; Elise Giuliano, "Secessionists from the Bottom Up," *World Politics* 58 (2006): 276–310; Shelef, *Evolving Nationalism*; and Goddard and Krebs, "Rhetoric, Legitimation, and Grand Strategy."

50. Joshua D. Kertzer, Jonathan Renshon, and Keren Yarhi-Milo, "How Do Observers Assess Resolve?," *British Journal of Political Science* (June 13, 2019): 1–23.

51. Jack L. Snyder, *Myths of Empire: Domestic Politics and International Ambition*, Ithaca, NY: Cornell University Press, 1991, 16; J. L. Snyder, *From Voting to Violence*; Toft, *Geography of Ethnic Violence*.

52. Finnemore and Sikkink, "Taking Stock," 402. See also Goddard and Krebs, "Rhetoric, Legitimation, and Grand Strategy"; and Krebs and Jackson, "Twisting Tongues and Twisting Arms."

53. Kuran, *Private Truths, Public Lies*, 199.

54. Huth and Allee, *Democratic Peace.*

55. See tables A.10 and A.11 in the appendix.

56. Goertz and Diehl, *Territorial Change*; Vasquez, "Why Do Neighbors Fight?"; Huth, *Standing Your Ground*; Douglas M. Gibler, "Alliances That Never Balance: The Territorial Settlement Treaty," *Conflict Management and Peace Science* 15, no. 1 (1996): 75–97; Hensel, "Charting a Course to Conflict"; Vasquez and Henehan, "Territorial Disputes and the Probability of War"; Ted R. Gurr and Monty G. Marshall, *Peace and Conflict: A Global Survey of Armed Conflicts, Self-Determination Movements, and Democracy*, College Park, MD: Center for International Development and Conflict Management, 2005; Senese and Vasquez, "Assessing the Steps to War"; Senese and Vasquez, *Steps to War.*

57. Huth and Allee, *Democratic Peace.*

58. The results for the impact of the withdrawal of homeland territoriality are of a similar magnitude, though they no longer appear significant in this context. This is likely a product of the fact that limiting the analysis to these cases results in a loss of almost 50 percent of the observations and a corresponding loss of statistical power to detect a relationship even if one exists. See tables A.10 and A.11 in the appendix.

59. See, for example, B. Anderson, *Imagined Communities*; Gellner, *Nations and Nationalism*; and Michael Hechter, *Containing Nationalism*, Oxford: Oxford University Press, 2000.

60. The classification of ruling ethnic groups generally followed the Ethic Power Relations (EPR-ETH) dataset, with a ruling group defined as one that was in any government at the level of junior partner or higher. Andreas Wimmer, Lars-Erik Cederman, and Brian Min, "Ethnic Politics and Armed Conflict: A Configurational Analysis of a New Global Dataset," *American Sociological Review* 74, no. 2 (2009): 316–37. Where EPR-ETH does not list any groups, I used the largest group listed by the *CIA World Factbook*, https://www.cia.gov/library/publications/the-world-factbook/. See note 82 in chapter 5 for additional sources.

61. See tables A.10 and A.11 in the appendix.

62. See tables A.10 and A.11 in the appendix. The models do not converge for wars. As a result, we cannot be certain that the results are not endogenous when wars are the outcome of interest.

63. See tables A.10 and A.11 in the appendix.

64. J. L. Snyder, *From Voting to Violence*; Mansfield and Snyder, *Electing to Fight.*

65. See tables A.10 and A.11 in the appendix.

66. Weiner, "Macedonian Syndrome"; Ambrosio, *Irredentism*; Mylonas and Shelef, "Which Land Is Our Land?"

67. See tables A.10 and A.11 in the appendix.

68. For example, James D. Fearon and David D. Laitin, "Violence and the Social Construction of Ethnic Identity," *International Organization* 54, no. 4 (2000): 845–77.

CONCLUSION

1. Shelef, *Evolving Nationalism.*

2. See also Sosis, "Why Sacred Lands Are Not Indivisible."

3. For important work that has been done in this vein on ethnicity, see especially Kanchan Chandra, "A Constructivist Dataset on Ethnicity and Institutions," in *Measuring Identity: A Guide for Social Scientists*, ed. Rawi Abdelal et al., Cambridge: Cambridge University Press, 2009, 250–75; Chandra, *Constructivist Theories of Ethnic Politics*; and Lars-Erik Cederman, Andreas Wimmer, and Brian Min, "Why Do Ethnic Groups Rebel: New Data and Analysis," *World Politics* 62, no. 1 (2010): 87–119.

4. See also Michael O. Roark, "Homelands: A Conceptual Essay," *Journal of Cultural Geography* 13 (Spring/Summer 1993): 5–12.

5. Ziva Kunda, *Social Cognition: Making Sense of People*, Cambridge, MA: MIT Press, 1999; Haidt, *Righteous Mind*.

6. Krebs, "How Dominant Narratives Rise and Fall," 810–11. See also Kornprobst, *Irredentism in European Politics*.

7. Maoz and Russett, "Normative and Structural Causes of Democratic Peace, 1946–1986"; Huth and Allee, *Democratic Peace*; Dafoe, Oneal, and Russett, "Democratic Peace"; Gibler, *Territorial Peace*; Michael R. Tomz and Jessica L. P. Weeks, "Public Opinion and the Democratic Peace," *American Political Science Review* 107, no. 4 (2013): 849–65.

8. Vasquez and Valeriano, "Territory as a Source of Conflict," 193.

9. Hensel, "Charting a Course to Conflict." For other critiques of how the end of conflict is operationalized and complementary solutions, see D. Scott Bennett, "Measuring Rivalry Termination, 1816–1992," *Journal of Conflict Resolution* 41, no. 2 (1997): 227–54; and Fortna, "Scraps of Paper?"

10. For example, Kaufmann, "When All Else Fails"; and C. Johnson, "Partitioning to Peace."

11. For example, Sambanis, "Partition as a Solution to Ethnic War"; Chapman and Roeder, "Partition as a Solution."

12. The average number of annual battle deaths in the Israeli-Palestinian conflict (distinct from that between Israel and the Arab states) was 252 for the 1950–93 period and 553 for 1994–2008. Bethany Lacina and Nils Petter Gleditsch, "Monitoring Trends in Global Combat: A New Dataset of Battle Deaths," *European Journal of Population/Revue Européenne de Démographie* 21, nos. 2–3 (2005): 145–66, version 3.0. This difference is highly significant (p = 0.0000), but in the wrong direction for identifying 1993 as the end of the conflict.

13. Cf. Kaufmann, "Possible and Impossible Solutions"; Chaim Kaufmann, "An Assessment of the Partition of Cyprus," *International Studies Perspectives* 8, no. 2 (2007): 206–23; and Radha Kumar, "The Troubled History of Partition," *Foreign Affairs* 76 (1997): 22–34.

14. Brendan O'Leary, "Analyzing Partition: Definition, Classification and Explanation," *Political Geography* 26 (2007): 886–908.

15. See, for example, Bennett, "Measuring Rivalry Termination."

16. Vasquez, "Why Do Neighbors Fight?," 283; Gibler, "Bordering on Peace"; Gibler, *Territorial Peace*; Kornprobst, *Irredentism in European Politics*.

17. For example, John J. Mearsheimer and Robert A. Pape, "The Answer: A Three-Way Partition Plan for Bosnia and How the U.S. Can Enforce It," *New Republic* 208, no. 24 (1993): 22–28; John J. Mearsheimer and Stephen Van Evera, "When Peace Means War," *New Republic* 213, no. 25 (1995): 16–21; John J. Mearsheimer and Stephen Van Evera, "Redraw the Map, Stop the Killing," *New York Times*, April 19, 1999; Maynard Glitman, "US Policy in Bosnia: Rethinking a Flawed Approach," *Survival* 38, no. 4 (1996): 66–83; Kaufmann, "Possible and Impossible Solutions"; Kaufmann, "When All Else Fails"; Michael O'Hanlon, "Turning the Bosnia Ceasefire into Peace," *Brookings Review* 16, no. 1 (1998): 41–44; Mearsheimer, "Case for Partitioning Kosovo"; Downes, "Holy Land Divided"; Leslie H. Gelb, "The Three-State Solution," *New York Times*, November 25, 2003; and Joseph and O'Hanlon, "Case for Soft Partition in Iraq."

18. For example, William Pfaff, "Invitation to War," *Foreign Affairs* 72 (Summer 1993): 97–109; Flora Lewis, "Reassembling Yugoslavia," *Foreign Policy* 98 (Spring 1995): 132–44; Carl Bildt, "There Is No Alternative to Dayton," *Survival* 39 (Winter 1997): 19–21; Kumar, "Troubled History of Partition"; Susan L. Woodward, "Avoiding Another Cyprus or Israel: A Debate about the Future of Bosnia," *Brookings Review* 16 (Winter 1998): 45–48; Donald L. Horowitz, "The Cracked Foundations of the Right to Secede," *Journal of Democracy* 14, no. 2 (2003): 5–17; Brendan O'Leary, "Debating Partition: Justifications and Critiques," *Working Papers in British-Irish Studies* 78 (2006): 1–29; Henderson and Lebow,

"Conclusions"; Stefano Bianchini, "Partitions: Categories and Destinies," in Bianchini et al., *Partitions*, 47–91; Erin K. Jenne, "The Paradox of Ethnic Partition: Lessons from De Facto Partition in Bosnia and Kosovo," *Regional and Federal Studies* 19, no. 2 (2009): 273–89; Thomas E. Hachey, *The Problem of Partition: Peril to World Peace*, Chicago: Rand McNally, 1972; Hauptmann, "Problem of Partition"; and Samaddar, introduction.

19. Cf. Mearsheimer and Pape, "Answer"; Mearsheimer and Van Evera, "When Peace Means War"; and Mearsheimer, "Case for Partitioning Kosovo," on the one hand, and John Mearsheimer, "The Impossible Partition," *New York Times*, January 11, 2001, on the other.

20. Bianchini, "Partitions," 62. See also, James D. Fearon, "Separatist Wars, Partition, and World Order," *International Security* 13 (Summer 2004): 394–415; Frank Jacobs, "If at First You Don't Secede. . . : Will This Be the Summer of Separatism for Europe?," *Foreign Policy*, April 28, 2014; Samaddar, introduction. For an argument against the presence of domino effects, see Erika Forsberg, "Do Ethnic Dominoes Fall?: Evaluating Domino Effects of Granting Territorial Concessions to Separatist Groups," *International Studies Quarterly* 57, no. 2 (2013): 329–40.

21. These works include Kaufmann, "When All Else Fails"; Sambanis, "Partition as a Solution to Ethnic War"; Tir, "Dividing Countries to Promote Peace"; Chapman and Roeder, "Partition as a Solution"; C. Johnson, "Partitioning to Peace"; Sambanis and Schulhofer-Wohl, "What's in a Line"; and Kornprobst, *Irredentism in European Politics*.

22. The total number of partitions identified can be higher, but it is limited here to the time span covered by the data in chapter 5 to make comparison easier.

23. Kaufmann, "When All Else Fails"; Tir, "Dividing Countries to Promote Peace"; Chapman and Roeder, "Partition as a Solution"; C. Johnson, "Partitioning to Peace."

24. Sambanis, "Partition as a Solution to Ethnic War"; Sambanis and Schulhofer-Wohl, "What's in a Line."

25. See also T. Forsberg, "Explaining Territorial Disputes."

26. O'Leary, "Elements of Right-Sizing and Right-Peopling the State"; O'Leary, "Analyzing Partition."

27. On the distinction between secession and irredentism, see Donald L. Horowitz, "Irredentas and Secessions: Adjacent Phenomena, Neglected Connections," *International Journal of Comparative Sociology* 33, nos. 1–2 (1992): 118–30.

28. Kaufmann, "When All Else Fails," 125; Robert K. Schaeffer, *Warpaths: The Politics of Partition*, New York: Hill and Wang, 1990. Jaroslav Tir agrees that partition and secession are distinct but includes only secessions in his analysis, excluding externally imposed territorial divisions. Tir, "Dividing Countries to Promote Peace."

29. Sambanis, "Partition as a Solution to Ethnic War," 445; and C. Johnson, "Partitioning to Peace," 152, respectively.

30. Cf. O'Leary, "Analyzing Partition" (2007); and John McGarry and Brendan O'Leary, "Introduction: The Macro-Political Regulation of Ethnic Conflict," in *The Politics of Ethnic Conflict Regulation: Case Studies of Protracted Ethnic Conflicts*, ed. John McGarry and Brendan O'Leary, New York: Routledge, 1993, 1–47.

31. Ray E. Johnston, "Partition as a Political Instrument," *Journal of International Affairs* 27, no. 2 (1973): 159–74; he also noted that what might be a partition to one side in a conflict may not be to another (163).

32. Central Committee of the TPLF, "Statement by the Central Committee of the Tigray People's Liberation Front (TPLF) on the Occasion of the 24th Anniversary of the Armed Struggle in Eritrea," *Review of African Political Economy* 35 (1986): 93. Compare the exclusion of Eritrea from Ethiopia by the TPLF with the claim to Eritrea articulated by the Ethiopian Monarchy and the Mengistu regime that they overthrew: for example, Ministry of Foreign Affairs, Empire of Ethiopia, *Digest of Memoranda Presented by the Imperial Ethiopian Government to the Council of Foreign Ministers*, 1945; Ethiopia Ministry of

Information and National Guidance, *Ethiopia: Four Years of Revolutionary Process,* Addis Ababa: Propaganda and Information Committee, 1978; Provisional Military Government of Ethiopia, *Ethiopia Tikdem: Declaration of the Provisional Military government of Ethiopia,* 1974. See also Tadesse, *Eritrean-Ethiopian War;* and Berhe, *Political History.*

33. Kaufmann ("When All Else Fails") includes Algeria, but categorizes it as a case of secession, not partition. Chapman and Roeder ("Partition as a Solution") and Tir ("Dividing Countries to Promote Peace") include the division of Ireland (though the former use the 1994 division and the latter uses the 1922 division). Sambanis ("Partition as a Solution to Ethnic War," 446n42), Sambanis and Schulhofer-Wohl ("What's in a Line," 101n46), and C. Johnson ("Partitioning to Peace," 151) identify Ireland as a case of partition in the course of their argument, though they exclude it from the empirical analysis on the grounds that it takes place before 1945. In other words, had it taken place after 1945, it would have been included. On the relationship between Algeria, Ireland, and their metropoles, see Lustick, *Unsettled States, Disputed Lands.*

34. Lustick, *Unsettled States, Disputed Lands;* Goddard, *Indivisible Territory.* Tir ("Dividing Countries to Promote Peace") does use the different conceptualization of the land to distinguish between decolonization and other kinds of territorial divisions.

35. For examples of studies that conflate the two, see Kaufmann, "When All Else Fails"; and C. Johnson, "Partitioning to Peace." Sambanis's definition of partition ("Partition as a Solution to Ethnic War") does so as well, but, curiously, this is not reflected in the operationalization of the variable. Chapman and Roeder ("Partition as a Solution") also conflate demography and territory in their discussion of the notion of the fading of "identity incompatibility" as the most likely path to successful conflict resolution.

36. See Hartmunt Berghoff, "Population Change and Its Repercussions on the Social History of the Federal Republic," in Larres and Panayi, *Federal Republic of Germany since 1949,* 35–73, 37.

37. Kaufmann, "Possible and Impossible Solutions," 149. See also Downes, "Holy Land Divided"; Joseph and O'Hanlon, "Case for Soft Partition in Iraq"; Mearsheimer, "Case for Partitioning Kosovo"; Mearsheimer, "Impossible Partition"; Mearsheimer and Pape, "Answer"; Mearsheimer and Van Evera, "When Peace Means War"; and Mearsheimer and Van Evera, "Redraw the Map, Stop the Killing."

38. Kaufmann, "When All Else Fails."

39. See, for example, Sambanis, "Partition as a Solution to Ethnic War"; Sambanis and Schulhofer-Wohl, "What's in a Line"; Chapman and Roeder, "Partition as a Solution"; and C. Johnson, "Partitioning to Peace."

40. Samaddar, introduction.

41. Kumar, "Troubled History of Partition"; Horowitz, "Cracked Foundations of the Right to Secede"; O'Leary, "Analyzing Partition"; Woodward, "Avoiding Another Cyprus or Israel"; Sambanis, "Partition as a Solution to Ethnic War"; Sambanis and Schulhofer-Wohl, "What's in a Line."

42. Arjun Chowdhury and Ronald R. Krebs, "Making and Mobilizing Moderates: Rhetorical Strategy, Political Networks, and Counterterrorism," *Security Studies* 18, no. 3 (2009): 371–99.

APPENDIX

1. Janet M. Box-Steffensmeier, Suzanna De Boef, and Kyle A. Joyce, "Event Dependence and Heterogeneity in Duration Models: The Conditional Frailty Model," *Political Analysis* 15, no. 3 (2007): 237–56.

2. Andersen and Gill, "Cox's Regression Model for Counting Processes," 1100–1120; Cleves, "Stata."

3. See, for example, Janet M. Box-Steffensmeier and Christopher J. W. Zorn, "Duration Models and Proportional Hazards in Political Science," *American Journal of Political Science* 45, no. 4 (2001): 972–88; Virginia Page Fortna, "Does Peacekeeping Keep Peace?: International Intervention and the Duration of Peace after Civil War," *International Studies Quarterly* 48, no. 2 (2004): 269–92; Giacomo Chiozza and Hein E. Goemans, "International Conflict and the Tenure of Leaders: Is War Still Ex Post Inefficient?," *American Journal of Political Science* 48, no. 3 (2004): 604–19; and Jason Webb Yackee and Susan Webb Yackee, "Administrative Procedures and Bureaucratic Performance: Is Federal Rule-Making 'Ossified'?," *Journal of Public Administration Research and Theory* 20, no. 2 (2009): 261–82.

4. Box-Steffensmeier, De Boef, and Joyce, "Event Dependence and Heterogeneity in Duration Models"; G. David Garson, *Cox Regression*, Asheboro, NC: Statistical Associates, 2013, 36–37.

5. Vogt et al., "Integrating Data on Ethnicity, Geography, and Conflict"; Alesina et al., "Fractionalization"; Gartzke and Gleditsch, "Identity and Conflict."

6. The modified version contains the following cases that were coded as sharing an ethnic group. Some of these include decolonization dyads that are excluded from the main analysis as described in the text, but are included when testing robustness to alternative universes of cases: Czech Republic–Slovakia, Cameroon-UK, Spain-Morocco where Spain is engaged in incomplete decolonization and in Western Sahara, Oman-Yemen, UK-Zimbabwe, Egypt-Syria, India-UK, Pakistan-UK, Jamaica-UK, Trinidad and Tobago–UK, Malaysia-UK, Jordan–Saudi-Arabia, Grenada-UK, Kuwait–Saudi Arabia, Israel-Syria, Saudi Arabia–Oman, Philippines-USA, Myanmar-UK, Sri Lanka–UK, USA-Panama, USA–South Korea, Guyana-UK, Yemen Arab Republic–Yemen People's Republic, Uganda-Sudan, Burkina Faso–Mali, Benin–Togo, Mauritania-Senegal, Tanzania-UK, Uganda-Tanzania, UK-Zambia, UK-Botswana, Ukraine-Moldova, Austria-Germany. The following missing cases were updated from the *CIA World Factbook* and other sources: Kiribati, Comoros, Equatorial Guinea, Seychelles, West Samoa, Dominica, Solomon Islands, St. Lucia, St. Kitts and Nevis, Brunei, Cape Verde, Maldives, Antigua and Barbuda, Belize, Vanuatu, St. Vincent and Grenadines, Marshall Islands, Palau, Micronesia, Tonga, Qatar, Bahamas, Barbados, Cape Verde.

7. The original data was modified as follows: Where cases were coded as sharing a religion partway through the data, I coded them as sharing a religion the entire time. Data for Czechoslovakia is missing after 1993, and I assume that Slovakia and the Czech Republic share its cultural characteristics. Likewise, Germany data is missing before 1949, and I assume that Germany prior to that point shares the cultural characteristics after 1949. Cases of incomplete decolonization coded as "1" in all three categories until the last one.

8. Braumoeller, "Hypothesis Testing and Multiplicative Interaction Terms"; Brambor, Clark, and Golder, "Understanding Interaction Models."

9. Unfortunately, there are not enough cases to conduct the analysis in which there are no coethnics in the lost homeland territory.

10. Gibler, *Territorial Peace*, 126.

Bibliography

Abdelal, Rawi, Yoshiko M. Herrera, Alastair Iain Johnston, and Rose McDermott. "Identity as a Variable." *Perspectives on Politics* 4, no. 4 (2006): 695–711. https://doi.org/10.1017/S1537592706060440.

——, eds. *Measuring Identity: A Guide for Social Scientists.* Cambridge: Cambridge University Press, 2009.

Abu Iyad. "Abu Iyad on the PNC Session and Other Topics." *Journal of Palestine Studies* 8, no. 3 (1979): 137–48. https://doi.org/10.2307/2536235.

——. *My Home, My Land: A Narrative of the Palestinian Struggle.* New York: Times Books, 1980.

Abu-Shanab, Ismail H. "An Islamic Approach of the Resistance against Israeli Occupation in Palestine: The Strategy of 'Hamas' in the Present and in the Future." In *Palestinian Perspectives*, edited by Wolfgang Freund, 165–73. Frankfurt: Peter Lang, 1999.

Abu Sharif, Bassam. *Arafat and the Dream of Palestine: An Insider's Account.* New York: Macmillan, 2009.

Aburish, Said K. *Arafat: From Defender to Dictator.* New York: Bloomsbury, 1999.

Adler, Emanuel. "Seizing the Middle Ground: Constructivism in World Politics." *European Journal of International Relations* 3, no. 3 (1997): 319–63. https://doi.org/10.1177/1354066197003003003.

Agnew, John A. "Borders on the Mind: Re-Framing Border Thinking." *Ethics and Global Politics* 1, no. 4 (2008): 175–91. https://doi.org/10.3402/egp.v1i4.1892.

——. "No Borders, No Nations: Making Greece in Macedonia." *Annals of the Association of American Geographers* 97, no. 2 (2007): 398–422. https://doi.org/10.1111/j.1467-8306.2007.00545.x.

——. *Reinventing Geopolitics: Geographies of Modern Statehood.* Heidelberg: Department of Geography, University of Heidelberg, 2001.

——. "The Territorial Trap: The Geographical Assumptions of International Relations Theory." *Review of International Political Economy* 1, no. 1 (1994): 53–80. https://doi.org/10.1080/09692299408434268.

Agosti, Aldo. *Palmiro Togliatti: A Biography.* New York: I. B. Tauris, 2008.

Ahonen, Pertti. *After the Expulsion: West Germany and Eastern Europe 1945–1990.* Oxford: Oxford University Press, 2003.

——. "Domestic Constraints on West German Ostpolitik: The Role of the Expellee Organizations." *Central European History* 31, no. 1/2 (1998): 31–63. https://doi.org/10.1017/S0008938900016034.

Akenson, Donald H. *God's People: Covenant and Land in South Africa, Israel, and Ulster.* Ithaca, NY: Cornell University Press, 1992.

Alami, Musa. "The Lesson of Palestine." *Middle East Journal* 3, no. 4 (1949): 373–405.

Albrecht-Carrié, René. *Italy at the Paris Peace Conference.* Hamden, CT: Archon Books, 1966.

Albright, David E. "Soviet Economic Development and the Third World." *Soviet Studies* 43, no. 1 (1991): 27–59. https://doi.org/10.1080/09668139108411910.

Alesina, Alberto, Arnaud Devleeschauwer, William Easterly, Sergio Kurlat, and Romain Wacziarg. "Fractionalization." *Journal of Economic Growth* 8, no. 2 (2003): 155–94.

Alesina, Alberto, and Enrico Spolaore. *The Size of Nations.* Cambridge, MA: MIT Press, 2003.

Aliboni, Roberto, and Ettore Greco. "Foreign Policy Re-Nationalization and Internationalism in the Italian Debate." *International Affairs* (Royal Institute of International Affairs) 72, no. 1 (1996): 43–51. https://doi.org/10.2307/2624748.

Allcock, John B., Guy Arnold, Alan J. Day, D. S. Lewis, Lorimer Poultney, Roland Rance, and D. J. Sagar, eds. *Borders and Territorial Disputes.* 3rd ed. Essex: Longman Current Affairs, 1992.

Allen, Debra J. *The Oder-Neisse Line: The United States, Poland, and Germany in the Cold War.* Westport, CT: Praeger, 2003.

Allen, William Sheridan. "The Collapse of Nationalism in Nazi Germany." In Breuilly, *State of Germany*, 141–53.

Alpher, Joseph. *Ve-gar ze'ev 'im ze'ev: Ha-mitnahalim veha-Palestinim* [And the wolf shall dwell with the wolf: The settlers and the Palestinians]. Tel Aviv: Hakibbutz Hameuchad, 2001.

Al-Shuaibi, Issa. "The Development of Palestinian Entity-Consciousness: Part I." *Journal of Palestine Studies* 9, no. 1 (1979): 67–84. https://doi.org/10.2307/2536319.

——. "The Development of Palestinian Entity-Consciousness: Part III." *Journal of Palestine Studies* 9, no. 3 (1980): 99–124. https://doi.org/10.2307/2536552.

Alter, Peter. "Nationalism and German Politics after 1945." In Breuilly, *State of Germany*, 154–76.

Ambrosio, Thomas. *Irredentism: Ethnic Conflict and International Politics.* Westport, CT: Praeger, 2001.

American Community Survey. *S0201—Selected Population Profile in the United States.* May 2012.

Andersen, P. K., and R. D. Gill. "Cox's Regression Model for Counting Processes: A Large Sample Study." *Annals of Statistics* 10, no. 4 (1982): 1100–1120.

Anderson, Benedict. *Imagined Communities: Reflections on the Origin and Spread of Nationalism.* New York: Verso, 1991.

Anderson, Ewan W. *International Boundaries: A Geopolitical Atlas.* New York: Psychology Press, 2003.

Anderson, James. "Nationalist Ideology and Territory." In Johnston, Knight, and Kofman, *Nationalism, Self-Determination, and Political Geography*, 18–39.

Anderson, Malcolm. *Frontiers: Territory and State Formation in the Modern World.* Cambridge: Polity Press, 1996.

Anno, Tadashi. "Collective Identity as an 'Emotional Investment Portfolio': An Economic Analogy to Psychological Process." In *Beyond Boundaries?: Disciplines, Paradigms, and Theoretical Integration in International Studies*, edited by Rudra Sil and Eileen M. Doherty, 117–41. Albany: SUNY Press, 2000.

Asal, Victor, Amy Pate, and Jonathan Wilkenfeld. *Minorities at Risk Organizational Behavior Data and Codebook Version 9/2008.* http://www.mar.umd.edu/mar_data.asp.

Ash, Timothy Garton. *In Europe's Name: Germany and the Divided Continent.* New York: Random House, 1993.

Ashbrook, John E. "'Istria Is Ours, and We Can Prove It': An Examination of Istrian Historiography in the Nineteenth and Twentieth Centuries." *Carl Beck Papers in Russian and East European Studies*, no. 1707 (2006): 1–43.

Ashrawi, Hanan. *This Side of Peace: A Personal Account.* New York: Simon and Schuster, 1996.

Asiwaju, A. I. "The Conceptual Framework." In Asiwaju, *Partitioned Africans,* 1–18.

——, ed. *Partitioned Africans: Ethnic Relations across Africa's International Boundaries, 1884–1984.* London: C. Hurst, 1985.

Association of Expellee Landsmannschaften. *The European Significance of the Oder-Neisse Territories.* Bonn: Association of Expellee Landsmannschaften, 1955.

Atran, Scott, Robert Axelrod, Richard Davis, et al. "Sacred Barriers to Conflict Resolution." *Science* 317 (2007): 1039–40. https://doi.org/10.1126/science.1144241.

Atzili, Boaz. *Good Fences, Bad Neighbors: Border Fixity and International Conflict.* Chicago: University of Chicago Press, 2011.

Atzili, Boaz, and Anne Kantel. "Accepting the Unacceptable: Lessons from West Germany's Changing Border Politics." *International Studies Review* 17, no. 4 (2015): 588–616. https://doi.org/10.1111/misr.12256.

Ballinger, Pamela. *History in Exile: Memory and Identity at the Borders of the Balkans.* Princeton, NJ: Princeton University Press, 2003.

Banchoff, Thomas F. *The German Problem Transformed: Institutions, Politics, and Foreign Policy, 1945–1995.* Ann Arbor: University of Michigan Press, 1999.

Barnhart, Joslyn. "Humiliation and Third-Party Aggression." *World Politics* 69, no. 3 (2017): 532–68. https://doi.org/10.1017/s0043887117000028.

Barrington, Lowell W. "'Nation' and 'Nationalism': The Misuse of Key Concepts in Political Science." *PS: Political Science and Politics* 30, no. 4 (1997): 712–16. https://doi.org/10.2307/420397.

Baumgarten, Helga. "The Three Faces/Phases of Palestinian Nationalism, 1948–2005." *Journal of Palestine Studies* 34, no. 4 (2005): 25–48.

Beck, Nathaniel, Jonathan N. Katz, and Richard Tucker. "Taking Time Seriously: Time-Series-Cross-Section Analysis with a Binary Dependent Variable." *American Journal of Political Science* 42, no. 4 (1998): 1260–88. https://doi.org/10.2307/2991857.

Becker, Josef, and Franz Knipping, eds. *Power in Europe?: Great Britain, France, Italy and Germany in a Postwar World, 1945–1950.* Berlin: Walter de Gruyter, 1986.

Belci, Corrado. *Quel confine mancato: La linea Wilson, 1919–1945* [The missing border: The Wilson line, 1919–1945]. Brescia: Morcelliana, 1996.

Belloni, Frank P. "Dislocation in the Italian Political System: An Analysis of the 1968 Parliamentary Elections." *Western Political Quarterly* 24, no. 1 (1971): 114–35. https://doi.org/10.2307/446269.

Benardelli, Mainardo. *La questione di Trieste: Storia di un conflitto diplomatico (1945–1975)* [The question of Trieste: History of a diplomatic conflict (1945–1975)]. Udine: Del Bianco, 2006.

Ben-Israel, Hedva. "Irredentism: Nationalism Reexamined." In Chazan, *Irredentism and International Politics,* 9–22.

Bennett, D. Scott. "Measuring Rivalry Termination, 1816–1992." *Journal of Conflict Resolution* 41, no. 2 (1997): 227–54. https://doi.org/10.1177/0022002797041002002.

Berghahn, Volker, and Uta Poiger. "Occupation and the Emergence of Two States (1945–1961)." 2018. Accessed August 1, 2018. http://germanhistorydocs.ghi-dc.org/section.cfm?section_id=14.

Berghoff, Hartmunt. "Population Change and Its Repercussions on the Social History of the Federal Republic." In Larres and Panayi, *Federal Republic of Germany since 1949,* 35–73.

Berhe, Aregawi. *A Political History of the Tigray People's Liberation Front (1975–1991): Revolt, Ideology and Mobilisation in Ethiopia.* Los Angeles: Tsehai, 2009.

Berkovitch, Jacob, and Richard Jackson. *International Conflict: A Chronological Encyclopedia of Conflicts and Their Management, 1945–1995*. Washington, DC: CQ Press, 1997.

Bettcher, Kim Eric. "Factionalism and the Adaptation of Dominant Parties: Japan's Liberal Democratic Party and Italy's Christian Democracy." PhD diss., Johns Hopkins University, 2001.

Beyme, Klaus von. "The Legitimation of German Unification between National and Democratic Principles." *German Politics and Society*, no. 22 (1991): 1–17.

——. "National Consciousness and Nationalism: The Case of the Two Germanies." *Canadian Review of Studies in Nationalism* 8, no. 2 (1986): 227–48.

Bianchini, Stefano. "Partitions: Categories and Destinies." In Bianchini et al., *Partitions*, 47–91.

Bianchini, Stefano, Sanjay Chaturvedi, Rada Iveković, and Ranabir Samaddar, eds. *Partitions: Reshaping States and Minds*. New York: Frank Cass, 2005.

Biger, Gideon, ed. *The Encyclopedia of International Boundaries*. New York: Facts on File, 1995.

Biggs, Michael. "Putting the State on the Map: Cartography, Territory, and European State Formation." *Comparative Studies in Society and History* 41, no. 2 (1999): 374–405. https://doi.org/10.1017/S0010417599002121.

Bildt, Carl. "There Is No Alternative to Dayton." *Survival* 39 (Winter 1997): 19–21. https://doi.org/10.1080/00396339708442939.

Billig, Michael. *Banal Nationalism*. London: Sage, 1995.

Bishai, Linda S. *Forgetting Ourselves: Secession and the (Im)Possibility of Territorial Identity*. Lanham, MD: Lexington Books, 2004.

Black, Jeremy. *Maps and History: Constructing Images of the Past*. New Haven, CT: Yale University Press, 2000.

——. *Maps and Politics*. Chicago: University of Chicago Press, 2002.

Blackmer, Donald L. M. "The International Strategy of the Italian Communist Party." In *The International Role of the Communist Parties of Italy and France*, edited by Donald L. M. Blackmer and Annie Kriegel. Cambridge, MA: Center for International Affairs, Harvard University, 1975.

Blackmore, Susan. *The Meme Machine*. Oxford: Oxford University Press, 2000.

Bognetti, Giovanni. "The Role of Italian Parliament in the Treaty-Making Process—Europe." *Chicago-Kent Law Review* 67, no. 2 (1991): 391–412.

Bolzon, Irne. "Da Roma alla Zona B: Il Comitato di liberazione nazionale dell'Istria, l'Ufficio per le zone de confine e le comunitá istriane tra informazioni, propaganda e assistenza." [From Rome to Zone B: The National Liberation Committee of Istria, the Office for Border Areas and Istrian Communities with information, propaganda and assistance]. In D'Amelio, Di Michele, and Mezzalira, *La difesa dell'italianitá*, 487–509.

Boria, Edoardo. "Violence beyond Trenches: Ethnographical Maps from Science to Propaganda and the Case of the Julian March." In *The First World War: Analysis and Interpretation*, edited by Antonello Biagini and Giovanna Motta, 199–212. Newcastle: Cambridge Scholars, 2015.

Bornemann, John. *Belonging in the Two Berlins: Kin, State, Nation*. Cambridge: Cambridge University Press, 1992.

Boswell, Thomas D. "The Cuban-American Homeland in Miami." *Journal of Cultural Geography* 13, no. 2 (1993): 133–48. https://doi.org/10.1080/08873639309478394.

Bowman, Isaiah. "The Strategy of Territorial Decisions." *Foreign Affairs* 24, no. 2 (1946): 177–94.

Box-Steffensmeier, Janet M., Suzanna De Boef, and Kyle A. Joyce. "Event Dependence and Heterogeneity in Duration Models: The Conditional Frailty Model." *Political Analysis* 15, no. 3 (2007): 237–56. https://doi.org/10.1093/pan/mpm013.

Box-Steffensmeier, Janet M., and Christopher J. W. Zorn. "Duration Models and Proportional Hazards in Political Science." *American Journal of Political Science* 45, no. 4 (2001): 972–88. https://doi.org/10.1.1.475.4731.

Brambor, Thomas, William Roberts Clark, and Matt Golder. "Understanding Interaction Models: Improving Empirical Analyses." *Political Analysis* 14, no. 1 (2005): 63–82. https://doi.org/10.1093/pan/mpi014.

Branch, Jordan. *The Cartographic State: Maps, Territory, and the Origins of Sovereignty*. Cambridge: Cambridge University Press, 2013.

——. "Mapping the Sovereign State: Technology, Authority, and Systemic Change." *International Organization* 65, no. 1 (2011): 1–36. https://doi.org/10.1017/S0020818310000299.

Brandt, Willy. *My Life in Politics*. London: Hamish Hamilton, 1992.

——. *A Peace Policy for Europe*. London: Weidenfeld and Nicolson, 1969.

——. *People and Politics: The Years 1960–1975*. New York: Harper Collins, 1978.

Brass, Paul R. *Ethnicity and Nationalism: Theory and Comparison*. London: Sage, 1991.

Braumoeller, Bear F. "Hypothesis Testing and Multiplicative Interaction Terms." *International Organization* 58, no. 4 (2004): 807–20. https://doi.org/10.1017/S0020818304040251.

Breakwell, Glynis M. "Identity Processes and Social Changes." In *Changing European Identities: Social Psychological Analyses of Social Change*, edited by Glynis M. Breakwell and Evanthia Lyons, 13–27. Oxford: Butterworth Heinemann, 1996.

Breit, Peter K. "Case Studies of West German Views on Reunification." PhD diss., University of Massachusetts, 1967.

Bremer, Stuart A. "Dangerous Dyads: Conditions Affecting the Likelihood of Interstate War, 1816–1965." *Journal of Conflict Resolution* 36, no. 2 (1992): 309–41. https://doi.org/10.1177/0022002792036002005.

Breuilly, John, ed. *The State of Germany: The National Idea in the Making, Unmaking and Remaking of a Nation-State*. New York: Longman, 1992.

Bröning, Michael. *The Politics of Change in Palestine: State-Building and Non-Violent Resistance*. New York: Pluto Press, 2011.

Brown, Nathan. *Is Hamas Mellowing?* Carnegie Endowment for International Peace. January 17, 2012. http://carnegieendowment.org/2012/01/17/is-hamas-mellowing-pub-46488.

Brubaker, Rogers. *Citizenship and Nationhood in France and Germany*. Cambridge: Cambridge University Press, 1992.

——. "Ethnicity, Race, and Nationalism." *Annual Review of Sociology* 35 (2009): 21–42. https://doi.org/10.1146/annurev-soc-070308-115916.

——. *Nationalism Reframed: Nationhood and the National Question in the New Europe*. Cambridge: Cambridge University Press, 1996.

Bruk, Solomon I., and V. S. Apenchenko, eds. *Atlas Narodov Mira* [Atlas of the peoples of the world]. Moscow: Glavnoe Upravlenie Geodezii i Kartografi, 1964.

Bucarelli, Massimo. "Détente in the Adriatic: Italian Foreign Policy and the Road to the Osimo Treaty." In Bucarelli, Micheletta, Monzali, and Riccardi, *Italy and Tito's Yugoslavia*, 217–48.

Bucarelli, Massimo, Muca Micheletta, Luciano Monzali, and Luca Riccardi, eds. *Italy and Tito's Yugoslavia in the Age of International Détente*. Brussels: Peter Lang, 2016.

Bueno de Mesquita, Bruce, James D. Morrow, Randolph M. Siverson, and Alastair Smith. "An Institutional Explanation of the Democratic Peace." *American Political Science Review* 93, no. 4 (1999): 791–807. https://doi.org/10.2307/2586113.

Bueno de Mesquita, Bruce, Alistair Smith, Randolph Siverson, and James Morrow. *The Logic of Political Survival*. Cambridge, MA: MIT Press, 2003.

Bufon, Milan. "The Changeable Political Map of the Upper Adriatic Region: From Conflict to Harmony." *Revija za geografijo* 1, no. 3 (2008): 9–23.

Bufon, Milan, and Julian Minghi. "The Upper Adriatic Borderland: From Conflict to Harmony." *GeoJournal* 52, no. 2 (2000): 119–27. https://doi.org/10.1023/A:1013374204149.

Buhaug, Halvard, Lars-Erik Cederman, and Jan Ketil Rød. "Disaggregating Ethno-Nationalist Civil Wars: A Dyadic Test of Exclusion Theory." *International Organization* 62, no. 3 (2008): 531–51. https://doi.org/10.1017/S0020818308080181.

Buhaug, Halvard, and Scott Gates. "The Geography of Civil War." *Journal of Peace Research* 39, no. 4 (2002): 417–33. https://doi.org/10.1177/0022343302039004003.

Bühler, Phillip A. *The Oder-Neisse Line: A Reappraisal under International Law*. Boulder, CO: East European Monographs, 1990.

Bukovansky, Mlada. *Legitimacy and Power Politics: The American and French Revolutions in International Political Culture*. Princeton, NJ: Princeton University Press, 2002.

Burghardt, Andrew F. "The Bases of Territorial Claims." *Geographical Review* 63, no. 2 (1973): 225–45.

——. "Boundaries: Setting Limits to Political Areas." In *Concepts in Human Geography*, edited by Carville Earle, Kent Mathewson, and Martin S. Kenzer, 213–30. Lanham, MD: Rowman and Littlefield, 1996.

Calhoun, Craig. *Nationalism*. Minneapolis: University of Minnesota Press, 1997.

——. "Nationalism and Ethnicity." *Annual Review of Sociology* 19 (1993): 211–39. https://doi.org/10.1146/annurev.so.19.080193.001235.

Calzini, Paolo, ed. *Italo-Yugoslav Relations*. Rome: Istituto affari internazional, 1970.

Campbell, John Creighton. *Successful Negotiation, Trieste 1954: An Appraisal by the Five Participants*. Princeton, NJ: Princeton University Press, 1976.

Capano, Fabio. "Between the Local and the National: The Free Territory of Trieste." PhD diss., West Virginia University, 2014.

——. "Cold-War Trieste: Metamorphosing Ideas of Italian Nationhood, 1945–1975." *Modern Italy* 21, no. 1 (2016): 51–66. https://doi.org/10.1017/mit.2015.4.

——. "Resisting Détente: The Associative Network and the Osimo Treaty." In Bucarelli, Micheletta, Monzali, and Riccardi, *Italy and Tito's Yugoslavia*, 367–96.

Cappuzzo, Umberto. "The New Italian Perception of Security." *International Spectator* 19, nos. 3–4 (1984): 133–36. https://doi.org/10.1080/03932728408456545.

Carey, Jane Perry Clark, and Andrew Galbraith Carey. "The Italian Elections of 1958: Unstable Stability in an Unstable World." *Political Science Quarterly* 74, no. 4 (1958): 566–89.

——. "The Varying Seasons of Italian Politics, 1956–57." *Political Science Quarterly* 72, no. 2 (1957): 200–223. https://doi.org/10.2307/2145773.

Carstensen, Martin B. "Ideas Are Not as Stable as Political Scientists Want Them to Be: A Theory of Incremental Ideational Change." *Political Studies* 59 (2011): 596–615. https://doi.org/10.1111/j.1467-9248.2010.00868.x.

Carter, David B., and Hein E. Goemans. "The Making of the Territorial Order: New Borders and the Emergence of Interstate Conflict." *International Organization* 55, no. 2 (2011): 275–309. https://doi.org/10.1017/S0020818311000051.

Carter, David B., and Curtis S. Signorino. "Back to the Future: Modeling Time Dependence in Binary Data." *Political Analysis* 18, no. 3 (2010): 271–92. https://doi.org/10.1093/pan/mpq013.

Cattaruzza, Marina. *L'Italia e il confine orientale* [Italy and the eastern border]. Bologna: Il Mulino, 2007.

CDU Federal Office. *The Election Program of the CDU and CSU.* 1976.

Cederman, Lars-Erik. *Emergent Actors in World Politics: How States and Nations Develop and Dissolve.* Princeton, NJ: Princeton University Press, 1997.

——. "Nationalism and Ethnicity in International Relations." In *Handbook of International Relations*, edited by Walter Carlsnaes, Thomas Risse, and Beth A. Simmons, 530–54. Los Angeles: Sage, 2013.

Cederman, Lars-Erik, Andreas Wimmer, and Brian Min. "Why Do Ethnic Groups Rebel: New Data and Analysis." *World Politics* 62, no. 1 (2010): 87–119. https://doi.org/10.1017/S0043887109990219.

Central Committee of the TPLF. "Statement by the Central Committee of the Tigray People's Liberation Front (TPLF) on the Occasion of the 24th Anniversary of the Armed Struggle in Eritrea." *Review of African Political Economy* 35 (1986): 92–94. https://doi.org/10.1080/03056248608703672.

Chandra, Kanchan. "A Constructivist Dataset on Ethnicity and Institutions." In *Measuring Identity: A Guide for Social Scientists*, edited by Rawi Abdelal, Yoshiko M. Herrera, Alastair Iain Johnston, and Rose McDermott, 250–75. Cambridge: Cambridge University Press, 2009.

——, ed. *Constructivist Theories of Ethnic Politics.* Oxford: Oxford University Press, 2012.

——. "Ethnic Parties and Democratic Stability." *Perspectives on Politics* 3, no. 2 (2005): 235–52. https://doi.org/10.1017/S1537592705050188.

Chapman, Thomas, and Philip G. Roeder. "Partition as a Solution to Wars of Nationalism: The Importance of Institutions." *American Political Science Review* 101, no. 4 (2007): 677–91. https://doi.org/10.1017/S0003055407070438.

"Charters of Hamas." *Contemporary Review of the Middle East* 4, no. 4 (2017): 393–418.

Chatterji, Joya. *Bengal Divided: Hindu Communalism and Partition, 1932–1947.* Cambridge: Cambridge University Press, 1994.

Chazan, Naomi, ed. *Irredentism and International Politics.* Boulder, CO: Lynne Rienner, 1991.

Cheibub, José Antonio, Jennifer Gandhi, and James Raymond Vreeland. "Democracy and Dictatorship Revisited." *Public Choice* 143, nos. 1–2 (2010): 67–101. https://doi.org/10.1007/s11127-009-9491-2.

Chiozza, Giacomo, and Hein E. Goemans. "International Conflict and the Tenure of Leaders: Is War Still Ex Post Inefficient?" *American Journal of Political Science* 48, no. 3 (2004): 604–19. https://doi.org/10.1111/j.0092-5853.2004.00090.x.

Chowdhury, Arjun, and Ronald R. Krebs. "Making and Mobilizing Moderates: Rhetorical Strategy, Political Networks, and Counterterrorism." *Security Studies* 18, no. 3 (2009): 371–99. https://doi.org/10.1080/09636410903132961.

Christia, Fotini. *Alliance Formation in Civil Wars.* Cambridge: Cambridge University Press, 2012.

Christian Democratic Union of Germany, The. *The CDU: History, Idea, Program, Constitution.* Bonn: Christian Democratic Union of Germany, 1961.

Citrin, Jack, Ernst B. Haas, Christopher Muste, and Beth Reingold. "Is American Nationalism Changing?: Implications for Foreign Policy." *International Studies Quarterly* 38, no. 1 (1994): 1–31. https://doi.org/10.2307/2600870.

Clemens, Clay. *CDU Deutschlandpolitik and Reunification, 1985–1989*. Washington, DC: German Historical Institute, 1992.

——. *Reluctant Realists: The Christian Democrats and West German Ostpolitik*. Durham, NC: Duke University Press, 1989.

Cleves, Mario. "Stata: Analysis of Multiple Failure-Time Survival Data." *Stata Technical Bulletin* 49 (1999): 30–39.

Cobban, Helena. *The Palestinian Liberation Organisation: People, Power and Politics*. Cambridge: Cambridge University Press, 1984.

Coggins, Bridget. "Friends in High Places: International Politics and the Emergence of States from Secessionism." *International Organization* 65, no. 3 (2011): 433–67. https://doi.org/10.1017/s0020818311000105.

Cohen, Saul B., and Nurit Kliot. "Place-Names in Israel's Ideological Struggle over the Administered Territories." *Annals of the Association of American Geographers* 82, no. 4 (1992): 653–80. https://doi.org/10.2307/2563694.

Colarizi, Simona, and Guido Panvini. "From Enemy to Opponent: The Politics of Delegitimation in the Italian Christian Democratic Party (1945–1992)." *Journal of Modern Italian Studies* 22, no. 1 (2017): 57–70. https://doi.org/10.1080/13545 71x.2017.1267982.

Collier, David S., and Kurt Glaser. *The Conditions for Peace in Europe: Problems of Detente and Security*. Washington, DC: Public Affairs Press, 1969.

Committee for the Defense of the Italian Character of Trieste and Istria. *Trieste—November 1953: Facts and Documents*. Trieste, 1953.

Connor, Walker. *Ethnonationalism: The Quest for Understanding*. Princeton, NJ: Princeton University Press, 1994.

——. "Homelands in a World of States." In *Understanding Nationalism*, edited by Montserrat Guibernau and John Hutchinson, 53–73. Malden, MA: Polity Press, 2001.

Conradt, David P. "Changing German Political Culture." In *The Civic Culture Revisited*, edited by Gabriel Almond and Sidney Verba, 212–72. Boston, MA: Little, Brown, 1980.

Conzen, Michael P. "Culture Regions, Homelands, and Ethnic Archipelagos in the United States: Methodological Considerations." *Journal of Cultural Geography* 13 (Spring/Summer 1993): 13–29. https://doi.org/10.1080/ 08873639309478386.

Coppedge, Michael, John Gerring, Staffan I. Lindberg, Svend-Erik Skaaning, Jan Teorell, David Altman, Michael Bernhard et al. *Varieties of Democracy (V-Dem) Dataset Version 7.1*. 2017. https://www.v-dem.net/en/data/data-version-7/.

Cordell, Karl. "The Basic Treaty between the Two German States in Retrospect." *Political Quarterly* 61, no. 1 (1990): 36–50. https://doi.org/10.1111/j.1467-923X.1990. tb00794.x.

Corni, Gustavo. "The Exodus of Italians from Istria and Dalmatia, 1945–56." In Reinisch and White, *Disentanglement of Populations*, 71–90.

Crawford, Neta. *Argument and Change in World Politics: Ethics, Decolonization, and Humanitarian Intervention*. Cambridge: Cambridge University Press, 2002.

Croan, Melvin. "Dilemmas of Ostpolitik." In *West German Foreign Policy: Dilemmas and Directions*, edited by Peter Merkl, 35–52. Chicago: Chicago Council on Foreign Relations, 1982.

Croci, Osvaldo. "Search for Parity: Italian and Yugoslav Attitudes toward the Question of Trieste." *Slovene Studies* 12, no. 2 (1992): 141–55. https://doi.org/10.7152/ssj. v12i2.14516.

——. "The Trieste Crisis, 1953." PhD thesis, McGill University, 1991.

Csergo, Zsuzsa, and James M. Goldgeier. "Nationalist Strategies and European Integration." *Perspectives on Politics* 2, no. 1 (2004): 21–37. https://doi.org/10.1017/S153759270400060X.

Cunningham, Kathleen Gallagher. *Inside the Politics of Self-Determination*. Oxford: Oxford University Press, 2014.

Cunningham, Kathleen Gallagher, Kristin M. Bakke, and Lee J. M. Seymour. "Shirts Today, Skins Tomorrow: Dual Contests and the Effects of Fragmentation in Self-Determination Disputes." *Journal of Conflict Resolution* 56, no. 1 (2012): 67–93. https://doi.org/10.1177/0022002711429697.

Cunningham, Kathleen Gallagher, Marianne Dahl, and Anne Frugé. "Strategies of Resistance: Diversification and Diffusion." *American Journal of Political Science* 61, no. 3 (2017): 591–605. https://doi.org/10.1111/ajps.12304.

Cunsolo, Ronald S. *Italian Nationalism: From Its Origins to World War II*. Malabar, FL: Krieger, 1990.

Cvijic, Jovan. *Ethnographic Map of the Balkan Peninsula*, 1918.

Dafoe, Allan, John R. Oneal, and Bruce Russett. "The Democratic Peace: Weighing the Evidence and Cautious Inference." *International Studies Quarterly* 57, no. 1 (2013): 201–14. https://doi.org/10.1111/isqu.12055.

Dalmatia, Fiume and the Other Unreedemed [sic] Lands of the Adriatic: A Historical and Statistical Study . . . with a Map of the Eastern Frontier of Italy. Rome: L'Universelle, 1916.

D'Amelio, Diego. "Frontiere in transizione: Il lungo dopoguerra dei confini Italiani fra ereditá, emergenze e distensioni" [Frontiers in transition: The long postwar period of Italian borders between inheritance, emergencies and distension]. In D'Amelio, Di Michele, and Mezzalira, *La difesa dell'italianitá*, 539–94.

———. "Imperfect Normalization: The Political Repercussions of the Treaty of Osimo." In Bucarelli, Micheletta, Monzali, and Riccardi, *Italy and Tito's Yugoslavia*, 343–66.

D'Amelio, Diego, Andrea Di Michele, and Giorgio Mezzalira, eds. *La difesa dell'Italianitá: L'ufficio per le zone di confine a Bolzano, Trento e Trieste (1945–1954)* [The defense of Italian culture: The office for the border areas in Bolzano, Trento and Trieste (1945–1954)]. Bologna: Il Mulino, 2015.

Dannenberg, Julia von. *The Foundations of Ostpolitik: The Making of the Moscow Treaty between West Germany and the USSR*. Oxford Historical Monographs. Oxford: Oxford University Press, 2008.

Darwish, Mahmoud, ed. *Palestinian Leaders Discuss the New Challenges for the Resistance*. Beirut: Palestine Research Center, 1974.

De Agostini's Geographical Institute, ed. *L'Europe ethnique et linguistique* [Ethnicity and language of Europe]. Novara, Italy: De Agostini's Geographical Institute, 1917.

De Castro, Diego. *La questione di Trieste: L'azione politica e diplomatica italiana dal 1943 al 1954* [The Trieste issue: Italian political and diplomatic action from 1943 to 1954]. Trieste: LINT, 1981.

Demographic Research Center Institute of Social Sciences. *The Population of Yugoslavia: 1974 World Population Year*. Belgrade: Demographic Research Center Institute of Social Sciences, 1975. http://www.cicred.org/Eng/Publications/pdf/c-c55.pdf.

Dennett, Daniel C. *Darwin's Dangerous Idea: Evolution and the Meaning of Life*. New York: Simon and Schuster, 1995.

Diab, Zuhair, ed. *International Documents on Palestine, 1968*. Beirut: Institute for Palestine Studies, 1971.

Diamanti, Ilvo, and Luigi Ceccarini. "Catholics and Politics after the Christian Democrats: The Influential Minority." *Journal of Modern Italian Studies* 12, no. 1 (2007): 37–59. https://doi.org/10.1080/13545710601132912.

Diehl, Paul F. "What Are They Fighting For?: The Importance of Issues in International Conflict Research." *Journal of Peace Research* 29, no. 3 (1992): 333–44. https://doi.org/10.1177/0022343392029003008.

Dijink, Gertjan. *National Identity and Geopolitical Visions: Maps of Pride and Pain.* London: Routledge, 2002.

"Documents and Source Material: Arab Documents on Palestine, June 1–September 1, 1973." *Journal of Palestine Studies* 3 (Autumn 1973): 187–89. https://doi.org/10.2307/2535547.

Downes, Alexander B. "The Holy Land Divided: Defending Partition as a Solution to Ethnic Wars." *Security Studies* 10, no. 4 (2001): 58–116. https://doi.org/10.1080/09636410108429445.

Doyle, Michael W. *Empires.* Ithaca, NY: Cornell University Press, 1986.

Duggan, Christopher. *The Force of Destiny: A History of Italy since 1796.* Boston, MA: Houghton Mifflin Harcourt, 2008.

Duke of Litta-Visconti-Arese. "Unredeemed Italy." *North American Review* 206, no. 743 (1917): 561–74.

Dumont, Louis. *German Ideology: From France to Germany and Back.* Chicago: University of Chicago Press, 1994.

Dunning, Thad. "Conditioning the Effects of Aid: Cold War Politics, Donor Credibility, and Democracy in Africa." *International Organization* 58, no. 2 (2004): 409–23. https://doi.org/10.1017/S0020818304582073.

Duroselle, Jean Baptiste. *Le conflit de Trieste, 1943–1954* [The Trieste conflict, 1943–1954]. Brussels: Éditions de l'Institut de sociologie de l'Université libre de Bruxelles, 1966.

Dzurek, Daniel J. "What Makes Territory Important: Tangible and Intangible Dimensions." *GeoJournal* 64 (2005): 263–74. https://doi.org/0.1007/s10708-005-5802-4.

Edelman, Maurice. "Italy's Foreign Policy." *Political Quarterly* 21, no. 4 (1950): 374–84. https://doi.org/10.1111/j.1467-923X.1950.tb01080.x.

Eiran, Ehud. "Explaining the Settlement Project: We Know More but What More Should We Know?" *Israel Studies Forum* 25, no. 2 (2010): 102–15.

——. *Post-Colonial Settlement Strategy.* Edinburgh: Edinburgh University Press, 2019.

Ejobowah, John Boye. "Who Owns the Oil?: The Politics of Ethnicity in the Niger Delta of Nigeria." *Africa Today* 47, no. 1 (2000): 28–47.

Elden, Stuart. *The Birth of Territory.* Chicago: University of Chicago Press, 2013.

Ellwood, David W. "Italy, Europe and the Cold War: The Politics and Economics of Limited Sovereignty." In *Italy in the Cold War: Politics, Culture and Society 1948–1958*, edited by Christopher Duggan and Christopher Wagstaff, 25–46. Oxford: Berg, 1995.

Esman, Milton J. *Ethnic Politics.* Ithaca, NY: Cornell University Press, 1994.

Ethiopia Ministry of Information and National Guidance. *Ethiopia: Four Years of Revolutionary Process.* Addis Ababa: Propaganda and Information Committee, 1978.

Ezbidi, Basem. "'Arab Spring': Weather Forecast for Palestine." *Middle East Policy* 20, no. 3 (2013): 99–110. https://doi.org/10.1111/mepo.12036.

Fabry, Mikulas. *Recognizing States: International Society and the Establishment of New States since 1776.* Oxford: Oxford University Press, 2010.

Fall, Juliet J. "Artificial States?: On the Enduring Geographical Myth of Natural Borders." *Political Geography* 29, no. 3 (2010): 140–47. https://doi.org/10.1016/j.polgeo.2010.02.007.

Farnetti, Paolo. *The Italian Party System*. London: Pinter, 1985.

Fateh Revolutionary Council. "Political Statement, Tunis, 15 November 1993." *Journal of Palestine Studies* 23, no. 2 (1994): 133–36.

Fazal, Tanisha M. *State Death: The Politics and Geography of Conquest, Occupation, and Annexation*. Princeton, NJ: Princeton University Press, 2007.

Fazal, Tanisha M., and Ryan Griffiths. "A State of One's Own: The Rise of Secession since World War II." *Brown Journal of World Affairs* 15 (2008): 199–209.

Fearon, James D. "Rationalist Explanations for War." *International Organization* 49, no. 3 (1995): 379–414. https://doi.org/10.1017/S0020818300033324.

——. "Separatist Wars, Partition, and World Order." *International Security* 13 (Summer 2004): 394–415. https://doi.org/10.1080/09636410490945965.

Fearon, James D., and David D. Laitin. "Explaining Interethnic Cooperation." *American Political Science Review* 90, no. 4 (1996): 715–35. https://doi.org/10.2307/2945838.

——. "Violence and the Social Construction of Ethnic Identity." *International Organization* 54, no. 4 (2000): 845–77. https://doi.org/10.1162/002081800551398.

Fegiz, Pierpaolo Luzzatto. *Il volto sconosciuto dell'Italia: Dieci anni di sondaggi Doxa* [The unknown face of Italy: Ten years of Doxa surveys]. Milan: Giuffrè, 1966.

Fella, Stefano, and Carlo Ruzza. *Re-Inventing the Italian Right: Territorial Politics, Populism and 'Post-Fascism.'* New York: Routledge, 2009.

Finnemore, Martha, and Kathryn Sikkink. "International Norm Dynamics and Political Change." *International Organization* 52, no. 4 (1998): 887–917. https://doi.org/10.1162/002081898550789.

——. "Taking Stock: The Constructivist Research Program in International Relations and Comparative Politics." *Annual Review of Political Science* 4, no. 1 (2001): 391–416. https://doi.org/10.1146/annurev.polisci.4.1.391.

Fiske, Alan Page, and Philip E. Tetlock. "Taboo Trade-Offs: Reactions to Transactions That Transgress the Spheres of Justice." *Political Psychology* 18, no. 2 (1997): 255–97. https://doi.org/10.1111/0162-895X.00058.

Fornasier, Roberto. *The Dove and the Eagle*. Newcastle: Cambridge Scholars, 2012.

Forsberg, Erika. "Do Ethnic Dominoes Fall?: Evaluating Domino Effects of Granting Territorial Concessions to Separatist Groups." *International Studies Quarterly* 57, no. 2 (2013): 329–40. https://doi.org/10.1111/isqu.12006.

Forsberg, Tuomas. "Explaining Territorial Disputes: From Power Politics to Normative Reasons." *Journal of Peace Research* 33, no. 4 (1996): 433–49. https://doi.org/10.1177/0022343396033004005.

Fortna, Virginia Page. "Does Peacekeeping Keep Peace?: International Intervention and the Duration of Peace after Civil War." *International Studies Quarterly* 48, no. 2 (2004): 269–92.

——. "Scraps of Paper?: Agreements and the Durability of Peace." *International Organization* 57, no. 2 (2003): 337–72. https://doi.org/10.1017/S0020818303572046.

Fox, Jon E., and Cynthia Miller-Idriss. "Everyday Nationhood." *Ethnicities* 8, no. 4 (2008): 536–63. https://doi.org/10.1177/1468796808088925.

Fravel, Taylor M. "International Relations Theory and China's Rise: Assessing China's Potential for Territorial Expansion." *International Studies Review* 12, no. 4 (2010): 505–32. https://doi.org/10.1111/j.1468-2486.2010.00958.x.

Free Palestine. "Editorial: The Struggle Continues." *Free Palestine* 5, nos. 3–4 (April 1977): 1.

Freymond, Jacques. *The Saar Conflict, 1945–1955*. London: Stevens, 1960.

Friedenwald, Herbert, and H. G. Friedman, eds. *The American Jewish Year Book*. Philadelphia: Jewish Publication Society of America, 1913.

Frisch, Hillel. "Ethnicity, Territorial Integrity, and Regional Order: Palestinian Identity in Jordan and Israel." *Journal of Peace Research* 34, no. 3 (1997): 257–69. https://doi.org/10.1177/0022343397034003002.

———. "From Armed Struggle over State Borders to Political Mobilization and Intifada within It: The Transformation of PLO Strategy in the Territories." *Plural Societies* 19, nos. 2–3 (1990): 92–115.

Fritsch-Bournazel, Renata. *Confronting the German Question: Germans on the East-West Divide*. New York: Berg, 1988.

Fulbrook, Mary. *German National Identity after the Holocaust*. Cambridge: Polity Press, 1999.

———. "Nation, State and Political Culture in Divided Germany, 1945–90." In Breuilly, *State of Germany*, 177–200.

Galante, Severino. "In Search of Lost Power: The International Policies of the Italian Christian Democrat and Communist Parties in the Fifties." In Nolfo, *Power in Europe?*, 407–34.

———. "The Genesis of Political Impotence: Italy's Mass Political Parties in the Years between the Great Alliance and the Cold War." In Becker and Knipping, *Power in Europe?*, 185–206.

Garson, G. David. *Cox Regression*. Asheboro, NC: Statistical Associates, 2013.

Gartzke, Erik, and Kristian Skrede Gleditsch. "Identity and Conflict: Ties That Bind and Differences That Divide." *European Journal of International Relations* 12, no. 1 (2006): 53–87. https://doi.org/10.1177/1354066106061330.

Gasiorowski, Mark J. *US Foreign Policy and the Shah: Building a Client State in Iran*. Ithaca, NY: Cornell University Press, 1991.

GDR and Poland—Friends and Battle Comrades Forever. Dresden: Panorma DDR, 1975.

Gehrig, Sebastian. "Cold War Identities: Citizenship, Constitutional Reform, and International Law between East and West Germany, 1967–1975." *Journal of Contemporary History* 49, no. 4 (2014): 794–814.

Geiss, Imanuel. "The Federal Republic of Germany in International Politics before and after Unification." In Larres and Panayi, *Federal Republic of Germany since 1949*, 137–68.

———. *The Question of German Unification, 1806–1996*. New York: Routledge, 1997.

Gellner, Ernest. "Do Nations Have Navels?" *Nations and Nationalism* 3, no. 2 (1996): 366–70. https://doi.org/10.1111/j.1469-8219.1996.tb00003.x.

———. "Nationalism in the Vacuum." In *Thinking Theoretically about Soviet Nationalities: History and Comparison in the Study of the USSR*, edited by Alexander J. Motyl, 243–54. New York: Columbia University Press, 1992.

———. *Nations and Nationalism*. Ithaca, NY: Cornell University Press, 1983.

Gendzier, Irene L. "The Palestinian Revolution, the Jews, and Other Matters." *New Middle East* (January 1971): 38–41.

Gentile, Emilio. *La Grande Italia: The Myth of the Nation in the Twentieth Century*. Madison: University of Wisconsin Press, 1997.

Gentili, Anna Maria, and Angelo Panebianco. "The PCI and International Relations, 1945–1975: The Politics of Accommodation." In *The Italian Communist Party: Yesterday, Today, and Tomorrow*, edited by Simon Serfaty and Lawrence Gray, 109–27. Westport, CT: Greenwood Press, 1980.

Geyer, David Curtis, and Bernd Schaefer, eds. *American Détente and German Ostpolitik, 1969–1972*. Washington, DC: German Historical Institute, 2004.

Ghanem, As'ad. "Palestinian Nationalism: An Overview." *Israel Studies* 18, no. 2 (2013): 11–29.

Gibler, Douglas M. "Alliances That Never Balance: The Territorial Settlement Treaty." *Conflict Management and Peace Science* 15, no. 1 (1996): 75–97. https://doi.org/10.1177/073889429601500104.

——. "Bordering on Peace: Democracy, Territorial Issues, and Conflict." *International Studies Quarterly* 51, no. 3 (2007): 509–32. https://doi.org/10.1111/j.1468-2478.2007.00462.x.

——. *International Military Alliances, 1648–2008*. Thousand Oaks, CA: CQ Press, 2009.

——. *The Territorial Peace: Borders, State Development, and International Conflict*. Cambridge: Cambridge University Press, 2012.

Giese, Ernst. *Ostdeutschland, unvergessenes Land: Pommern, Schlesien, Ostpreussen* [Eastern Germany, unforgotten country: Pomerania, Silesia, East Prussia]. Frankfurt: Wochenschau Verlag, 1957.

Gilmore, Elisabeth, Nils Petter Gleditsch, Päivi Lujala, and Jan Ketil Rød. "Conflict Diamonds: A New Dataset." *Conflict Management and Peace Science* 22, no. 3 (2005): 257–72. https://doi.org/10.1080/07388940500201003.

Gilpin, Robert. *War and Change in World Politics*. Cambridge: Cambridge University Press, 1981.

Ginges, Jeremy, and Scott Atran. "Noninstrumental Reasoning over Sacred Values: An Indonesian Case Study." *Psychology of Learning and Motivation* 50 (2009): 193–206. https://doi.org/10.1016/S0079-7421(08)00406-4.

Ginges, Jeremy, Scott Atran, Douglas Medin, and Khalil Shikaki. "Sacred Bounds on the Rational Resolution of Violent Political Conflict." *Proceedings of the National Academy of Sciences* 104, no. 18 (2007): 7357–60.

Giuliano, Elise. "Secessionists from the Bottom Up." *World Politics* 58 (2006): 276–310.

Gleditsch, Kristian Skrede. "Expanded Trade and GDP Data." *Journal of Conflict Resolution* 46, no. 5 (2002): 712–24. https://doi.org/10.1177/002200202236171.

Gleditsch, Nils Petter, Peter Wallensteen, Mikael Eriksson, Margareta Sollenberg, and Håvard Strand. "Armed Conflict 1946–2001: A New Dataset." *Journal of Peace Research* 39, no. 5 (2002): 615–37. https://doi.org/10.1177/0022343302039005007.

Gleis, Joshua L., and Benedetta Berti. *Hezbollah and Hamas: A Comparative Study*. Baltimore: Johns Hopkins University Press, 2012.

Glennon, John P., ed. *Foreign Relations of the United States, 1955–1957*. Vol. 27, *Western Europe and Canada*. Washington, DC: United States Government Printing Office, 1992.

Glitman, Maynard. "US Policy in Bosnia: Rethinking a Flawed Approach." *Survival* 38, no. 4 (1996): 66–83.

Goddard, Stacie E. *Indivisible Territory and the Politics of Legitimacy: Jerusalem and Northern Ireland*. Cambridge: Cambridge University Press, 2010.

——. "Uncommon Ground: Indivisible Territory and the Politics of Legitimacy." *International Organization* 60, no. 1 (2006): 35–68. https://doi.org/10.1017/s0020818306060024.

Goddard, Stacie E., and Ronald R. Krebs. "Rhetoric, Legitimation, and Grand Strategy." *Security Studies* 24, no. 1 (2015): 5–36. https://doi.org/10.1080/09636412.2014.1001198.

Goemans, Hein E. "Bounded Communities: Territoriality, Territorial Attachment, and Conflict." In *Territoriality and Conflict in an Era of Globalization*, edited by

Miles Kahler and Barbara F. Walter, 25–61. Cambridge: Cambridge University Press, 2006.

Goemans, Hein E., and Kenneth A. Schultz. "The Politics of Territorial Claims: A Geospatial Approach Applied to Africa." *International Organization* 71, no. 1 (2017): 31–64. https://doi.org/10.1017/S0020818316000254.

Goemans, Henk E., Kristian Skrede Gleditsch, and Giacomo Chiozza. "Introducing Archigos: A Dataset of Political Leaders." *Journal of Peace Research* 46, no. 2 (March 1, 2009): 269–83. https://doi.org/10.1177/0022343308100719.

Goertz, Gary, and Paul F. Diehl. *Territorial Change and International Conflict.* New York: Routledge, 1992.

Golan, Galia. "Moscow and the PLO: The Ups and Downs of a Complex Relationship, 1964–1994." In Sela and Ma'oz, *PLO and Israel,* 121–41.

Goldstone, Jack A. "Toward a Fourth Generation of Revolutionary Theory." *Annual Review of Political Science* 4, no. 1 (2001): 139–87. https://doi.org/10.1146/annurev.polisci.4.1.139.

Gottmann, Jean. "The Political Partitioning of Our World: An Attempt at Analysis." *World Politics* 4, no. 4 (1952): 512–19. https://doi.org/10.2307/2008963.

——. *The Significance of Territory.* Charlottesville: University Press of Virginia, 1973.

Government of Italy. *Trieste: The Italian Viewpoint.* Rome: Government of Italy, 1946.

Gramsci, Antonio. *Selections from the Prison Notebooks of Antonio Gramsci.* Edited by Quintin Hoare and Geoffrey Nowell Smith. New York: International, 1971.

Granieri, Ronald J. *The Ambivalent Alliance: Konrad Adenauer, the CDU/CSU, and the West, 1949–1966.* New York: Berghahn Books, 2003.

Grass, Günter. *Two States—One Nation?* New York: Harcourt Brace Jovanovich, 1990.

Gray, Richard T., and Sabine Wilke, eds. *German Unification and Its Discontents: Documents from the Peaceful Revolution.* Seattle: University of Washington Press, 1996.

Gray, William G. "West Germany and the Lost German East: Two Narratives." In *The Germans and the East,* edited by Charles W. Ingrao and Franz A. J. Szabo, 402–20. West Lafayette, IN: Purdue University Press, 2008.

Graziano, Manlio. *The Failure of Italian Nationhood: The Geopolitics of a Troubled Identity.* New York: Springer, 2010.

Great Britain. *Palestine Royal Commission: Minutes of Evidence Heard at Public Sessions.* London: H.M.S.O., 1937.

Greco, Ettore. "Italy, the Yugoslav Crisis and the Osimo Agreements." *International Spectator* 29, no. 1 (1994): 13–31. https://doi.org/10.1080/03932729408458038.

Greenfeld, Liah. *Nationalism: Five Roads to Modernity.* Cambridge, MA: Harvard University Press, 1992.

Gresh, Alain. *The PLO: The Struggle within: Towards an Independent Palestinian State.* London: Zed Books, 1985.

Griffith, William E. *The Ostpolitik of the Federal Republic of Germany.* Cambridge, MA: MIT Press, 1978.

Gross, Feliks. *Ethnics in a Borderland: An Inquiry into the Nature of Ethnicity and Reduction of Ethnic Tensions in a One-Time Genocide Area.* Westport, CT: Greenwood Press, 1978.

Grzymala-Busse, Anna. "Time Will Tell?: Temporality and the Analysis of Causal Mechanisms and Processes." *Comparative Political Studies* 44, no. 9 (2011): 1267–97. https://doi.org/10.1177/0010414010390653.

Guehenno, Jean-Marie. *The End of the Nation-State.* Minneapolis: University of Minnesota Press, 1995.

Guibernau, Montserrat. "Nationalism and Intellectuals in Nations without States: The Catalan Case." *Political Studies* 48, no. 5 (2000): 989–1005. https://doi.org/10.1111/1467-9248.00291.

Gurr, Ted R., and Monty G. Marshall. *Peace and Conflict: A Global Survey of Armed Conflicts, Self-Determination Movements, and Democracy.* College Park, MD: Center for International Development and Conflict Management, 2005.

Gutman, Emanuel. "Concealed or Conjured Irredentism: The Case of Alsace." In Chazan, *Irredentism and International Politics*, 37–50.

Hachey, Thomas E. *The Problem of Partition: Peril to World Peace.* Chicago: Rand McNally, 1972.

Haftendorn, Helga. *Coming of Age: German Foreign Policy since 1945.* Lanham, MD: Rowman and Littlefield, 2006.

Haidt, Jonathan. *The Righteous Mind: Why Good People Are Divided by Politics and Religion.* New York: Pantheon Books, 2012.

Haklai, Oded, and Neophytos Loizides, eds. *Settlers in Contested Lands: Territorial Disputes and Ethnic Conflicts.* Stanford, CA: Stanford University Press, 2015.

Häkli, Jouni. "In the Territory of Knowledge: State-Centred Discourses and the Construction of Society." *Progress in Human Geography* 25, no. 3 (2001): 403–22. https://doi.org/10.1191/030913201680191745.

Hall, Rodney Bruce. *National Collective Identity: Social Constructs and International Systems.* New York: Columbia University Press, 1999.

Hamad, Jamil. "Palestinian Future: New Directions." *New Middle East* (August 1971): 20–22.

Hametz, Maura Elise. *Making Trieste Italian, 1918–1954.* Woodbridge: Boydell and Brewer, 2005.

Hanrieder, Wolfram F. "The Foreign Policies of the Federal Republic of Germany, 1949–1989." *German Studies Review* 12, no. 2 (1989): 311–32. https://doi.org/10.2307/1430097.

——. *Germany, America, Europe: Forty Years of German Foreign Policy.* New Haven, CT: Yale University Press, 1989.

——, ed. *West German Foreign Policy, 1949–1979.* Boulder, CO: Westview Press, 1980.

——. "West German Foreign Policy, 1949–1979: Necessities and Choices." In Hanrieder, *West German Foreign Policy, 1949–1979*, 15–36.

Harkabi, Yehoshafat. "The Meaning of 'A Democratic Palestinian State.'" *Wiener Library Bulletin* 24, no. 2 (1970): 1–6.

Harkabi, Yehoshafat, and Matti Steinberg. *The Palestinian Covenant: In the Test of Time and Reality; Explanations and Implications.* Jerusalem: Leonard Davis Center, Hebrew University, 1987.

Harley, J. B. "Maps, Knowledge, and Power." In *The Iconography of Landscape: Essays on the Symbolic Representation, Design and Use of Past Environments*, edited by Denis Cosgrove and Stephen Daniels, 277–312. Cambridge: Cambridge University Press, 1988.

Harrison, Hope M. "The Berlin Wall, Ostpolitik, and Détente." In Geyer and Schaefer, *American Détente and German Ostpolitik, 1969–1972*, 5–18.

Hassner, Ron E. "'To Halve and to Hold': Conflicts over Sacred Space and the Problem of Indivisibility." *Security Studies* 12, no. 4 (2003): 1–33. https://doi.org/10.1080/09636410390447617.

——. *War on Sacred Grounds.* Ithaca, NY: Cornell University Press, 2009.

Hauptmann, Jerzy. "The Problem of Partition." In Collier and Glaser, *Conditions for Peace in Europe*, 87–93.

Hechter, Michael. *Containing Nationalism*. Oxford: Oxford University Press, 2000.

Heidenheimer, Arnold J. *Adenauer and the CDU: The Rise of the Leader and the Integration of the Party*. The Hague: Martinus Nijhoff, 1960.

Henderson, Gregory, and Richard Ned Lebow. "Conclusions." In Henderson, Lebow, and Stoessinger, *Divided Nations*, 433–56.

Henderson, Gregory, Richard Ned Lebow, and John G. Stoessinger, eds. *Divided Nations in a Divided World*. New York: David McKay, 1974.

Hensel, Paul R. "Charting a Course to Conflict: Territorial Issues and Interstate Conflict, 1816–1992." *Conflict Management and Peace Science* 15, no. 1 (1996): 43–73. https://doi.org/10.1177/073889429601500103.

——. "Contentious Issues and World Politics: Territorial Claims in the Americas, 1816–1992." *International Studies Quarterly* 45, no. 1 (2001): 81–109. https://doi.org/10.1111/0020-8833.00183.

——. "Territory: Theory and Evidence on Geography and Conflict." In Vasquez, *What Do We Know About War?*, 57–84.

Hensel, Paul R., and Sara McLaughlin Mitchell. "Issue Indivisibility and Territorial Claims." *GeoJournal* 64 (2005): 275–85. https://doi.org/10.1007/s10708-005-5803-3.

Herb, Guntram Henrik. "Double Vision: Territorial Strategies in the Construction of National Identities in Germany, 1949–1979." *Annals of the Association of American Geographers* 94, no. 1 (2004): 140–64. https://doi.org/10.1111/j.1467-8306.2004.09401008.x.

——. *Under the Map of Germany: Nationalism and Propaganda 1918–1945*. London: Routledge, 1997.

Herbst, Jeffrey. "The Creation and Maintenance of National Boundaries in Africa." *International Organization* 43, no. 4 (1989): 673–92.

Herz, John H. "Germany." In Henderson, Lebow, and Stoessinger, *Divided Nations*, 3–42.

Hiltermann, Joost R. *Behind the Intifada: Labor and Women's Movements in the Occupied Territories*. Princeton, NJ: Princeton University Press, 1991.

Hobsbawm, Eric, and Terence Ranger, eds. *The Invention of Tradition*. Cambridge: Cambridge University Press, 1983.

Holmes, John W. "Italian Foreign Policy in a Changing Europe." In *Italian Politics: A Review*, vol. 8, edited by Stephen Hellman and Gianfranco Pasquino, 165–77. New York: Pinter, 1993.

Hooson, David, ed. *Geography and National Identity*. Cambridge: Blackwell, 1994.

Horowitz, Donald L. "The Cracked Foundations of the Right to Secede." *Journal of Democracy* 14, no. 2 (2003): 5–17.

——. *Ethnic Groups in Conflict*. Berkeley: University of California Press, 1985.

——. "Irredentas and Secessions: Adjacent Phenomena, Neglected Connections." *International Journal of Comparative Sociology* 33, nos. 1–2 (1992): 118–30. https://doi.org/10.1163/002071592X00086.

Hroub, Khaled. "A 'New Hamas' through Its New Documents." *Journal of Palestine Studies* 35, no. 4 (2006): 6–27. https://doi.org/10.1525/jps.2006.35.4.6.

Hunt, Jennifer. "The Economics of German Reunification." National Bureau of Economic Research, 2006. http://www.rci.rutgers.edu/jah357/Hunt/Transition_files/german_unification.pdf.

Hurrelmann, Achim. "Empirical Legitimation Analysis in International Relations: How to Learn from the Insights—and Avoid the Mistakes—of Research in EU Studies." *Contemporary Politics* 23, no. 1 (2017): 63–80. https://doi.org/10.1080/13569775.2016.1213077.

Husmann, Lisa E. "'National Unity' and National Identities in the People's Republic of China." In Hooson, *Geography and National Identity*, 141–57.

Huth, Paul K. *Standing Your Ground: Territorial Disputes and International Conflict*. Ann Arbor: University of Michigan Press, 1996.

——. "Territory: Why Are Territorial Disputes between States a Central Cause of International Conflict." In Vasquez, *What Do We Know About War?*, 85–110.

Huth, Paul K., and Todd Allee. *The Democratic Peace and Territorial Conflict in the Twentieth Century*. Cambridge: Cambridge University Press, 2002.

Ignatieff, Michael. *Blood and Belonging: Journeys into the New Nationalism*. New York: Farrar, Straus and Giroux, 1993.

Instituto per le Recerche Statistiche e l'Analisi dell'Opinione Pubblica. *DOXA Survey 1958–5801: Political and Social Research*. Ithaca, NY: Roper Center for Public Opinion Research, 1958.

International Crisis Group. *Dealing with Hamas*. 2004. Accessed July 30, 2018. https://www.crisisgroup.org/middle-east-north-africa/eastern-mediterranean/israel-palestine/dealing-hamas.

IPS Research and Documents Staff, ed. *International Documents on Palestine, 1977*. Beirut: Institute for Palestine Studies, 1979.

——, ed. *International Documents on Palestine, 1978*. Beirut: Institute for Palestine Studies, 1980.

——, ed. *International Documents on Palestine, 1979*. Beirut: Institute for Palestine Studies, 1981.

——, ed. *International Documents on Palestine, 1980*. Beirut: Institute for Palestine Studies, 1983.

——, ed. *International Documents on Palestine, 1981*. Beirut: Institute for Palestine Studies, 1983.

Italy and the Free Territory of Trieste. Special Supplement of *Esteri: Quindicinale di politica estera*. May 1953.

Jabber, Fuad A., ed. *International Documents on Palestine, 1967*. Beirut: Institute for Palestine Studies, 1970.

Jacobs, Frank. "If at First You Don't Secede . . . : Will This Be the Summer of Separatism for Europe?" *Foreign Policy*, April 28, 2014.

Jamal, Amal. "The Palestinian Media: An Obedient Servant or a Vanguard of Democracy?" *Journal of Palestine Studies* 29 (Spring 2000): 45–59. https://doi.org/10.2307/2676455.

James, Harold. *A German Identity, 1770–1990*. New York: Weidenfeld and Nicolson, 1989.

Jaraunsch, Konrad H., Hinrich C. Seeba, and David P. Conradt. "The Presence of the Past: Culture, Opinion, and Identity in Germany." In *After Unity: Reconfiguring German Identities*, edited by Konrad H. Jaraunsch, 25–60. Providence, RI: Berghahn Books, 1997.

Jenne, Erin K. "A Bargaining Theory of Minority Demands: Explaining the Dog That Did Not Bite in 1990s Yugoslavia." *International Studies Quarterly* 48, no. 4 (2004): 729–54. https://doi.org/10.1111/j.0020-8833.2004.00323.x.

——. *Ethnic Bargaining: The Paradox of Minority Rights*. Ithaca, NY: Cornell University Press, 2006.

——. "The Paradox of Ethnic Partition: Lessons from De Facto Partition in Bosnia and Kosovo." *Regional and Federal Studies* 19, no. 2 (2009): 273–89. https://doi.org/10.1080/13597560902789853.

Jiryis, Sabri. "On Political Settlement in the Middle East: The Palestinian Dimension." *Journal of Palestine Studies* 7, no. 1 (1977): 3–25. https://doi.org/10.2307/2536526.

Johnson, Carter. "Partitioning to Peace: Sovereignty, Demography, and Ethnic Civil Wars." *International Security* 32, no. 4 (2008): 140–70. https://doi.org/10.1162/isec.2008.32.4.140.

Johnson, Dominic D.P., and Monica Duffy Toft. "Grounds for War: The Evolution of Territorial Conflict." *International Security* 38, no. 3 (2014): 7–38. https://doi.org/10.1162/ISEC_a_00149.

Johnston, Ray E. "Partition as a Political Instrument." *Journal of International Affairs* 27, no. 2 (1973): 159–74.

Johnston, Ronald John, David B. Knight, and Eleonore Kofman, eds. *Nationalism, Self-Determination and Political Geography*. New York: Croom Helm, 1988.

———. "Nationalism, Self-Determination, and the World Political Map: An Introduction." In Johnston, Knight and Kofman, *Nationalism, Self-Determination and Political Geography*, 1–17.

Jones, Daniel M., Stuart A. Bremer, and J. David Singer. "Militarized Interstate Disputes, 1816–1992: Rationale, Coding Rules, and Empirical Patterns." *Conflict Management and Peace Science* 15, no. 2 (1996): 163–213. https://doi.org/10.1177/073889429601500203.

Joseph, Edward P., and Michael E. O'Hanlon. "The Case for Soft Partition in Iraq." *Saban Center for Middle East Policy at the Brookings Institution* 12 (2007): 1–45.

Juergensmeyer, Mark. *Terror in the Mind of God: The Global Rise of Religious Violence*. Berkeley: University of California Press, 2003.

Kaddoumi, Farouk. "Kaddumi [*sic*]: Confidence in Armed Struggle." *Free Palestine* 4, nos. 1–2 (January–February 1976): 7.

Kardelj, Edvard. *Trieste and Yugoslav-Italian Relations*. New York: Yugoslav Information Center, 1953.

Karlsen, Patrick. "La 'terra di mezzo' del comunismo adriatico alla vigilia della rottura fra Tito e Stalin" [The "middle ground" of Adriatic communism on the eve of the rupture between Tito and Stalin]. *Qualestoria: Rivista di storia contemporanea* 45, no. 1 (2017): 19–41.

Kaufman, Stuart J. *Nationalist Passions*. Ithaca, NY: Cornell University Press, 2015.

Kaufmann, Chaim. "An Assessment of the Partition of Cyprus." *International Studies Perspectives* 8, no. 2 (2007): 206–23. https://doi.org/10.1111/j.1528-3585.2007.00281.x.

———. "Possible and Impossible Solutions to Ethnic Civil Wars." *International Security* 20, no. 4 (1996): 136–75. https://doi.org/10.1162/isec.20.4.136.

———. "When All Else Fails: Ethnic Population Transfers and Partitions in the Twentieth Century." *International Security* 23, no. 2 (1998): 120–56. https://doi.org/10.1162/isec.23.2.120.

Kedourie, Elie. *Nationalism*. New York: Praeger, 1961.

Kelen, Christopher, and Aleksandar Pavković. "Of Love and National Borders: The Croatian Anthem 'Our Beautiful Homeland.'" *Nations and Nationalism* 18, no. 2 (2012): 247–66. https://doi.org/10.1111/j.1469-8129.2011.00529.x.

Kellerman, Henry J. "Party Leaders and Foreign Policy." In *West German Leadership and Foreign Policy*, edited by Hans Speier and W. Phillips Davison, 57–95. Evanston, IL: Row, Peterson, 1957.

Kennedy, Dennis. *Widening Gulf: Northern Attitudes to the Independent Irish State, 1919–49*. Belfast: Blackstaff Press, 1988.

Kertzer, David I., and Dominique Arel, eds. *Census and Identity: The Politics of Race, Ethnicity, and Language in National Censuses*. Cambridge: Cambridge University Press, 2002.

Kertzer, Joshua D, Jonathan Renshon, and Keren Yarhi-Milo. "How Do Observers Assess Resolve?" *British Journal of Political Science* (June 13, 2019): 1–23. https://doi.org/10.1017/S0007123418000595.

Khadduri, Walid, ed. *International Documents on Palestine, 1969*. Beirut: Institute for Palestine Studies, 1972.

———, ed. *International Documents on Palestine, 1970*. Beirut: Institute for Palestine Studies, 1973.

Khalidi, Rashid. *The Iron Cage: The Story of the Palestinian Struggle for Statehood*. Boston, MA: Beacon Press, 2006.

———. *Palestinian Identity: The Formation of National Consciousness*. New York: Columbia University Press, 1998.

Killinger, Charles L. *The History of Italy*. Westport, CT: Greenwood, 2002.

Kimmerling, Baruch, and Joel S. Migdal. *The Palestinian People: A History*. Cambridge, MA: Harvard University Press, 2003.

King, Geoff. *Mapping Reality: An Exploration of Cultural Cartographies*. New York: St. Martin's Press, 1996.

Kissinger, Henry A. *Years of Upheaval*. Boston: Little, Brown, 1979.

Klein, Menachem. "Against the Consensus: Oppositionist Voices in Hamas." *Middle Eastern Studies* 45, no. 6 (2009): 881–92. https://doi.org/10.1080/00263200903268629.

Kleinfeld, Margo. "Destabilizing the Identity-Territory Nexus: Rights-Based Discourse in Sri Lanka's New Political Geography." *GeoJournal* 64, no. 4 (2005): 287–95. https://doi.org/10.1007/s10708-005-5806-0.

Klinghoffer, Arthur Jay. *The Power of Projections: How Maps Reflect Global Politics and History*. Westport, CT: Praeger, 2006.

Kocs, Stephen A. "Territorial Disputes and Interstate War, 1945–1987." *Journal of Politics* 57, no. 1 (1995): 159–75. https://doi.org/10.2307/2960275.

Kohl, Philip L. "Nationalism and Archaeology: On the Constructions of Nations and the Reconstructions of the Remote Past." *Annual Review of Anthropology* 27 (1998): 223–46. https://doi.org/10.1146/annurev.anthro.27.1.223.

Kohn, Hans. *The Mind of Germany: The Education of a Nation*. New York: Charles Scribner's Sons, 1960.

———. "The Nature of Nationalism." *American Political Science Review* 33, no. 6 (1939): 1001–21. https://doi.org/10.2307/1948728.

Kokot, Józef. *The Logic of the Oder-Neisse Frontier*. Warsaw: Wydawn Zachodnie, 1959.

Koppel, Thomas Paul. "Sources of Change in West German Ostpolitik: The Grand Coalition, 1966–1969." PhD diss., University of Wisconsin, 1972.

Korbel, Josef. *Detente in Europe: Real or Imaginary*. Princeton, NJ: Princeton University Press, 1972.

Kornprobst, Markus. *Irredentism in European Politics: Argumentation, Compromise and Norms*. Cambridge: Cambridge University Press, 2008.

Kornprobst, Markus, and Martin Senn. "Arguing Deep Ideational Change." *Contemporary Politics* 23, no. 1 (2017): 100–119. https://doi.org/10.1080/13569775.2016.1213078.

Korte, Karl-Rudolf. "The Art of Power: The 'Kohl System,' Leadership and *Deutschlandpolitik*." In *The Kohl Chancellorship*, edited by Clay Clemens and William E. Paterson, 64–90. London: Frank Cass, 1998.

Krasner, Stephen D. *Sovereignty: Organized Hypocrisy*. Princeton, NJ: Princeton University Press, 1999.

Krause, Peter. "The Structure of Success: How the Internal Distribution of Power Drives Armed Group Behavior and National Movement Effectiveness." *Security Studies* 38, no. 3 (2014): 72–116. https://doi.org/10.1162/ISEC_a_00148.

Krause, Peter, and Ehud Eiran. "How Human Boundaries Become State Borders: Radical Flanks and Territorial Control in the Modern Era." *Comparative Politics* 40, no. 4 (2018): 479–99. https://doi.org/10.5129/001041518823565632.

Krebs, Ronald R. "How Dominant Narratives Rise and Fall: Military Conflict, Politics, and the Cold War Consensus." *International Organization* 69, no. 4 (2015): 809–45. https://doi.org/10.1017/s0020818315000181.

——. *Narrative and the Making of US National Security*. Cambridge: Cambridge University Press, 2015.

Krebs, Ronald R., and Patrick Thaddeus Jackson. "Twisting Tongues and Twisting Arms: The Power of Political Rhetoric." *European Journal of International Relations* 13, no. 1 (2007): 35–66. https://doi.org/10.1177/1354066107074284.

Krebs, Ronald R., and Jennifer Lobasz. "The Sound of Silence: Rhetorical Coercion, Democratic Acquiescence, and the Iraq War." In *American Foreign Policy and the Politics of Fear: Threat Inflation since 9/11*, edited by A. Trevor Thrall and Jane K. Cramer, 117–34. New York: Routledge Taylor and Francis Group, 2009.

Kreile, Michael. "Ostpolitik Reconsidered." In *The Foreign Policy of West Germany: Formation and Contents*, edited by Ekkehart Krippendorff and Volker Rittberger, 123–46. London: Sage, 1980.

Kristof, Ladis K. D. "The Image and the Vision of the Fatherland: The Case of Poland in Comparative Perspective." In Hooson, *Geography and National Identity*, 221–32.

Kumar, Radha. "The Troubled History of Partition." *Foreign Affairs* 76 (1997): 22–34.

Kunda, Ziva. *Social Cognition: Making Sense of People*. Cambridge, MA: MIT Press, 1999.

Kunz, Josef L. "The Free Territory of Trieste." *Western Political Quarterly* 1, no. 2 (1948): 99–112. https://doi.org/10.1177/106591294800100201.

Kupferschmidt, Uri M. *The Supreme Muslim Council: Islam under the British Mandate for Palestine*. Leiden: Brill, 1987.

Kuran, Timur. "Preference Falsification, Policy Continuity and Collective Conservatism." *Economic Journal* 97, no. 387 (1987): 642–65. https://doi.org/10.2307/2232928.

——. *Private Truths, Public Lies: The Social Consequences of Preference Falsification*. Cambridge, MA: Harvard University Press, 1995.

Kydd, Andrew, and Barbara F. Walter. "Sabotaging the Peace: The Politics of Extremist Violence." *International Organization* 56, no. 2 (2002): 263–96. https://doi.org/10.1162/002081802320005487.

Lacina, Bethany, and Nils Petter Gleditsch. "Monitoring Trends in Global Combat: A New Dataset of Battle Deaths." *European Journal of Population/Revue Européenne de Démographie* 21, nos. 2–3 (2005): 145–66. https://doi.org/10.1007/s10680-005-6851-6.

Lamme, Ary J., III, and Douglas B. McDonald. "The 'North Country' Amish Homeland." *Journal of Cultural Geography* 13, no. 2 (1993): 107–18. https://doi.org/10.1080/08873639309478392.

Landau, Jacob. "The Ups and Downs of Irredentism: The Case of Turkey." In Chazan, *Irredentism and International Politics*, 81–96.

Laqueur, Walter, and Barry Rubin, eds. *The Israeli-Arab Reader: A Documentary History of the Middle East Conflict*. New York: Penguin Books, 2001.

Larres, Klaus, and Panikos Panayi, eds. *The Federal Republic of Germany since 1949: Politics, Society and Economy before and after Unification*. New York: Longman, 1996.

Lee, Seokwoo. *Boundary and Territory Briefing: Territorial Disputes among Japan, China and Taiwan concerning the Senkaku Islands*. Boundary and Territory Briefing vol. 3, no. 7. Durham: International Boundaries Research Unit, 2002.

Legum, Colin. "Somali Liberation Songs." *Journal of Modern African Studies* 1, no. 4 (1963): 503–19. https://doi.org/10.1017/s0022278x00001415.

Leibfritz, Willi. "Economic Consequences of German Unification." *Business Economics* 25, no. 4 (1990): 5–9.

Leonardi, Robert, and Douglas A. Wertman. *Italian Christian Democracy: The Politics of Dominance*. New York: Macmillan, 1989.

Lesch, Ann Mosely. *Political Perceptions of the Palestinians on the West Bank and the Gaza Strip*. Washington, DC: Middle East Institute, 1980.

Lewis, Flora. "Reassembling Yugoslavia." *Foreign Policy* 98 (Spring 1995): 132–44.

Lewis, Orion A., and Sven Steinmo. "How Institutions Evolve: Evolutionary Theory and Institutional Change." *Polity* 44, no. 3 (2012): 314–39. https://doi.org/10.1057/pol.2012.10.

Lieberman, Evan S. "Nested Analysis as a Mixed-Method Strategy for Comparative Research." *American Political Science Review* 99, no. 3 (2005): 435–52. https://doi.org/10.1017/S0003055405051762.

Litvak, Meir. "Inside versus Outside: The Challenge of the Local Leadership, 1967–1994." In Sela and Ma'oz, *PLO and Israel*, 171–95.

Livingston, Robert Gerald, ed. *West German Political Parties: CDU, CSU, FDP, SPD, The Greens*. German Issues Series, no. 4. Washington, DC: American Institute for Contemporary German Studies, 1986.

Lodge, Juliet. *The European Policy of the SPD*. Beverly Hills, CA: Sage, 1976.

Lujala, Paivi, Jan Ketil Rød, and Nadja Thieme. "Fighting over Oil: Introducing a New Dataset." *Conflict Management and Peace Science* 24, no. 3 (2007): 239–56. https://doi.org/10.1080/07388940701468526.

Lukacs, Yehuda, ed. *The Israeli-Palestinian Conflict: A Documentary Record*. Cambridge: Cambridge University Press, 1992.

Lustick, Ian S. "Taking Evolution Seriously: Historical Institutionalism and Evolutionary Theory." *Polity* 43, no. 2 (2011): 179–209. https://doi.org/10.1057/pol.2010.26.

——. *Unsettled States, Disputed Lands: Britain and Ireland, France and Algeria, Israel and the West Bank–Gaza*. Ithaca, NY: Cornell University Press, 1993.

Luthar, Oto. *The Land Between: A History of Slovenia*. Brussels: Peter Lang, 2008.

Maier, Charles S. *Once within Borders: Territories of Power, Wealth, and Belonging since 1500*. Cambridge, MA: Harvard University Press, 2016.

Mannheim, Karl. "The Problem of Generations." In *Essays on the Sociology of Knowledge*, edited by Karl Mannheim, 276–320. London: Routledge and Kegan Paul, 1952.

Mansfield, Edward D., and Jack L. Snyder. *Electing to Fight: Why Emerging Democracies Go to War*. Cambridge, MA: MIT Press, 2007.

Ma'oz, Moshe. "The Palestinian Guerrilla Organizations and the Soviet Union." In *Palestinian Arab Politics*, edited by Moshe Ma'oz, 91–106. Jerusalem: Academic Press, 1975.

Maoz, Zeev. *Dyadic MID Dataset* (Version 2.0), 2005. http://psfaculty.ucdavis.edu/
zmaoz/dyadmid.html.
Maoz, Zeev, and Bruce Russett. "Normative and Structural Causes of Democratic
Peace, 1946–1986." *American Political Science Review* 87, no. 3 (1993): 624–38.
https://doi.org/10.2307/2938740.
Marshall, Barbara. *Willy Brandt: A Political Biography*. New York: St. Martin's Press,
1997.
Marshall, Monty G., Keith Jaggers, and Ted Robert Gurr. *Polity IV Dataset*, 2004.
http://www.systemicpeace.org/inscr/p4v2018.xls.
Martin, James. "Situating Speech: A Rhetorical Approach to Political Strategy." *Political
Studies* 63, no. 1 (2015): 25–42. https://doi.org/10.1111/2F1467-9248.12039.
Mathews, Jessica. "Power Shift." *Foreign Affairs* 76, no. 1 (1997): 50–66.
McAdams, A. James. *Germany Divided: From the Wall to Reunification*. Princeton, NJ:
Princeton University Press, 1994.
McGarry, John, and Brendan O'Leary. "Introduction: The Macro-Political Regulation
of Ethnic Conflict." In *The Politics of Ethnic Conflict Regulation: Case Studies of
Protracted Ethnic Conflicts*, edited by John McGarry and Brendan O'Leary, 1–47.
New York: Routledge, 1993.
McGraw, A. Peter, and Philip Tetlock. "Taboo Trade-Offs, Relational Framing, and the
Acceptability of Exchanges." *Journal of Consumer Psychology* 15, no. 12 (2005):
2–15. https://doi.org/10.1207/s15327663jcp1501_2.
McGraw, A. Peter, Philip E. Tetlock, and Orie V. Kristel. "The Limits of Fungibility:
Relational Schemata and the Value of Things." *Journal of Consumer Research* 30,
no. 2 (2003): 219–29.
Mearsheimer, John J. "Back to the Future: Instability in Europe after the Cold War."
International Security 15, no. 1 (1990): 5–56.
———. "The Case for Partitioning Kosovo." In *NATO's Empty Victory: A Postmortem
on the Balkan War*, edited by T. G. Carpenter, 133–38. Washington, DC: CATO
Institute, 2000.
Mearsheimer, John J., and Robert A. Pape. "The Answer: A Three-Way Partition Plan
for Bosnia and How the U.S. Can Enforce It." *New Republic* 208, no. 24 (1993):
22–28.
Mearsheimer, John J., and Stephen Van Evera. "When Peace Means War." *New Republic*
213, no. 25 (1995): 16–21.
Merkl, Peter H. "The Role of Public Opinion in West German Foreign Policy." In
Hanrieder, *West German Foreign Policy, 1949–1979*, 157–80.
Merritt, Anna J., and Richard L. Merritt. *Public Opinion in Semisovereign Germany:
The HICOG Surveys, 1949–1955*. Urbana: University of Illinois Press, 1980.
Miklavcic, Alessandra. "Border of Memories, Memories of Borders: An Ethnographic
Investigation of Border Practices in the Julian Region (Italy, Slovenia)." PhD
thesis, University of Toronto, 2006.
Miller, Benjamin. *States, Nations, and the Great Powers: The Sources of Regional War
and Peace*. Cambridge: Cambridge University Press, 2007.
Miller, David. "In Defence of Nationality." *Journal of Applied Philosophy* 10, no. 1
(1993): 3–16. https://doi.org/10.1111/j.1468-5930.1993.tb00058.x.
Miller, James E. "Taking Off the Gloves: The United States and the Italian Elections of 1948." *Diplomatic History* 7, no. 1 (1983): 35–56. https://doi.
org/10.1111/j.1467-7709.1983.tb00381.x.
Millo, Anna. "Il 'filo nero': Violenza, lotta politica, apparti dello stato al confine orientale (1945–1954)" [The "black thread": Violence, political struggle, state

apparatus on the eastern border (1945–1954)]. In D'Amelio, Di Michele, and Mezzalira, *La difesa dell'italianitá*, 415–38.

Milton-Edwards, Beverley, and Alastair Crooke. "Waving, Not Drowning: Strategic Dimensions of Ceasefires and Islamic Movements." *Security Dialogue* 35, no. 3 (2004): 295–310. https://doi.org/10.1177/2F0967010604047528.

Ministry of Foreign Affairs, Empire of Ethiopia. *Digest of Memoranda Presented by the Imperial Ethiopian Government to the Council of Foreign Ministers*. 1945.

Mishal, Shaul, and Avraham Sela. *The Palestinian Hamas: Vision, Violence and Coexistence*. New York: Columbia University Press, 2000.

Mišić, Saša. "A Difficult Reconciliation on the Adriatic: The Yugoslav Road to the Osimo Agreements of 1975." In Bucarelli, Micheletta, Monzali, and Riccardi, *Italy and Tito's Yugoslavia*, 249–84.

Mitchell, Paul, Geoffrey Evans, and Brendan O'Leary. "Extremist Outbidding in Ethnic Party Systems Is Not Inevitable: Tribune Parties in Northern Ireland." *Political Studies* 57, no. 2 (2009): 397–421. https://doi.org/10.1111/j.1467-9248.2008.00769.x.

Mommsen, Hans. "History and National Identity: The Case of Germany." *German Studies Review* 6, no. 3 (1983): 559–82.

Monzali, Luciano. "Aldo Moro, Italian *Ostpolitik* and Relations with Yugoslavia." In Bucarelli, Micheletta, Monzali, and Riccardi, *Italy and Tito's Yugoslavia*, 199–216.

Morris, Benny. *Righteous Victims: A History of the Zionist-Arab Conflict, 1881–1998*. New York: Vantage Books, 2001.

Motyl, Alexander J., ed. *Thinking Theoretically about Soviet Nationalities: History and Comparison in the Study of the USSR*. New York: Columbia University Press, 1992.

Murdock, George Peter. *Africa: Its Peoples and Their Culture History*. New York: McGraw-Hill, 1959.

Murphy, Alexander B. "National Claims to Territory in the Modern State System." *Geopolitics* 7, no. 2 (2002): 193–241. https://doi.org/10.1080/714000938.

Muslih, Muhammad. "A Study of PLO Peace Initiatives, 1974–1988." In Sela and Ma'oz, *PLO and Israel*, 37–53.

——. "Towards Coexistence: An Analysis of the Resolutions of the Palestine National Council." *Journal of Palestine Studies* 19, no. 4 (1990): 3–29. https://doi.org/10.2307/2537386.

Myers, Kenneth A. *Ostpolitik and American Security Interests in Europe*. Washington, DC: Center for Strategic and International Studies, Georgetown University, 1972.

Myers, Paul F., and Arthur A. Campbell. *The Population of Yugoslavia*. International Population Statistics Report P-90, No. 5. Washington, DC: US Government Printing Office, 1954.

Mylonas, Harris. *The Politics of Nation-Building: Making Co-Nationals, Refugees, and Minorities*. Cambridge: Cambridge University Press, 2013.

Mylonas, Harris, and Nadav G. Shelef. "Methodological Challenges in the Study of Stateless Nationalist Territorial Claims." *Territory, Politics, Governance* 5, no. 2 (2017): 145–57.

——. "Which Land Is Our Land?: Domestic Politics and Change in the Territorial Claims of Stateless Nationalist Movements." *Security Studies* 23, no. 4 (2014): 754–86. https://doi.org/10.1080/09636412.2014.964996.

Nanda, B. R. "Nehru, the Indian National Congress and the Partition of India, 1937–1947." In *The Partition of India: Policies and Perspectives, 1935–1947*, ed.

C. H. Philips and Mary Doreen Wainwright, 148–87. London: George Allen and Unwin, 1970.

Neuberger, Benyamin. "Irredentism and Politics in Africa." In Chazan, *Irredentism and International Politics*, 97–109.

Newman, David. "Boundaries, Borders, and Barriers: Changing Geographic Perspectives on Territorial Lines." In *Identities, Borders, Orders: Rethinking International Relations Theory*, edited by M. Albert, D. Jacobson, and Y. Lapid, 137–52. Minneapolis: University of Minnesota Press, 2001.

———. "From National to Post-National Territorial Identities in Israel-Palestine." In *Israelis in Conflict: Hegemonies, Identities and Challenges*, edited by Adriana Kemp, David Newman, Uri Ram, and Oren Yiftachel, 21–46. Brighton: Sussex Academic Press, 2004.

Newman, David, and Anssi Paasi. "Fences and Neighbours in the Postmodern World: Boundary Narratives in Political Geography." *Progress in Human Geography* 22, no. 2 (1998): 186–207. https://doi.org/10.1191/2F030913298666039113.

Nickerson, Raymond S. "Confirmation Bias: A Ubiquitous Phenomenon in Many Guises." *Review of General Psychology* 2, no. 2 (1998): 175–220. https://doi.org/10.1037//1089-2680.2.2.175.

Niedhart, Gottfried. "The Federal Republic's Ostpolitik and the United States: Initiatives and Constraints." In *The United States and the European Alliance since 1945*, edited by Kathleen Burke and Melvyn Stokes, 289–312. Oxford: Berg, 1999.

———. "Ostpolitik: Phases, Short-Term Objectives, and Grand Design." In Geyer and Schaefer, *American Détente and German Ostpolitik, 1969–1972*, 118–36.

Nkrumah, Kwame. *Ghana: The Autobiography of Kwame Nkrumah*. New York: International, 1957.

Nolfo, Ennio Di, ed. *Power in Europe?: Great Britain, France, Germany, and Italy, and the Origins of the EEC, 1952–1957*. Berlin: Walter de Gruyter, 1992.

———. "'Power Politics': The Italian Pattern (1951–1957)." In Nolfo, *Power in Europe?*, 530–45.

———. "The Shaping of Italian Foreign Policy during the Formation of the East-West Blocs: Italy between the Superpowers." In Becker and Knipping, *Power in Europe?*, 485–502.

Nostrand, Richard L., and Lawrence E. Estaville Jr. "Introduction: The Homeland Concept." *Journal of Cultural Geography* 13 (Spring/Summer 1993): 1–4. https://doi.org/10.1080/08873639309478384.

Novak, Bogdan C. "American Policy toward the Slovenes in Trieste, 1941–1974." *Slovene Studies*, no. 1 (1978): 1–25. http://dx.doi.org/10.7152/ssj.v0i1.3422.

———. *Trieste, 1941–1954: The Ethnic, Political, and Ideological Struggle*. Chicago: University of Chicago Press, 1970.

Nuti, Leopoldo. "Italian Foreign Policy in the Cold War: A Constant Search for Status." In *Italy in the Post–Cold War Order: Adaptation, Bipartisanship, Visibility*, edited by Maurizio Carbone, 25–47. Lanham, MD: Lexington Books, 2011.

O'Hanlon, Michael. "Turning the Bosnia Ceasefire into Peace." *Brookings Review* 16, no. 1 (1998): 41–44.

O'Leary, Brendan. "Analyzing Partition: Definition, Classification and Explanation." *Political Geography* 26 (2007): 886–908.

———. "Debating Partition: Justifications and Critiques." *Working Papers in British-Irish Studies* 78 (2006): 1–29.

———. "The Elements of Right-Sizing and Right-Peopling the State." In O'Leary, Lustick, and Callaghy, *Right-Sizing the State*, 15–73.

O'Leary, Brendan, Ian S. Lustick, and Thomas Callaghy, eds. *Right-Sizing the State: The Politics of Moving Borders*. Oxford: Oxford University Press, 2001.

Orlow, Dietrich. "Delayed Reaction: Democracy, Nationalism, and the SPD, 1945–1966." *German Studies Review* 16, no. 1 (1993): 77–102.

———. "The GDR's Failed Search for a National Identity, 1945–1989." *German Studies Review* 29, no. 3 (2006): 537–58.

Osborne, Jason. *Best Practices in Logistic Regression*. London: Sage, 2015. https://doi.org/10.4135/9781483399041.

Paasi, Anssi. "Deconstructing Regions: Notes on Scales of Spatial Life." *Environment and Planning A* 23 (1991): 239–56.

———. *Territories, Boundaries, and Consciousness: The Changing Geographies of the Finnish-Russian Border*. New York: John Wiley and Sons, 1996.

Padgett, Stephen. "The SPD: The Decline of the Social Democratic *Volkspartei*." In Larres and Panayi, *Federal Republic of Germany since 1949*, 230–53.

Pagel, Karl, ed. *The German East*. Berlin: K. Lemmer, 1954.

Palestine National Council. "Political Communique, Algiers, 15 November 1988." *Journal of Palestine Studies* 18, no. 2 (1989): 216–23.

———. "Political Programme for the Present Stage of the Palestine Liberation Organization Drawn Up by the Palestinian National Council, Cairo, June 9, 1974." *Journal of Palestine Studies* 3, no. 4 (1974): 224.

———. "Political Resolutions, Algiers, 22 February 1983." In Lukacs, *Israeli-Palestinian Conflict*, 357–64.

Palmowski, Jan. *Inventing a Socialist Nation: Heimat and the Politics of Everyday Life in the GDR, 1945–1990*. Cambridge: Cambridge University Press, 2009.

Park, Sunhee, and David J. Hendry. "Reassessing Schoenfeld Residual Tests of Proportional Hazards in Political Science Event History Analyses." *American Journal of Political Science* 59, no. 4 (2015): 1072–87. https://doi.org/10.1111/ajps.12176.

Parness, Diane L. *The SPD and the Challenge of Mass Politics: The Dilemma of the German Volkspartei*. Boulder, CO: Westview Press, 1991.

Paterson, William E. "The Ostpolitik and Regime Stability in West Germany." In Tilford, *Ostpolitik and Political Change in Germany*, 23–44.

———. *The SPD and European Integration*. Farnborough: Saxon House, 1974

Pearlman, Wendy. "Spoiling Inside and Out: Internal Political Contestation and the Middle East Peace Process." *International Security* 33, no. 3 (2009): 79–109. https://doi.org/10.1162/isec.2009.33.3.79.

Penrose, Jan. "Nations, States and Homelands: Territory and Territoriality in Nationalist Thought." *Nations and Nationalism* 8, no. 3 (2002): 277–97. https://doi.org/10.1111/1469-8219.00051.

Pew Research Center. *End of Communism Cheered but Now with More Reservations*. http://www.pewglobal.org/2009/11/02/chapter-5-views-of-german-reunification/#standard-of-living-in-east-germany.

Pfaff, William. "Invitation to War." *Foreign Affairs* 72 (Summer 1993): 97–109.

Pickett, Ralph Hall. *Germany and the Oder-Neisse Line*. Clarkson, ON: Canadian Peace Research Institute, 1968.

Pirjevec, Jože. "Italian Policy toward the Slovenes from 1915 to 1994." *Slovene Studies* 12, nos. 1–2 (1993): 63–73.

———. "Slovene Nationalism in Trieste, 1848–1982." *Nationalities Papers* 11, no. 2 (1983): 152–61. https://doi.org/10.1080/00905998308407963.

PLO. "Executive Committee Statement, Tunis, 7 March 1986." *Journal of Palestine Studies* 15, no. 4 (1986): 232–41.

———. "Palestinian National Council Political Statement, Damascus, 21 April 1981." In Lukacs, *Israeli-Palestinian Conflict*, 350–57.

PLO Central Committee. "Statement, Baghdad, 9 January 1988." *Journal of Palestine Studies* 17, no. 3 (1988): 181–84.

Plock, Ernest D. *The Basic Treaty and the Evolution of East-West German Relations*. Boulder, CO: Westview Press, 1986.

Pond, Elizabeth. *Beyond the Wall: Germany's Road to Unification*. Washington, DC: Brookings Institution Press, 1993.

Posner, Daniel N. "Measuring Ethnic Fractionalization in Africa." *American Journal of Political Science* 48, no. 4 (2004): 849–63. https://doi.org/10.1111/j.0092-5853.2004.00105.x.

Potthoff, Heinrich, and Susanne Miller. *The Social Democratic Party of Germany, 1848–2005*. Bonn: Dietz, 2006.

Prati, Giulia. *Italian Foreign Policy, 1947–1951: Alcide De Gasperi and Carlo Sforza between Atlanticism and Europeanism*. Göttingen: Vandenhoeck and Ruprecht, 2006.

Pridham, Geoffrey. *Christian Democracy in Western Germany: The CDU/CSU in Government and Opposition, 1945–1976*. New York: St. Martin's Press, 1977.

Provisional Military Government of Ethiopia. *Ethiopia Tikdem: Declaration of the Provisional Military Government of Ethiopia*. 1974.

Pullé, Francesco L. *Italia genti e favelle (disegno antropologico-linguistico) atlante* [Italy people and languages (anthropological-linguistic design) atlas]. Turin: Fratelli Bocca Editori, 1927.

Pupo, Raoul. "Gli esodi e la realtá politica dal dopoguerra a oggi" [The exoduses and the political reality from the post-war period to today]. In *Storia d'Italia: Le regioni dall'Unitá a oggi; Il Friuli-Venezia Giulia* [History of Italy: Regions from unity to today; Friuli-Venezia Giulia], 663–758. Torino: Einaudi, 2002.

———. "A Mistaken History?: A Survey of the Short Century of Italian-Yugoslav Relations." In Bucarelli, Micheletta, Monzali, and Riccardi, *Italy and Tito's Yugoslavia*, 133–58.

Quandt, William B., Paul Jabber, and Ann Mosely Lesch. *The Politics of Palestinian Nationalism*. Berkeley: University of California Press, 1973.

Rabushka, Alvin, and Kenneth A. Shepsle. *Politics in Plural Societies: A Theory of Democratic Instability*. Columbus, OH: Merrill, 1972.

Radunski, Peter. "The Christian Democratic Union." In Livingston, *West German Political Parties*, 16–28.

Rau, Johannes. *Zunkunft für alle: Arbeiten für soziale Gerechtigkeit und Frieden* [A future for all: Working for social justice and peace]. Bonn: Social Democratic Party Press and Information Department, 1987.

Readman, Kristina Spohr. "National Interests and the Power of 'Language': West German Diplomacy and the Conference on Security and Cooperation in Europe, 1972–1975." *Journal of Strategic Studies* 29, no. 6 (2006): 1077–1120. https://doi.org/10.1080/01402390601016626.

"The Real German Question." *Time* 78, no. 16 (1961): 21.

Reinisch, Jessica, and Elizabeth White, eds. *The Disentanglement of Populations: Migration, Expulsion and Displacement in Post-War Europe, 1944–9*. New York: Palgrave Macmillan, 2011.

Reiter, Yitzhak. "Islam and the Question of Peace with Israel." In *Muslim Attitudes to Jews and Israel: The Ambivalences of Rejection, Antagonism, Tolerance and Cooperation*, edited by Moshe Ma'oz, 90–112. Brighton: Sussex Academic Press, 2010.

Riall, Lucy. *Garibaldi: Invention of a Hero*. New Haven, CT: Yale University Press, 2007.

——. *The Italian Risorgimento: State, Society, and National Unification*. New York: Routledge, 1994.

Risse, Thomas. "'Let's Argue!': Communicative Action in World Politics." *International Organization* 54, no. 1 (2000): 1–39. https://doi.org/10.1162/002081800551109.

Roark, Michael O. "Homelands: A Conceptual Essay." *Journal of Cultural Geography* 13 (Spring/Summer 1993): 5–12. https://doi.org/10.1080/08873639309478385.

Robertis, Antonio Giulio M. de. *La frontiera orientale italiana nella diplomazia della seconda guerra mondiale* [The Italian eastern frontier in the diplomacy of the Second World War]. Naples: Edizioni Scientifiche Italiane, 1981.

Roeder, Philip G. *Where Nation-States Come from: Institutional Change in the Age of Nationalism*. Princeton, NJ: Princeton University Press, 2007.

Ronai, Andras, ed. *Atlas of Central Europe*. Budapest: Society of St. Steven-Puski, 1993.

Roy, Olivier. *The New Central Asia: Geopolitics and the Birth of Nations*. New York: I. B. Tauris, 2007.

Royston, Patrick, and Paul C. Lambert. *Flexible Parametric Survival Analysis Using Stata: Beyond the Cox Model*. College Station, TX: Statacorp, 2011.

Rusinow, Dennison I. *What Ever Happened to the "Trieste Question"?: De-Fusing a Threat to World Peace*. Hanover, NH: American Universities Field Staff, 1969.

Russett, Bruce M. *Grasping the Democratic Peace: Principles for a Post–Cold War World*. Princeton, NJ: Princeton University Press, 1995.

Ruzicic-Kessler, Karlo. "Comunismi di frontiera: L'Alto Adige e la Venezia Giulia in una prospettiva transnazionale" [Border communisms: Alto Adige and Venezia Giulia in a transnational perspective]. *Qualestoria: Rivista di storia contemporanea* 45, no. 1 (2017): 123–38.

Sack, Robert David. *Human Territoriality: Its Theory and History*. Cambridge: Cambridge University Press, 1986.

Saideman, Stephen M. "Inconsistent Irredentism?: Political Competition, Ethnic Ties, and the Foreign Policies of Somalia and Serbia." *Security Studies* 7, no. 3 (1998): 51–93. https://doi.org/10.1080/09636419808429351.

Saideman, Stephen M., and R. William Ayers. "Determining the Causes of Irredentism: Logit Analyses of Minorities at Risk Data from the 1980s and 1990s." *Journal of Politics* 62, no. 4 (2000): 1126–44. https://doi.org/10.1111/0022-3816.00049.

——. *For Kin or Country: Xenophobia, Nationalism, and War*. New York: Columbia University Press, 2008.

Samaddar, Ranabir. "Introduction: The Infamous Event." In Bianchini et al., *Partitions*, 1–12.

Sambanis, Nicholas. "Partition as a Solution to Ethnic War: An Empirical Critique of the Theoretical Literature." *World Politics* 52, no. 4 (2000): 437–83. https://doi.org/10.1017/S0043887100020074.

Sambanis, Nicholas, Micha Germann, and Andreas Schädel. "SDM: A New Data Set on Self-Determination Movements with an Application to the Reputational Theory of Conflict." *Journal of Conflict Resolution* 62, no. 3 (2017): 656–86. https://doi.org/10.1177/0022002717735364.

Sambanis, Nicholas, and Jonah Schulhofer-Wohl. "What's in a Line?: Is Partition a Solution to Civil War?" *International Security* 34, no. 2 (2009): 82–118. https://doi.org/10.1162/isec.2009.34.2.82.

Sandler, Shmuel. "Territoriality and Nation-State Formation: The Yishuv and the Making of the State of Israel." *Nations and Nationalism* 3, no. 4 (1997): 667–88. https://doi.org/10.1111/j.1354-5078.1997.00667.x.

Sarkees, Meredith Reid, and Frank Whelon Wayman. *Resort to War: A Data Guide to Inter-State, Extra-State, Intra-State, and Non-State Wars, 1816–2007*. Thousand Oaks, CA: CQ Press, 2010.

Sassoon, Donald. *The Strategy of the Italian Communist Party: From the Resistance to the Historic Compromise*. London: Pinter, 1981.

Sayigh, Yezid. *Armed Struggle and the Search for State: The Palestinian National Movement, 1949–1993*. Oxford: Oxford University Press, 1997.

Schaeffer, Robert K. *Warpaths: The Politics of Partition*. New York: Hill and Wang, 1990.

Schellenger, Harold Kent. *The SPD in the Bonn Republic: A Socialist Party Modernizes*. The Hague: Martinus Nijhoff, 1968.

Schiffrer, Carlo. *Historic Glance at the Relations between Italians and Slavs in Venezia Giulia*. Trieste: Istituto di storia dell'Università di Trieste, 1946.

Schimmelfennig, Frank. "The Community Trap: Liberal Norms, Rhetorical Action, and the Eastern Enlargement of the European Union." *International Organization* 55, no. 1 (2001): 47–80. https://doi.org/10.1162/002081801551414.

Schoch, Bernd. *The Islamic Movement: A Challenge for Palestinian State-Building*. Jerusalem: PASSIA (Palestinian Academic Society for the Study of International Affairs), 1999.

Schoenbaum, David, and Elizabeth Pond. *The German Question and Other German Questions*. New York: St. Martin's Press, 1996.

Schultz, Kenneth A. "Looking for Audience Costs." *Journal of Conflict Resolution* 45, no. 1 (2001): 32–60. https://doi.org/10.1177/0022002701045001002.

Schulz, Helena Lindholm. *The Reconstruction of Palestinian Nationalism: Between Revolution and Statehood*. Manchester: Manchester University Press, 1999.

Schulze, Max-Stephan, and Nikolaus Wolf. "On the Origins of Border Effects: Insights from the Habsburg Empire." *Journal of Economic Geography* 9, no. 1 (2009): 117–36. https://doi.org/10.1093/jeg/lbn040.

Schuman, Howard, and Cheryl Rieger. "Historical Analogies, Generational Effects, and Attitudes toward War." *American Sociological Review* 57, no. 3 (1992): 315–26.

Schwarz, Hans-Peter. "Adenauer's Ostpolitik." In Hanrieder, *West German Foreign Policy, 1949–1979*, 127–43.

Schweigler, Gebhard. *National Consciousness in Divided Germany*. Beverly Hills, CA: Sage, 1975.

Sedmak, V., and J. Mejak. *Trieste, the Problem Which Agitates the World*. Belgrade: Edition Jugoslavija, 1953.

Sela, Avraham, and Moshe Ma'oz, eds. *The PLO and Israel: From Armed Conflict to Political Solution, 1964–1994*. New York: St. Martin's Press, 1997.

Senese, Paul D., and John Vasquez. "Assessing the Steps to War." *British Journal of Political Science* 35, no. 4 (2005): 607–33. https://doi.org/10.1017/S0007123405000323.

———. *The Steps to War: An Empirical Study*. Princeton, NJ: Princeton University Press, 2008.

Service Geographique de l'Indochine. *L'Indochine, Carte Linguistique*. 1928.

Seton-Watson, Christopher. "Italy's Imperial Hangover." *Journal of Contemporary History* 15, no. 1 (1980): 169–79. https://doi.org/10.1177/2F002200948001500111.

Shamir, Jacob, and Khalil Shikaki. "Determinants of Reconciliation and Compromise among Israelis and Palestinians." *Journal of Peace Research* 39, no. 2 (2002): 185–202. https://doi.org/10.1177/2F0022343302039002003.

Shelef, Nadav G. *Evolving Nationalism: Homeland, Religion, and National Identity in Israel, 1925–2005*. Ithaca, NY: Cornell University Press, 2010.

——. "From 'Both Banks of the Jordan' to the 'Whole Land of Israel': Ideological Change in Revisionist Zionism." *Israel Studies* 9, no. 1 (2004): 125–48.

—— "How Homelands Change." *Journal of Conflict Resolution* 64, no. 2–3 (2020): 490–517. https://doi.org/10.1177/0022002719863470.

——. "Unequal Ground: Homelands and Conflict." *International Organization* 70, no. 1 (2016): 33–63. https://doi.org/10.1017/s0020818315000193.

Shelef, Nadav G., and Yael Zeira. "Recognition Matters!: UN State Status and Attitudes towards Territorial Compromise." *Journal of Conflict Resolution* 61, no. 3 (2017): 537–63. https://doi.org/10.1177/0022002715595865.

Shihadeh, Aziz. "Must History Repeat Itself?: The Palestinian Entity and Its Enemies." *New Middle East* (January 1971): 36–37.

——. "The Palestinian Demand Is for Peace, Justice and an End to Bitterness—the Initiative Is with Israel—the Time to Negotiate Is Now." *New Middle East* (August 1971): 16–19.

Shikaki, Khalil. "Refugees and the Legitimacy of Palestinian-Israeli Peace Making." In *Arab-Jewish Relations: From Conflict to Resolution?; Essays in Honour of Professor Moshe Ma'oz*, edited by Elie Podeh and Asher Kaufman, 363–74. Brighton: Sussex Academic Press, 2006.

Shlaim, Avi. "Israel and the Arab Coalition in 1948." In *The War for Palestine: Rewriting the History of 1948*, edited by Eugene L. Rogan and Avi Shlaim, 79–103. Cambridge: Cambridge University Press, 2001.

Shoup, Paul. "Yugoslavia's National Minorities under Communism." *Slavic Review* 22, no. 1 (1963): 64–81. https://doi.org/10.2307/3000388.

Shukeiri, Ahmad. *Liberation—Not Negotiation*. Beirut: Palestine Liberation Organization Research Centre, 1966.

Siboni, Giorgio Federico. *Il confine orientale: Da campoformio all'approdo europeo* [The eastern border: From Camp Formio to the European landing]. Sestri Levante: Oltre Edizioni, 2012.

Singer, J. David. "Reconstructing the Correlates of War Dataset on Material Capabilities of States, 1816–1985." *International Interactions* 14 (1987): 115–32. https://doi.org/10.1080/03050628808434695.

Singh, Sonali, and Christopher R. Way. "The Correlates of Nuclear Proliferation: A Quantitative Test." *Journal of Conflict Resolution* 48, no. 6 (2004): 859–85. https://doi.org/10.1177/0022002704269655.

Siroky, David S., and Christopher W. Hale. "Inside Irredentism: A Global Empirical Analysis." *American Journal of Political Science* 61, no. 1 (2017): 117–28. https://doi.org/10.1111/ajps.12271.

Sluga, Glenda. *The Problem of Trieste and the Italo-Yugoslav Border: Difference, Identity, and Sovereignty in Twentieth-Century Europe*. Albany: SUNY Press, 2001.

Smith, Anthony D. "Culture, Community and Territory: The Politics of Ethnicity and Nationalism." *International Affairs* 72, no. 3 (1996): 445–58. https://doi.org/10.2307/2625550.

——. *The Ethnic Origins of Nations*. New York: Basil Blackwell, 1987.

——. "Gastronomy or Geology?: The Role of Nationalism in the Reconstruction of Nations." *Nations and Nationalism* 1, no. 1 (1995): 3–23. https://doi.org/10.1111/j.1354-5078.1995.00003.x.

——. "The 'Sacred' Dimension of Nationalism." *Millennium: Journal of International Studies* 29, no. 3 (2000): 791–814. https://doi.org/10.1177/2F03058298000290030301.

——. *Theories of Nationalism*. London: Duckworth, 1971.

Smith, Helmut Walser. *The Continuities of German History: Nation, Religion, and Race across the Long Nineteenth Century*. Cambridge: Cambridge University Press, 2008.

Smith, Jean Edward. "The Berlin Wall in Retrospect." *Dalhousie Review* 47, no. 2 (1967): 173–84.

Smith, Monica L. "Networks, Territories, and the Cartography of Ancient States." *Annals of the Association of American Geographers* 95, no. 4 (2005): 832–49. https://doi.org/10.1111/j.1467-8306.2005.00489.x.

Snyder, Jack L. "Dueling Security Stories: Wilson and Lodge Talk Strategy." *Security Studies* 24, no. 1 (2015): 171–97. https://doi.org/10.1080/09636412.2015.1003723.

——. *From Voting to Violence: Democratization and Nationalist Conflict*. New York: W. W. Norton, 2000.

——. *Myths of Empire: Domestic Politics and International Ambition*. Ithaca, NY: Cornell University Press, 1991.

Snyder, Louis Leo. *Roots of German Nationalism*. Bloomington: Indiana University Press, 1978.

Social Democratic Party. *A Programme for Government: Presented by Willy Brandt, Governing Mayor of Berlin and Chancellor-Candidate, April 28, 1961*. Bonn: Social Democratic Party of Germany, 1961.

——. *Das Regierungsprogramm der SPD, 1961* [The SPD's Government Program, 1961].

——. *Das Regierungsprogramm der SPD, 1983–1987* [The SPD's Government Program, 1983–1987]. 1983.

——. *Sicherheit für Deutchland: Leistungen für Deutschland ein Leistunsbericht zum Whalprogramm 1980* [Security for Germany: Benefits for Germany, a performance report on the election program]. 1980.

——. *SPD Party Conference 1966: The State of the Nation*. Bonn: Social Democratic Party of Germany, 1966.

——. *Weiter arbeiten am Modell Deutschland: Regierungsprogramm 1976–1980* [Continue to work on the German model: Government program]. 1976.

Sosis, Richard. "Why Sacred Lands Are Not Indivisible: The Cognitive Foundations of Sacralising Land." *Journal of Terrorism Research* 2, no. 1 (2011): 17–44. https://doi.org/10.15664/jtr.172.

Speier, Hans. "Magic Geography." *Social Research* 8, no. 3 (1941): 310–30.

Spinelli, Altiero. "Remarks on Italian Foreign Policy." In Calzini, *Italo-Yugoslav Relations*, 22–35.

Staniland, Paul. "Between a Rock and a Hard Place: Insurgent Fratricide, Ethnic Defection, and the Rise of Pro-State Paramilitaries." *Journal of Conflict Resolution* 56, no. 1 (2012): 16–40. https://doi.org/10.1177/0022002711429681.

Starr, Harvey. *On Geopolitics: Space, Place, and International Relations*. New York: Routledge, 2015.

Steininger, Rolf. *The German Question: The Stalin Note of 1952 and the Problem of Reunification*. New York: Columbia University Press, 1990.

Sterpellone, Alfonso. "Italy and Yugoslavia." In Calzini, *Italo-Yugoslav Relations*, 42–61.

Stopford, John M., Susan Strange, and John Henley. *Rival Firms, Rival States: Competition for World Market Shares*. Cambridge: Cambridge University Press, 1991.

Stourzh, Gerald. *From Vienna to Chicago and Back: Essays on Intellectual History and Political Thought in Europe and America*. Chicago: University of Chicago Press, 2010.

Strange, Susan. *States and Markets*. 2nd ed. New York: Continuum, 1994.

Strassoldo, Raimondo. "Perspectives on Frontiers: The Case of Alpe Adria." In *The Frontiers of Europe*, edited by Malcolm Anderson and Eberhard Bort, 75–90. London: Pinter, 1998.

Süddeutsche Zeitung. "Das deutsche Weißbuch zur Saarfrage" [The German white paper on the Saar question]. March 10, 1950. Accessed July 30, 2018. http://www.cvce.eu/obj/the_german_white_paper_on_the_saar_question_from_the _suddeutsche_zeitung_10_march_1950-en-94e43ff0-ac8b-4cc5–85a3– 22651f37ecd7.html.

Swidler, Ann. "Culture in Action: Symbols and Strategies." *American Sociological Review* 51, no. 2 (1986): 273–86. https://doi.org/10.2307/2095521.

Sylvan, David J., and Stephen J. Majeski. "What Choices Do US Foreign Policy Makers Actually Face?" 2011. Paper presented at the Annual Conference of the American Political Science Association. Available at SSRN: https://ssrn.com/abstract=1902551.

Szaz, Z. Michael. *Germany's Eastern Frontiers: The Problem of the Oder-Neisse Line.* Chicago: Regnery, 1960.

Tadesse, Medhane. *The Eritrean-Ethiopian War: Retrospect and Prospects; Reflections on the Making of Conflicts in the Horn of Africa, 1991–1998.* Addis Ababa: Mega, 1999.

Tamimi, Azzam. *Hamas: A History from Within.* Northhampton, MA: Olive Branch Books, 2007.

Tarrow, Sidney. "Inside Insurgencies: Politics and Violence in an Age of Civil War." *Perspectives on Politics* 5, no. 3 (2007): 587–600. https://doi.org/10.1017/S1537592707071575.

Taylor, Peter J. "The State as Container: Territoriality in the Modern World-System." *Progress in Human Geography* 18, no. 2 (1994): 151–62. https://doi.org/10.1177/2F030913259401800202.

Teltschik, Horst. "Gorbachev's Reform Policy and the Outlook for East-West Relations." *Aussenpolitik*, no. 3 (1989): 201–14.

Terzuolo, Eric R. *Red Adriatic: The Communist Parties of Italy and Yugoslavia.* Boulder, CO: Westview, 1985.

Tessmer, Carsten. "'Thinking the Unthinkable' to 'Make the Impossible Possible': Ostpolitik, Intra-German Policy, and the Moscow Treaty, 1969–1970." In Geyer and Schaefer, *American Détente and German Ostpolitik, 1969–1972*, 53–66.

Tetlock, Philip E. "Thinking the Unthinkable: Sacred Values and Taboo Cognitions." *Trends in Cognitive Sciences* 7, no. 7 (2003): 320–24. https://doi.org/10.1016/s1364-6613(03)00135-9.

Tetlock, Philip E., Orie V. Kristel, S. Beth Elson, Melanie C. Green, and Jennifer S. Lerner. "The Psychology of the Unthinkable: Taboo Trade-Offs, Forbidden Base Rates, and Heretical Counterfactuals." *Journal of Personality and Social Psychology* 78, no. 5 (2000): 853–70. https://doi.org/10.1037//0022-3514.78.5.853.

Thomas, Louis B. "Maps as Instruments of Propaganda." *Surveying and Mapping* 9, no. 2 (1949): 75–81.

Tilford, Roger. Introduction to Tilford, *Ostpolitik and Political Change in Germany*, 1–22.

——, ed. *The Ostpolitik and Political Change in Germany.* Lexington, MA: Lexington Books, 1975.

Tingley, Dustin H., and Barbara F. Walter. "Can Cheap Talk Deter?: An Experimental Analysis." *Journal of Conflict Resolution* 55, no. 6 (2011): 996–1020. https://doi.org/10.1177/0022002711414372.

Tir, Jaroslav. "Dividing Countries to Promote Peace: Prospects for Long-Term Success of Partitions." *Journal of Peace Research* 42, no. 5 (2005): 545–62. https://doi.org /10.1177/2F0022343305056228.

Tir, Jaroslav, Philip Schafer, Paul Diehl, and Gary Goertz. "Territorial Changes, 1816– 1996: Procedures and Data." *Conflict Management and Peace Science* 16, no. 1 (1998): 89–97. https://doi.org/10.1177/2F073889429801600105.

Todd, Jennifer. "Partitioned Identities?: Everyday National Distinctions in Northern Ireland and the Irish State." *Nations and Nationalism* 21, no. 1 (2015): 21–42. https://doi.org/10.1111/nana.12083.

Toft, Monica Duffy. *The Geography of Ethnic Violence: Identity, Interests, and the Indivisibility of Territory*. Princeton, NJ: Princeton University Press, 2003.

Tomz, Michael R., and Jessica L. P. Weeks. "Public Opinion and the Democratic Peace." *American Political Science Review* 107, no. 4 (2013): 849–65. https://doi. org/10.1017/s0003055413000488.

Toset, Hans Petter Wollebæk, Nils Petter Gleditsch, and Håvard Hegre. "Shared Rivers and Interstate Conflict." *Political Geography* 19, no. 8 (2000): 971–96. https:// doi.org/10.1016/s0962-6298(00)00038-x.

Touval, Saadia. "Partitioned Groups and Inter-State Relations." In Asiwaju, *Partitioned Africans*, 223–32.

Trieste e la Venezia Giula [Trieste and Venezia Giulia]. Rome: Istituto Editoriale Julia Romana, 1951.

United States. Central Intelligence Agency. *The CIA World Factbook: Jordan*. 2012.

———. *The CIA World Factbook: West Bank*. May 2012.

———. *Peoples of Yugoslavia: Distribution by Opstina 1981 Census*. 1983.

———. "The Current Situation in the Free Territory of Trieste." ORE 23-48. April 15, 1948.

United States. Department of State. *Documents on Germany, 1944–1985*. Washington, DC: Office of the Historian, Bureau of Public Affairs, US Department of State, 1985.

———. *Foreign Relations of the United States, 1952–1954*. Edited by William Z. Slany, David M. Baehler, Evans Gerakas, Ronald D. Landa, and Charles S. Sampson. Washington, DC: US Government Printing Office, 1988. https://history.state. gov/historicaldocuments/frus1952-54v08.

United States. Office of Strategic Services (OSS). *Borneo: Indonesian Peoples and Christian Missions*, 1945.

———. *Indochina Linguistic Groups: Adapted from L'Indochine, carte linguistique, Paris 1929*, 1945.

United States. Office of the Geographer, Bureau of Intelligence and Research. *Limits in the Seas, No. 9. Continental Shelf Boundary: Italy-Yugoslavia*. US Department of State, 1970. https://www.state.gov/documents/organization/61999.pdf.

United States. Senate Committee on Foreign Relations. *Documents on Germany, 1944–1959: Background Documents on Germany, 1944–1959, and a Chronology of Political Developments Affecting Berlin, 1945–1956*. Washington, DC: United States Government Printing Office, 1959.

United States. War Department General Staff, Military Intelligence Division. "Feature Section: The Security Council and Trieste." *Intelligence Review* 59 (April 3, 1947): 17–24.

Valinakis, Yannis. "Italian Security Concerns and Policy." *International Spectator* 19, no. 2 (1984): 110–14. https://doi.org/10.1080/03932728408456541.

Van Evera, Stephen. "Hypotheses on Nationalism and War." *International Security* 18, no. 4 (1994): 5–39.

Varsori, Antonio. "De Gasperi, Nenni, Sforza and Their Role in Post-War Italian Foreign Policy." In Becker and Knipping, *Power in Europe?*, 89–116.

Vasquez, John A. *The War Puzzle*. Cambridge: Cambridge University Press, 1993.

——, ed. *What Do We Know About War?* Lanham, MD: Rowman and Littlefield, 2000.

——. "Why Do Neighbors Fight?: Proximity, Interaction, or Territoriality." *Journal of Peace Research* 32, no. 3 (1995): 277–93. https://doi.org/10.1177 /2F0022343395032003003.

Vasquez, John A., and Marie T. Henehan. "Territorial Disputes and the Probability of War, 1816–1992." *Journal of Peace Research* 38, no. 2 (2001): 123–38. https://doi. org/10.1177/2F0022343301038002001.

Vasquez, John A., and Brandon Valeriano. "Territory as a Source of Conflict and a Road to Peace." In *The Sage Handbook of Conflict Resolution*, edited by Jacob Bercovitch, Viktor A. Kremeniuk, and William I. Zartman, 193–209. Thousand Oaks, CA: Sage, 2009.

Velikonja, Joseph. "The Quest for Slovene National Identity." In Hooson, *Geography and National Identity*, 249–56.

Vigezzi, Brunello. "Italy: The End of a 'Great Power' and the Birth of a 'Democratic Power.'" In Becker and Knipping, *Power in Europe?*, 67–88.

Vogt, Manuel, Nils-Christian Bormann, Seraina Rüegger, Lars-Erik Cederman, Philipp Hunziker, and Luc Girardin. "Integrating Data on Ethnicity, Geography, and Conflict: The Ethnic Power Relations Dataset Family." *Journal of Conflict Resolution* 59, no. 7 (2015): 1327–42. https://doi.org/10.1177/0022002715591215.

Walter, Barbara F. "Bargaining Failures and Civil War." *Annual Review of Political Science* 12 (2009): 243–61. https://doi.org/10.1146/annurev. polisci.10.101405.135301.

——. *Reputation and Civil War: Why Separatist Conflicts Are So Violent*. Cambridge: Cambridge University Press, 2009.

Wang, Yan. "Globalization and Territorial Identification: A Multilevel Analysis across 50 Countries." *International Journal of Public Opinion Research* 28, no. 3 (2016): 401–14. https://doi.org/10.1093/ijpor/edv022.

Warner, Carolyn M. *Confessions of an Interest Group: The Catholic Church and Political Parties in Europe*. Princeton, NJ: Princeton University Press, 2000.

Waterman, Stanley. "Partitioned States." *Political Geography Quarterly* 6, no. 2 (1987): 151–70. https://doi.org/10.1016/0260-9827(87)90005-X.

Weber, Eugen. *Peasants into Frenchmen: The Modernization of Rural France, 1870–1914*. Stanford, CA: Stanford University Press, 1976.

Weidmann, Nils B. "Geography as Motivation and Opportunity: Group Concentration and Ethnic Conflict." *Journal of Conflict Resolution* 53, no. 4 (2009): 526–43. https://doi.org/10.1177/0022002709336456.

Weidmann, Nils B., Jan Ketil Rød, and Lars-Erik Cederman. "Representing Ethnic Groups in Space: A New Dataset." *Journal of Peace Research* 47, no. 4 (2010): 491–99. https://doi.org/10.1177/2F0022343310368352.

Weiner, Myron. "The Macedonian Syndrome: An Historical Model of International Relations and Political Development." *World Politics* 23, no. 4 (1971): 665–83. https://doi.org/10.2307/2009855.

Wertman, Douglas A. "The Catholic Church and Italian Politics: The Impact of Secularisation." *West European Politics* 5, no. 2 (1982): 87–107. https://doi. org/10.1080/01402388208424359.

West, Richard. *Tito and the Rise and Fall of Yugoslavia*. New York: Carroll and Graf, 1994.

White, George W. *Nation, State, and Territory: Origins, Evolution, and Relationships.* Lanham, MD: Rowman and Littlefield, 2004.

Wiegand, Krista Eileen. *Enduring Territorial Disputes: Strategies of Bargaining, Coercive Diplomacy, and Settlement.* Athens: University of Georgia Press, 2011.

Wilkens, Andreas. "New Ostpolitik and European Integration: Concepts and Policies in the Brandt Era." In *European Integration and the Cold War: Ostpolitik-Westpolitik, 1965–1973,* edited by Piers Ludlow, 67–80. New York: Routledge, 2007.

Wilpert, Friedrich von. *The Oder-Neisse Problem: Towards Fair Play in Central Europe.* Bonn: Atlantic Forum, 1964.

Wimmer, Andreas, Lars-Erik Cederman, and Brian Min. "Ethnic Politics and Armed Conflict: A Configurational Analysis of a New Global Dataset." *American Sociological Review* 74, no. 2 (2009): 316–37. https://doi.org/10.1177/2F000312240907400208.

Wimmer, Andreas, and Nina Glick Schiller. "Methodological Nationalism and Beyond: Nation-State Building, Migration and the Social Sciences." *Global Networks* 2, no. 4 (2002): 301–34. https://doi.org/10.1111/1471-0374.00043.

Winichakul, Thongchai. *Siam Mapped: A History of the Geo-Body of a Nation.* Honolulu: University of Hawai'i Press, 1994.

Wiskemann, Elizabeth. *Germany's Eastern Neighbours: Problems Relating to the Oder-Neisse Line and the Czech Frontier Regions.* Oxford: Oxford University Press, 1956.

——. *Italy since 1945.* New York: MacMillan, 1971.

Wolff, Stefan. *The German Question since 1919: An Analysis with Key Documents.* Westport, CT: Greenwood, 2003.

Wolffsohn, Michael. *West-Germany's Foreign Policy in the Era of Brandt and Schmidt, 1969–1982: An Introduction.* Frankfurt: Peter Lang Gmbh Internationaler Verlag der Wissenschaften, 1986.

Wood, Denis. *Rethinking the Power of Maps.* New York: Guilford Press, 2010.

Wood, Denis, and John Fels. *The Power of Maps.* New York: Guilford Press, 1992.

Woodward, Susan L. "Avoiding Another Cyprus or Israel: A Debate about the Future of Bosnia." *Brookings Review* 16 (Winter 1998): 45–48.

Yaari, Ehud. "Al Fath's Political Thinking." *New Outlook* 11, no. 9 (102) (November–December 1968): 20–33.

Yackee, Jason Webb, and Susan Webb Yackee. "Administrative Procedures and Bureaucratic Performance: Is Federal Rule-Making 'Ossified'?" *Journal of Public Administration Research and Theory* 20, no. 2 (2009): 261–82. https://doi.org/10.1093/jopart/mup011.

Yiftachel, Oren. "The Homeland and Nationalism." In *Encyclopedia of Nationalism,* edited by A. J. Motyl, 359–83. London: Academic Press, 2001.

Young, Crawford. *The Politics of Cultural Pluralism.* Madison: University of Wisconsin Press, 1976.

Zaccaria, Benedetto. *The EEC's Yugoslav Policy in Cold War Europe, 1968–1980.* London: Palgrave MacMillan, 2016.

Zacher, Mark W. "The Territorial Integrity Norm: International Boundaries and the Use of Force." *International Organization* 55, no. 2 (2001): 215–50. https://doi.org/10.1162/00208180151140568.

Zariski, Raphael. "Intra-Party Conflict in a Dominant Party: The Experience of Italian Christian Democracy." *Journal of Politics* 27, no. 1 (1965): 3–34. https://doi.org/10.2307/2127999.

Zerubavel, Yael. *Recovered Roots: Collective Memory and the Making of Israeli National Tradition.* Chicago: Chicago University Press, 1995.

Zuckerman, William D. "The Germans: What's the Question?" *International Affairs* 61, no. 3 (1985): 465–70.

Zunes, Stephen, and Jacob Mundy. *Western Sahara: War, Nationalism, and Conflict Irresolution*. Syracuse, NY: Syracuse University Press, 2010.

Zurayk, Constantine K. *The Meaning of the Disaster*. Beirut: Khayat's College Book Cooperative, 1956.

Index